Contents

What's Queer about Queer Studies Now?
Special Issue Editors David L. Eng, Judith Halberstam, José Esteban Muñoz

Introduction: What's Queer about Queer Studies Now?
David L. Eng with Judith Halberstam and José Esteban Muñoz 1

Punk'd Theory Tavia Nyong'o 19

The Joy of the Castrated Boy Joon Oluchi Lee 35

Time Binds, or, Erotohistoriography Elizabeth Freeman 57

Tarrying with the Normative: Queer Theory and *Black History* Amy Villarejo 69

Of Our Normative Strivings: African American Studies and the Histories of Sexuality Roderick A. Ferguson 85

Asian Diasporas, Neoliberalism, and Family: Reviewing the Case for Homosexual Asylum in the Context of Family Rights Chandan Reddy 101

Queer Times, Queer Assemblages Jasbir K. Puar 121

Race, Violence, and Neoliberal Spatial Politics in the Global City Martin F. Manalansan IV 141

Bollywood Spectacles: Queer Diasporic Critique in the Aftermath of 9/11 Gayatri Gopinath 157

You Can Have My Brown Body and Eat It, Too! Hiram Perez 171

JJ Chinois's Oriental Express, or, How a Suburban Heartthrob Seduced Red America Karen Tongson 193

Shame and White Gay Masculinity Judith Halberstam 219

Gay Rights versus Queer Theory: What Is Left of Sodomy after *Lawrence v. Texas*? Teemu Ruskola 235

Uncivil Wrongs: Race, Religion, Hate, and Incest in Queer Politics Michael Cobb 251

Policing Privacy, Migrants, and the Limits of Freedom Nayan Shah 275

Sex + Freedom = Regulation: Why? Janet R. Jakobsen 285

Contributors

Michael Cobb is an assistant professor of English at the University of Toronto. His essays have appeared, or soon will appear, in *Callaloo*, *GLQ*, *University of Toronto Quarterly*, *Criticism*, and *boundary 2*. His book *God Hates Fags: The Rhetorics of Religious Violence* is forthcoming from New York University Press.

David L. Eng is an associate professor of English at Rutgers University. He is the author of *Racial Castration: Managing Masculinity in Asian America* (Duke University Press, 2001). In addition, he is coeditor with David Kazanjian of *Loss: The Politics of Mourning* (University of California Press, 2003) and coeditor with Alice Y. Hom of *Q & A: Queer in Asian America* (Temple University Press, 1998), which was the winner of a 1998 Lambda Literary Award and the 1998 Cultural Studies Book Award of the Association for Asian American Studies. He is completing a book titled "Queer Diasporas/Psychic Diasporas," which explores the impact of Asian transnational and queer social movements on family and kinship in the late twentieth century.

Roderick A. Ferguson is an associate professor of race and critical theory in the Department of American Studies at the University of Minnesota, Twin Cities. He is the author of *Aberrations in Black: Toward a Queer of Color Critique* (University of Minnesota Press, 2004).

Elizabeth Freeman is an associate professor of English at the University of California, Davis. She is the author of *The Wedding Complex: Forms of Belonging in Modern American Culture* (Duke University Press, 2002) and is working on a second book tentatively titled "Time Binds: Essays in Queer Temporality." She has also published or copublished articles in nineteenth-century American literature and queer studies in journals including *American Literary History*, *American Literature*, *boundary 2*, *New Literary History*, *Radical Teacher*, and *Women and Performance*.

Gayatri Gopinath is an associate professor of women's and gender studies at the University of California, Davis. She is the author of *Impossible Desires: Queer Diasporas and South Asian Public Cultures* (Duke University Press, 2005). Her work on diasporic sexualities has appeared in journals such as *GLQ*, *positions*, *Diaspora*, *Amerasia*, and *Gender and History*.

Judith Halberstam is a professor of English and director of the Center for Feminist Research at the University of Southern California. She is the author of *Skin Shows: Gothic Horror and the Technology of Monsters* (Duke University Press, 1995) and *Female Masculinity* (Duke University Press, 1998) and has a new book of essays titled *In a Queer Time and Place: Transgender Bodies, Subcultural Lives* (New York University Press, 2005). Halberstam is working on a book titled "Dude, Where's My Theory? The Politics of Knowledge in an Age of Stupidity."

Janet R. Jakobsen is director of the Center for Research on Women at Barnard College. She is the author of *Working Alliances and the Politics of Difference* (Indiana University Press, 1998), coauthor (with Ann Pellegrini) of *Love the Sin: Sexual Regulation and the Limits of Religious Tolerance* (New York University Press, 2003), and coeditor (with Elizabeth A. Castelli) of *Interventions: Activists and Academics Respond to Violence* (Palgrave/Macmillan, 2004).

Joon Oluchi Lee is assistant professor of gender studies and English at the Rhode Island School of Design. He is working on a book about gay male effeminacy and black femininity titled "rainbowbaby-woman: poethics of racial-sexual cross-identification."

Martin F. Manalansan IV is an associate professor of anthropology and Asian American studies at the University of Illinois, Urbana-Champaign. He is the author of *Global Divas: Filipino Gay Men in the Diaspora* (Duke University Press, 2003). In addition to essays in journals and anthologies, he has edited two volumes of essays: *Cultural Compass: Ethnographic Explorations of Asian America* (Temple University Press, 2001) and (with Arnaldo Cruz-Malave) *Queer Globalizations: Citizenship and the Afterlife of Colonialism* (New York University Press, 2002).

José Esteban Muñoz is an associate professor in the Department of Performance Studies at New York University. He is the author of *Disidentifications: Queers of Color and the Performance of Politics* (University of Minnesota Press, 1999). He is also the coeditor (with Celeste Delgado) of *Everynight Life: Culture and Dance in Latin/o America* (Duke University Press, 1997) and (with Jennifer Doyle and Jonathan Flatley) of *Pop Out: Queer Warhol* (Duke University Press, 1996).

Tavia Nyong'o is an assistant professor of performance studies at New York University. He has written on racial kitsch in cinema and collecting, on the cyber-performance artist Pamela Z, and on the performance of blackness in U.S. politics. His work has appeared in the *Yale Journal of Criticism*, *3x3*, and *Women and Performance.*

Hiram Perez is an assistant professor of English at Montclair State University, where he also teaches courses in women's studies and African American studies. He is completing a manuscript that explores the relationship between shame and racial embodiment.

Jasbir K. Puar is an assistant professor of women's and gender studies at Rutgers University. She works on queer globalizations, South Asian diasporas, gay and lesbian tourism, and sexual scripts of terrorism. Her articles have appeared in *GLQ*, *Signs*, *Society and Space*, *Feminist Review*, *Radical History Review*, *Antipode*, and *Gender, Place and Culture.*

Chandan Reddy is an assistant professor of English at the University of Washington, Seattle. He is completing a manuscript on the rise of postemancipation black publics in the age of U.S. wars in Asia, 1898–1952. The essay published here is part of a second project on queer of color cultural formations and U.S. neoliberalism.

Teemu Ruskola is a professor of law at American University. His writings on the cultural study of law have appeared, among other places, in *Michigan Law Review*, *Stanford Law Review*, *Yale Journal of Law and Feminism*, and *Yale Law Journal.*

Nayan Shah is an associate professor in the Department of History at the University of California, San Diego. He is the author of *Contagious Divides: Epidemics and Race in San Francisco's Chinatown* (University of California Press, 2001).

Karen Tongson is an assistant professor of English and gender studies at the University of Southern California. She has published various articles on queer theory and aesthetics from the nineteenth century to the present and is working on two book projects: one on Victorian aesthetics and homonormativity, and another on contemporary queer of color suburban subcultures.

Amy Villarejo teaches film and directs the Feminist, Gender, and Sexuality Studies Program at Cornell University, where she is an associate professor. Her most recent book is *Lesbian Rule: Cultural Criticism and the Value of Desire* (Duke University Press, 2003).

Mie Yim was born in South Korea in 1963 and currently lives and works in New York City. Her work has been displayed in numerous international solo and group exhibitions. Most recently, she had solo exhibitions at Galleria In Arco in Turin, Italy, in 2004 and at Metaphor Contemporary Art in New York City in 2003. She is represented by the Lehmann Maupin Gallery in New York City.

Introduction

WHAT'S QUEER ABOUT QUEER STUDIES NOW?

David L. Eng with Judith Halberstam and José Esteban Muñoz

Around 1990 *queer* emerged into public consciousness. It was a term that challenged the normalizing mechanisms of state power to name its sexual subjects: male or female, married or single, heterosexual or homosexual, natural or perverse. Given its commitment to interrogating the social processes that not only produced and recognized but also normalized and sustained identity, the political promise of the term resided specifically in its broad critique of multiple social antagonisms, including race, gender, class, nationality, and religion, in addition to sexuality.

Fourteen years after *Social Text*'s publication of "Fear of a Queer Planet," and eight years after "Queer Transexions of Race, Nation, and Gender," this special double issue reassesses the political utility of queer by asking "what's queer about queer studies now?" The contemporary mainstreaming of gay and lesbian identity—as a mass-mediated consumer lifestyle and embattled legal category—demands a renewed queer studies ever vigilant to the fact that sexuality is intersectional, not extraneous to other modes of difference, and calibrated to a firm understanding of queer as a political metaphor without a fixed referent. A renewed queer studies, moreover, insists on a broadened consideration of the late-twentieth-century global crises that have configured historical relations among political economies, the geopolitics of war and terror, and national manifestations of sexual, racial, and gendered hierarchies.

The following sixteen essays—largely authored by a younger generation of queer scholars—map out an urgent intellectual and political terrain for queer studies and the contemporary politics of identity, kinship, and belonging. Insisting on queer studies' intellectual and political relevance to a wide field of social critique, these essays reassess some of the field's most important theoretical insights while realigning its political attentions, historical foci, and disciplinary accounts. Broadly, these scholars examine the limits of queer epistemology, the denaturalizing potentials of queer diasporas, and the emergent assumptions of what could be called queer liberalism. Collectively, they rethink queer critique in relation to a number of historical emergencies, to borrow from Walter Benjamin, of both national and global consequence.

Social Text 84–85, Vol. 23, Nos. 3–4, Fall–Winter 2005. © 2005 by Duke University Press.

What does queer studies have to say about empire, globalization, neoliberalism, sovereignty, and terrorism? What does queer studies tell us about immigration, citizenship, prisons, welfare, mourning, and human rights?

Such emergencies include the triumph of neoliberalism and the collapse of the welfare state; the Bush administration's infinite "war on terrorism" and the acute militarization of state violence; the escalation of U.S. empire building and the clash of religious fundamentalisms, nationalisms, and patriotisms; the devolution of civil society and the erosion of civil rights; the pathologizing of immigrant communities as "terrorist" and racialized populations as "criminal"; the shifting forms of citizenship and migration in a putatively "postidentity" and "postracial" age; the politics of intimacy and the liberal recoding of freedom as secularization, domesticity, and marriage; and the return to "moral values" and "family values" as a prophylactic against political debate, economic redistribution, and cultural dissent. Indeed, in this intense time of war and death, and of U.S. unilateralismand corporate domination, queer studies now more than ever needs to refocus its critical attentions on public debates about the meaning of democracy and freedom, citizenship and immigration, family and community, and the alien and the human in all their national and their global manifestations.

What does queer studies have to say about empire, globalization, neoliberalism, sovereignty, and terrorism? What does queer studies tell us about immigration, citizenship, prisons, welfare, mourning, and human rights? What is the relationship between *Lawrence v. Texas*, the exalted June 2003 Supreme Court decision decriminalizing gay sex, and the contemporaneous USA PATRIOT Act? If mainstream media attention to queer lives and issues has helped to establish the social and legal foundation for the emergence of gay marriage, family, and domesticity, what are the social costs of this new visibility? And how does the demand for marriage and legal rights affect, run counter to, or in fact converge with conservative promotion of traditional marriage?

While queer studies in the past has rarely addressed such broad social concerns, queer studies in the present offers important insights. In recent years, scholars in the field have produced a significant body of work on theories of race, on problems of transnationalism, on conflicts between global capital and labor, on issues of diaspora and immigration, and on questions of citizenship, national belonging, and necropolitics.[1] The various essays gathered here insist that considerations of empire, race, migration, geography, subaltern communities, activism, and class are central to the continuing critique of queerness, sexuality, sexual subcultures, desire, and recognition. At the same time, these essays also suggest that some of the most innovative and risky work on globalization, neoliberalism, cultural politics, subjectivity, identity, family, and kinship is happening in the realm of queer studies. As a whole, this volume reevaluates the utility of queer as an engaged mode of critical inquiry. It charts some of the notable historical shifts in the field since its inception while recognizing different pasts, alternative presents, and new futures for queer scholarship.

What's queer about queer studies now?

A lot.

Queer Epistemology

In her 1993 essay "Critically Queer," Judith Butler writes that the assertion of "queer" must never purport to "fully describe" those it seeks to represent. "It is necessary to affirm the contingency of the term," Butler insists, "to let it be vanquished by those who are excluded by the term but who justifiably expect representation by it, to let it take on meanings that cannot now be anticipated by a younger generation whose political vocabulary may well carry a very different set of investments." That queerness remains open to a continuing critique of its privileged assumptions "ought to be safeguarded not only for the purposes of continuing to democratize queer politics, but also to expose, affirm, and rework the specific historicity of the term."[2] The operations of queer critique, in other words, can neither be decided on in advance nor be depended on in the future. The reinvention of the term is contingent on its potential obsolescence, one necessarily at odds with any fortification of its critical reach in advance or any static notion of its presumed audience and participants.

That queerness remains open to a continuing critique of its exclusionary operations has always been one of the field's key theoretical and political promises. What might be called the "subjectless" critique of queer studies disallows any positing of a proper subject *of* or object *for* the field by insisting that queer has no fixed political referent. Such an understanding orients queer epistemology, despite the historical necessities of "strategic essentialism" (Gayatri Spivak's famous term), as a continuous deconstruction of the tenets of positivism at the heart of identity politics. Attention to queer epistemology also insists that sexuality—the organizing rubric of lesbian and gay studies—must be rethought for its positivist assumptions. A subjectless critique establishes, in Michael Warner's phrase, a focus on "a wide field of normalization" as the site of social violence. Attention to those hegemonic social structures by which certain subjects are rendered "normal" and "natural" through the production of "perverse" and "pathological" others, Warner insists, rejects a "minoritizing logic of toleration or simple political interest-representation in favor of a more thorough resistance to regimes of the normal."[3]

Today, we find ourselves at an ironic historical moment of what might be described as "queer liberalism." Mechanisms of normalization have endeavored to organize not only gay and lesbian politics but also the internal workings of the field itself, attempting to constitute its governing logic around certain privileged subjects, standards of sexual conduct, and political and intellectual engagements (a subject discussed in greater detail below). At such a historical juncture, it is crucial to insist yet again on the capacity of queer studies to mobilize a broad social critique of race, gender, class, nationality, and religion, as well as sexuality. Such a theoretical project demands that queer epistemologies not only rethink the relationship between intersectionality and normalization from multiple points of view but also, and equally important, consider how gay and lesbian rights are being reconstituted as a type of reactionary (identity) politics of national and global consequence.

At such a historical juncture, it is crucial to insist yet again on the capacity of queer studies to mobilize a broad social critique of race, gender, class, nationality, and religion, as well as sexuality.

Roderick A. Ferguson observes in his contribution to this special issue, "Of Our Normative Strivings: African American Studies and the Histories of Sexuality" that while queer studies "has had the most concentrated engagement with the category of sexuality," its institutional advances should not convince queer studies that "its engagements with sexuality are the only and most significant pursuits of that formation." In other words, if interdisciplinary sites such as queer studies isolate sexuality within one epistemic terrain (such as psychoanalysis), or attempt to arrogate the study of sexuality to themselves alone, these "sites prove interdisciplinarity's complicity with disciplinarity rather than interdisciplinarity's rebellion against the disciplines." Ferguson's observations move us away from an exclusive focus on how sexuality becomes the "propertied" object of queer studies, its privileged site of critical inquiry. Instead, he focuses on normalization and intersectionality at once, by asking "in what ways has the racialized, classed, and gendered discourse known as sexuality dispersed itself to constitute this particular discipline or interdiscipline?" Configuring queer epistemology in such a manner insists on a sustained consideration of what happens to sexuality when it is resituated as the effect not only of queer studies but also other fields of inquiry, such as women of color feminism, queer of color critique, or queer diasporas.[4] Hence critical attentions are drawn to the governing logics of knowledge production, the constitutive assumptions that form the foundation of disciplinary fields, rendering them internally coherent while giving social and political difference their discursive power.

In "Time Binds, or, Erotohistoriography," Elizabeth Freeman expands on Ferguson's epistemological investigation in a different register. Freeman brings queer studies together with one of the most important epistemological inquiries in postcolonial studies: the disparate mappings of time and space. Nation-states, she observes, "still track and manage their own denizens through an official time line, effectively shaping the contours of a meaningful life by registering some events like births, marriages, and deaths, and refusing to record others like initiations, friendships, and contact with the dead." Freeman's crossing of queer studies with postcolonial concerns of individual and group "development" reformulates certain basic tenets of the field such that "queer subjectivity and collectivity demand, and take as their reward, particularly inventive and time-traveling forms of grief and compensation." Reconsidering the spatial and temporal dimensions of queer traumas, including AIDS, Freeman suggests that the incorporation of lost others need not be haunted solely by melancholy and depression. In a historical moment of intense political conservatism, residues of "positive affect"—"erotic scenes, utopias, memories of touch"—must become available for queer counterhistories of space and time, alternative narratives of development that have become central to the notion of queer subcultures, counterpublics, and utopias.

Queer epistemology insists that we embark on expanded investigations of normalization and intersectionality. In this regard, Tavia Nyong'o's opening essay, "Punk'd Theory," proffers yet another take on "intersectionality," one interrupting the everyday practices and "litigious process through which subjects petition for admission to queer theoretical attention." Proffering "Punk'd Theory" as, in the words of Eve Sedgwick, a "nonce taxonomy" full of unrationalized hypotheses about what kinds of people there are to be found in the world, Nyong'o rewrites a now frozen dialectic between black and white, as well as straight and gay. He observes that it is not enough "to take up the simultaneity of race, class, gender, and sexuality, which it is my argument that the vernacular does constantly in keywords like *punk* and *punked*." Instead, Nyong'o contends, we must investigate "the subject transformed by law that nevertheless exists nowhere within it, the figure of absolute abjection that is, paradoxically, part of our everyday experience." Here, queer epistemology rethinks intersectionality not just as racial, sexual, or class simultaneity but as "a meeting of two streets, and in a landscape long given over to automotivity . . . a place of particular hazard for the pedestrian." According to Nyong'o, "punk'd" pedestrians must demand both their "rights and *more* than their rights, simply to preserve a portion of the mobility they had prior to enclosure": workers become "illegal immigrants"; poor mothers, "welfare queens"; protestors, "potential terrorists." While all must attack the presumption of their criminality merely to preserve their way of life, intersectionality will become positively hazardous to everyone's health if we choose to adjudicate among these differences rather than to nurture them all at once.

Extending Nyong'o's nonce taxonomy of what kinds of people there are to be found in the world, Joon Oluchi Lee's essay, "The Joy of the Castrated

Boy," draws our critical attention, along the lines of Freeman, to queer pleasures and desires. Lee suggests that the contemporary mainstreaming of queerness in both popular culture and the social imaginary has resulted in the embracing of a "mainstream ethics of gender" in queer studies. Indeed, like several other contributors to this special issue, Lee insists that certain prevailing epistemological paradigms, such as gay shame, have been implicitly universalized in queer studies to great social and political harm. Refusing the disavowal of castration and effeminacy that underwrites D. A. Miller's reading of the Broadway musical *Gypsy*, for instance, Lee posits an alternative to the anxious glorification of white masculinity that Miller erects as a defense against the feminine forms of identification that *Gypsy* demands and circulates. "I have always considered myself a castrated boy," Lee writes in relation to a stereotypical Asian masculinity, "and learned to be happy in that state because that was the only way I could live my life as the girl I knew myself to be." Simply put, Lee offers an "ecstatic" politics of racial castration in the place of an anxious phallic restoration of whiteness. Suggesting that the "joy" of the castrated boy might abet in the project of "undoing" gender—undoing, that is, the idealization of white masculinity in queer studies—Lee asserts that racial castration preserves a space of alterity to embrace "femininity as race" and "race as femininity." In this regard, Lee advances the groundbreaking project laid out by Eve Sedgwick in her 1991 essay, "How to Bring Your Kids Up Gay."[5]

Like cultural, postcolonial, and critical race studies, queer studies has been a privileged site for the explicit reconsideration of disciplinarity and knowledge production. All the essays in this special issue contend in some way or another with the question of queer epistemology, reorienting the field's potential to engage with a wide field of normalization precisely through a critical reengagement with intersectionality in its manifold forms and locations. The social and political potential of such a critique is "precisely calibrated to the degree to which 'queer' is deployed as a catachresis," Amy Villarejo observes in her essay, "Tarrying with the Normative: Queer Theory and *Black History*." Investigating the 1968 documentary *Black History: Lost, Stolen, or Strayed?* as a counterarchive for queer normalization, Villarejo posits a "queer of color" critique as making "good on the understanding of normativity as variegated, striated, contradictory," as the persistent tension "between systematization and desire, between reason and affect, between the literal and the figurative, between philosophy and literature." In these interstitial spaces, Villarejo discovers yet another caveat to the practice of queer intersectionality, encouraging us to abandon "a certain literal understanding of the role of abstraction as enforcing a logic of equivalence in the production of the symptom." Social and political differences cannot finally be equalized as analogous values or commensurate forms of domination; instead, they must be considered in and through their supplemental deployments.[6]

Queer Diasporas

Attention to queer epistemology generates alternate critical genealogies for queer studies outside its conventional relationship to francophone and Anglo-American literatures and literary studies, as well as its presumed white masculine subjects. "Women of color feminism" and "queer of color critique" collectively explored by Nyong'o, Lee, Ferguson, and Villarejo mark two such alternate critical genealogies for the investigation of normalization and difference. Queer diaspora is a third.

In their 1997 introduction to "Queer Transexions of Race, Nation, and Gender," the editors note that the "theorization of divergent sexualities offered by contemporary queer critique and the interrogation of race and ethnicity undertaken within postcolonial studies and critical race theory are among the most significant recent developments in social analysis and cultural criticism. While the best work in these fields have emphasized that their objects of study cannot be understood in isolation from one another, the critical ramifications of this fact have nevertheless gone largely unexplored."[7] Eight years later, the critical ramifications of such a project have become part of our intellectual consciousness largely because of a critical mass of scholarship in queer of color critique as well as queer diasporas. Collectively, these two fields have systematically rethought critical race theory (which takes the U.S. nation-state as its conceptual frame) and postcolonial studies alongside scattered deployments of sexuality—its uneven mappings of time and space across domestic as well as diasporic landscapes.

For instance, in its denaturalizing of various origin narratives, such as "home" and "nation," queer diasporas "investigates what might be gained politically by reconceptualizing diaspora not in conventional terms of ethnic dispersion, filiation, and biological traceability, but rather in terms of queerness, affiliation, and social contingency." By doing so, queer diasporas emerges as a critical site "providing new ways of contesting traditional family and kinship structures—of reorganizing national and transnational communities based not on origin, filiation, and genetics but on destination, affiliation, and the assumption of a common set of social practices or political commitments."[8]

In the shadows of postcoloniality, globalization, and the now infinite "war on terrorism," queer diasporas have also become a concerted site for the interrogation of the nation-state, citizenship, imperialism, and empire.

In the shadows of postcoloniality, globalization, and the now infinite "war on terrorism," queer diasporas have also become a concerted site for the interrogation of the nation-state, citizenship, imperialism, and empire.

It has examined the numerous ways in which racialized heteropatriarchy has been universalized as a Western discourse of (sexual) development, as a project of modernity and modernization, as a colonial and civilizing mission, as an index of political and social advancement, and as a story of human liberty and freedom. In this regard, the concerns of queer diasporas have worked, borrowing Dipesh Chakrabarty's term, to "provincialize" queer studies, bringing problems of citizenship, sovereignty, migration, asylum, welfare, the public sphere, and civil society to questions of sexuality and sexual development at the heart of the modern liberal nation-state. In the process, queer diasporas brings to conceptual crisis contradictions of global and domestic politics, as it broadens studies of migration in the Black Atlantic to consider other areas such as South Asia, East Asia, and Latin America. It shifts critical attention to the incommensurabilities of sexuality and national belonging while marking the false equivalences of the nation-state as well as the constitutive limits of "Queer Nation."

In her contribution to this special issue, "Bollywood Spectacles: Queer Diasporic Critique in the Aftermath of 9/11," Gayatri Gopinath delineates the methodology of queer diasporic critique through figurations of the impure, the inauthentic, and the nonreproductive. If queer diasporic critique, Gopinath observes, takes to task the "implicit heteronormativity within some strands of area studies," it also powerfully challenges "the parochialism of some strands of queer studies by making the study of sexuality central to an anti-imperialist, antiracist project." Reading the ascension and global circulation of Bollywood cinema as a spectacle to be safely consumed in a post-9/11 U.S. national imaginary, Gopinath posits the queer South Asian female diasporic subject as an impossible figure, one who stands in contradistinction to the neoliberal citizen-subject. The incommensurability of these two figures, Gopinath contends, creates a conceptual space for challenging the binary construction of South Asian bodies as either "terrorists" or "model minorities," as "inherently criminal and antinational or multicultural and assimilationist."

In similar regard, Jasbir K. Puar examines the "queer" figures of Sikh and Muslim terrorists. In "Queer Times, Queer Assemblages," Puar explores how the Bush administration's "war on terrorism" reconciles queerness to the liberal demands of rational subject formation, employing a rhetoric of sexual modernization that constructs the imperialist center as "tolerant" while castigating the backward other as "homophobic" and "perverse." In our contemporary political moment, exceptionalist discourses on sexual freedom all too easily conspire with U.S. nationalism and patriotism in the service of empire. Queer nationalism, Puar observes, "colludes with U.S. exceptionalisms embedded in nationalist foreign policy via the articulation and production of whiteness as a queer norm and the tacit acceptance of U.S. imperialist expansion." In short, nationalist debates on marriage and gays in the military come to replace any and all principled objections to state violence and torture, exemplified by Guantànamo and Abu Ghraib, on the global stage. Examining the figure of the suicide bomber as a "queer assemblage" resisting the demands of rational subject formation—the sanctioned binaries of subject and object—in favor of affective "temporal, spatial, and corporeal schisms," Puar suggests that the ontologies of such figures reorient a diasporic imaginary that queers the habitus of the nation-state, its geopolitical mandates and imperialist ambitions.

In "Asian Diasporas, Neoliberalism, and Family: Reviewing the Case for Homosexual Asylum in the Context of Family Rights," Chandan Reddy extends Puar's notion of "tolerance," queer nationalism, and U.S. exceptionalisms in a different direction. Reddy explores how the figure of the gay Pakistani asylum seeker works to challenge any contemporary understanding of the U.S. nation-state as the central guarantor of "freedom, destigmatization, and normality" in the global context of human rights or in the national arena of gay marriage political debate. Noting how recent U.S. immigration policy has worked to produce a racialized and gendered low-wage workforce precisely through the rubric of "family reunification" and its idealization of the heteropatriarchal family unit, he investigates how the state codes this migration as produced by the petitioning families themselves. In the process, the state projects itself as "a benevolent actor reuniting broken families or an overburdened and effete agent unable to prevent immigrants' manipulation of its (mandatory) democratic and fair laws." Either way, Reddy points out, the state gets to have its cake and eat it, too: such policies satisfy capital's need for an ever-expanding low-wage workforce while exacerbating the conditions of noncitizen life through the dismantling of economic and social resources for immigrant communities. In an ever-shrinking civil society, Reddy concludes, family reunification enables state power to "create heteropatriarchal relations for the recruitment and socialization of labor while justifying the exclusion of immigrant communities from state power through a liberal language of U.S. citizenship as the guarantor of individual liberty and sexual freedom."

Such guarantees to individual liberty and sexual freedom provide little security for undocumented queers, as well as queers of color, in urban metropoles, an issue Martin F. Manalansan takes up in his essay "Race, Violence, and Neoliberal Spatial Politics in the Global City." Manalansan explores the decimation of queer diasporic immigrant space in Jackson Heights, Queens. He notes how the disappearance of Arab as well as Muslim communities from neighborhood streets after the events of 9/11 coincided with the simultaneous gentrification of Jackson Heights as a "new exotic gay mecca" for Manhattanites to visit and to consume as aestheticized commodity. Speculating that the (de)politicizing of nationalist politics about terrorism and race is in part shored up through the neoliberal recoding of queer life and lifestyle as the freedom to travel, tour, and consume safely in various settings and locales, Manalansan delineates the urban processes by which global politics in a post-9/11 world come to be embedded into the built environment. Neoliberalism short-circuits the politics of queer diaspora precisely through the "stabilizing and normalizing of specific forms of capitalist inequalities" in the guise of economic opportunity and similitude. In the process, queer diasporics, queers of color, the feminized, the foreign, the colored, and the poor are left with the short end of the political stick, as discourses of "personal responsibility" serve to excuse state obligation toward collective, public caretaking.

If Manalansan focuses on how neoliberal and nationalist U.S. politics post-9/11 eviscerate queer diasporic spaces in the urban metropole, Karen Tongson's attention to the suburban and rural periphery in her essay "JJ Chinois's Oriental Express, or, How a Suburban Heartthrob Seduced Red America" relocates queer diasporic critique in the "heartland" of America. Tongson notes how queerness as hip metrosexuality configures these other areas as spaces of either departure or bypass. She examines the performance art of Lynne Chan, a second-generation Asian American artist, whose transgendered alter ego JJ Chinois denaturalizes a normative trajectory of queer development as the unidirectional migration from suburban to urban space by relocating his heartland adventures in the indeterminate zone of cyberspace. Through his domain name and virtual space, Tongson tracks JJ Chinois's exploits in "Red America," observing how this "dykeaspora" explodes "sentimental narratives" of longing inherent in not just heteronormative but certain queer renderings of diaspora.

Queer Liberalism

Is "queer liberalism" no longer a paradox?

As numerous essays in this special issue point out, the emergence of "queer liberalism" marks an unsettling though perhaps not entirely unexpected attempt to reconcile the radical political aspirations of queer studies' subjectless critique with the contemporary liberal demands of a nationalist gay and lesbian U.S. citizen-subject petitioning for rights and recognition before the law. Indeed, our current historical moment is marked by a particular coming together of economic and political spheres that form the basis for liberal inclusion: the merging of a certain queer consumer lifestyle first established in the 1980s (and now typified by Bravo's *Queer*

Eye for the Straight Guy) with recent juridical protections for gay and lesbian domesticity established by the landmark 2003 U.S. Supreme Court decision *Lawrence v. Texas* decriminalizing gay sodomy as well as the Commonwealth of Massachusett's legalizing of same-sex marriage in the same year. While in prior decades gays and lesbians sustained a radical critique of family and marriage, today many members of these groups have largely abandoned such critical positions, demanding access to the nuclear family and its associated rights, recognitions, and privileges from the state. That such queer liberalism comes at a historical moment of extreme right-wing nationalist politics should give us immediate pause.

While in prior decades gays and lesbians sustained a radical critique of family and marriage, today many members of these groups have largely abandoned such critical positions.

Given the negative referendum on gay marriage in the 2004 presidential election that witnessed George W. Bush's "reelection" on a platform of "moral values," such rights, recognitions, and privileges might indeed be, to borrow from Gayatri Spivak, something gays and lesbians "cannot not want." At the same time, queer intellectuals must untangle national forms of homophobia from the Republicans' wholesale economic assault on the poor. Doing so would help to clarify the meaning of anti–gay marriage votes. For instance, Lisa Duggan's recent work on the politics of gay marriage suggests that most people in the United States are in favor of limited domestic partnership rights. However, they oppose gay marriage because traditional marriage is increasingly the only way to access federal welfare benefits in the United States. What Duggan has aptly labeled "homonormativity," the gay and lesbian liberal platform advocating for gay marriage while rhetorically remapping and recoding freedom and liberation in narrow terms of privacy, domesticity, and the unfettered ability to consume in the "free" market, collaborates with a mainstreamed nationalist politics of identity, entitlement, inclusion, and personal responsibility, while abandoning a more global critique of capitalist exploitation and domination, state violence and expansion, and religious fundamentalisms and hate.[9]

The turning away from a sustained examination of the vast inequalities in civil society and commercial life that mark the paradoxes of queer liberalism find an unwitting accomplice in certain strands of contemporary queer studies. As numerous essays in this special issue emphasize, the problems of political economy cannot be abstracted away from the racial, gendered, and sexual hierarchies of the nation-state but must in fact be understood as operating in and through them. Yet the current return to an unapologetic and rapacious white masculine heteropatriarchy in a putatively "postidentity" and "postracial" U.S. nation-state finds some odd bedfellows in mainstream queer studies.

For instance, both Hiram Perez and Judith Halberstam take the occasion of an international "Gay Shame" conference at the University of Michigan in March 2003 to analyze how queer studies has evolved over the last fifteen years to produce, and to reproduce, its own canonical set of proper subjects and objects, as well as intellectual methods and institutional spaces. In "You Can Have My Brown Body and Eat It, Too!" Perez resists queer liberalism's demand for the "active untroubling" of race in queer studies. He notes that the conference occurred within a week of the U.S. invasion of Iraq and in the midst of the *Grutter v. Bollinger* (2003) and *Gratz v. Bollinger* (2003) affirmative action cases involving the University of Michigan, yet it was a conference that included only one queer person of color out of forty invited participants. Perez speculates that our conservative historical moment finds an unfortunate parallel in the attempts to entrench a "transparent white subject" at the heart of queer studies: "Queer theorists who can invoke that transparent subject, and choose to do so," Perez writes, "reap the dividends of whiteness." "Brown" is what needs to be exploited and maintained for a weak multiculturalism to inhere, the "fixity" of race providing the ground for queer theory's performative sexuality, the ground against which the figure of complex (white) gay male sexuality and shame unfolded. "The chronic failure of establishmentarian queer theory to revisit its fundamental collusions with American liberalism," Perez concludes, "consolidates indivisibilities—white, patriarchal, heteronormative—contrary to any professed anti-identity."

Like Perez, Halberstam recognizes the political and intellectual promises of queer studies as yet unfulfilled to the extent that queer too quickly collapses back into "gay and lesbian" and, more often than not, a "possessive individualism" that simply connotes "gay," "white," and "male." In "Shame and White Gay Masculinity," Halberstam contends that the future of queer studies "depends absolutely on moving away from white gay male identity politics and learning from the radical critiques offered by a younger generation of queer scholars who draw their intellectual inspiration from feminism and ethnic studies rather than white queer studies." Observing that feminism and queer of color critique offer a rich critical vocabulary for female and racialized subjects to respond to the politics of shame and neoliberal claims to rights, Halberstam notes that "the only people really lacking a politically urgent language with which to describe and counter shame are gay white men." Indeed, it is gay white male shame, Halberstam concludes, "that has proposed 'pride' as the appropriate remedy and that focuses its libidinal and other energies on simply rebuilding the self that shame dismantled rather than taking apart the social processes that project shame onto queer subjects in the first place."

Much of queer theory nowadays sounds like a metanarrative about the domestic affairs of white homosexuals. Surely, queer studies promises more than a history of gay men, a sociology of gay male sex clubs, an anthropology of gay male tourism, a survey of gay male aesthetics. The emergence of queer liberalism challenges us to reconsider some of the canonical ideas of the field—shame and intimacy, normal and antinormal, publics and counterpublics—for their contemporary liberal deployments. As crucial as these intellectual paradigms have been to the establishment of queer studies, it is important to insist on their continuing reevaluation in both their historical applications and their contemporary contexts. The discourse of publics and counterpublics, for instance, traces itself to a Habermasian analysis of the emergence of the bourgeois public sphere and the rise of liberal society in eighteenth-century Enlightenment thought. The homogeneity of Habermas's public sphere—its assumptions of an abstract citizen-subject who inhabits and moves with ease through civil society—reprises the universalizing tendencies of "gay shame" as well as progress narratives of Western modernity and development that postcolonial, feminist, and critical race studies have effectively deconstructed.

The dialectic of public and counterpublic loses any critical edge to account for "perverse" modernities, those queer bodies and knowledges that exist outside the boundaries of sanctioned time and space, legal status, citizen-subjecthood, and liberal humanism. In this regard, Nayan Shah's contribution, "Policing Privacy, Migrants, and the Limits of Freedom," rethinks the liberation narrative of *Lawrence v. Texas* in the context of early-twentieth-century sodomy cases involving racialized migrant workers in the rural West. Shah contends that, historically, "sexual identity is not the determining factor in prosecuting sodomy, but, rather, differentials of class, age, and race shape the policing that leads to sodomy and public morals arrests." Finding a contemporary parallel in the mixed-race "couple" of John Lawrence (who is white) and Tyrone Garner (who is black), petitioners in the *Lawrence v. Texas* case, Shah asks where and for whom does privacy, mobility, and freedom of intimate contact apply historically and legally. He observes that the gay male subject assumed by contemporary queer theorists in public-counterpublic debates "has both free access to participate in the public world of the intimate and may also retreat to a private realm of intimacy." In turn, Shah posits Samuel Delany's queer ethnography of the radical transformation of Times Square beginning in the mid-1980s as situating "inequality and interclass and interethnic contact at the center of his analysis of public sex and sexual publics."[10]

Tackling the liberatory assumptions of *Lawrence v. Texas* from another angle, Teemu Ruskola's "Gay Rights versus Queer Theory: What Is Left of Sodomy after *Lawrence v. Texas*?" asks to "what extent are commitments to queerness and liberal rights compatible?" Noting how *Lawrence v. Texas* anxiously inscribes a discourse of "dignity" and "respect" to gay and lesbian relationships rather than to gay and lesbian sex, Ruskola insists that an "intimate personal relationship should not be a requirement for having a constitutionally protected sex life." The insistent analogizing of homosexual intimacy to heterosexual marriage in Justice Kennedy's majority decision in *Lawrence v. Texas* belies the resilience of compulsory heterosexuality in its "new, second-generation form." Gay liberation and rights do not connote "freedom," however useful or politically necessary they might be. Instead, *Lawrence v. Texas* leaves queer subjects in an underregulated and nebulous space between "criminalization and legitimization through marriage."

Both Michael Cobb's and Janet R. Jakobsen's essays round out the issue by exploring queer liberation in the context of religion and regulation. In "Uncivil Wrongs: Race, Religion, Hate, and Incest in Queer Politics," Cobb investigates religious hate speech as the "limits of liberalism." Exploring the various religious arguments against homosexuality as the "horror of incest" and the "decline of the traditional, heterosexual family," he observes that the alignment of homosexuality with "like race" analogies provides a political opportunity to expose the liberal limits of tolerance and free speech.

Extending Cobb's insights, Jakobsen's essay, "Sex + Freedom = Regulation: Why?" offers a careful genealogy of "freedom" in relation to the institution of marriage. Jakobsen traces how the Protestant Reformation linked the idea of individual freedom to the institution of marriage. "Marriage, then, like the market," she writes, "is part of the freedom from the church that marks the beginning of modernity." Yet it would be foolish to think that in the capitalist marketplace freedom is the antithesis of sexual regulation and that the marketplace is "value-free." The incitement to matrimony and reproductive sexuality—the option to wed a partner of one's own "choosing"—becomes the *only* expression of sexual freedom in the secular age and is thus "constitutive of freedom as we know it." In the era of queer liberalism, it would be a mistake to believe that, since sexual regulation seems to be based in religious intolerance and hate, the answer would be to defend secular freedom. "Our problem," Jakobsen concludes, "is as much secular freedom as it is religious regulation." That gay identity, which starts with freedom from the family, has led us so inexorably and vehemently back to the institution of same-sex marriage ironically symptomizes this confusion. It is through marriage that gay people fully become individuals, and this discourse of individualism is precisely the point at which sexual regulation and gay "liberation" meet.

Where Now?

In her closing comments at the "Gay Shame" conference at the University of Michigan, Gayle Rubin suggested that the event's participants might shift for a moment their attentions from "gay shame" to "gay humility." In an age of queer liberalism, Rubin's call for "gay humility" serves as heuristic device for a return to what a desirably queer world might look like. In our putatively "postidentity" and "postracial" age such a turn is urgent. In this regard, our attention to queer epistemology, queer diasporas, and queer liberalism might be considered one modest attempt to frame queer studies more insistently and productively within a politics of epistemological humility.

Our attention to queer epistemology, queer diasporas, and queer liberalism might be considered one modest attempt to frame queer studies more insistently and productively within a politics of epistemological humility.

Such a politics must also recognize that much of contemporary queer scholarship emerges from U.S. institutions and is largely written in English. This fact indicates a problematic dynamic between U.S. scholars whose work in queer studies is read in numerous sites around the world. Scholars writing in other languages and from other political and cultural perspectives read but are not, in turn, read. These uneven exchanges replicate in uncomfortable ways the rise and consolidation of U.S. empire, as well as the insistent positing of a U.S. nationalist identity and political agenda globally. We propose epistemological humility as one form of knowledge production that recognizes these dangers.

From a similar perspective, and in regard to a virulent post–9/11 U.S. militarism that dominates contemporary politics, Judith Butler observes that the "very fact that we live with others whose values are not the same as our own, or who set a limit to what we can know, or who are opaque to us, or who are strange, or are partially understood, that just means we live with a kind of humility."[11] Butler suggests that that to take responsibility in democratic polity does not mean to take responsibility for "the entirety of the world" but to place ourselves "in a vividly de-centered way" in a world marked by the differences of others. An ethical attachment to others insists that we cannot be the center of the world or act unilaterally on its behalf. It demands a world in which we must sometimes relinquish not only our epistemological but also our political certitude. Suffice it to say that to appreciate "what's queer about queer studies now" is to embrace such a critical perspective and to honor such an ethics of humility.

Notes

For their thoughtful feedback and comments, we would like to thank Brent Edwards, Katherine Franke, Janet R. Jakobsen, David Kazanjian, Ann Pellegrini, Teemu Ruskola, Josie Saldaña, and Leti Volpp, as well as the *Social Text* collective.

1. See, for instance, Samuel R. Delany, *Times Square Red, Times Square Blue* (New York: New York University Press, 1999); David L. Eng, *Racial Castration: Managing Masculinity in Asian America* (Durham, NC: Duke University Press, 2001); Roderick A. Ferguson, *Aberrations in Black: Toward a Queer of Color Critique* (Minneapolis: University of Minnesota Press, 2004); Phillip Brian Harper, *Are We Not Men? Masculine Anxiety and the Problem of African-American Identity* (New York: Oxford University Press, 1996); Licia Fiol-Matta, *A Queer Mother for the Nation: The State and Gabriela Mistral* (Minneapolis: University of Minnesota Press, 2002); Gayatri Gopinath, *Impossible Desires: Queer Desire and South Asian Public Cultures* (Durham, NC: Duke University Press, 2005); Martin F. Manalansan, *Global Divas: Filipino Gay Men in the Diaspora* (Durham, NC: Duke University Press, 2003); José Esteban Muñoz, *Disidentifications: Queers of Color and the Performance of Politics* (Minneapolis: University of Minnesota Press, 1999); José Quiroga, *Tropics of Desire: Interventions from Queer Latino America* (New York: New York University Press, 2000); Robert Reid-Pharr, *Black Gay Man: Essays* (New York: New York University Press, 2001); Juana Maria Rodriguez, *Queer Latinidad: Identity Practices, Discursive Spaces* (New York: New York University Press, 2003); and Mary Pat Brady, *Extinct Lands, Temporal Geographies: Chicana Literature and the Urgency of Space* (Durham, NC: Duke University Press, 2002).

2. Judith Butler, "Critically Queer," in *Bodies That Matter: On the Discursive Limits of "Sex"* (New York: Routledge, 1993), 230.

3. Michael Warner, introduction to *Fear of a Queer Planet: Queer Politics and Social Theory*, ed. Michael Warner (Minneapolis: University of Minnesota Press, 1993), xxvi.

4. In his book *Aberrations in Black*, for instance, Ferguson explores how both Marxist and liberal theories of social power implicitly configure subject formation through their reliance on an "organic" distinction between adult heterosexuality and "immature" and "deviant" forces of aberrant sexual practices. It is on the terrain of heteropatriarchy that these seemingly divergent theories of social power in fact converge. "Put plainly," Ferguson writes, "racialization has helped to articulate heteropatriarchy as universal" (6).

5. Eve Kosofsky Sedgwick, "How to Bring Your Kids Up Gay: The War on Effeminate Boys," *Social Text*, no. 29 (1991): 18–27.

6. See Gayatri Chakravorty Spivak, "Scattered Speculations on the Theory of Value," in her *In Other Worlds: Essays in Cultural Politics* (New York: Routledge, 1988), 154–75.

7. Phillip Brian Harper, Anne McClintock, José Esteban Muñoz, and Trish Rosen, "Queer Transexions of Race, Nation, and Gender: An Introduction," *Social Text*, nos. 52/53 (1997): 1.

8. David L. Eng, "Transnational Adoption and Queer Diasporas," *Social Text*, no. 76 (2003): 4.

9. See Lisa Duggan, *The Twilight of Equality? Neoliberalism, Cultural Politics, and the Attack on Democracy* (Boston: Beacon, 2003).

10. Ground-level sites of queer belonging are theory-generating spaces. Thus we think of the collective political organizing of groups like the Audre Lorde Project and the South Asian Lesbian and Gay Association in New York City as offering us valuable knowledge that queer intimacy in a diasporic setting may have considerable theoretical heft.

11. European Graduate School Faculty, "Judith Butler: Quotes," www.egs.edu/faculty/butler-resources.html.

Punk'd Theory

Tavia Nyong'o

I said I was a nerd, but I'm not a punk.
—N.E.R.D., *In Search Of . . .*

The political scientist Cathy Cohen has proposed that queer theory and politics be reconceptualized and made more relevant to the lives and struggles of "punks, bulldaggers, and welfare queens."[1] In speaking of—and on behalf of—punks, bulldaggers, and welfare queens, and in asking where one might find them located within the political project of queer theory, Cohen does not simply challenge us to pay attention to previously ignored identities. Rather, in proposing the nonce taxonomy of "punks, bulldaggers, and welfare queens,"[2] Cohen attempts to interrupt the litigious process through which subjects petition for admission to queer theoretical attention and political concern. She proposes instead an antiauthoritarian process of subject formation closer in spirit to what, on the punk scene, is called D.I.Y., or do it yourself.[3]

Cohen's discontent with the radical aspirations of queer politics (which I collate with queer theory for present purposes) registers an additional irony. As is now commonplace to observe, "queer" theory first emerged as a vernacular-tinged protest against the more rarified operations of "theory" as such. That queer theory should have in turn emerged as the target of vernacular scorn, one indexed by the alternative nomination of a series of street taxonomies that have not, like "queer," been elevated to the status of an academic discipline but have instead been abandoned to the tender mercies of the neoliberal state, ought to give pause. That this perceived transformation of queer theory from "street" to "straight" theorizing (more on this contrast in a moment) should have come so rapidly—at times it seems as if queer theory was greeted at birth with castigations of academic insularity—ought to become the occasion for further sustained reflection. But at the same time, recent declarations of the death of theory, however dubious, do remind us not to take the permanency of such transformations for granted.[4] The fate of the theorist today, wandering around unwilling to repent her or his irrelevancy, complicates any assumptions about academic privilege or security. In calling attention to such hostile framings of theorizing as irrelevant, exhausted, etc., I evoke a dimension

Social Text 84–85, Vol. 23, Nos. 3–4, Fall–Winter 2005.

of the punk experience with abjection that might be fruitful for theory to ponder.

In this essay I take up some implications and ironies of Cohen's critique by investigating the intersection of punk and queer. In contrast to the standard mode of intersectionality,[5] I want to speculate upon another sort of intersection implied but not fully articulated in Cohen, one that is perhaps more phenomenological than sociological in nature. Cohen calls for an accounting within queer analysis for the simultaneity of racism and class oppression alongside sexism and homophobia. Such a call might be read as proposing the addition of further dimensions to the queer problematic, in an almost geometric effort to more accurately picture the social whole. I want to suggest, however, that the word *intersectional* might also point in another direction. What if we take "punks, bulldaggers, and welfare queens" as neither exhaustive nor programmatic, still less as a grand unifying theory of social oppression, but instead used this nonce taxonomy to express creative discontent with settled categories and an identification with the punk spirit? Might we theorize the intersection of punk and queer as an encounter between concepts both lacking in fixed identitarian referent, but which are nonetheless periodically caught up and frozen, as it were, within endemic modern crises of racialization? Might a reanimation of this other intersectionality better equip us to revivify both street and straight theorizing?

The figure of the punk in Anglo-American culture is a venerable but mercurial one, and to trace it fully would exceed my present effort. In my nonce proposal for a punk or punk'd theory, I do not take up the more expected sites of investigation. I do not, for instance, consider punk rock directly.[6] Although in a longer treatment of this topic such a consideration would be essential, I begin here by focusing on some less-expected cultural moments at which punk has been figured. Such figurations of punk have more than a nominal relation to the canonical ones, and understanding something more of the connections between them—and the discourses of race and sex that simultaneously make and mask such connections—is an important part of the project of "punking" theory.

But what do punks and queers have in common, other than the obvious? And what might be the gain, for academic theory, and perhaps also for activism, in building upon this commonalty? Can we, as scholars, contribute to the cultivation of a punk spirit of anticapitalist subculture, art, and politics? It is with these questions in mind that I offer this preliminary and prospective mapping of an intellectual and perhaps political project.[7] I broach this topic as a queer scholar and not at all, to be candid, as a current or former punk. In addition to this caveat, there are two other obvious objections to address. The first is that I have willfully misread

Cohen's use of *punk* as African American slang for a gay man. Her purpose is to distinguish a punk from a queer, the latter being racially unmarked and therefore presumptively white. Admitting this misreading, I defend it below through an etymological retangling of these two supposedly distinct types of punk. My aim here is to call attention to a preexisting conflation that I feel provides an intellectual opportunity.

The second objection is that, in commending punk to the attention of queer theorists, my terms of pop reference are out of date. Hip-hop surely, or rave culture, or the Internet, would all provide more relevant and timely sources for the kind of "street theorizing" that the queer studies scholar Kath Weston has argued for.[8] But in an urbanized and overdeveloped culture that wants to live nowhere but at the cutting edge, a defiantly backward glance just might prove revivifying.[9] And, ultimately, the two objections answer each other, for it is in the racialization of the figure of the punk that the question of its present currency is justified. Since Cohen wrote, the black inflection on punk has been mainstreamed in contemporary American culture to the point where it may possibly be eclipsing prior associations with the likes of Sid and Nancy. Let me begin, then, with this contemporary American "Africanization" of the meanings of punk.

"Punked" as American Africanism

> *Punked* (v) : 1. When you make fun of someone so bad they have nothing else to say back. 2. When you hook up with a guy and he doesn't call you ever again. 3. While detained in a prison or jail, to be raped by a fellow inmate.
> —UrbanDictionary.com

> And of course, one can hardly afford to be put down too often, or one is beat, one has lost one's confidence, one has lost one's will, one is impotent in the world of action and so closer to the demeaning flip of becoming a queer.
> —Norman Mailer, "The White Negro: Superficial Reflections on the Hipster"

The diverse usages of punk as verb and noun mark it as a folk variant of what Raymond Williams called a "keyword." In contrast to the keywords Williams discussed in his famous book of the same name, punk is folk culture and does not keep company with serious words like *folk* or *culture*.[10] That punk nonetheless counts as "street theorizing" can be seen in the proposed homology that the above definitions for *punked*—drawn from the populist Web site UrbanDictionary.com[11]—propose between the

The core meaning of getting "put down," "flipped," "ripped off," or "punked"—from at least the late 1950s to the early 2000s—appears to be getting scapegoated within an erotic and masculinized economy of scarcity.

experiences of (1) being teased, (2) not being called after sex, and (3) being raped in prison. As Norman Mailer puts it in "The White Negro,"[12] punk is "a prime symbol" (225), cheerfully serving the lexicon with flexibility comparable to the word *fuck* and with some noticeable denotative overlap to that latter word as well.[13] Although *punk* is not of central concern to Mailer, a related word, *beat*, is. The meaning Mailer ascribes to *beat*—"the demeaning flip of becoming a queer"—makes it perfectly clear that the homology drawn by street theorizing on punking and getting punked resembles the "situation beyond one's experience, impossible to anticipate" (225) that is Mailer's hipster's prime symbol of dread.

The core meaning of getting "put down," "flipped," "ripped off," or "punked"—from at least the late 1950s to the early 2000s—appears to be getting scapegoated within an erotic and masculinized economy of scarcity. In this economy, another's pleasure comes at the cost of your pain. Ass fucking serves as a "prime symbol" of this economy. Sodomy, in the homophobic imagination, is the "situation beyond one's experience, impossible to anticipate," and is associated with extreme forms of unfreedom like imprisonment, slavery, and rape.[14]

It is not sufficient, however, to arrest our theorization of sodomy at the level of homophobia. Street theorizing around the word *punk* marks a discursive space in which the possibility of desiring sodomy, desiring to be sodomized, is unthinkable but, nevertheless, unavoidable. The very sexual practice, which serves as metaphor for almost any mundane humiliation, is itself intermittently exempted from its own connotational penumbra. Mailer, for instance, speaks not of the fear of being "put down" but rather of being "put down too often." In similar fashion, UrbanDictionary.com inserts between two meanings of *punked* that indicate a dread of getting fucked a third meaning—a sort of etymological Lucky Pierre—signaling the dread of *not* getting fucked: "When you hook up with a guy and he doesn't call you ever again." One is punked in this case because, by not calling you afterward, the "guy" is retroactively minimizing your enjoyment of the mutual sex by making it clear that he was just "using" you. But this meaning of punked makes no sense unless you wanted the hookup in the first place and, indeed, were sort of looking forward to further hookups. That is, it makes no sense unless, in some sense, you wanted to get flipped.

Of course, it is precisely upon its ambiguity that the power of slang pivots. So I would be naive to imagine that deconstructing slang will in itself erode its force. What we need is thicker descriptions of the experiences that these ambiguities account for. Part of this thicker description entails grasping the racial dimension of the epithets "punk" and "punked." I have mentioned that one of the several significances of Cohen's essay is its marking of "punk" as black vernacular for "faggot" or "queer."[15] Clarence Major's authoritative compendium of black slang, *Juba to Jive: A Dictionary of African-American Slang*, defines *punk* as a "derogatory term for male homosexual" and a "male pejorative term for any other male without similar interest; a weak man; any male who gives in to anal intercourse in prison."[16] It is this American Africanism, I argue, that has been popularized on the practical joke television show *Punk'd* that has aired on the MTV network since the spring of 2003. On the show, the white actor Ashton Kutcher—a deodorized simulacrum of Mailer's hipster—leads a gang who "punk" hapless celebrities. Their targets have included both male and female celebrities of many races.

In the context of contemporary U.S. mass culture, Kutcher's use of "punk'd" has a specific frisson. It was made possible by the mainstreaming of hip-hop slang and the ensuing wave of new "white Negroes."[17] *Punk'd*, however, does not fit the model of a surreptitious African retention in English, such as *okay*.[18] No source I consulted could definitively trace the origin of the word *punk*, but a representative etymology reports that "the word originated in British slang around the end of the 17th century when it was used to denote a *whore* and later a precursor to the modern *rent boy*."[19] Although this account does not preclude an African origin for the word, I read the evidence as indicating that *punk'd* emerges from within what Dick Hebdige has called the "frozen dialectic between black and white cultures," that is, a word for which the memory of its English provenance has been surrogated by the imagination of a black resonance.[20] Telltale evidence of this faux-African origin is the use of "eye dialect," ungrammatical spellings indistinguishable in audible speech from grammatical ones (e.g., "punk'd" for "punked").[21] Such a graphic practice has characterized white transcription of black speech since slavery times, so MTV's eye dialect notifies us that we are in the presence of what the novelist Toni Morrison has termed an "American Africanism."

Such usages, Morrison notes, make "a playground of the imagination" out of "the dramatic polarity created by skin color" and "impute African meanings—black meanings—as a way of simultaneously acknowledging and distancing a shared experience, state, or desire through spuriously ascribing it to black people."[22] Morrison's central point—that "race" is produced out of an ongoing avoidance of an ongoing history of racist domination, rather than being the product of a benign diversity of "ethnic heritages"—is somewhat unfashionable today, despite the popularity of her novels. But it is this relational model of "race" and racism (which is not, I would say, reducible or equivalent to the bankrupt model "race relations") that I want to argue is needed to unpack the cultural meanings of *punk* in contemporary U.S. and British cultures.

Only a dialectical approach can account for the incongruity of MTV endorsing Cohen's reclamation of punk as black language. That is to say, where in its early days MTV hysterically disavowed any black influence on the musical forms it marketed (it took no smaller a phenomenon than Michael Jackson to break the channel's color bar), black style has come to dominate the network's offerings, and proscriptive markings of blackness appear only to whet the mainstream appetite. Such a white embrace of ostensibly exclusionary black style is neither new nor specifically American. Speaking of the British punk scene in the late 1970s, Hebdige notes that "paradoxically it was here, in the exclusiveness of Black West Indian style, in the virtual impossibility of authentic white identification, that reggae's attraction for the punks was strongest. . . . Reggae's blackness was proscriptive. It was an alien essence, a foreign body which implicitly threatened British culture from within and as such it resonated with punk's adopted values" (64). In interpreting this passage, we should remember Paul Gilroy's critique of naturalizing such language of "foreign bodies" in "British culture."[23] But we should also note that, in the opening pages of *Subculture: The Meaning of Style*, Hebdige felt the need to apologize for the amount of attention his text on punk pays to "the largely neglected dimension of race and race relations." Remarkably, the same word that Cohen could assume circa 1997 would firmly connote blackness to her readers could, just two decades earlier, just as clearly mark a cultural style awaiting an overdue racial perspective. I believe this situation is not accidental. That is to say, and this is a major argument of my essay, I think Cohen and Hebdige are discussing a single, complex phenomena—frozen dialectically between black and white—and not two distinct topics. I think the linkage is deeper than just the reappearance of a word, but rather the reappearance of an experiential field that the word indexes.

The enduring strength of Hebdige's reading is the agility with which it pivots between the object of subcultural style and its meaning. He reads this object in terms of its historical context and, at the same time, how it revolts, through style, against that context. He is thereby able to read "race" into styles that conspicuously dismiss black style.[24] Most persuasively, he argues that punk "translated" the concept of a victimized "ethnicity" from a black to a white context, a move economically summarized in a quotation the punk rocker Richard Hell gave to the *New Musical Express* (as reported by Hebdige): "Punks are niggers."[25]

But what kinds of "niggers" are punks, exactly? Apparently, they are "niggers" as opposed to "queers." According to Hebdige, "the scruffiness and earthiness of punk ran directly counter to the arrogance, elegance, and verbosity of the glam rock superstars" (63), above all, David Bowie.[26] Here is a point where a useful queer intervention can be made into Hebdige's analysis. According to Hebdige, the punk-as-nigger identifies against the glamorous homosexual. Indeed, Hebdige associates the rise of "glam and glitter rock" (59) with both the musical "atrophy into vacuous disco-bounce and sugary ballads" (60) as well as the "segregation" of British youth culture into black-and-white camps (59). The "new sexually ambiguous image" (60) of Bowie, Hebdige reports, represented

> a deliberate avoidance of the "real" world and the prosaic language in which that world was habitually described, experienced and reproduced. . . . Bowie's meta-message was escape—from class, from sex, from personality, from obvious commitment—into a fantasy past (Isherwood's Berlin peopled by a ghostly cast of doomed bohemians) or a science-fiction future. (61)

Such passages leave one with the impression that punk hostility to glam paid homage to an imagined black-white alliance. And yet Hebdige admits black-white solidarity was made possible "only by continually monitoring trouble spots (e.g., the distribution of white girls) and by scapegoating other alien groups ('queers,' hippies, and Asians)" (59). But why did the "extreme foppishness" of the queers block youth subcultures from unifying black and white working-class men? Why did "the prosaic language in which that world was habitually described, experienced and reproduced" exclude queer experience? Here a critique of masculinity—and its distortions of both language and culture—is needed.

In an odd and perhaps telling turn of phrase, Hebdige argues that punk was "designed to puncture glam rock's extravagantly ornate style" (63). Hebdige does not explicitly endorse this puncturing—or punking—of the utopic and nostalgic dimensions of queer style, this phallic refusal of the political possibilities of "morbid pretensions to art and intellect" (62). But neither does he subject it to critical scrutiny. This is so despite the fact that queer objects are oddly central to his account. The work opens with an excerpt from Jean Genet's *Thief's Journal*, in which Hebdige locates the ideal-type for the subcultural object: Genet's "tube of vaseline [. . . a] 'dirty wretched object'" that "proclaim[s] his homosexuality to the world" (1). Hebdige's choice is not unjustifiable in terms of actual punk object choices, such as "offensive" T-shirts of two naked cowboys kissing, or naming a band *The Homosexuals*, a name that was meant as a "fuck you" rather than an identification. But, ironically for a text that rigidly proscribes the "ornate style" of glam, such queer objects are purely ornamental to Hebdige's main theoretical project. Much as a desire to be punked appears in the absent center of the vernacular horror of getting punked, a queer object appears in the absent center of an analysis largely devoted to explaining away the capacity of queer objects to revolt through style. It is through the eliding of queer affect, I suggest, that Hebdige's analysis reproduces the dominant figure of masculinity that constantly transmits the "racial" meanings Morrison critiqued and identified.

Punk City

This use of an underinterpreted contrast between the punk and the queer recurs in other examples of the "frozen dialectic" between black and white. In the Academy Award–winning U.S. documentary, *Scared Straight!* (1978), a group of adolescent men and women are "sentenced" to spend three hours in Rahway State Prison, during which they are berated and threatened by the Lifers, a group of long-term convicts. The filming portrays the youths as narcissistic and unrepentant. Because they do not respond to shame, they must instead be punked. They are abandoned to the topsy-turvy world of prison, where convicted criminals literally run the show. The documentary depicts prison as the way society itself might be without the protections of law and norm.[27] The punks, in being exposed to this truly anomic violence, will, it is hoped, revert to good behavior. The success or failure of this strategy provides the theme of the many and highly sentimental follow-up episodes appended to the documentary throughout the 1980s and 1990s. I focus here on the original documentary, as an example of a cultural text, contemporaneous to the emergence of punk rock, in which the American Africanist connotation of "punk" is already manifested. But *Scared Straight!* is also a transitional text, insofar as what is now seen as black slang was primarily understood then as prison slang. The film thus represents an early figuration of the rise of the prison-industrial complex within the distorting mirror of law-and-order ideology and its racializing imperatives. As a film it provides the template followed by popular shows of the 1990s like *Oz* and, more elliptically, by shows like *Punk'd*, which share *Scared Straight!*'s interest in exposing a zone of anomic violence—always figured with the "help" of unwilling black participants—underlying and threatening the social order.[28]

The highly scripted character of the inmates' conduct (and perhaps also the youths' responses) makes the encounter feel ritualistic. In particular, the session resembles an ersatz initiation rite, in which the inmates play the role of adult male villagers, guiding the youths into responsible adulthood. A primary mode of that ritualized violence is, perhaps predictably, the threat to "do bodily harm to your asshole." The articulation between this lawless behavior and the lawful future lives of heterosexual domesticity the documentary is intended to produce cries out for further exploration.

Scared Straight! maps a bifurcated society traversed by two forces: the silent power of the penal apparatus (which the documentary film crew identifies itself and its viewers with) and the loud, offensive sound of what the film calls "street talk." The temporary disruption of the normal bounds of propriety (the profanity-laced film was broadcast unexpurgated on television) is marked by a slang figured as the only language that can reach the youth. The link that "street talk" establishes between prison and the street renders the latter a sort of extrusion of the former. The lawlessness of prison spills out into the streets, the site of crime. The film thus operates through the same voyeuristic technology of panopticism that the evening news continuously resorts to, in which we see crime but remain unseen to it.

The link that "street talk" establishes between prison and the street renders the latter a sort of extrusion of the former.

The spectacle of street talk masks the surveillance of the penal apparatus. Prison guards are hardly depicted. At a key moment, an inmate histrionically yells at the camera, as if it were not his performance's occasion. Street talk is enlisted to the work of penology. The street theorizing of the Lifers—don't come to jail or you're going to get punked—is rendered supplemental to disciplinary power, which is allowed to operate behind the scenes as a silent partner.[29] The Lifers present themselves as bogeyman images of the youths' own dystopian futures. And the Lifers portray their desires to punk the youths in the universalizing terms of an animalistic state of nature. One (unnamed) inmate shouts, "Well, we got sexual desires too. We're just like you. We're made of flesh and blood. You tough guy, take a wild guess. When we got sexual desires, who do you think we kick, and don't tell me each other! Who?" As he asks this question, the inmate sticks his face up close to that of one of the young men and then veers up again to answer it, in case there was any doubt: "I gotta tell you, I've been down here ten years, and I'm going to die in this stinking joint, and if they wanted to give me these three bitches right here [gestures toward the three women in the group] I would leap over them like a kangaroo, just to get to one pretty young fat butt boy." His voice dropping nearly to a whisper as he ends that sentence, he leans again into the face of another of the young men. The other Lifers voice their agreement.

The concept of "situational homosexuality" (an oddly redundant term: what kind of homosexuality could occur outside a situation?) is especially ill equipped to theorize the deployment of sexuality in such disciplinary performances. What the inmate "confesses" to is his readiness to play the "masculine" role in prison society, and his readiness to feminize the youth, to turn them into women (which is one reason the inmates do not threaten the young women with rape: as women, they are already feminized, and the threat of rape upon them is not one restricted to the dystopian space of the prison but one that characterizes the ostensibly "free" space outside the prison, which it is the function of the film to idealize). Male rape, along with "coarse street talk," is called forth to supplement the social order.

What the film aptly calls "homosexual taunts" serve not to produce queer subjectivities but to deter them at all costs. The efficacy of scaring straight, negligible in terms of deterring street crime, seems to come rather in the production of sodomy without sodomites.[30] When both media and the state have been engaged in such practices of sexualized domination of the urbanized and racialized dispossessed since the 1970s, are we at least entitled to speak of the social construction of the punk? What would it mean to identify the authentic language of the street, its theorizing, not as some autonomous space that the law must at all costs come to dominate but rather as the active site of the law's production, through the street's supplemental provision of terror?[31]

There are no actual homosexuals in *Scared Straight!* except in one place: protective custody or, as the Lifers call it, "punk city." Punk city exists because of a contradiction in the logic of imprisonment: where do you place the victim and agent of a crime that occurs in prison? It is not that the Lifers tell the youths that this is where they might go if they happen to be gay. No such "natural" gayness is even speculated upon by the film. Rather, punk city represents a kind of no-place or blind spot within the bifurcated theorization of the social, a place of unthinkability. Beyond the state of exception that the film maps and determines—the straight-street nexus—there is this third space that seems to exist beyond a relation to either form of knowledge or experience. In my conclusion, I revision this third space. But first, I want to take one step further back into the genealogy of punk, revisiting Mailer's canonical performance of the frozen dialectic.

Punk'd Theory

The third space beyond the street-straight binary is both evoked and avoided in Mailer's essay "The White Negro." Here the homosexual appears as an example of a "condition of psychopathy" shared by "politicians, professional soldiers, newspaper columnists, entertainers, artists, jazz musicians, call girls, promiscuous homosexuals, and half the executives of Hollywood, television and advertising" (218). An alternative grouping of psychopaths Mailer provides is "the homosexual, the orgiast, the drug-addict, the rapist, the robber, and the murderer" (219). Such absurd lists of deviants share a surface resemblance to the "nonce taxonomies" through which, Eve Sedgwick suggests, "the precious, devalued arts of gossip [refine the] necessary skills for making, testing, and using unrationalized and provisional hypotheses about what *kinds of people* there are to be found in one's world."[32] This surface resemblance is mitigated by the leaden masculinism of the prose, which has its back up against the queer even as it proposes all sorts of queer-sounding scenarios (on which more in a moment). In Mailer's virtuosic prose, I suggest, a different configuration of street-straight fusion coagulates, as his effort to draw the cool of jazz into the prestigious orbit of psychoanalysis and sociology ultimately falls totally flat.

Just as Hebdige's punk "punctures" glam rock, Mailer's hip jazz acts like a cock: its "knifelike entrance into culture" has a "penetrating influence" (213). The figure of the black man stereotypically functions as the ultimate in macho, his "lifemanship" (223) providing the model for the hipster and for Mailer's style as well. But in its relentless pursuit of macho, Mailer's prose perpetually needs to cover its ass. In the very first pages Mailer describes hip as the product of a "ménage-à-trois" between "the Negro," the "bohemian," and the "juvenile delinquent" (213); just so we do not miss the point, he calls marijuana "the wedding ring" and reports that "the Negro . . . brought the cultural dowry" (213). Indeed, Mailer's inexplicable sprinklings of homosexuals (promiscuous and otherwise) among the people who possess the "new kind of personality" he champions can be interpreted as a slightly desperate attempt at keeping queerness at bay by condensing its meanings onto a socially marginal figure, permitting the very queer metaphors he deploys elsewhere in the text to escape untainted by embodied specificity. Employing a "street theorizing" still current in our usages of "getting punked," Mailer asserts that the hipster knows that "there is not nearly enough sweet for everyone" (221) and deploys his lifemanship to grasp what little he can at the cost of others. The virile figure of the black man functions in Mailer's economy as the catastrophic sign of the shattering of the street-straight nexus: "If the Negro can win his equality, he will possess a potential superiority, a superiority so feared that the fear itself has become the underground drama of domestic politics. . . . the Negro's equality would tear a profound shift into the psychology, the sexuality, and the moral imagination of every white alive" (228). Of course, wherever the words *fear* and *Negro* appear in one sentence, the word *miscegenation* is never far behind. And so it comes: "So, when it comes, miscegenation will be a terror" (228). But what could this possibly mean? How could the story of the U.S. racial formation, beginning in the forced labor and rape of black people, continuing apparently through the cultural ménage à trois of hip jazz in the 1950s, somehow produce miscegenation as a *future* terror? How does a discourse ostensibly about "the 'real' world and the prosaic language in which that world was habitually described,

"The White Negro" serves as an object lesson of how a keen eye on the gritty realities of the street can go deeply wrong. But it does not, of course, license us to retreat entirely into theoretical towers.

experienced and reproduced" manage to conjure up its own fantasy future in which, apparently, apocalyptically, the "races" mix?

No wonder that, in his commentary on his erstwhile friend Mailer, James Baldwin noted that "I could not, with the best will in the world, make any sense out of *The White Negro*."[33] The danger of street-cum-straight theorizing in the idiom of a writer like Mailer is that at least part of the intense energy of its sophistication is directed at occluding entire dimensions of social experience. Among them, black men who are not walking phallic symbols or psychopaths; men or women of any race who are okay with being punk or beat, and so on. Baldwin's essay "The Black Boy Looks at the White Boy" constitutes a kind of diva reading of Mailer's macho, an arch dismissal of a condescending theory of "race" that only perpetuates outmoded definitions of masculinity. Baldwin speaks of his "fury that so antique a vision of the blacks should, at this late hour, and in so many borrowed heirlooms, be stepping off the A train."[34] Mailer's essay represents for Baldwin the very figure of a totalizing and synthesizing theoretical project that reinscribes the very thought it was attempting to transcend: the stereotypical freezing of black masculinity that we still see, for example, in shows like *Punk'd*, or in any number of marketing campaigns for new hip-hop performers. "The White Negro" serves as an object lesson of how a keen eye on the gritty realities of the street can go deeply wrong. But it does not, of course, license us to retreat entirely into theoretical towers. How, then, to approach street theorizing differently?

I have argued that theory—of both the street variety spoken on *Scared Straight!* and the straight variety, literate, well read, culturally authoritative, that Mailer exemplifies—can present itself as being explicitly "about" race, class, and sexuality while continuing to serve the function of regulation and discipline. A major aspect of this regulation, I have argued, is the frozen dialectic between black and white, and, I should add, between straight and queer, that is produced and reproduced within cultural forms both sophisticated and otherwise. It is not enough, in other words, to take up the simultaneity of race, class, gender, and sexuality, which it is my argument that the vernacular does constantly in keywords like *punk* and *punked*. Rather, we must investigate the subject transformed by law that nevertheless exists nowhere within it, the figure of absolute abjection that is, paradoxically, part of our everyday experience.

Here, the very metaphor of intersectionality can provide us with its alternative. An intersection is also a meeting of two streets, and in a landscape long given over to automotivity, it is a place of particular hazard for the pedestrian. The discipline and surveillance of vernacular mobility at such intersections of course include such postmodern devices as the surveillance camera. But this discipline does not begin there but rather, I would argue, in the very process of enclosure through which the space for walking has been given over to automotivity in the first place. The rights of the pedestrian (to cross with the light, etc.) balance the right of way of the automobile. Yet, as any streetwalker will tell you, enforcing any of these rights against the legal and illegal incursions of car culture requires continuous tactics of everyday resistance (try actually getting traffic to stop for you at a striped "zebra" crossing, for example). Additionally, over many acts of vernacular mobility hovers the nebulous crime of jaywalking, rarely enforced, but pregnant in its enforceability. So, in the practice of everyday life, the vernacularly mobile are required to demand both their rights and *more* than their rights, simply to preserve a portion of the mobility they had prior to enclosure. Examples proliferate: workers become illegal immigrants; poor mothers become welfare queens; protestors become potential terrorists. All must attack the presumption of their criminality merely to preserve their way of life from the ongoing incursions of disciplinary power. Our responses will by definition be manifold: the purpose of radical theory and politics is not to adjudicate among these responses but to nurture them. At the intersection, in the streets, we are all in punk city.

Notes

I want to thank David Eng, José Muñoz, and my anonymous reviewer for comments that helped sharpen this essay.

1. Cathy J. Cohen, "Punks, Bulldaggers, and Welfare Queens: The Radical Potential of Queer Politics?" *GLQ* 3 (1997): 437–65.

2. On nonce taxonomies, see Eve Kosofsky Sedgwick, *Epistemology of the Closet* (Berkeley: University of California Press, 1990), 22–27.

3. On D.I.Y. culture, see Craig O'Hara, *The Philosophy of Punk* (San Francisco: AK, 1999), 153–66.

4. See, for example, "Theory Is Finished," *New York Times Sunday Magazine*, 14 December 2003, 94.

5. See Kimberlé Crenshaw, "The Intersection of Race and Gender," in *Critical Race Theory: The Key Writings That Formed the Movement*, ed. Kimberlé Crenshaw, Neil Gotanda, Garry Peler, and Kendall Thomas (New York: New Press, 1995), 357–83.

6. On the history of punk rock, see the following accounts, uniformly partisan to their respective city and national contexts: Greil Marcus, *Lipstick Traces: A Secret History of the Twentieth Century* (Cambridge, MA: Harvard University Press, 1989); Legs McNeil and Gillian McCain, *Please Kill Me: The Uncensored Oral History of Punk* (New York: Grove, 1996); Jon Savage, *England's Dreaming: Anarchy, Sex Pistols, Punk Rock, and Beyond* (New York: St. Martin's, 2002); Marc Spitz and Brenden Mullen, *We Got the Neutron Bomb: The Untold Story of L.A. Punk*

(New York: Three Rivers, 2001). In reading these texts, it pays to be mindful of Judith Halberstam's caution against privileging white male punk rock as the only or the most important example of subcultural resistance. See Judith Halberstam, *In a Queer Time and Place* (New York: New York University Press, 2005), 165.

7. Halberstam is one queer theorist contributing to such a direction; see her new book of essays, *In a Queer Time and Place: Transgender Bodies, Subcultural Lives*. A classic queer analysis of youth culture still awaiting a contemporary readership is Paul Goodman, *Growing Up Absurd: Problems of Youth in the Organized System* (New York: Random House, 1960).

8. Weston contrasts street theory with straight theory, by which she means academic or intellectual theory. See Kath Weston, "Theory, Theory, Who's Got the Theory?" *GLQ* 2 (1995): 347–49.

9. An additional incentive to engage punk is that it has already been studied by at least one previous radical critical tendency—British cultural studies—and this study has produced at least one enduring classic, Dick Hebdige's *Subculture: The Meaning of Style*. This book not only deserves a queer reading, it deserves to be queered. Furthermore, the historical arc of the cultural studies tendency, while of course not identical to that of queer theory, possesses some illuminating commonalties. Reflecting upon the combined and uneven trajectory of these disciplines may provide object lessons in the chances for politically attuned, culturally fluent, and activist-oriented scholarship today. The invitation to make the connection I am attempting was provided by *The Lesbian and Gay Studies Reader* in 1993, which reprinted germinal essays from the British cultural studies tradition written by Stuart Hall, among others. See, for example, Stuart Hall, "Deviance, Politics, and the Media," in *The Lesbian and Gay Studies Reader*, ed. Henry Abelove, Michèle Aina Barale, and David M. Halperin (New York: Routledge, 1993), 62–90.

10. Raymond Williams, *Culture and Society, 1780–1950* (New York: Columbia University Press, 1983); Williams, *Keywords: A Vocabulary of Culture and Society* (New York: Oxford University Press, 1983).

11. The epigraph gives the three most popular definitions, based on Internet voting, at www.urbandictionary.com (accessed 23 January 2004).

12. Norman Mailer, "The White Negro: Superficial Reflections on the Hipster," in *The Time of Our Time* (New York: Random House, 1998), hereafter cited in text.

13. See the chapter on *punk* in Paul Dickson, *Words: A Connoisseur's Collection of Old and New, Weird and Wonderful, Useful and Outlandish Words* (New York: Delacorte, 1982), 228–35.

14. For a book that really runs away with this idea, see Richard C. Trexler, *Sex and Conquest: Gendered Violence, Political Order, and the European Conquest of the Americas* (Cambridge: Polity, 1995).

15. Similarly, Cohen marks *bulldagger* as black vernacular for *dyke*. These markings, I should note, are implicit: she does not define or discuss either term at length in the essay. From her context, it is clear that it is the black vernacular usage she intends.

16. Clarence Major, ed., *Juba to Jive: A Dictionary of African-American Slang* (New York: Viking, 1994).

17. Greg Tate, ed., *Everything but the Burden: What White People Are Taking from Black Culture* (New York: Broadway, 2003).

18. Joseph E. Holloway, *Africanisms in American Culture, Blacks in the Diaspora* (Bloomington: Indiana University Press, 1990).

19. This definition also notes, "In the 20th century the term punk fell out of use in Britain, being reintroduced via the American media and later by way of the punk phenomenon of 1976 and 1977." See Tony Thorne, ed., *Dictionary of Contemporary Slang* (New York: Pantheon, 1990), 408, emphasis in original. Dickson notes that this usage of punk appears twice in Shakespeare (*Words: A Connoisseur's Collection*, 230). When Joey Ramone sang about "trying to turn a trick" on 53rd and 3rd, one sees that the connection between sex work punking and punk rock is quite direct (The Ramones, *Ramones*, music CD [1976]).

20. Dick Hebdige, *Subculture: The Meaning of Style* (1979; repr., London: Routledge, 2002), 70, hereafter cited in text.

21. Ira Berlin, Marc Favreau, and Steven F. Miller, eds., *Remembering Slavery* (New York: New Press, 1998), 1.

22. Toni Morrison, *Playing in the Dark: Whiteness and the Literary Imagination* (Cambridge, MA: Harvard University Press, 1992), 38. The recent banishing of *punked* from the English language by the Lake Superior State University Word Banishment selection committee provides odd confirmation of its status as an American Africanism. This annual list of new words that "annoy" its committee of stewards of what they call "the Queen's English" very reliably catches Africanisms like *bling bling* (2004), *got game* (2003), *yo* (1990), and *chill out* (1980). The full archive is kept online at www.lssu.edu/banished.

23. Paul Gilroy, *"There Ain't No Black in the Union Jack": The Cultural Politics of Race and Nation* (London: Hutchinson, 1987).

24. "The succession of white subcultural forms can be read as a series of deep-structural adaptations which symbolically accommodate or expunge the black presence from the host community" (44). James Spooner's 2003 documentary, *Afro-Punk: The "Rock N Roll Nigger" Experience*, is another attempt to read this seeming deep-structural adaptation. It does so, however, fairly literally (interviewing black participants in the contemporary U.S. and Canadian punk scene) and does not go much further to analyze the centrality of "race" and black style to the construction of punk even in the absence of black participants. The redundancy of the word *afro-punk* signals this difficulty. See Spooner, *Afro-Punk*.

25. Hebdige, *Subculture*, 62. In 1978 Patti Smith released the song "Rock & Roll Nigger" on her LP *Easter*, comparing her place as a woman in rock to the plight of "niggers." In 1995 the shock rocker Marilyn Manson released a cover of Smith's song on the CD *Smells Like Children*.

26. Bowie was, ironically, even more directly influenced by black American music and performance than the white ethnicity of the punks. When he performed in San Francisco, Bowie apocryphally noted that they did not need him because they already had Sylvester, the influential openly gay African American R&B, rock, and disco performer.

27. André Carrington correctly points out the film's Hobbesian logic: the prison society of Rahway is presented as a "state of nature" in which life is "nasty, brutish, and short" (Carrington, conversation with the author). I am grateful in general to the students in my class Punks and Divas for many of the insights about *Scared Straight!* that I make in the following paragraphs.

28. For those who have not seen the show, *Punk'd* specializes in getting celebrities to lose their cool on camera. While it does not exclusively target black celeb-

rities, there is in my view a preponderance of targets drawn from the world of hip-hop. Given the title of the show, I would argue that *Punk'd* takes the figure of the black male as its prototypical target, and its other targets exist in relation to this prototypical one. The white soul singer Justin Timberlake, for instance, is punked by revealing that, when the chips are down, he quickly drops his black affectations and performs whiteness to solicit empathy from law enforcement officials. Whether or not one accepts my view, the show undoubtedly charts the rise to prominence of a new cohort of black celebrities who are *equally* targeted alongside their white counterparts, and not studiously excluded, as many other forms of celebrity media often exclude black stars.

29. It almost goes without saying that recent criminologists have discredited such efforts at youth correction. See Anthony Petrosino, Carolyn Turpin-Petrosino, and James O. Finckenauer, "Well-Meaning Programs Can Have Harmful Effects! Lessons from Experiments of Programs Such as Scared Straight," *Crime and Delinquency* 46, no. 3 (2000): 354–79.

30. I am borrowing this phrasing from Sander L. Gilman, *On Blackness without Blacks: Essays on the Image of the Black in Germany* (Boston: Hall, 1982).

31. Here the work of Giorgio Agamben on the state of exception is essential. See Giorgio Agamben, *Homo Sacer: Sovereign Power and Bare Life* (Stanford, CA: Stanford University Press, 1998).

32. Sedgwick, *Epistemology of the Closet*, 23.

33. James Baldwin, "The Black Boy Looks at the White Boy," in *Collected Essays* (New York: Library of America, 1998), 276.

34. Ibid., 277.

The Joy of the Castrated Boy

Joon Oluchi Lee

The girly things I wanted when I was a little boy (things that made me girly):

Pink- and heart-covered *manhwa* (Korean comic) books for girls, filled with love stories starring medusa-curled girls with huge galaxies for eyes, filled with stars and rainbows and tears, of happiness and depression.

My little sister's smart winter jacket (red).

My little sister's beige coat, which I wore once with a sash around the middle to make a temporary dress.

Barbie dolls (in Korea, they looked like my *manhwa* girls: sixteen years old, flat chested and startled).

Wonder Woman paper dolls (my mother made them for me).

Lipstick (addicted from the moment I slathered my mother's on in bathroom secrecy).

Ankle socks (bought for me).

Mary Jane sandals (bought for me, in beige leather).

A sewing kit (never bought for me; I improvised one out of an old cookie tin).

When I was six years old, my mother began filling me with horror stories to snap me out of my girlhood: If you don't stop acting like a girl and start being a boy, then we'll have to take you to the hospital and get your pee-pee cut off so that you can become a girl. I was appropriately terrorized by this threat: what six-year-old isn't scared of hospitals, knife blades, operations—especially on the tender private flesh between the legs? Apparently, my mother understood the cultural uses of castration. In "Medusa's Head," Freud suggests that a "terror of castration" occurs "when a boy, who has hitherto been unwilling to believe the threat of castration, catches sight of the female genitals, probably those of an adult, surrounded by hair, and essentially those of his mother."[1] The mother-Medusa barges into the boy's psyche and provides evidence of the castration threat posed by the father. Invoking the myth of Medusa, Freud then articulates how the threat and terror of castration are used to create a heterosexualized male subject: just as Medusa's victims turn to stone, the boy finds his penis hardened at the sight of the female nude. Thus castration is invoked in order to be

Social Text 84–85, Vol. 23, Nos. 3–4, Fall–Winter 2005.

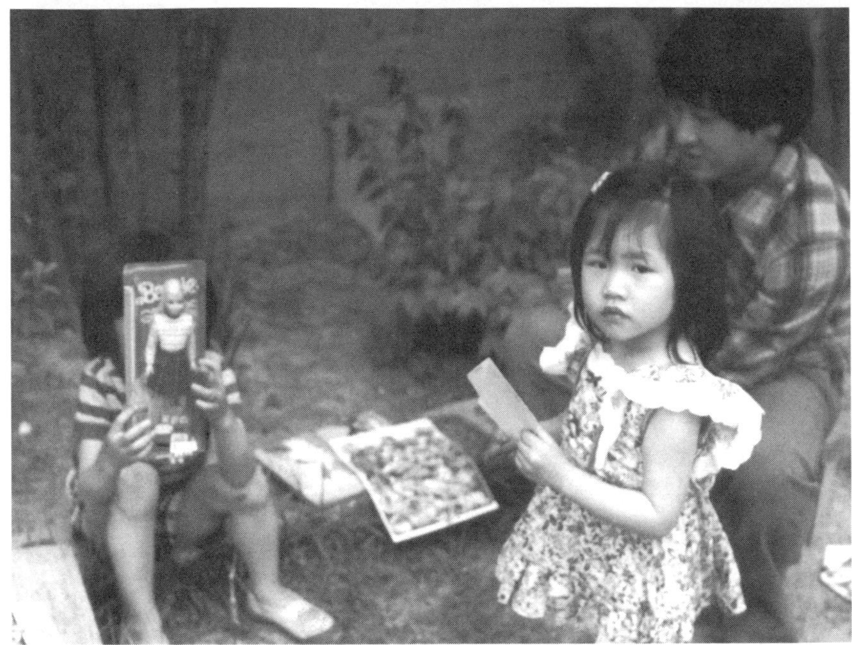

Family photo, November 1979. Courtesy the author

debunked as fiction: the frightening Medusa, with her hair of snakes, is really "a mitigation of the horror, for [the snakes] replace the penis, the absence of which is the cause of horror" (273). In effect, this mitigation is one that replaces the potentially lopped-off penis.

But, really, the horror story of *my* mother's castration threat doesn't sound as harsh in Korean as it may in English. Plus, with each repeated telling—and never finding myself on top of an operating table—the tale grew on me; castration grew on me. Because I was already a protogay kid, the eventual mitigation of my castration terror relied not on the magic of penile reclamation but on the gradual acclimation to the castration threat, and thus acclimation to the state of castration: having a feminine body, having a feminine psyche, being a feminine boy. This suggests an alternative reading of the boy's terror at seeing the nude female body. Freud identifies as the moment of castration terror the boy's "turning to stone" (273): as in, turning "stiff" as stone. But what if we took another path with the image of turning to stone? Not "stiff," but "still." If the boy can be seen as still rather than stiff, then we can begin to think about his interest in the nude female body not as an object for sex but as an object for being.[2] For me, the terror of castration that merged into an indicator of interest in identification was not produced by a nude female body but a raw female imagination, which narrated explicitly and scientifically the terms of castration. Castration was not a private fantasy that I could disprove in my brain with an erection but a public discourse in our family, imaginatively articulated as medical reality. The threatened castration was not mythic—my mother, with her cool engineer's logic, made it very scientific. I never disbelieved my mother; I just grew accustomed to the fear and the violence as part of my life as a girl. I never stopped believing in the possibility that I could be castrated simply because it was a fact. Eventually I learned that, although it was not as simple as my mother made it out to be—it was not an appendectomy or something—it could happen to me, and in my teens I knew I could make myself do it, by becoming a transsexual. In the meantime, my brain steeled itself: the six-year-old me did not give up dolls and pink because he couldn't. So even though I was never forcibly castrated, even though I never became an MTF (male-to-female) transsexual, I have always considered myself a castrated boy and learned to be happy in that state because that was the only way I could live my life as the girl I knew myself to be.

The threatened castration was not mythic—my mother, with her cool engineer's logic, made it very scientific.

This was not—is not—an easy way of living in a heteronormative world, with its hatred of effeminate boys.[3] As "Medusa's Head" shows, the castrated boy, as a negative image of the heterosexual male, is so abjected that he cannot even be imagined to exist. The negative valuation of castration indicates a continuing overvaluation of the penis-as-phallus: to invoke a male castrated is tantamount to seeing him as powerless or, at least, disempowered in the social-emotional-representational fields. When a male is castrated, something is always lost, whereas for me (not to mention a legion of MTFs who often see their penises as superfluous or ugly), something was always gained with that loss: mainly, my body, the body that remains after the operation.

To escape the soul-snuffing hatred and abjection that hunts him in the heterosexual world, the castrated boy turns to a homosexual world but, surprisingly, finds not solace but spies from the other side of the mirror. First, the gay "culture" created since the 1990s has radically evolved commercially but devolved emotionally and ethically. As homosexuality finds its place in mainstream culture, it also absorbs mainstream ethics of gender. Television shows and advertisements that make gay people visible push as desirable only a certain, usually white, upper-middle class, masculine version of gayness. This alienation may be compounded by the tradition, specifically in gay male life, which defines male femininity as the antithesis of sexiness. This is why the castrated boy, even within the homosexual world, may turn to the academic province of queer theory, attracted to and trusting in its epistemophilia to provide him, finally, a psychic sanctuary.

> The gay male who identifies as "female" is a doubly inadequate subject, inadequately male and inadequately female.

But a second surprise awaiting the castrated boy is that queer theory often offers not affirmation but only another kind of marginalization for his femme psyche: he finds himself the negative image of both heterosexual and homosexual males. While queer theory has made tremendous efforts to interweave the political discourses of race, class, and gender in the theorization of queer identification, it is rarely the case that such "generous" theoretical gestures actually make it out of the box into the practiced lives of sexualities and genders. The gay male critics who have invoked the female subjectivity to produce a gay one usually do so by first finding commonalities between the female and the gay male subject, then finish by adamantly disavowing that moment of identification. The gay subject produced thus may look like a woman, but, we are told, it is definitely not a woman. That is, the gay male subject is rarely, if ever, a castrated boy. This disavowal has many names, none of which is "female": for some, it is to become feminist, and for others, it is to *deny effeminacy.* Gay male critics fear "female"—and in this they have an ally in second-wave feminism—because the work of gender identification is ultimately seen as a system of impermeable biological boundaries, whose operation is totalizingly hierarchical. This can be most readily seen in the refusal of some feminists to recognize MTF transsexuals as "women," thus excluding them from feminist communities. On the other hand, a gay male who "becomes"—is mistaken for—female fears the endless sense of subjugation and insecurity in being "inadequately" so. The gay male who identifies as "female"—its French version, *femme,* turned into a moniker of homosexual self-styling—is a doubly inadequate subject, inadequately male and inadequately female.

Actually, that certain feminist reluctance to count particular, feminized XY humans as "female" is, I think, sometimes justified and important. Because this sense of gender inadequacy can create, even in a queer body, the masculinist instinct for violence against women, it is a situation we castrated boys must try hard to avoid, especially considering queer theory's great indebtedness to feminism. This determination for ethical vigilance is an important lesson for the castrated boy's self-definition as psychically "female." It means that the castrated boy has to make something positive out of that double inadequacy. This work may be thought of as what Jessica Benjamin would call "splitting the ego":

> [The] capacity to split the ego and take up antithetical positions, may, in certain conditions, be potentially creative. . . . a benign form of splitting the ego in relation to gender may well be an important accomplishment. . . . [in order to accomplish this, one has to] be able to . . . retain the ability to imagine it without being threatened or undone by it. Identification must be tolerated in order that the other's qualities not evoke intolerable envy or fear.[4]

Male queer theorists' abjection of the castrated boy is usually an expression of the gay male refusal or inability to thus be "threatened or undone" by femininity; it is understandable, but ultimately a finessed expression of gynophobia. Symptomatic of this critical phenomenon is D. A. Miller's *A Place for Us*, which uses the Broadway musical *Gypsy* to create a gay but antifemme male subjectivity from femininity. Based on the memoirs of the burlesque star Gypsy Rose Lee, *Gypsy* relates how the shy kid who only wanted to go to school, sew, and support her more talented vaudevillian child-star sister became, under the fierce and forceful imagination of her stage mother from hell, the most famous stripper ever. For Miller, this story narrates a world experienced by the protogay boy who longs to escape enforced heterosexualization: the vaudeville and burlesque scenes, with their privileging of female stars, marginalize the boy who longs to become that female star. Louise, the young Gypsy Rose Lee, although biologically female, does not herself possess the feminine sparkle necessary for vaudeville stardom and is thus marginalized as if she were a protogay boy: "A rebus of a sissy."[5] Miller astutely reads Louise as a boy castrated by her mother, like the other "mutilated figures, strewn by the way . . . like so many atrocities on a warpath, . . . Nerd, Sissy, or Snot," with "hideous scars—sores rather, . . . [that] never heal" (79–80). In this scenario, the castrated boy is abjected for wanting to become the girl he could never be, his femininity recognized only as unclotting and ugly flesh wounds. While this accounts accurately for how a heteronormative society abjects the castrated boy, Miller ultimately seems to agree with it. He offers no recovery, no emotional support or even cautious celebration of the femme boy. Instead, there is violence in the language. When he writes that "a man who did take the place of a woman could hardly be more abhorrent here than one who appears lacking in sufficient assertiveness to take it *from* her" (80), Miller is voicing a desire for a gay male subjectivity that could never be mistaken for that of a girl; the boy wanting to be a girl must "take the place" of the girl. This gay boy must not become castrated, so that he can have sufficient power to rape the coveted feminine position from the biological female. The abjected status of a castrated boy stems from his inability for violence; he is a boy not butch or aggressive enough to take it from her.

This is why for Miller, it is the chorus boy Tulsa's solo, "All I Need Is the Girl," that provides the gay male subject its ideal. In this scene, Tulsa demonstrates—with a dildolike broom as his imaginary future partner—a dance act of his own creation narrating the ritual of heterosexual dating. Completely rebellious to the beautifully shrill feminine ethos of the story thus far, this act makes the girl partner incidental to the boy's virtuosic dancing. In an ultimate act of revenge, Tulsa corrupts the very girl star he had been backing: Louise's little sister June becomes his incidental, on stage and off: he elopes with her and will make her stand in for that damned broom. And Miller celebrates: "Tulsa pulled it off! Tulsa got away! . . . Wily Tulsa—truly the most intelligent, the most resourceful boy in the act!—on you alone it dawned how male performance might be detached from secrecy, shame, and secondariness" (92, 94). "Male performance" now signals a refusal of femininity. It is, instead, a thievery of stage and spotlight from the female star. But Tulsa can be seen as such a queer hero only if we agree with Miller's interpretation of *Gypsy*'s feminine world as a quicksand, a veritable hell of or for sissies and snots. For some, the quicksand is a buttery and yummy thing, an ecstatic falling feeling:

> Sula picked him up by his hands and swung him outward then around and around. His knickers ballooned and his shrieks of frightened joy startled the birds and the fat grasshoppers. When he slipped from her hands and sailed out over the water they could still hear his bubbly laughter.
>
> The water darkened and closed quickly over the place where Chicken Little sank.[6]

This scene from Toni Morrison's *Sula* (1973) articulates the singular joy of the castrated boy missing from Miller's story. Morrison states the boy's masochistic affect with telling terseness: "frightened joy." There is no further elaboration, no justification for the boy's feeling: his "bubbly laughter" overwhelms his terror and eventual sinking. And even though he sinks and dies, as he is flung about in the air by the novel's eponymous heroine, the boy experiences the sensation of flight, the euphoria corresponding to and challenging that of Tulsa's escape from femininity.

Like *Gypsy*, *Sula* is a text gooey with feminine energy: the portrait of a girl as creator of a renegade and subversive femininity.[7] It's a novel that charts the process of such a feminine subjectivity as the thickening friendship between two black girls: Nel, who becomes the proper bourgeois wife; and Sula, who grows up to be the sexual-aesthetic adventuress as social outcast, Sula the egoless: "She was completely free of ambition, with no affection for money, property or things, no greed, no desire to command attention or compliments—no ego" (119). The friends' conflicting femininities are nevertheless brought together by the novel's famous ending: "We was girls together . . . girl, girl, girlgirlgirl" (174). The syntax of these words, cried out by Nel at Sula's death by self-willed illness, acts out in poetry the technically last lines of the novel, in which the third-person narrator describes Nel's girlsong: "It was a fine cry—loud and long—but it had no bottom and it had no top, just circles and circles of sorrow." The *girlgirlgirl* is a lament of egoless femininity with subversive social potential.

It is three girls who take a single verb. It is "loud and long": a voice whose volume allows it to be heard in the present moment and whose length extends its message into a future. And the message is a dream of a world with "no bottom and . . . no top," one in which the sharp verticality of hierarchies has been replaced with the curve of "circles and circles."[8]

The "girl" that is the building block for the subversively feminine *girlgirlgirl* takes a radical departure from the "girl" exemplified by Miller's reading of *Gypsy*. The difference is race; paradoxically, the girl identity implied by *girlgirlgirl* originates from the racist interpellation of "gal." When the grown-up version of Sula emerges in the narrative, she is as glossy and idealized as Gypsy Rose Lee: she is, we are told, "dressed in a manner that was as close to a movie star as anyone would ever see" (90). Topping off Sula's stylish dress was "a black felt hat with the veil of net lowered over one eye." One eye veiled by hat or hair: it is an iconically glamorous style—think of any star from Garbo to Veronica Lake to Aaliyah. But in Sula, this small but crucial gesture is actually an aesthetic mimesis that redresses a site of African American women's social trauma. Early in the novel, Nel's mother, Helene, finds her carefully crafted femininity as a proud black bourgeoisie pulled down—literally—when she is called, in front of her daughter, "gal" by an evil white train conductor. That word—embodying all the oppressive weight of what it means to be racially feminized as a black female in America—takes on corporeal form and restyles her: "She had heard only that one word ["gal"]; it dangled above her wide-brimmed hat, which had slipped, in her exertion, from its carefully leveled placement and was now tilted in a bit of a jaunt over her eye" (20). The hateful "gal" actually seems to produce a sexually saucy "jaunt" over one eye, an unwanted accident magically picked up and replicated by Sula as a style of subversion. The specific femme style of a racialized, *black*, girl, like the castrated boy, has its origin in violence: not the pleasure of feminine stardom but the pain of living in a racist society.

The specific femme style of a racialized, *black*, girl, like the castrated boy, has its origin in violence: not the pleasure of feminine stardom but the pain of living in a racist society.

Part of the violence of being black and female in America is that one's happily auto-authored self is always vulnerable to abjection and humiliation—a woman can be reduced to "gal"—by the normative social order through the fact of her racial difference. This psychically pejorative infantilizing of Helene can be thought of as what David L. Eng has importantly named "racial castration." Eng elaborates on and complicates Richard Fung's contention that "Asian and anus is conflated"; the gay Asian man who is a sexual bottom for a white man is a racially castrated boy, who seems to participate in his own abjection:

> [The] Asian male is psychically emasculated, foreclosed from an identification with normative heterosexuality, so as to guarantee the white male's claim to

> this location. As such, the potential trauma of sexual difference is not arrested at the site of the female body (as in the case of classic fetishism). Instead, sexual difference is managed through the arrest, disavowal, and projection of racial difference at the site of the Asian male body.[9]

In thinking thus about how the perceived passivity of femininity contributes to and elides with an unwhite racialization, Helene can be seen as the "Asian male body." Eng identifies racial castration as a "reverse fetishism" in which a white male subject practices a "blatant refusal to see on the body of an Asian male the penis that *is* clearly there for him to see" (150). When the white male conductor does not recognize Helene's adult sexuality, he is refusing the material reality of Helene's physical sexuality just as the white male rice queen does to the Asian femme bottom. The disturbing aspect of Helene's racial castration, however, is that she embraces it. Helene responds to the violent infantilizing call of the white male with sexualized receptiveness: "Helene smiled. Smiled dazzlingly and coquettishly at the salmon-colored face of the conductor" (21). To use Eng's outline: Helene's smile heterosexualizes the white male ("sexual difference is managed") by racializing herself as the other ("projection of racial difference").

However, while Eng locates the system and mechanics of racial castration, he does not provide an instance in which the sociopsychic position of the castrated boy is so embraced.[10] Helene's acceptance of her racial castration challenges, first of all, the notion that racial castration is always an interracial phenomenon. As Nel witnesses it, Helene's humiliating erotic and masochistic response is a politically abject one for a black woman, a fact mirrored by the other, unintended receivers of Helene's gaze, the two black soldiers seated in the car behind the conductor: "[The soldiers, who] had been watching the scene with what appeared to be indifference, now looked stricken" (21). Morrison then portrays Helene as Medusa: the black soldiers' stricken face flesh turns "from blood to marble," their gaze "a hard wetness" (22). A hard wetness, a wet hardness: the black males' hardening is the penile "stiffening" caused by Freud's Medusa. As Helene's performance heterosexualizes the white man, it heterosexualizes the black men. This heterosexualization is a racialization that phallicizes the black men: their racial politics—their disgust at Helene's coquettishness—merges here with a metaphor of potentially violent male heterosexuality.[11] The soldiers' disgust with Helene's femininity produces them as a phallic authority over her: they are simultaneously politically proper black subjects and heterosexual males. That the female Nel identifies with these men suggests that a politically proper black femininity must not be feminine, in the sense that it must not only continue to disavow castration but perform a particular redress of that psychic wound by a rephallicizing.

But redressing the psychic wound of racism—or antiracist politics in general, for that matter—is neither that simple nor that monolithic. Saidiya V. Hartman's interpretation as "acts of redress" the enslaved's apparently self-hating performance of contentedness with his social death is vital for reconsidering Helene's own embrace of racial castration:

> [These] acts of redress are undertaken with the acknowledgment that conditions will most likely remain the same. This acknowledgment implies neither resignation nor fatalism but a recognition of the enormity of the breach instituted by slavery and the magnitude of domination.
>
> Redressing the pained body encompasses operating in and against the demands of the system, negotiating the disciplinary harnessing of the body, and counterinvesting in the body as a site of possibility.[12]

In the case of the black soldiers, privileging a resistance that operates within the normative economy of the phallus ends up with one that relies structurally on potentially violent, gynophobic masculinity. That Helene's feminine style is taken up by Sula—as a girl, she actually loves Helene's severe domestic aesthetic, which Nel finds oppressive—suggests that while appearing complicit with a dominant order, this embracing of castration has the subversive potential invoked by Hartman. Sula's "girl" self takes up Hartman's challenge in incorporating Helene's ambiguous racial femininity into her own body and turning it into that "site of possibility" that is *girlgirlgirl*.

That Sula would take up the very femininity rendered ineffectual or unwanted by normatively gendering and racializing forces makes her a "girl," as Jessica Benjamin defines it. Benjamin argues that in the oedipal process of gender identification, the femininity that becomes synonymous with passivity—which is the core of Helene's racial castration—emerges in the "split" or "perversion" of the mother. The male child who will identify defensively toward castration, overwhelmed by the nurturing and creative omnipotence of his mother, greedily attempts to incorporate it into his own psyche. He siphons off this power—essentially, over him—into the father figure, leaving the mother as simply the object of love on which the suckling baby or fucking husband can act, rather than the subject of love who squirts milk into the baby. Nel's reaction to her mother's racial castration can be viewed as such a splitting that renders her a "boy." By contrast, Sula's identification with Helene renders her a "girl": "The girl can only be feminine by identifying with the part of the mother not kept by the boy."[13] *Girl*: the marginalized digester and collector of the unwanted, a psychic recycler. For Benjamin, this identification renders the resulting girl hopelessly helpless: "The 'content' of femininity is to contain this unwanted, primitively feared experience ["passivity and helplessness"] and make of it an exciting invitation, something that the phallus can now act upon, control, and structure" (58). But, as embodied by Sula, the girl's femininity is able to accomplish the first two elements of its content (containment and glamorization) without the last—becoming victim to a phallic control. Then, if we see Helene's racial castration as gesturing toward *girlgirlgirl* from the pained starting point of "gal," we have already two creative and creating components of that final persona: Nel, who identifies against her mother and with Sula; and Sula herself, who, like a Möbius strip twistingly connecting the estranged mother and daughter, identifies with Nel's mother. Deborah E. McDowell writes that "[*Sula*'s] narrative insistently blurs and confuses these [black/white, male/female, good/bad, positive/negative, self/other] and other binary oppositions, blurs the boundaries they create, boundaries separating us from us from others and rendering us 'others' to ourselves."[14] This idea of the defamiliarized self as the complement of a familiarized other is at the core of the politics of *girlgirlgirl*, which dreams of doing away with not only hierarchies but the very invisible barriers put up between bodies: the existent gender taxonomies that constitute the very egos that we have become so acculturated into protecting. Embracing racial castration can be a potentially libratory willingness to embrace femininity as a race and, vice versa, race as femininity.

With its breathless refusal of comma'd boundaries, *girlgirlgirl* is the murky water into which the boy Chicken Little falls and sinks in joy. Chicken Little's death is misinterpreted by the white man who finds his body as just another example of "the way niggers did [things]" (63). Chicken Little's death performs a posthumous racial castration: as with Helene, his feminine act (bonding with Sula) leads to a racialization that serves to stabilize white male subjectivity. However, this subtle racial castration also allows the estranged Nel and Sula to be reunited as "girls": when the adult Nel "clarifies" to Sula's grandmother Eva that it was Sula, not she, who sunk Chicken Little, Eva replies in recognition of their *girlgirlgirl* bond: "You. Sula. What's the difference?" (168).[15] This triplicate identity of "girl," which iconically marks Sula and Nel, is what the protogay Chicken Little desires also. *Chicken Little*: the little boy named simultaneously for the fairy-tale protagonist who fears apocalypse—the sky's falling down—and for fresh young meat, in gay sex culture. He can be read as a little protogay boy. Telegraphing Miller's "Snot" of a femme boy, Chicken Little is first seen by Sula and Nel picking his nose: "Your mamma tole you to stop eatin' snot, Chicken," Nel yells (59). But this is a boy who refuses to stop being a "Snot": he keeps picking. While Nel—foreshadowing her eventual role as the figurehead of normative socialization—mimics the voice of a proper parent, Sula ignores his snotty nose and helps Chicken up a high tree, leading him to see the world from an unexpected, previously undreamed of, perspective:

> Sula pointed to the far side of the river.
> "See? Bet you never saw that far before, did you?"
> "Uh uh." (60)

With the imaginative girl's guidance, Chicken Little is able to see a view of the world not enclosed by narrow social strictures. Instead of the paranoid "sky's falling down" of the fairy tale, this Chicken Little self-assuredly declares: "*I* ain't never coming *down*" (60, emphasis added). But even when he eventually does, as everyone knows one day he must, Sula continues to help him in re-creating that floating feeling of freedom—the broadened perspective of an unfalling sky—by flinging him around and around, never letting him down.

That Chicken Little's joyous bonding with Sula ends in his death suggests that there is a silent, dangerous contract that must be signed by the boy who desires for himself a female's femininity. This contract outlines the terms of his psychic castration: he is allowed to be feminine, incorporate her essence and aspects into the process of his own self-creation, but in exchange he must understand that the newly subversive narratives and shapes of femininity formed on him (as his "maleness" mixes up with "femininity," transforming the assumed cultural history and meaning of both) can at any time be repossessed by its original owner, the imaginative female. The implication of this clause maintains the delicate political balance between the biologically male boy who can, at any time, turn into the violent aggressor or oppressor of the female who has gifted him with the femininity of her own imagining. Thus a salient part of his girlhood is his own acceptance that his membership into the female tribe is not guaranteed.

For certain gay males, the mandated lack of a contractual guarantee that the castrated boy can be a socially legitimate female—this necessary contractual inequality—is totally unacceptable. This is where the queer male subject, though retaining a homosexuality, ceases to be "queer" as we learned it in the 1990s: its signifying desire to imaginatively transform the lexicon of social taxonomies is erased, and the gay male subject emerges simply as a male subject. The femininity desired by the male in such a case is, to me, a sham: simply another instance of the totalizing masculine appetite to own everything that seems glittering or valuable. What Angela Carter writes about D. H. Lawrence we could say about Miller's Tulsa: "[He] can put all these lovely garments he himself desires so much on the girls he has invented and yet cunningly evade the moral responsibility of having to go out in them himself and face the rude music of the mob."[16]

For certain gay males, the mandated lack of a contractual guarantee that the castrated boy can be a socially legitimate female—this necessary contractual inequality—is totally unacceptable.

In contrast to Miller, Carter proposes that if a male wants to perform femininity, the phrase "male performance" has to become meaningless. The castrated boy must become vulnerable. He must willingly give up the sociopsychic privilege of maleness—its claim to aggressive self-promotion and preservation—and risk psychic and bodily danger as a girl.

This psychic masochism is the very means by which the castrated boy can create a sense of his male body that does not conform to the masculine tradition; how a human with a penis can become as female as he can be. Freud writes, stereotypically but as an astute social realist, of femininity:

> The suppression of women's aggressiveness which is prescribed for them constitutionally and imposed on them socially favours the development of powerful masochistic impulses, which succeed, as we know, in binding erotically the destructive trends which have been diverted inwards. Thus masochism, as people say, is truly feminine.[17]

As a "girl," a collector/recycler of psychic waste, the castrated boy must collect that certain masochism that has been cast off by females who have politically evolved to refusing monolithic feminine identification through masochism. The potential subversiveness of the castrated boy is that he denies the very impulse of aggressive self-preservation that has traditionally marked masculinity. The castrated boy proudly wears his subjugation to the female imagination—which looks like a manacle from afar—as a heavy silver chastity lock in the shape of a heart, dangling from his wrist, the weight of which makes him as girly as a Chloé bracelet does for its wearer. In the case of Chicken Little, the contract falls, by chance, on the side of its risk. Instead of being held forever aloft in the girl's air, having the chance to find a different, physical, life-sustaining kind of female quagmire, he dies in his falling, weighed down by the shining contract. But he is a valuable sacrifice—to the creation of *girlgirlgirl*.

This reincarnating "save" of Chicken Little is symbolized by the swarm of butterflies that invades his funeral, where Sula and Nel keep their distance from the grave itself:

> They held hands and knew that only the coffin would lie in the earth; the bubbly laughter and the press of fingers would stay aboveground forever. At first, as they stood there, their hands were clenched together. They relaxed slowly until during the walk back home their fingers were laced in as gentle a clasp as that of any two young girlfriends trotting up the road on a summer day wondering what happened to butterflies in the winter. (66)

The funeral of the little sacrificial femme boy has a marginalized, secret, and less formal ritualistic counterpoint between the two girls who would create each other. The girls' holding each other's hands performs the magic of lodging the little femme boy in their psyches as melancholic objects for their own nascent girlhood: in remembering Chicken Little—the joy in his "bubbly laughter"—they also mimic his last grip. Indeed, the diction of the girlfriends' handclasp replicates his: "The pressure of his hard and tight little fingers was still in Sula's palms as she stood looking at the closed place in the water" (61). The grip's relaxing indicates not an eventual forgetting of the meaning of the little hand but a remembering of its affect—the comfort of its relaxing and gentleness. As such, the gesture symbolizes an eventual integration, fluid introjection—a return—of the boy's femininity into the girls' own. The butterflies that storm the funeral are multiple reincarnations of the joyous, fluttering, floating Chicken Little and his gossamer ballooning knickers. They stay on the girls' brains, not only as aesthetic object or memory but as a promise of the future: what does happen to butterflies in the winter? What happens to a delicate thing in a material world that discourages its survival?

A clue: in addition to *girlgirlgirl*, the butterflies also invoke the deweys, three boys of varying shades of African American who, on informal adoption by Sula's grandmother Eva, "came out of whatever cocoon he was in at the time his mother or somebody gave him away" (38). They share one name—Dewey King—and "spoke with one voice, thought with one mind, and maintained an annoying privacy" (39). The deweys—Morrison writes their name in lowercase and plural—can be seen as the prototype of *girlgirlgirl*: they refuse the erection of individual male egos, preferring instead the beauty and comfort of murky self-erasure. The three boys are/is "a trinity with a plural name . . . inseparable, loving nothing and no one but themselves" (38). Shared onanism turns homoerotic and gives them a protogay aura.[18] Their egoless shared identity, a trial run for *girlgirlgirl*, is, like Chicken Little's death, an instance of subtle racial castration: the white schoolteacher, exasperated by the deweys' refusal to buckle under the normative imperative toward individuality, finally dismisses them as yet another example of "the ways of the colored people in town" (39).

Like the deweys, Chicken Little is a promise of the circular future spoken by *girlgirlgirl*. Immediately following his death, Chicken Little is characterized repeatedly in Sula's thoughts as "something newly missing" (61). Newly Missing: when something recently missing is thought of as newly, the unpresent boy is given a new life, precisely through his disappearance: the boy's psyche is projected into the future, signaling a promise of something better. At the moment of Chicken Little's death, Nel and Sula notice a shadowy figure across the lake and deduce it to be Shadrack, the town crazy, whose house occupies the opposite shore. Sula runs into the house and eventually confronts the smiling man. Shadrack gives her only one, but significant, word, "Always" (62), which she remembers years later as she lay dying: "Always. Who said that? She tried hard to think. Who was it that had promised her a sleep of water always?" (149). By confusing her own oncoming death with the death of Chicken Little, she completes the inclusive curve of *girlgirlgirl*, to which now Chicken Little is finally bonded. In facilitating this bond, Shadrack also represents that new life promised to Chicken Little.

If we read Shadrack as integral a *girlgirlgirl* as Chicken Little, then we can fully flesh out the subtext of a femme boy's femininity and see a case in which the boy's "becoming" a girl through psychic castration does not set off the violent warfare instinct that leads to his normalization as a masculine subject. When we first meet Shadrack—who is in fact the first human character we encounter in the novel—it is as the boy protagonist of Freud's "Medusa's Head": a boy who realizes the possibility of castration. Shadrack is not yet twenty years old, fighting in World War I, "running with his comrades across a field in France" (7), when he

> saw the face of a soldier near him fly off. Before he could register shock, the rest of the soldier's head disappeared under the inverted soup bowl of his helmet. But stubbornly, taking no direction from the brain, the body of the headless soldier ran on, with energy and grace, ignoring altogether the drip and slide of brain tissue down its back. (8)

As in "Medusa's Head," the boy who witnesses decapitation/castration in war is led toward initiation into normative masculinity. He must learn to be hard and erect, not only in the blood-filled penile tissue way of heterosexual desire but in its ugly underbelly: the upright, gun-toting, fearless way of a male waging violent conflict on another. This ritual is given the italicized, succinctly significant title of "*it*": "Shellfire was all around him, and though he knew that this was something called *it*, he could not muster up the proper feeling—the feeling that would accommodate *it*. He expected to be terrified or exhilarated—to feel *something* very strong" (7, emphasis in original). That Shadrack consciously anticipates the emotional effects of witnessing Medusa's decapitation cues us to rethink the preconceived meaning of psychic castration. As a young male, Shadrack is already socialized into a knowledge of what emotions the manly pursuit of warfare and murder should produce in a properly gendered male: terror (of his own castration or death) or exhilaration (at the sight of another thus mutilated)—that is, seeing a female genital or defeating a foe. Which is why it makes no real difference that the Medusa figure here is male: the male fucked over in battle is tantamount to the woman fucked.

Male Medusa: that he feels neither exhilaration nor terror marks Shadrack as a protogay figure who will pursue a different path of psychic gendering. Rather than becoming a man—an injured war hero, let's say—Shadrack instead returns to his home "permanently astonished, . . . his head full of nothing and his mouth recalling the taste of lipstick" (7). Morrison's portrait of the shell-shocked Shadrack makes me think of Jacqueline Kennedy Onassis's witnessing the assassination of her husband, JFK. Writing about Jackie's iconicity, Wayne Koestenbaum conjectures that "Jackie's face, like the Medusa's, partly fascinates because JFK's missing head lurked behind it. Jackie, frozen or 'astonished' by JFK's assassination/decapitation, in turn astonishes us."[19] Jackie's astonishment at her Medusa-husband leads her to discover her own power to astonish, making her a Medusa as well. In the same way, Shadrack, too, is "astonished" by the spectacle of the Medusa-soldier, and this reaction is "permanent": he reacts as a female would to the Medusa. His run-in with Medusa does not form a male psyche fighting to escape the fate of the decapitated woman but leads him to become her: Shadrack's head is as "full of nothing" as the leaky soup bowl of the Medusa-soldier's skull.

His run-in with Medusa does not form a male psyche fighting to escape the fate of the decapitated woman but leads him to become her.

Specifically feminizing this spectacular identification is Shadrack's memory of "the taste of lipstick." I guess this could be read as a moment of heterosexualization—remembering some preteen kiss. However, given that he is only nineteen at that point, it seems unlikely that any female lips he touched would have been lipsticked—of course, older woman notwithstanding. But this is just what he may be recalling into his current psyche: the older woman who is the original referent of the soldier-Medusa he witnessed in France: his mother. I think of Shadrack as the "beautiful son" of Courtney Love and her band Hole's song "Beautiful Son": "He had ribbons in his hair / And lipstick was everywhere / You look good in my dress / My beautiful son, my beautiful son."[20] The root of Shadrack's memory of "the taste of lipstick": he gets his mother's lipstick "everywhere" because he sneaked it on and then licked his lips, just as Helene had licked hers at the moment of her racial castration (21). Shadrack remembers the taste of lipstick not as a budding heterosexual but as a baby femme. For example: when I put on a lipstick I bought myself at age twenty-seven—Nars Roman Holiday, a candy-heart pink—my lips immediately remembered sneaking on, twenty years earlier, my mother's left-behind lipstick, a Korean brand of bing cherry magenta. It was shocking how consistent the technology of lipstick actually is; twenty years and a hemisphere were crossed, yet lipstick tasted the same! All this is not to simply say that Shadrack is a closet drag queen, although, who knows, had he the clarity of consciousness and lived in a different time and place, he, too, may have found a lipstick of his own. What is significant here is that the traditionally masculinizing psychic ritual has been turned upside down by a protogay male subject, who takes away from it a desire for embodying femininity.

It seems no coincidence that Morrison describes the Medusa-soldier's headless, running body as if it were that of a dancer, with "energy and grace." This Medusa is psychically valuable not for the trophylike head, with its phallic snakes (the brain cells that here unceremoniously "drip and slide" off) but for its headless body. Morrison's dancing male Medusa inspires us to imagine life as a castrated boy: how can the state of castration become beautiful, powerful, important for living?[21] Shadrack manifests his feminizing masochism through the creation and enactment of Suicide Day, in which he parades through town, making what Helene astutely calls "this headless display" (160). This display he celebrates with the other nonnormative males of the town: Tar Baby, the lonely, feminine, alcoholic, suicidal white boy with an angelic singing voice; and the aforementioned deweys.[22] So what does a Medusa become after decapitation/castration? Does it simply die off, collapse? No; it becomes a headless display; it becomes a *her.*

The aesthetic pleasance of the castration dance comes from a seemingly willful disregard for "direction from the brain," that is, the stereotypically and usually exaggerated masculine quality of cold rationality. What governs this dancing body is not even its epistemic inverse, wild emotion (Shadrack is astonished into another totally unfamiliar state; he doesn't feel), but a different, altogether alternative system of logic. The only thing that governs him in his miming of Medusa is the rhythm of pain: "[He] *felt only* the bite of the nail in his boot, which pierced the ball of his foot whenever he came down on it" (7–8, emphasis added). The pain is neither biological reaction nor consciously processed emotion but a rhythm: his running turns the pain of the piercing boot nail into a beat box of masochism. The repeated puncture of his foot flesh is the constant threat of castration that the femme boy accepts as a part of his girly life.

It's important to name this rhythmic piercing of flesh as a newly imagined feminizing masochism of a girl because it is a motif repeated for an explicitly political effect later on in the novel: the scene in which the young Sula protects herself and Nel against a gang of violent white boys. Sula pulls out her paring knife, but instead of aiming it toward the aggressive boys, she turns it upon herself with a "determined but inaccurate" aim: "She slashed off only the tip of her finger. The four boys stared open-mouthed at the wound and the scrap of flesh, like a button mushroom, curling in the cherry blood" (54). Here the terms of the castrated boy's contract are realized, without his death: the life experience of the feminized boy (in this case, the masochistic rhythm of the castration threat felt by Shadrack) returns to the female. If Shadrack can be seen as a castrated boy who has become the headless, dancing Medusa, forever creating a "headless display" of himself, then Sula, in her girlhood, has followed the same path. She says to herself:

> When I was a little girl the heads of my paper dolls came off, and it was a long time before I discovered that my own head would not fall off if I bent my neck. I used to walk around holding it very stiff because I thought a strong wind or a heavy push would snap my neck. Nel was the one who told me the truth. But she was wrong. I did not hold my head stiff enough when I met [Jude, Nel's husband with whom Sula has sex] and so I lost it just like the dolls. (136)

Contrary to our normative expectations—and Nel's own wishes—the slightly wistful tone of Sula's musing on her head loss does not at all render it a sad regret. Instead, it is a declaration of her egoless state. Her psyche has created a world in which "truth" can be "wrong" and humans are basically dolls. Like the paper dolls, like Shadrack, like the soldier-Medusa in France, like the original Medusa herself, Sula, too, has been decapitated: yet still she lives.

Because Shadrack and Sula cross paths only for a moment, and exchange only one word, this lesson of feminine masochism is not really a lesson at all. Sula herself must construct meaning for Shadrack's single, puzzling "Always" and do with it what she eventually will. Shadrack and Sula are connected in their feminine masochism not by a one-way trajectory or progression or transfer of knowledge: such a flow of information, which could serve to hierarchize the older male Shadrack over the younger female Sula, is a concept totally uninteresting to the novel's ethos. What matters is that both bodies come to resemble each other—both are suicidal pariahs intent on paving their own paths to living. In the end, it is the precisely feminine *girlgirlgirl*, with its original suggestion that race and gender can meld into each other, which dissolves the boundaries between male and female. As Sula is with Nel, Sula is Shadrack, as both are with Chicken Little, and with all three: they are "girls together."

Let us return to *Gypsy* with this feeling. Miller convincingly suggests that the musical makes femininity enticing for protogay boys, who bear and wear the threat of castration. However, as *Sula* shows, the castrated boy who does not mitigate his fear through a penile reclamation is not forever lost in abjection. The castrated boy has a chance to help forge a new meaning of "female" through the crucible of his own crazed imagination and frustrated, male but feeling-female body. Such a boy in *Gypsy* is the bitchy stage manager Pastey, who contributes to the birth of the show's female star by misreading—consciously or not—Louise's new stage name: "Gypsy Rose Lee," he says, instead of "Gypsy Rose Louise." In a brilliantly generous reading, Miller suggests that "by rechristening her, Pastey insinuates Louise's shady male past into her brilliant new career as all girl—or GRL, if we prefer the spelling on her monogram" (77). Yet for Miller, Pastey is still one of the mutilated corpses on the path to female

The castrated boy has a chance to help forge a new meaning of "female" through the crucible of his own crazed imagination and frustrated, male but feeling-female body.

femininity and represents the abject converse of the butch Tulsa. Pastey's limp-wristed kvetching, however creative, belies a desire to actually occupy the feminine star space of the stripper, but he only pathetically succeeds in opening the curtain for her, giving her her cues, announcing her stardom. In other words, he is his name: a bunch of sequins on the girl's nipple, "basic item of striptease paraphernalia."[23]

That Pastey never gets on stage seems to me, though, a moot point. Tori Amos sings about the joys of being "the sweetest cherry in an apple pie," which articulates well this situation.[24] A cherry in an apple pie has no need to strive toward supersweetness: however sweet it is, it is only ultimately a detractor and misfit to the taste bud craving an apple pie. And besides, even the sweetest cherry will be lost in the heady flood of sugared and cinnamoned apples. But what does a sense of alienation or inadequacy matter when you are contributing to such a delicious product? You may be mistaken for a bite of apple! In this way, and as Shadrack's performativity returns as support for young Sula's performance against her potential rapists, Pastey is not a loser but a happy cherry in an apple pie: a good team player of femininity. Think of Pastey as a version of Chicken Little: if, indeed, Pastey reads his own experience as a girl into his naming of Louise as Gypsy Rose Lee, then she cannot be "all girl" as Miller contends. She, too, is an incomplete girl, and her monogram tells this truth with glossy nakedness: *GRL*. If Gypsy Rose Lee looks like a girl, she is the GIRL without the all-important *I*. Like the *girlgirlgirl* Sula, she is an egoless thing, a female who has found a sense of empowerment in the erasure of the ego: a girl who does not want or need to mimic a masculine psyche in expressing herself.

So, despite the violent rivalry that Miller writes into the Pastey-GRL bond, it is not true that "whereas the boy wishing to be a star in this world must imagine himself in female dress, the girl may just take off her clothes" (75). Because the very novelty of GRL's stripping—that which turns her into a superstar—actually puts the inevitable meaning of "naked" into hazy unfocus: GRL never *shows* her breasts and vagina. GRL becomes a socially subversive paradox because, as Miller says, while stripping does affirm the boyish Louise's status as female, some prop—a hat, a curtain, a boa—always covers those biological parts that would mark her conventionally female. Thus the revolutionary act of this stripping is a transitioning tranny's dream: not that "boy-Louise" becomes a female *by* taking off her clothes, but that "he" can be female *in spite of* taking off "his" clothes. Miller sees boy-Louise's "boysister" status as psychically unsatisfying: "Being *only* the rebus of a sissy" (75, emphasis added). But this is not so. A rebus is a pictorial version of written narrative: not shorthand but a linguistic system that can open avenues to alternative, revolutionary interpretations of the signified concept. GRL's boy-passing stripping reveals that she truly is a rebus: she is what she looks like.

In the end, the joy of the castrated boy is that which he initially dreaded: to be mistaken for someone that you are.

I was a little boy who looked like a little girl. I had my hair cut in a bowl cut: long bangs that extended all the way around my skull. When we came to America, I loved my hair because it reminded me of my idol, Charlene on the television sitcom *Diff'rent Strokes*, who was played by the teenage Janet Jackson and was everything I had never had the chance to dream a girl could be. And now I could dream: pretty in purple plaid pussy bow-collared blouse with leg-of-mutton sleeves and tight indigo jeans, smarter than her cute boyfriend, sassily articulate, and black. And I had her hairdo! (Kinda: without the ends ironed up into curly wings.) People used to mistake me for a girl because of all that hair nearly hanging to my shoulders, framing my face. They would mistake me even more when, on hot summer days, my mother would pin away my long bangs with a steel barrette. As I grew older, I began to resent all this mistaking because in my older wisdom, I figured that I was "really" a boy because I had a penis, after all. So when I turned twelve, three years after coming to America, after two years of steady playground torture

[comes up behind me and snaps at my spine through my shirt]

"Hey, Tinkerbell! Are you wearing a bra?"

I asked my mother to chop off my hair. So began my career as a boy. Even though the torture, playground and beyond, never really stopped, my hair kept getting shorter and shorter until it was shaved off, although by that time, in college, I progressed in my girlhood a bit: I had enough courage to wear big gold doorknocker earrings à la Salt-N-Pepa. I was not a girl, not yet a man, I thought. What I did not realize was that I was a male, not yet a woman.

In the end, the joy of the castrated boy is that which he initially dreaded: to be mistaken for someone that you are. In the much maligned film *Showgirls* (1996), Elizabeth Berkley plays Nomi Malone, a dancing girl who comes to Las Vegas to be a cabaret star. Along the way to her eventual stardom, she must pay her dues by working in a sleazy strip club, and, because of that labor, people around her call her to her face, or mistake her, for a whore. Over and over, Nomi asserts: "I'm not a whore!" Shockingly (or not), it is revealed at the end of the film that Nomi was indeed a whore: she is from Oakland and has been hooking since her preteen years. Nomi Malone is a *girlgirlgirl*. She is, in fact, a GRL: *No Me* Malone. Like Sula, Nomi is an egoless girl, whose very power and subversive potential in that egoless performance of hyperfemininity confuses and discombobulates her audience. Critics and lay people alike love to rip this film to shreds by laughing at the utter intensity of Berkley's performance as Nomi; somehow when the film comes up on screen, everyone becomes an expert on camp. I've never found those "comic" scenes, in which Berkely-as-Nomi grapples with her life of prostitution, particularly comic. Berkely's performance—filled with emotional intensity and real, really good dancing (the actress herself is a trained dancer)—reminds me of me: we both got laughed at for looking exactly like what we actually were. And because laughter is very killing to the soft soul of the young, we tried to get away from the shame and pain of laughter by denouncing that identity. And yet: just as Nomi can never really not look like a whore in long, elaborately self-painted acrylic nails and a red fringe dress that barely covers her pussy; just as I could never really not look like a sissy girl faggot with my flopping wrist and hip-shaking walk, the escape is never effective—or satisfying. What works is to accept that mistakability as not only a fact of life but a point of joy and liberation. It can be powerful to be what you look like. It can be wonderful to be mistaken for something that the rest of the world calls horrible, ugly, embarrassing.

Finally, this past year, as I cornered thirty, I got around to growing my hair again. It became long enough to reach past my shoulders. Tossable, brushable, my hair made me my own doll. At first, my hair grew from laziness. Then, slowly, I realized that I had also reverted to my kid days, days of the long bangs: feeling and often looking like a girl—to homeless people asking for change, to sloppy-eyed construction workers, to confused patrons of the public men's restroom. A few months ago, while visiting me in San Francisco, my mother complimented me on how "pretty" my hair looked, then said, as a punch line to one of her philosophical musings: I don't know if you are a son or a daughter. She said it with an easy carelessness that made me very, very happy.

Notes

1. Sigmund Freud, "Medusa's Head," in *The Standard Edition of the Complete Psychological Works of Sigmund Freud*, trans. James Strachey (London: Hogarth, 1955), 19:273.

2. The psychoanalyst Silvan Tomkins suggests that the physical manifestation of the negative affect of "Fear-Terror" is superficially similar or even indistinguishable to that of "Surprise-Startle," which, as a "Resetting" affect, functions as a transition between affects, positive or negative. Thus the "Surprise-Startle" affect is often a precursor to the positive "Interest-Excitement." See *Shame and Its Sisters: A Silvan Tomkins Reader*, ed. Eve Kosofsky Sedgwick and Adam Frank (Durham, NC: Duke University Press, 1995), chap. 1, "What Are Affects?" and chap. 4, "Surprise-Startle."

3. For a detailed account of this phenomenon, see Tim Bergling, *Sissyphobia: Gay Men and Effeminate Behavior* (New York: Harrington Park, 2001); and Eve Kosofsky Sedgwick, "How to Bring Your Kids Up Gay: The War on Effeminate Boys," in *Tendencies* (Durham, NC: Duke University Press, 1994).

4. Jessica Benjamin, "'Constructions of Uncertain Content': Gender and Subjectivity beyond the Oedipal Complementaries," in *Shadow of the Other: Intersubjectivity and Gender in Psychoanalysis* (New York: Routledge, 1998), 64.

5. D. A. Miller, *A Place for Us: Essay on the Broadway Musical* (Cambridge, MA: Harvard University Press, 1998), 75.

6. Toni Morrison, *Sula* (1973; repr., New York: Plume, 1982), 61.

7. *Sula*'s critical history is usually centered on this point: Sula as an artist of the psyche and body, who creates on herself the idea of "black woman" that resists racist and sexist normativity. See Hortense J. Spillers, "A Hateful Passion, a Lost Love," *Feminist Studies* 9 (1983): 293–323; Gloria Wade-Gayles, "Giving Birth to Self: The Quests for Wholeness of Sula Mae Peace and Meridian Hill," in *No Crystal Stair: Visions of Race and Sex in Black Women's Fiction* (New York: Pilgrim, 1984), 184–215; Deborah E. McDowell, "Boundaries, or, Distant Relations and Close Kin—*Sula*," in *"The Changing Same": Black Women's Literature, Criticism, and Theory* (Bloomington: Indiana University Press, 1995), 101–17.

8. Through *Sula*, Kathryn Bond Stockton asserts that being the absolute "bottom" of a white and male-valuing society has paradoxically allowed black women to create an alternate economy: that which is valuable is precisely what is devalued or debased by the normative social order. Although Stockton, exploring the various ways in which such an inverted or "bottom" economy is elaborated in *Sula*, does not gesture toward what I see as the implicit effect of *girlgirlgirl*, doing away with hierarchical valuative systems altogether, such an inversion can be seen as a precursor or preparatory step to it. See Kathryn Bond Stockton, "Heaven's Bottom: Anal Economics and the Critical Debasement of Freud in Toni Morrison's *Sula*," *Cultural Critique* (Spring 1993), 81–118.

9. David L. Eng, *Racial Castration: Managing Masculinity in Asian America* (Durham, NC: Duke University Press, 2001), 151.

10. Eng's project—through a reading of *M. Butterfly*—is to articulate how white and heteronormative society deploys castration. Anne Anlin Cheng reads both *M. Butterfly* and Eng's reading of it to suggest that we consider the possibly subversive pleasure of the Asian bottom. See Anne Anlin Cheng, "Fantasy's Repulsion and Investment: David Henry Hwang and Ralph Ellison," in *The Melancholy of Race* (New York: Oxford University Press, 2000), 103–38.

11. Like the black male soldiers who perform a violence of their own on the castrated boy Helene, the black townspeople refuse, as a gesture of hatred against her polished, glossy black bourgeoise femininity, to pronounce the final *e* in her name. Morrison spells this out to us: "The people in the Bottom refused to say Helene. They called her Helen Wright and left it at that" (18). The black folks' phallic victory of the black woman castrated boy: leaving Helene nipped of her bit of a last letter by pronouncing her name without the extended "eene."

12. Saidiya V. Hartman, *Scenes of Subjection: Terror, Slavery, and Self-Making in Nineteenth-Century America* (New York: Oxford University Press, 1997), 51. See in particular chapter 2, "Redressing the Pained Body: Toward a Theory of Practice."

13. Benjamin, "Constructions of Uncertain Content," 58.

14. McDowell, "Boundaries, or, Distant Relations," 104.

15. Eva actually seems to be the other model for the racial-sexual blurring of *girlgirlgirl*: she renames her effeminate ("a beautiful, slight, quiet man who never spoke above a whisper" [39]) whiteboy tenant "Tar Baby." His previous name reflected his protoqueer, femme aspect: "Pretty Johnnie."

16. Angela Carter, "Lorenzo the Closet-Queen," *Nothing Sacred* (London: Virago, 1982), 211.

17. Sigmund Freud, "Femininity," in *New Introductory Lectures on Psycho-Analysis*, trans. James Strachey (New York: Norton, 1964), 144.

18. Interestingly, "Dewey" is a name that Morrison also used in her first novel, *The Bluest Eye* (1970). There it is not "Dewey King" but "Dewey Prince": the dreamlover—it is not clear whether he actually exists—of the prostitute Miss Marie/Maginot Line, who is one of the few people who actually loves the heroine Pecola Breedlove.

19. Wayne Koestenbaum, *Jackie under My Skin: Interpreting an Icon* (New York: Farrar, Straus and Giroux, 1995), 37.

20. Hole, "Beautiful Son" (1992), *My Body, The Hand Grenade*, audio recording, City Slang Records (1997).

21. Hélène Cixous has considered this question, although still focusing on the Medusa's head rather than body, in "The Laugh of the Medusa," *Signs* (1976): 880.

22. These other participants of Suicide Day were named (literally) and live under the roof of a particularly intense female imagination: that of Eva, Sula's own renegade grandmother, whose amputated one-leggedness renders her a Medusa of another kind. For more on Eva, see Rosemarie Garland Thomson, "Disabled Women as Powerful Women in Petry, Morrison, and Lorde," in *Extraordinary Bodies: Figuring Disability in American Culture and Literature* (New York: Columbia University Press, 1997), 103–34. There is another misfit male resident in Eva's house—her son Plum, who also returns from war shell-shocked. But unlike Shadrack, he seems to revert to infantilism rather than a protogay subjectivity: he longs to crawl back inside his mother, who eventually burns him alive rather than see her son as a "baby." Given this, it makes sense that Plum never gets the chance to join the Suicide Day parade.

23. Miller, *Place for Us*, 75.

24. Tori Amos, "In the Springtime of His Voodoo," *Boys for Pele*, audio recording, Atlantic Records (1996).

Time Binds, or, Erotohistoriography

Elizabeth Freeman

> At the national level, the struggle over control of meaning concerns making people's life constructions coterminous with periodizations given by the state.
>
> —John Borneman, *Belonging in the Two Berlins: Kin, State, Nation*

Years ago now, writing about interactions between individuals and small-scale social groups, Pierre Bourdieu declared that strategies of power consist of "playing on the time, or rather the *tempo*, of the action," mainly through managing delay and surprise.[1] Yet this chronopolitics extends beyond local conflicts to the management of entire populations: both the state and the market produce biopolitical status relations not only through borders, the establishment of private and public zones, and other strategies of spatial containment, but also and crucially through temporal mechanisms. Some groups have their needs and freedoms deferred or snatched away, and some don't. Some cultural practices are given the means to continue; others are squelched or allowed to die on the vine. Some events count as historically significant, some don't; some are choreographed as such from the first instance and thereby overtake others. Most intimately, some human experiences officially count as a life or one of its parts, and some don't. Those forced to wait or startled by violence, whose activities do not show up on the official time line, whose own time lines do not synchronize with it, are variously and often simultaneously black, female, queer.

More specifically, as numerous scholars have recognized, bourgeois-liberal entities from nations to individuals are defined within a narrow chronopolitics of development at once racialized, gendered, and sexualized. Western "modernity," for instance, has represented its own forward movement against a slower premodernity figured as brown-skinned, feminine, and erotically perverse.[2] On the material level, large-scale periodizing mechanisms have shaped what can be lived as a social formation, or an individual life. To take only one example: even before the hourly wage had quantified time, the colonial state intervened early into temporality, inscribing itself into and as the bodies of "the people" directly via the calendar, skewing indigenous rhythms of sacred and profane and

Social Text 84–85, Vol. 23, Nos. 3–4, Fall–Winter 2005. © 2005 by Duke University Press.

representing these rhythms as backward and superstitious.[3] And, as John Borneman suggests in my epigraph, supposedly postimperial nation-states still track and manage their own denizens through an official time line, effectively shaping the contours of a meaningful life by registering some events like births, marriages, and deaths, and refusing to record others like initiations, friendships, and contact with the dead.[4] In many places, the neoliberalist project continues to reconstruct time in these ways as it "develops" new regions for profit, and additionally depends upon the idea of capital's movement as itself an inexorable progress that will eventually accommodate select women, people of color, and queers. Neoliberalism describes the needs of everyone else, everyone it exploits, as simply, generically, deferred: the phrase "No Child Left Behind" suggests that there is, indeed, a behind in which the unlucky shall dwell.

Homi Bhabha has elegantly described this *unheimlich* "place" of anteriority, where in the postcolony time is always several and any historical moment correspondingly consists of many.[5] But it is also a crucial one within which queer politics and theory must dismantle the chronopolitics of development. If in 1990 or so, "queer" named a pressure against the state's *naming* apparatus, particularly against the normalizing taxonomies of male and female, heterosexual and homosexual, now it must include pressure against state and the market *periodizing* apparatuses.[6] I say "queer" not to overwrite postcolonial theory with a singular focus on sexuality—indeed, there is an emerging body of powerful work on the intersection of these two domains. Rather, my version of queer insists, following Cesare Casarino, that "we need to understand and practice time as fully incorporated, as nowhere existing outside of bodies and their *pleasures*."[7] Thus while this essay argues for a deviant chronopolitics obviously indebted to the work of postcolonial thinkers, it also insists that pleasure is central to the project—that queers survive through the ability to invent or seize pleasurable relations between bodies. We do so, I argue, across time.

I also emphasize a Foucauldian notion of pleasure and bodily contact over a Freudian model of pain and ego formation in response to recent reevaluations of negative affect in queer theory. So far, a simultaneously psychoanalytic and historicist loss—perhaps replacing or subsuming structuralist lack—has emerged as one of fin de siècle queer theory's key terms. A number of scholars have tracked the way that queer subjectivity and collectivity demand, and take as their reward, particularly inventive and time-traveling forms of grief and compensation that neither the normalizing work of the ego nor the statist logic of sequential generations can contain.[8] I would like to suggest, however, that this powerful turn toward loss—toward failure, shame, negativity, grief, and other structures of feeling historical—may also be a premature turn away from a seemingly obsolete politics of pleasure that could, in fact, be renewed by attention to temporal difference. That is, melancholic queer theory may acquiesce to the idea that pain—either a pain we do feel or a pain we should feel but cannot, or a pain we must laboriously rework into pleasure if we are to have any pleasure at all—is the proper ticket into historical consciousness. Eroticism and materialist history, pleasure and the dialectic, are too often cast as theoretical foils: was it not the distinctly unqueer Fredric Jameson who wrote, albeit in a very different context, that "history is what hurts. It is what refuses desire"?[9] Perhaps theorizing queerness on the basis of grief and loss acquiesces, however subtly, to a Protestant ethic in which pleasure cannot be the grounds of anything productive at all, let alone of such a weighty matter as the genuinely historical.

Against the chronopolitics of development, and also extending postcolonial notions of temporal heterogeneity beyond queer melancholic historiography, this essay advances what I call erotohistoriography: a politics of unpredictable, deeply embodied pleasures that counters the logic of development. Particularly in light of the liberal transformation of a queer sex revolution into gay marriage reform and Marxist condemnations of queer theory's focus on matters libidinal,[10] I would like to take the risk of the inappropriate response to ask: how might queer practices of pleasure, specifically, the bodily enjoyments that travel under the sign of queer sex, be thought of as temporal practices, even as portals to historical thinking? Freud's "uncanny" has offered one powerful model for a dialectic between bodily feelings and temporal alterity, but its "feelings" are both unpleasant and at one remove from the body (with the exception of goose bumps). Perhaps more important, the productive sense of alternate times in the uncanny—so fruitful for postcolonial theory—centers on the distinctly heterosexualized chronotopes of home, family, and mother.[11] In contrast, Foucault has famously written that queers should "use sexuality henceforth to arrive at a multiplicity of relationships," while Bourdieu would insist that these relationships inevitably play with and on time.[12] As a mode of reparative criticism, then, erotohistoriography indexes how queer relations complexly exceed the present. It insists that various queer social practices, especially those involving enjoyable bodily sensations, produce form(s) of time consciousness, even historical consciousness, that can intervene upon the material damage done in the name of development.[13] Against pain and loss, erotohistoriography posits the value of surprise, of pleasurable interruptions and momentary fulfillments from elsewhere, other times.

Against pain and loss, erotohistoriography posits the value of surprise, of pleasurable interruptions and momentary fulfillments from elsewhere, other times.

Bind Me Up, Bind Me Down

> Were I a writer, and dead, how I would love it if my life, through the pains of some friendly and detached biographer, were to reduce itself to a few details, a few preferences, a few inflections, let us say: to "biographemes" whose distinction and mobility might come to touch, like Epicurian atoms, some future body, destined to the same dispersion.
> —Roland Barthes, *Sade, Loyola, Fourier*

As a way in, let me momentarily exhume a body all too familiar to queer theory, particularly the literary-critical sort: Frankenstein's monster. The monster's physique, a patchwork of remnants from corpses his creator robs from the grave, is itself an index of temporal nonsynchronicity—specifically, of dead bodies persisting in the present and the future, of nonreproductive, yet still insistently corporeal kinship with the departed. His body literalizes Carolyn Dinshaw's model of the queer touch of time, of past bodies palpably connecting with present ones.[14] But in a low-budget independent film I saw a few years ago, Frankenstein's monster momentarily appeared to suggest the possibility of a sensual connection with futurity as well. In Hillary Brougher's 1997 *The Sticky Fingers of Time*, a woman mentions a scene in a novel her best friend has written: "I love that part, when Frankenstein splits his stitches and he dies, fertilizing the earth where that little girl grows tomatoes."[15] In contrast to the original novel, here the monster secures his future, joining the human scheme of obligations and dependencies rather than escaping on an ice floe. Though he seems to inseminate the little girl (for his body fluids will indirectly enter the orifice of her mouth when she eats the tomatoes), he transcends both the supposedly natural pain of childbirth and the cyclical time of reproduction. Like Walt Whitman, he disseminates himself.[16] Together, his body and the act he performs with it suggest a historiographical practice wherein the past takes the form of something already fragmented, "split," and decaying, and the present and future appear equally porous. Indeed, they seem to answer Roland Barthes's call, in my second epigraph, for a model of dispersed but insistently carnal continuity,[17] which I call binding. In this sense, the monster's body is not a "body" at all but a figure for relations between bodies past and present, for the insistent return of a corporealized historiography and future making of the sort to which queers might lay claim.

The scene that this woman calls forth, then, figures almost everything I mean by this essay's title "Time Binds." At the simplest level, "binds" are predicaments: like Frankenstein's monster, we cannot reproduce little queers with sperm and eggs, even if we do choose to give birth or parent:

making other queers is a social matter. In fact, sexual dissidents must create continuing queer lifeworlds while not being witness to this future or able to guarantee its form in advance, on the wager that there will be more queers to inhabit such worlds: we are "bound" to queer successors whom we might not recognize. "Binds" also suggests the bonds of love, not only attachments in the here and now but also those forged across both spatial and temporal barriers: to be "bound" is to be going somewhere. Yet even as it suggests connectivity, "binds" also names a certain fixity in time, a state of being timebound, belated, incompletely developed, left behind or not there yet, going nowhere. This nowhere has everything to do with sex, for "binds" is the present-tense English of a German verb employed by Freud, *Binden*, meaning to contain otherwise freely circulating libidinal energies. Yet there are pleasures here, too, for "binding" is, of course, one among many queer bodily practices, which include not only the painful enjoyment of bondage but also, in the scene I have described, the digestive work the little girl's body will eventually do upon the tomatoes.

Binding, we might say, makes predicament into pleasure, fixity into a mode of travel across time as well as space. Like "dissemination," it counters the fantasy of castration that subtends melancholic historiography, for it foregrounds attachments rather than loss. Furthermore, the monster's body and bodily act provide a queer alternative to the two most heterosexually gendered figures for "progress": the fecund maternal body that supposedly engenders natural history and the heroic male body that supposedly engenders national history. Consider the monster in terms of Freud's theory that a bodily imago and eventually the ego itself bind, indeed are caused by the binding of, raw and unpleasant sensory effects into legible somatic and psychic form. Freud argues that subjectivity begins when the libido invests in an uncomfortable bodily sensation by means of which it doubles back upon itself to delineate body parts as such. His example is a toothache, though he suggests that the genitals are perhaps the most insistent locale for such libidinal fixations.[18] From within this Möbius loop of attachment to sensitive areas, an increasingly unified sense of bodily contours emerges, and these contours materialize the ego that is "at first, a bodily ego," an interconnected set of perceived surfaces and boundaries.[19] Opening these terms out into the social, we can certainly think of engroupment—the collective form of the ego—as engendered by just this process. Here, the monster's wounds become metonymic of any number of physical lacerations suffered by queer bodies: beatings, unwanted heterosexual sex, medical "corrections" to the intersexed. These injuries, among others, are the violent foundation of collective queer being, the morphological imaginary, as Judith Butler calls it, for a wounded socius whose very wounding enables its being at all.[20]

History thus emerges as textual, humanmade, and linear only in contradistinction to a mute female body laboring "naturally" and recurrently in childbirth.

But even the scene as I have narrated it thus far succumbs to the logic that time binding would counter. As L. O. Aranye (Louise) Fradenburg has argued, history, coded as male, supersedes reproduction, coded as female, insofar as the former charts the work of men injured in war who tell tales to one another across generations.[21] History thus emerges as textual, humanmade, and linear only in contradistinction to a mute female body laboring "naturally" and recurrently in childbirth. In *The Sticky Fingers of Time*, within a conversation between two women, the singular and irreplaceable event of a wounded male body installs the deep time of a "before" and an "after," marks the potential historicity of this time and facilitates human agency over it in the form of a narrative that our fictional writer hands over to her friend and she hands over to the filmic audience. Significantly, one speaker is murdered soon after the conversation, suggesting that two women cannot be the bearers of a future thought outside the context of reproduction. Or, this is what you get when you look at the speakers and not at the little girl who does not actually materialize in this scene: as a figure for the queer undead, the monster is temporally linked—timebound—to the little girl who is not a child at all but a queer unborn, a future we cannot see but upon which we bet. Her speculated presence, I would argue, inaugurates a different reading of the monster, one leading to the "eroto-" in erotohistoriography.

Returning to Fradenburg's and Freud's analyses, both pivot on the transformation of a wound into phallic power. Authority over what counts as history, Fradenburg argues, compensates for bodily injury. As Butler has noted, Freud eventually recasts the originary bodily discomfort that creates the individual (and I would argue, social) imago as a tumescence or engorgement, the kind that only penises experience. Part of Butler's project is to unglue the phallic ego from the penis by relocating the grounds for a morphological imaginary, a bodily ego, onto any number of possible bodily surfaces: the lesbian phallus might emerge in relation to "an arm, a tongue, a hand (or two), a knee, a thigh, a pelvic bone, an array of purposefully instrumentalized body-like things."[22] But where in this model is the toothache's interestingly aching hole and other symptoms of a certain desire to be filled up, not all of which can be reduced to wounds? What is the morphological imaginary for that? Another essay about the lesbian phallus allows us to see that the Freudian hole seems to reappear in Butler's work on and as the audience. Jordana Rosenberg has recently argued that in Butler's essay, the audience's hunger for lesbian presence, the dumb literalist dyke's wish to be taken by the clumsy, dildonic visual referent, can only disgust and amuse the professional deconstructionist for whom the phallus is, of course, the very sign of nonpresence.[23] Our monster's extravagant bodily gesture similarly relocates the hole: the little girl, his "audience," will have her hunger satiated directly by the tomato and indirectly by his blood, which also carries with it the DNA of multiple dead. Of course, her queer hunger for tactile contact with the past is open to similar charges of vulgar historicism, the ugly twin of vulgar homosexuality. But the monster's wounds themselves pass over from his pain to her satisfaction, his openings to hers, without necessarily having to become either lack or presence. The monster's transfer of energy across time appears not as masculine sacrifice but rather as a gender-undifferentiated but nevertheless localized bodily effusion: in short, holes beget holes.

The great surprise of this scene, then, lies in the missing feast it suggests: a taste of the idea that pleasure may be as potentially generative of a future as pain, trauma, loss, or foreclosure. In fact, Giorgio Agamben has suggested that pleasure could found a new concept of time, one presently missing from historical materialism. But he has more problematically located that pleasure in "man's originary home," which sounds, again, like a return to the plenitude of a maternal body.[24] In contrast, the scene I have described offers neither mother nor father in its imagining of relations across time and between times, no original womb, but only a scarred and striated body on the one side, an absent prepubescent body on the other, and a dumb, juicy, not-yet-born vegetable in between, with no portable text mediating the transfer. And, crucially, it offers the mouth as a tactile rather than just a verbal instrument for temporal transactions, for temporal binding. The question is how this might become historical.

Surprise! On the Inappropriate Response

In its recorporealizing of the mouth and its use of this "hole" to bind a differential past to an uninevitable future, the figure of the little girl invokes Nicholas Abraham and Maria Torok's description of melancholia—one that has the power to reinscribe pleasure into the melancholic historiographical interventions that queer theory is already making. Abraham and Torok describe melancholia in particularly corporeal terms, as a way to preserve a prior scene or object in the form of a symptom usually connected to the mouth—sometimes a set of behaviors like bingeing on food or starving, but most often a fetish word, even a way of speaking, that simultaneously preserves and obscures the loss. In this process, which they call incorporation, the subject mimes its repossession of a lost object by eating or speaking awry, attempting literally to embed the object into or make it part of the body itself.[25] Incorporation, Abraham and Torok argue, is the pathological form of a process they call introjection, where the lost object serves as a means for the subject to rework its originary erotic autonomy.[26] In introjection, the object becomes a mere placeholder for the self, whom the subject must return to loving as in primary narcissisim, but this time the self must be permeable enough to integrate new objects, too. This is, notably, a much less phallic model of the ego than Freud's, or even Butler's. In fact, opened out from individual psyche to collective process, both the process of incorporation and that of introjection suggest what might be called a "bottom" historiography. If our absent little girl is a receptacle for queer history, what she receives is not a transmission of authority or custom but a transmission of receptivity itself, of a certain pleasurably porous relation to new configurations of the past and unpredictable futures.[27]

In fact, opened out from individual psyche to collective process, both the process of incorporation and that of introjection suggest what might be called a "bottom" historiography.

In Abraham and Torok's model, melancholia is cured when the lost object finally disappears, when incorporation yields to introjection, and time synchs up again such that the uninterrupted present corresponds to an integrated self open to the future but over the past. Yet like melancholia itself, the so-called pathological form of incorporation seems eminently more queer; it preserves the past *as* past, in a crypt imperfectly sealed off from the present. Incorporation imagines a psyche with unpredictable leakages, a body at semiotically and sexually productive temporal odds with itself. Despite Abraham and Torok's flattening of time in the "normal" model of introjection, the past they suggest interrupts the present to trigger eating and speaking is not wholly defined in terms of trauma. Instead, it consists of latent excitations not yet traversed by the binary between pain and pleasure. In this sense, what is preserved and suspended within the mouth is also capable of being released as pleasure rather than simply being repeated as incomplete mastery over pain.

In fact, Torok addresses the most opaque part of Freud's essay on mourning and melancholia, in which Freud notes but fails to theorize the problem of the inappropriate response. While we would expect tears or numbness in the face of death, Freud remarks that the grieving subject often experiences a surge of frenzied joy: "The most remarkable peculiarity of melancholia, and one most in need of explanation, is the tendency it displays to turn into mania accompanied by a completely opposite symptomatology."[28] He notes that mourning does not have the same tendency, which eliminates the possibility that mania is simply energy unbound from the lost object once its loss has been recognized and worked through. Torok considers a series of letters in which Freud's contemporary Karl Abraham pressed him to consider the question of this mania and suggested several times that it often consisted of a sudden influx of erotic feelings. But Freud seems not to have answered this call to examine the phenomenon. Taking up where he left off, Torok suggests that the melancholic's entombed secret may not be a loss at all. Rather, it is an erotic effusion repressed and mnemonically preserved: "*The illness of mourning* [i.e., melancholia] *does not result, as might appear, from the affliction caused by the objectal loss itself, but rather from the feeling of an irreparable crime of having been overcome with desire, of having been surprised by an overflow of libido at the least appropriate moment, when it would behoove us to be grieved in despair.*"[29] She goes on to claim that melancholic incorporation itself "perpetuate[s] a clandestine pleasure," a long-ago interrupted scene of erotic contact with the lost object.[30] For Torok, then, the melancholic psyche is a doubled effect of pleasures past: first, pleasure is severed and remade as unpleasure or trauma; then, the object that gave pleasure itself disappears. The scene's affect and object secret themselves in body and psyche, to be released in the grieving subject's sudden feeling of carnal desire. In short, as a component of melancholia, mania revisits an inappropriate sexual response from the past.

With Torok's sense of melancholia as a lost erotic encounter preserved, then, we can imagine the "inappropriate" response of eros in the face of sorrow as a trace of past forms of pleasure located in specific historical moments. A recent video by Nguyen Tan Hoang, an emerging artist, makes this possibility tangible: *K.I.P.* (2002) cuts between a 1970s pornographic videotape and an image of Nguyen's face reflected in a television set. Speaking of this work recently, Nguyen described his fascination with the way that the original videotape had deteriorated in the places where viewers had rewound the tape to look at particularly sexy scenes, so that the tape now skipped and the action was punctuated by grainy blank spots.[31] Reappearing in Nguyen's video, these blank spots suggest the impossibility of returning to the short-lived era when gay men could have unprotected sex with multiple partners without fear. Floating over this scene, Nguyen's face is the sign of his generation, born too late. At the same time, the image of Nguyen's face indexes the fact that, given how Asian American men have been stereotyped as feminine in the United States, he would not necessarily have had access anyway to this particular sex scene or to the "scene" of urban macho man cruising: Nguyen's reflection also looks like the ghosts of those condemned to watch from the sidelines during the era of the taping, waiting for their moment of inclusion. Yet this is not a tape about inclusion, ultimately, for a trace of pleasure is also visible: the surface of the television also simply reflects a voyeur taking his enjoyments where he finds them. Given the historical framing of this video by AIDS and racism against Asian Americans, it might seem politically inappropriate for the videomaker-character to experience any bliss by looking at white gay men barebacking. Yet there he is, watching. The audience cannot know for sure what personal or political experiences rush into his head to fill the gaps in the tape that once contained white gay men, to bind him to the surrounding scenes and bind these to events in his own life.

Nguyen's video registers something akin to Toni Morrison's concept of "skin memory, the body's recollection of pleasure," combined with the claim of her earlier works that the skin might index historical moments as well as personal encounters.[32] But what Abraham and Torok describe as maniac memory is hardly emotion recollected in tranquillity—instead, it is an irruption of strange plenitude in the present, like Nguyen's bliss amid generational and racial grief. In this and other erotohistoriographical works, we see Walter Benjamin's concept of the shock of modernity, which even he linked to ephemeral encounters with sexualized figures such as prostitutes and sailors, met by his concept of the past flashing up to illuminate the present.[33] Following the lead of Abraham and Torok, of Benjamin, of works like these two films, we might imagine ourselves haunted by ecstasy and not just by loss; residues of positive affect (erotic scenes, utopias, memories of touch) might be available for queer counter- (or para-) historiographies. As I have argued elsewhere, within this paradigm we might see camp performance as a kind of historicist *jouissance*, a friction of dead bodies upon live ones, obsolete constructions upon emergent ones, which I have called "temporal drag."[34] Or, we might look for what Annamarie Jagose has called "the figure of 'history'—its energizing of the very tropes of before and after" in queer patterns of courtship and cruising, in sexual and more broadly tactile encounters, even in identity formations such as butch/femme or FTM.[35] Or (and), historicity itself might appear as a structure of *tactile* feeling, a mode of touch, even a sexual practice. In particular, we may want to glimpse traces of historically specific forms of pleasure—whether they have been lost, repressed, disavowed, or subsumed into institutional forms of supposedly benign supervision like marriage—in our present, precisely because they once counted in the lesbian and gay imaginary, if not the national one, as part of what it meant to have a life.

Notes

Many thanks to those who offered comments on this essay in its various incarnations: Bishnu Ghosh, Judith Halberstam, Heather Love, Dana Luciano, H. N. Lukes, Kara Thompson, readers and editors at *Social Text*, and audiences at Harvard University, the Pembroke Center for Teaching and Research on Women at Brown University, and the University of California at Davis Scholars' Symposium.

1. Pierre Bourdieu, *Outline of a Theory of Practice*, trans. Richard Nice (New York: Cambridge University Press, 1977), 7.

2. Exemplary recent critiques of the intertwined racial, gendered, and sexualized politics of developmental time include Rod Ferguson, *Aberrations in Black: Toward a Queer of Color Critique* (Minneapolis: University of Minnesota Press,

2004); and Martin F. Manalansan IV, *Global Divas: Filipino-American Men in the Diaspora* (Durham, NC: Duke University Press, 2003). The classic text is Anne McClintock, *Imperial Leather: Race, Gender, and Sexuality in the Colonial Contest* (New York: Routledge, 1995).

3. See Geeta Patel, "Ghostly Appearances: Time Tales Tallied Up," *Social Text* 64 (2000): 47–66; and Eviatar Zerubavel, *Hidden Rhythms: Schedules and Calendars in Social Life* (Chicago: University of Chicago Press, 1981).

4. John Borneman, *Belonging in the Two Berlins: Kin, State, Nation* (Cambridge: Cambridge University Press, 1992), 31.

5. Homi Bhabha, *The Location of Culture* (New York: Routledge, 1994), 1–18.

6. On queer as an anti-taxonomizing force, see Lauren Berlant and Elizabeth Freeman, "Queer Nationality," *boundary 2* 19 (1992): 149–80; and Eve Sedgwick, "Introduction: Axiomatic," in *Epistemology of the Closet* (Berkeley: University of California Press, 1990), 1–63. For provocative theorizations of how the state uses genealogical time to make lives intelligible as such, see Borneman, *Belonging in the Two Berlins*, and Elizabeth Povinelli, "Notes on Gridlock: Genealogy, Intimacy, Sexuality," in "New Imaginaries," ed. Dilip Gaonkar and Benjamin Lee, special issue, *Public Culture* 14 (2002): 215–38. An important theorization of queer temporality is Judith Halberstam, *In a Queer Time and Place: Transgender Bodies, Subcultural Lives* (New York: New York University Press, 2005), just published as this article went to press.

7. Cesare Casarino, "Time Matters: Marx, Negri, Agamben, and the Corporeal," *Strategies* 16 (2003): 185–206, 202 (emphasis added).

8. Particularly moving examples of this work include Christopher Nealon, *Foundlings: Lesbian and Gay Historical Emotion before Stonewall* (Durham, NC: Duke University Press, 2001); and Heather Love, "Feeling Backward: Loss and the Politics of Queer History" (unpublished manuscript).

9. Frederic Jameson, *The Political Unconscious: Narrative as a Socially Symbolic Act* (Ithaca, NY: Cornell University Press, 1981), 102.

10. See, e.g., the work of Donald Morton.

11. Sigmund Freud, "The Uncanny" (1925), reprinted in *The Standard Edition of the Complete Psychological Works of Sigmund Freud*, ed. and trans. James Strachey, vol. 17 (London: Hogarth, 1953), 219–52. The term *chronotope* is from Mikhail Bakhtin, "Forms of Time and of the Chronotope in the Novel," in *The Dialogic Imagination: Four Essays*, ed. Michael Holquist, trans. Caryl Emerson and Michael Holquist (Austin: University of Texas Press, 1981), 84–258.

12. Michel Foucault, "Friendship as a Way of Life," in *Foucault Live: Collected Interviews, 1961–1984*, ed. Sylvère Lotringer, trans. Lysa Hochroth and John Johnston (New York: Semiotext[e], 1996), 308–12, 310.

13. This formulation echoes and modifies J. G. Pocock, "Time, Institutions, and Action: An Essay on Traditions and Their Understanding," in *Politics, Language, and Time* (New York: Atheneum, 1971), 233–72, 256.

14. Carolyn Dinshaw, *Getting Medieval: Sexualities and Communities, Pre- and Postmodern* (Durham, NC: Duke University Press, 1999). Dinshaw also productively explores the remark on Roland Barthes I have used for an epigraph.

15. Hillary Brougher, *The Sticky Fingers of Time* (1997; New York: Strand Releasing Home Video DVD, 2001). The speaker has confused the monster and his creator.

16. See Michael Moon, *Disseminating Whitman: Revision and Corporeality in Leaves of Grass* (Cambridge, MA: Harvard University Press, 1991).

17. Roland Barthes, *Sade, Loyola, Fourier*, trans. Richard Miller (New York: Hill and Wang, 1976).

18. Sigmund Freud, "On Narcissism: An Introduction" (1914). Reprinted in *General Psychological Theory*, ed. Philip Reiff (New York: Macmillan, 1963), 56–82, esp. 64.

19. Sigmund Freud, *The Ego and the Id*, trans. Joan Riviere, rev. and ed. James Strachey (New York: Norton, 1962), 17.

20. See Judith Butler, "The Lesbian Phallus and the Morphological Imaginary," in *Bodies That Matter: On the Discursive Limits of "Sex"* (New York: Routledge, 1993), 57–91.

21. Louise O. Fradenburg (now L. O. Aranye) and Carla Freccero, "The Pleasures of History," *GLQ* 1 (1995): 371–84.

22. Butler, "The Lesbian Phallus," 88.

23. Jordana Rosenberg, "Butler's 'Lesbian Phallus'; or, What Can Deconstruction Feel?" *GLQ* 9 (2003): 393–414.

24. Giorgio Agamben, "Time and History: Critique of the Instant and the Continuum," in *Infancy and History: The Destruction of Experience*, trans. Liz Heron (New York: Verso, 1993), 91–105, esp. 104. Thanks to Gregory Dobbins for bringing this essay to my attention.

25. Nicolas Abraham and Maria Torok, "Mourning or Melancholia: Introjection versus Incorporation," in Abraham and Torok, *The Shell and the Kernel: Renewals of Psychoanalysis*, vol. 1, ed. and trans. Nicholas Rand (Chicago: University of Chicago Press, 1994), 125–38.

26. Maria Torok, "The Illness of Mourning and the Fantasy of the Exquisite Corpse," in *The Shell and the Kernel: Renewals of Psychoanalysis*, ed. Nicolas Abraham and Maria Torok (Chicago: University of Chicago Press, 1994), 112.

27. Ann Cvetkovich, "Recasting Receptivity: Femme Sexualities," in *Lesbian Erotics*, ed. Karla Jay (New York: New York University Press, 1995), 125–46.

28. Sigmund Freud, "Mourning and Melancholia" (1917). Reprinted in *General Psychological Theory*, ed. Philip Reiff (New York: Macmillan, 1963), 174.

29. Torok, "The Illness of Mourning," 107–24, 110 (emphasis in original).

30. Torok, "The Illness of Mourning," 131.

31. Nguyen Tan Hoang, "Queer Art" (roundtable presentation, Queer Locations conference, Irvine, CA, 11 May 2004).

32. Toni Morrison, *Love* (New York: Knopf, 2003), 67. See also Jay Prosser, *Second Skins: The Body Narratives of Transsexuality* (New York: Columbia University Press, 1998), 83.

33. See Dianne Chisholm, "The City of Collective Memory," *GLQ* 7 (2001): 195–203.

34. On temporal drag, see Elizabeth Freeman, "Packing History, Count(er)ing Generations," *New Literary History* 31 (2000): 727–44.

35. Annamarie Jagose, *Inconsequence: Lesbian Representation and the Logic of Sexual Sequence* (Ithaca, NY: Cornell University Press, 2002), xi.

Tarrying with the Normative

QUEER THEORY AND *BLACK HISTORY*

Amy Villarejo

> *Der Alptraum*: I am in a warmly lit room, spanned by banquet tables draped with white tablecloths. It's like an interior from *The West Wing*, the camera swooping across the amber room to reveal its sconces, its sideboard, its oriental carpet. The hum of conversation is pleasant, soothing, and I am vaguely contented to meet the woman seated next to me at the long table. Her manicured fingers grasp mine a second or two longer than necessary; her clasp feels seductive and inviting. Just as I draw back my hand, I become hot, sweaty, panicky. All of a sudden, I am seized with an anxiety about being in a room filled with well-heeled, well-groomed, well-mannered, and well-dressed putatively straight white people. I am a fraud, an imposter. I run screaming from the room. I wake up.

For me, queer studies has been one way to make this private, solitary, and inchoate feeling of being a fraud—a feeling that surges and subsides like a flare—into something like a critique. The feeling, it should be said, also erupts in gatherings of witty, edgy, and beautiful queer people. It is a more fundamental question of being, exploding when the decorousness of the normative, however indicated, becomes too much to bear.

I did have the above nightmare recently. It recurs periodically, blending its mise-en-scène from the habitual visual ingredients of my everyday life: film, television, and academic institutions. The result is that my dreamworld looks like a crossbreeding experiment between the Ivy League and *Law and Order*, the classroom and the morgue. If you get the picture, the point I would like to take up substantively here is a blunt one: normativity, like ideology, is a deviously expressive beast, deriving its form as well as its force from unexpected, unanticipated, unimaginable quarters. It confronts desire as well as power, and it seems curiously indifferent to rationalized, systematic, and scientific counterattacks. The place where *I* encounter normativity and its effects is conjugated as the pedagogy of the visual.

When I say "normativity," what I really mean is the terror of the normative: in its most benign form it appears as a bullying insistence toward obedience to social law and hierarchy, and in its most lethal form it carries the punishment of death for resistance to them. In my view, queer theory brings immense resources to the analysis of, engagement with, and cri-

Social Text 84–85, Vol. 23, Nos. 3–4, Fall–Winter 2005.

In what follows, I take up what I see as a fundamental challenge posed by queer of color analysis: making good on the understanding of normativity as variegated, striated, contradictory.

tique of normativity, resources precisely calibrated to the degree to which "queer" is deployed as a catachresis, as a metaphor without an adequate referent. To put it differently, queer theory seems to me most equipped to "tarry with the normative" when it forsakes its claims to the literal and makes for the more dangerous—but also more commodious—complications of relationality and variegation.[1] Queer is but one name, hurled back with pride, for social abjection, exclusion, marginalization, and degradation; it provides, by this logic, but one opening toward freedom.

In what follows, I take up what I see as a fundamental challenge posed by queer of color analysis: making good on the understanding of normativity as variegated, striated, contradictory. Queer of color critique, an emergent and open-ended task as well as an awkward if provisional name, takes the prismatic pressures of the normative as impossible to seize and to systematize simultaneously. To make more explicit what I have been allowing to play beneath the surface, what interests me is the persistent tension queer theory inherits from its forebears in critical theory between systematization and desire, between reason and affect, between the literal and the figurative, between philosophy and literature.

A particularly exciting recent book addresses this tension, Roderick Ferguson's *Aberrations in Black: Toward a Queer of Color Critique*. It is a serious and sure attempt to bring a Marxist inheritance into conversation with modes of pathologizing African American life, particularly through the logic of the symptom, through the hierarchies of value of gender and sexuality; it is part of a larger endeavor, which deserves our close attention, more explicitly to rewrite queer studies as a discourse about race and class, not simply as a bounded discourse about gender and sexuality. The book, in turn, sparked my reading of a peculiar 1968 film I have been struggling to understand through this multifaceted, layered conception of normativity: *Black History: Lost, Stolen, or Strayed?* (I should add here, by way of a stipulation as to my sanity or as to what constitutes "queer of color" matter or material, that the film is neither "queer" nor aggressively "heteronormative," but it takes hold of me in a way that helps me think about normativity in what might be a queer way.) Like Ferguson's book, the film is a survey of how twentieth-century African American life is naturalized as a pathologizing symptom and redeemed by masculinist identifications, in this case through the language of cinema itself. But the film differs from Ferguson's book in that it powerfully distinguishes between the terrors of the normative and the fantasies and practices of self-production through which we meet those terrors. I visit both the book and the film in turn, adhering neither to the form of the book review nor to the hermeticism of textual analysis. Instead, I want *Aberrations* to bleed into *History*, black and beautiful. Roderick Ferguson, meet Bill Cosby.

A brief word on my titular reference to Slavoj Žižek's work, which is motivated by a question this essay shares with *Tarrying with the Negative*: how to address questions of social conflict, particular racial or ethnic conflict, within the terms of ideology critique? Like Žižek, I share the sense that it is the task of the critical intellectual—if indeed one can still speak of him or her—to maintain a distance with respect to the Master-Signifier or, as he says, "to 'produce' the Master-Signifier, that is to say, to render visible its 'produced,' artificial, contingent character."[2] The movement into the realm of possibility from actuality belongs to the pedagogy of the visual: as Žižek's frequent brief analyses of films demonstrate, the cinema is as integral to the dialectic of *Bildung* as philosophical, sociological, or psychoanalytic discourses may be. While this short essay cannot possibly engage with the dense readings of the German tradition of philosophical idealism Žižek provides in his book, resonances of his work on the symptom may be heard elsewhere in the essay.

Aberrations in Black and the Sociological Institution

I admire Ferguson's book and would hope to engage it as it does the work of the thinkers Ferguson addresses: patiently, thoroughly, rigorously, lovingly. Ferguson's project, forging queer of color analysis that bridges the social sciences and the humanities (sociology and literature), displays the kind of thinking that some of the early work of British cultural studies did, particularly in its sense of unrelenting urgency and in the transformations it puts into play of academic categories (cultural studies, queer studies, critical race studies, queer of color critique). Like some critiques of that initial Birmingham Centre work, Ferguson also seeks to unmask the normative assumptions of Marxist traditions while disavowing the ideology of transparency of which such unmasking would seem to be an example. This produces an interesting and productive tension, mirroring that torque the project sustains between scientific sociological methodology and literary insight. Early in the book, Ferguson defines his project in this way: "Queer of color analysis denotes an interest in materiality, but refuses ideologies of transparency and reflection, ideologies that have helped to constitute marxism, revolutionary nationalism, and liberal pluralism."[3] Endorsing a more discursive procedure that would constitute different political subjects, Ferguson turns to Marx's own treatment in the *Economic and Philosophic Manuscripts of 1844* of the figure of the prostitute. He reads her figuration as an instance of naturalizing as "real" symptom (of the ravages of industrial capitalism) the potential *agent* of social change, a maneuver that sociology would later extend to African Americans in the twentieth century.

In opening with a reading of this figure and in more explicit ways, too (especially in his final chapter, "Something Else to Be: *Sula*, *The Moynihan Report*, and the Negations of Black Lesbian Feminism"), Ferguson marks his debt to feminism and its persistent work of undoing normative and naturalizing moves made in the name of the universal. In his words, queer of color analysis "extends women of color feminism by investigating how intersecting racial, gender, and sexual practices antagonize and/or conspire with the normative investments of nation-states and capital" (4). Since the mode of sociology—a privileged discourse in the sense that it has been, in Ferguson's view, the primary mechanism for obtaining knowledge about African American life in the twentieth century and beyond—is to naturalize as or while rendering *perverse*, it becomes necessary to fuse queer critique with the legacy of feminism's intersectional critique, building or accumulating a theoretical stance as well as a method through what I would call a kind of historical sedimentation. Ultimately, Ferguson cements feminist critique with queer critique through two key descriptors of his object, naturalized "heteropatriarchy" and its companion term, the "nonheteronormative." Ferguson's object, the naturalized and normative view of African American life proffered through the texts drawn from sociology and literature Ferguson reads, is constituted both by the perverting logic of "canonical" sociology and by Ferguson's critical feminist/queer position: "Looking at canonical sociology's relationship to African American nonheteronormative formations can help us see how U.S. capital has also been regarded as a site of pathologies and perversions that have designated racialized nonwhite communities as the often ominous outcome of capital's productive needs" (18–19).

All of this is to say that "nonheteronormative" comes to denote, for Ferguson, a symptom or sign of a relentless and pathologizing racial logic, itself produced through the circuits of industrial capitalism, as well as that which would seem to evade that logic. I have summarized his elegant argument quickly, and it would be important in a more extended treatment of his book to explore among other things the consequences of distinguishing carefully between sign and symptom, between logic and result, between industrial and urbanizing economies. But for my purposes in trying to open up a more nuanced understanding of normativity, what seems significant is that Ferguson seeks to forge a method (symptomatic reading) and an abstraction (nonheteronormative) that, on the one hand, can speak to the multiple forms that degradation takes in late capitalist America, where perversions and gender transgressions aplenty become inscribed in the mortar of racialized urban landscapes. On the other hand, he lends that same name to figures of defiance and critique. This conflation, lodged in his readings and in the term *nonheteronormative*, is, I want to argue, an effort to keep alive the intersectional, "accumulated" historical sedimentation whereby African American exploitation, degradation, abjection, and exploitation are figured through, naturalized by, and dependent on descriptive hierarchies of value of gender and sexuality (not to mention discourses of citizenship, ethics, and democracy). To insist on the fractured and contradictory nature of such sedimentation is an act, again in my view, of considerable intellectual bravery. At the same time, Ferguson wants *nonheteronormative* to mark a range of (to use some of his words) positions, formations, sites of knowledge production, and, well (to use a humbler category), kinds of people (like those black queens on the South Side of Chicago whom Ferguson invokes) who would be candidates for the kind of transformative agency Marx refused to see in the figure of the prostitute.

The questions, then, are these: How do we come to know about the pressures that the normative exerts on African American life, particularly in its relation to the looming forces and abstractions of the midcentury (from the thirties to the seventies, from *Native Son* to *Sula*)? Through what lenses, frameworks, disciplines, texts, stories, fragments? And how would we know what escapes the terror of the normative? Through what process of recovery, retrieval, critique, problematization, or alternative? Through what understanding of abstraction? By what vision?

Ferguson's contention is that American sociology has provided the most insistent narration and most privileged epistemology through which the state has gained access to, and produced knowledge about, African Americans. Furthermore, taking African American life as its putative object, sociology (in particular, what Ferguson calls "canonical sociology") seems able only to stabilize, rather than to trouble, the specifically normative tendencies of that dense text of midcentury African American life; the "nonheteronormative gender, sexual and familial formations" (46) encouraged by industrialization become pathological or perverse signs of capitalist exploitation that must be answered, corrected through sociological scrutiny. His further point, one I take especially seriously, is that when one says that "the state" has gained access to knowledge, one also and hauntingly means "the school" and "the university." This collection of sociological documents, from the work of Robert Park to the Moynihan Report, indeed function as social policy as much as they provide a pedagogical script for the reproduction of pathologizing and naturalizing lifeworlds, on the ground and in the mind.[4]

American sociology has provided the most insistent narration and most privileged epistemology through which the state has gained access to, and produced knowledge about, African Americans.

Since I am not a sociologist, I do not know whether looking, say, at the vibrant tradition of American radical sociology, or at the *émigré* sociology of the Frankfurt exiles, would yield a different story, although I certainly hope it would. Ferguson's own critical stance toward the sociological institution yields a careful reading of those specifically canonical or influential texts he chooses to illustrate his point, which again, to paraphrase, is that when sociology looks at African American "communal and corporeal difference" (41), it sees the degenerate and perverse results of industrializing and urbanizing economies. Symptom and nothing more: canonical sociology in its benevolence cannot read perversion as agency. But is it then literature that would offer another route: through the imagination, through the reshuffling of positions and desire according to new grammars and idioms rather than systematizing and scientific "canons" and logics?[5] Does literature appear in its difference, on which many of us would like to insist, from the systematizing imperatives of the (social) sciences? In Ferguson's view, the answer is a surprising "no." Here I want to take up the challenge that Ferguson lays out but leaves unfinished: to think, as it were, outside the symptom. I want to cleave apart the two senses of *nonheteronormative* Ferguson proposes, so that the politics of African American life and struggle are not forced to yield their lessons in the same terms in which these have been pathologized. In what follows, I would like to suggest that through cinema (perhaps as well as literature but, if so, then in different ways), one can find a rich vocabulary for parsing the distinction that I have argued is collapsed in *nonheteronormative* between symptom and agency.

Before I get to cinema, however, let me first look quickly but more closely at Ferguson's view of literature, which amounts to a view, in fact, of the canon. For it is Ferguson's contention that canonical sociology and canonical literature are *functionally* equivalent, continuous, and homologous:

> African American nonheteronormativity thus disrupts the idea that the literary and the sociological are discrete and discontinuous formations. Instead we must assume that canonical sociology and canonical literature arise out of the same system of power, one that presents normativity and humanity as the gifts of state compliance and heteropatriarchal belonging. (72)

Insofar as the literary collides with the sociological (and discourses of citizenship, state-formation, ethics, and aesthetics), it does so on very specific ground, where sanctioned, frequently read, or influential texts seem to share, almost tautologically, a genealogy of naturalizing the heteronormative. Because, for example, Richard Wright professed interest in the Chicago school of sociology—and to a great extent depended on it for *12 Million Angry Black Voices* as well as for *Native Son*, Ferguson reads the latter novel's attempts to anchor "nonheteronormative formations within the feminizing dysfunctions of capital" (44) as equivalent to sociological diagnoses of industrialization's perverse effects. Rather than contest it, Wright instead replicates sociology's bad logic; *Native Son* is thus understood as a kind of clone, offering through the character of Bigger a readable and straightforward symbol of nonheteronormative dysfunction. While Ferguson does offer readings of African American literary works that stand in a more critical relation to sociological distortion (by Ralph Ellison and Toni Morrison, for example), he retains his commitment to the functional equivalence of canonical formations precisely in order to bring them into conversation with one another, to read sociology alongside literature. Especially in his later chapters, then, Ferguson seeks to avoid one commonplace of liberal pluralist readings of canonical literature: a practice merely of exposing the literary text's complicity with hegemonic values.

But in Ferguson's readings, what is specifically "queer" *must* appear through the same rubric of nonheteronormativity that sociology discloses, and it is in insisting on this equivalence that Ferguson suppresses, I think, the critical potency of queer theory. Queer theory offers a view of relationality that is not strictly speaking symptomatic; it offers ways to fly with language and desire away from homology and continuity. Queer theory can offer, in other words, a way to grapple with feeling and with response (affect), a way to work in the interstices of contacts, affiliations, relations. Queer theory would do wonders with the differences and the tingles of the list of transgressions that sociology instead uniformly pathologizes in urban territory: "Prostitutes, homosexuals, rent parties, black and tans, interracial liaisons, speakeasies, and juvenile delinquency" (41) to take a few, interrogating a logic that would take these as *equivalent* signs of capital's perverting effects. This is not to say that literature cannot do wonders with these equivalences, too, or that literary language and literary criticism are not already well equipped to distinguish, for example, between Wright's naturalism and Ellison's modernism. It is, however, to say that Ferguson's particularly exciting contribution has been to point to the astonishing complicity of two discourses that would seem frequently to insist on their own autonomy and to see what happens when that autonomy is fractured, thereby opening up a set of relationships that has yet fully to be explored.

I am therefore interested in how to pull apart the two strands, symptom and agency, that Ferguson conjoins in *nonheteronormative* in the interest of producing a specifically queer understanding of the differences that might inhere in both pathologizing and revolutionary rhetorics. I would venture that such an understanding is as cinematic as it is sociological, by which I mean that the very mode of response engendered by urban and industrial life in midcentury America is marked by the language and social institution of the cinema. To examine the middle decades of the American twentieth

Queer theory offers a view of relationality that is not strictly speaking symptomatic; it offers ways to fly with language and desire away from homology and continuity.

century is, as Ferguson mentions in passing, to take the movie theater as itself a central technology of racialization, gendering, sexualization (47–48). To take up the question of agency of African American people following the migrations to the north is necessarily to meditate on movement itself: "Movies, parties, automobiles, and other features of urban life exposed the city's residents to other truths that provided both context and access to alternative subject and social formations" (34).

Cinema is perhaps a more congenial social institution than literature through which to understand the contradictory effects (at minimum, both dominant and alternative subject and social formations) of social reproduction, if only because we are in such wide agreement about its centrality to that process as we are about literature's marginality to it (to which the debates on canon formation bear witness).[6] Because the cinema has, from its inception, been a deforming agent of social life, explicitly marked as an industrial art par excellence used less explicitly but no less convincingly as an instrument of the state, its pleasures and dangers have been more difficult to acknowledge and calculate than those of literature. Because it is such a dominant cultural institution, its role as a pedagogical agent has been more difficult to assess, too, especially given the extent to which its address (as with television and now the Internet) has always been racialized, sexualized, gendered. But I think that too much focus on the representational politics of the commercial cinema has yielded a uniformity of commentary and response similar to what Ferguson ultimately produces by aligning the symbolic work of literary fiction with sociological diagnosis: we have gone from Eve Sedgwick's quip, "kinda subversive, kinda hegemonic," to "hegemonic-in-deeply-complicated-ways-complicit-with-normative-and-regulative-ideals-destructive-to-alternative-formations-and-imaginaries."[7] I think I can illustrate a different possibility of thinking about the variegated pressures of the normative through a single perplexing film.

The Scar of History

Black History: Lost, Stolen, or Strayed is a 1968 film made by CBS News in a series called "Of Black America." Its script was written by one Andrew Rooney (yes, that Andy Rooney, of *60 Minutes* fame), for which he won his first Emmy, and it is narrated by a young and sardonic Bill Cosby. As I have said, it is a peculiar film, which one can find here and there in university and secondary school libraries, on 16mm (on which it appears to have been released for distribution), on eBay now and again, as well as transferred to videocassette. What makes it peculiar is a certain schizophrenia or division in its form. It begins and extends for some forty-odd minutes with a lesson familiar to Black History Month (or Women's History Month, for that matter): history has been deformed by deliberate omission, what "didn't get into the history books," and that deformation has literal and tragic consequences for the future. If history is, as Napoleon is quoted in *Black History*, "fable agreed upon," that agreement fundamentally distorts children's conceptions of themselves, their work, their lives, and their futures. Childhood is thus imagined as the time to sow more fertile and vibrant (read, inclusive and whole, proud and true) conceptions of themselves and the world, not as inculcation but as organic ingredients of self-production. The introduction to *Black History* takes the primary school classroom as its mise-en-scène, the expansion of a pedagogy of history as its explicit task. It corrects the omissions of official history by insertion, taking a primary-school classroom in which children have made their own drawings and posters of contributions to black history as its initial model for correction.

History and pedagogy are furthermore taken as predominantly visual. The task of *Black History* is to expose the distorting effects of racist historiography, particularly and interestingly as we soon see through Cosby's eyes the history of African American people in the cinema, and to put the issue of representational justice as social reproduction on the national agenda through the wonders of its national medium, television. This is, in other words, a film about films, made for TV, during a moment of a certain optimism about television's national pedagogical role. The first sections of *Black History* thus make the following argument: official history (including sanctioned teaching practices and prescribed racist historiography) distorts; popular culture distorts; one must speak back in anger to distortion. Similar to Ferguson's own insistence on the alignment of sociology and literature, the film for most of its duration refuses for good reasons to separate the devastating effects of quantified or legitimated knowledges (such as sociology and institutionalized American history) from the arts of representation, such as film: both naturalize degradation, both do so effectively. Lethally and apparently equivalently.

At the end of the film, however, Cosby's narration mysteriously evaporates, and the film dwells for ten or so minutes on the efforts of one man in a Philadelphia storefront preschool to clothe African American children in the psychic and intellectual armor they will need to protect themselves against the ravages and scars of history as it is shaped by the victors. Those ten minutes of film are among the most riveting I have ever seen. They raise for me a structural question that arises directly from a reading of Ferguson: how ought we to make sense of the cleavage, the split between what the bulk of the film presents, through something I think it would be fair to

The task of *Black History* is to expose the distorting effects of racist historiography, particularly and interestingly as we soon see through Cosby's eyes the history of African American people in the cinema.

call sociological knowledge, as a crisis engendered by representation, and what the film finally presents as solution, which is a didactic pedagogy of self-determination hewing to black nationalist masculinism, presumptively heteronormative? Let me say this another way: on the model of Ferguson's argument, one would demonstrate that the sociological lens produces the same distortions as the nationalist one, that they both naturalize heteronormativity by pathologizing or rendering perverse nonheteronormative formations, racializing the perverse in the process. I want to propose a counterreading, emphasizing these ten minutes of pedagogy at the film's end as producing and circulating an affective value that cannot be caught in the logic of equivalence proposed through the systematic model. One can only make sense of affective value if one abandons a certain literal understanding of the role of abstraction as enforcing a logic of equivalence in the production of the symptom.

Let me review the film's movement up to those fascinating final ten minutes. It may not be surprising that *Black History: Lost, Stolen, or Strayed* relies on a psychotherapist in its opening reel to render "deformity" a literal and haunting image, since the method of psychotherapy engages the logic of the symptom I have been discussing. Dr. Emmanuel Hammer's studies of children's drawings (he was an art therapist at New York University) set the scene for the film's long review of the politics of African American representation in Hollywood film: he compared drawings done by "normal" children, that is, white children, against those done by "powerless Black children" (these are Hammer's phrases) juxtaposing cheerful images of home and family with horrifying self-portraits of amputated limbs and lynchings. Worrisome as such images are, the film steamrolls over them quickly, assuming that they function adequately as proof that representations yield knowledge about the psychic effects of unspecified and undifferentiated inequality, degradation, exploitation, and domination. At the same time, these images attest to the process by which the reality of African American life is concealed through false representations of America: a sunny stick-crayon drawing on every refrigerator door masks the wounds of a ravaging lifeworld.

So, too, do the movies: *Black History* spends the bulk of its two reels on how cinema or media become the central cultural organ for stealing history, for reproducing distortion. *Black History* thus finds itself in the same argumentative stance as Ferguson's book: it unmasks the errors of which it itself is likewise guilty. Perhaps doubly so: since this film about film circulates on television, and structures its address to a viewer calculated sociologically, it resists the hermetic readings a certain strain of high film theory might bring to it that would isolate its textual operations from its circulation on the small screen. From minstrel shows to *Birth of a*

Nation, *Black History* is off and running, furthermore, with an assessment of cinema's normative capacity to shape understanding, as well as to make money for white Americans on the backs of black men. Cinema feminizes, animalizes, infantilizes: "Everything suggested the Black man was nothing." Moving on to Stepin Fetchit, *Our Gang*, the films of Shirley Temple, and Bill "Bojangles" Robinson, *Black History* sees Hollywood icons as their master's pets, stars who nonetheless "had to come in a picture through the servant's entrance." (When current soi-disant leftist scholars try to retrieve exploitation—those servants, porters, chauffeurs—as subversive, this 1960s anger, reductive as it is, comes as a welcome reprieve.)[8] *Black History* is concerned with the visceral effects of degradation, too, with how history sears, pierces, penetrates. Cosby ends the first reel this way: "Hollywood folks didn't suspect that scenes like the one with Shirley Temple could make a lot of people, mostly black, sick to their stomachs. This is a lot of fun, isn't it?"

History hurts. Normativity kills. And the wound is inflicted on the black man: "It was always the women who were dominant," according to the logic of *Black History*. When the second reel turns to newsreels, to black cast pictures ("all Black but the white man's picture"), to Amos and Andy and to television, it is in order to sound the same note ("the patterns come jumping out") about the containment of black masculinity. From *Uncle Tom's Cabin* in 1903 to the contemporary film *Guess Who's Coming to Dinner* (1968), these representations function as the ground for knowledge about a certain form of inequality, a terrain on which to count up and display the repetitive marks of a people's psychic destruction. The lesson of the movies? Get rich, look white, succeed on the white man's terms, or die.

Not until almost halfway through the second reel does *Black History* reveal its own sense of its ultimate purpose: to explain something about this "new generation" that, in 1968, is asserting itself. It seeks, in other words and to a predominantly white audience, to explain black power, black nationalism, the coming into being of young, proud, and angry black American men. That the terms of an asserted humanity require legitimation, explication, and analysis testifies to the power of the sociological imagination on the nation's television screens. What is surprising, however, is the form in which the legitimation comes: the particular form in which the symptom (devastated masculinity) finds the cure (masculinism on the model of black nationalism). It is, of course, through film itself, and the affect film produces, circulates, sets in motion.

Again, the last ten minutes of *Black History: Lost, Stolen, or Strayed* focus on the efforts of one teacher, John Churchill, in a Philadelphia storefront school called the Freedom Liberty Day School, to give African American preschool children "the emotional armor they need to protect themselves." The film takes us, in other words, from one classroom, in which the distortions of history are reproduced yet corrected, to another classroom, in which the distortions of history are barred entrance. As I have said, Cosby's voice-over narration, which returns at the film's end, has by this point been entirely displaced without explication—as though this chunk of film was spliced onto quite a different project—and is replaced with a vérité-style record of the classroom activities, with the cameras held low and in the midst of the classroom exchanges among very young children. The sequence juxtaposes a question-and-answer routine in which Churchill engages with his students, a dialogue that occupies most of the screen time, with a short lesson Churchill teaches the students about mathematics, a lesson offered at a high level of abstraction for preschool students. "A number is a concept of quantity or amount," Churchill explains to his students, who repeat his explanation back to him, rather than, say, counting from one to ten.

The lesson's level of abstraction, about which more in a moment, reminds the viewer that these students are extremely bright and capable, a recognition that foregrounds, as a result, the rote and didactic nature of the dialogue, which is also obvious from the students' quick and formulaic answers to Churchill's questions, with variations on this basic theme:

> What is your nationality?
> My nationality is Afro-American.
> What do you want?
> I want freedom.
> When do you want it?
> I want it now.
> How are you going to get your freedom?
> By any means necessary.
> What is freedom?
> Freedom is Black Power.
> How old are you?
> Four years old.
> Are you sure you're four?
> Yes.
> You're six years old.
> No.

Are you being frightened by me?
No.
Are you a Negro?
No. I'm Afro-American.
Are you a flunkie? Are you a boy?
No. I'm a man.
What kind of man?
I'm Black, and I'm beautiful.

The didactic nature of the dialogue makes it no less compelling, no less astonishing. For what we are witnessing in this back-and-forth is the shaping of agency, the honing of some tools that will redress the forms of shame, loss, and delegitimation these children will face "after school." When the four-year-old Eric holds his ground, insisting that he is four and not six, he begins to pry apart symptom from agency, he distinguishes his degradation from his ability forcefully to enter into an assertion of the most definitive elements of his being, even if only for the moment before he must reoccupy the role of the little Man. The viewer witnesses that struggle up close, at about Eric's level, as he choreographs his defiant step into a realm beyond his own experience. Despite the centrifugal pressures toward a normative articulation of that agency, the sequence produces an affective charge, I want to argue, that carries in the opposite direction, building a core of pride against the forces of its dispersion.

Churchill explains the purposes of his badgering to the students in this way:

> What I did is what people are going to do to you in different ways when you leave this school. They're not going to come right up to you and give you a dollar and say, "If you say you're an American Negro, I'll give you a dollar." They're going to be very nice to you, some of them, and they're going to try to get you not to love Black people. They're going to try to get you to be something other than you are. They're going to try to make it seem as though you're different from Black people. You must reject that. Do you know what that means? You're not going to have the money you'd like to have. Money is not what matters. The only thing that makes a person worth being is being a man and being a woman, being strong in character, being straight, telling the truth and living the truth and doing the right thing.

This is a good lesson, it seems to me, in the powers of the normative and in their deadly pressures, even as it might seem also to reproduce normative gender and sexual value-codings. This lesson about "what's out there" is what haunts me at night, more than the particular forms in which the normative asserts itself: it is something, that is, that someone queer can hear, though the address is not packaged through the logic or language

This lesson about "what's out there" is what haunts me at night, more than the particular forms in which the normative asserts itself: it is something, that is, that someone queer can hear.

of non- or antiheteronormativity. The powers of the normative do not yield themselves at all times according to systematic rules of equivalence, where what is progressive lines up historically or theoretically with content alone. Churchill's didactic pedagogy here yields to an elaboration of its implications for living, staged in the film itself. The challenge is to parse the difference between prescription/symptom and living/agency, to resist the desire to tell the old story about how black nationalism is a ruthlessly masculinist enterprise, or to remark the heteronormative assumptions without moving on. The challenge is not, finally, to confuse similarity with equivalence.

I think these ten minutes of film show us how. Churchill is offering his student two lessons, after all: a mathematics lesson and a lesson in racial ontology. My thesis is that the two lessons speak to one another, and through that conversation, a model of agency emerges that has the capacity to linger, to tarry with the normative (to dwell there, for there is nowhere else). The mathematics lesson, as I have said, operates at a level of abstraction one might find surprising for three or four year olds. Churchill is essentially teaching his students a conceptual model of arithmetic derived from field theory or number theory; he is teaching them how to derive a so-called fact from a concept. "A number is a concept of quantity or amount" allows them also to understand the concept of greater or lesser numbers, hierarchy, based on an abstract understanding of quantity or amount. To put it in naive-experiential terms, Churchill is giving his teeny weeny students that "aha!" moment that college-level mathematics students get (or at least I got) in abstract algebra, after roughly two years of calculus, when one understands the foundation of elementary arithmetic in algebraic terms: arithmetic, that seemingly simple set of calculations that can be done by preschool children, is a particular case of a larger set of relations or field. Doing arithmetic, adding and subtracting, multiplying and dividing, maybe just counting, distinguishing between greater and lesser is not equivalent to understanding field theory or number theory; it is merely to perform in rote terms the rules that govern the system. But one does not need to understand algebra in order to do arithmetic.

To put it in more abstract terms, Churchill is offering his students a lesson in what happens when one ventures beyond the confines of one's own experience, when one gets caught up in the logic, identifications, abstractions, exchanges that lie beyond. Rather than bringing into being an understanding simply of sequential or consecutive relations (such as those at work in counting), Churchill models through his teaching of arithmetic a complicated relationship between the particular and the universal that is not about their contrariety but their imbrication. They are not static terms but dynamic ones, in play with one another as reason develops as self-consciousness entangled in the structures beyond itself. To return briefly to a resonance with Žižek's work, what Churchill is offering resembles the description Žižek offers of Kantian (mathematical and dynamic) antinomies, or of sexuality itself: the "crack in the universal," the "effect on the living being of the impasses which emerge when it gets entangled in the symbolic order, i.e., the effect on the living body of the deadlock or inconsistency that pertains to the symbolic order qua order of universality."[9]

Churchill's teaching sets that relationship between abstraction and instance in motion. His students perform in rote terms a set of counterattacks to racism, without understanding the systemic relations of power that give rise to their self-production. "That's kind of like brainwashing," Bill Cosby says, ventriloquizing the likely responses of the television audience, when he returns to close the film, without, at the same time, condemning it. But such repetition is not equivalent, at the same time, to inhabiting either a pathologized version of African American existence or a particular view of resistance to it. The affective charge of these minutes of film, I think, comes in the dissonance or lack of fit between theory and practice, between conception of the world and iteration of being-in-it. When the young student Travis tells Churchill that he is not a boy but a man, a man who is black and beautiful, he is obviously both right and wrong: he *is* a boy, after all, and the hope is that his words will become a prophesy, that he will think of himself as black and beautiful when he becomes a man, after school. One does not need algebra to do arithmetic: Travis can stage a becoming without its being yet accomplished.

I think we would do well to hang out in these gaps for a while, to tarry in the distance between the terrors of the normative and our nightmares of them. These, after all, may be similar but not equivalent, and we have much to learn from other struggles and other embattled lives of that difference.

Notes

1. My title is a pun on a different post-Marxian analysis of social antagonism in Slavoj Žižek, *Tarrying with the Negative: Kant, Hegel, and the Critique of Ideology* (Durham, NC: Duke University Press, 1993).

2. Ibid., 2.

3. Roderick A. Ferguson, *Aberrations in Black: Toward a Queer of Color Critique* (Minneapolis: University of Minnesota Press, 2003), 3, hereafter cited in text.

4. Hortense J. Spillers reads the Moynihan Report in an influential essay Ferguson ought to have cited, "Mama's Baby, Papa's Maybe: An American Grammar Book," republished in *Black, White, and in Color: Essays on American Literature and Culture*, by Hortense J. Spillers (Chicago: University of Chicago Press, 2003), 203–29.

5. See Gayatri Chakravorty Spivak, *Death of a Discipline* (New York: Columbia University Press, 2003), wherein she makes the case for the humanities, including the study of literature, as the "uncoercive rearrangement of desire" (101) against attempts, such as that made by John Guillory in his study of literary canons, to legitimate the humanities by making them scientific (see note 6).

6. John Guillory makes a similar point about the centrality of mass culture in *Cultural Capital: The Problem of Literary Canon Formation* (Chicago: University of Chicago Press, 1993), 80.

7. Eve Kosofsky Sedgwick, "Queer Performativity: Henry James' *Art of the Novel*," *GLQ* 1 (1993): 15.

8. See, for example, Lary May, *The Big Tomorrow: Hollywood and the Politics of the American Way* (Chicago: University of Chicago Press, 2000).

9. Žižek, *Tarrying with the Negative*, 56.

Of Our Normative Strivings

AFRICAN AMERICAN STUDIES AND THE HISTORIES OF SEXUALITY

Roderick A. Ferguson

In *Aberrations in Black: Toward a Queer of Color Critique*, I attempted to advance a materialist interrogation of racialized gender and sexuality. I tried to do so by theorizing the genealogy of women of color feminism as inspiration for intersectional analyses of nonheteronormative racial formations. *Aberrations* used women of color feminism to provoke new considerations around the natures of culture and capital, new considerations that summed up in queer of color critique. It has since occurred to me that women of color feminism also invites us to consider how we might reconsider the issue of sexuality's deployment in an effort to assess queer studies' management of that category and to usher queer studies into its full critical potential.

It is important to note, as I implied in *Aberrations*, that women of color feminism has the longest engagement with racialized sexuality. This single fact means that we must admit that there are other terrains for the interrogation of sexuality, terrains that do not begin and end with queer studies. Queer studies, to be sure, has had the most concentrated engagement with the category of sexuality and in doing so has made certain institutional advances within the academy. But those strides have, in many ways, convinced queer studies that its engagements with sexuality are the only and most significant pursuits of that formation. Queer studies has achieved this maneuver by taking Foucault's very important text *The History of Sexuality*, vol. 1, *An Introduction* as the principal engagement with the question of sexuality. Doing so has meant occluding critical sexual formations that preceded queer studies and Foucault's wonderful intervention, formations such as women of color feminism, an interrogation that theorized sexuality as a constitutive component of racial and class formations. In a moment characterized by the insistence of queer of color formations in and outside the academy, we must develop ways to put *The History of Sexuality* in dialogue with other histories and deployments of sexuality.

Foucault, in *The History of Sexuality*, understands sexuality as a discursive formation that arises epistemologically. In that text, he engages psychoanalysis as the domain of sexuality, using psychoanalysis to account for the hysterization of women's bodies, the pedagogization of children's sex,

Social Text 84–85, Vol. 23, Nos. 3–4, Fall–Winter 2005.

the socialization of procreative sex, and the psychiatrization of perverse pleasure. Continuing to designate psychoanalysis as a powerful episteme for sexuality's emergence, Foucault argues in an interview, "One finds in the West a medicalisation of sexuality itself, as though it were an area of particular pathological fragility in human existence. All sexuality runs the risk at one and the same time of being in itself an illness and of inducing illnesses without number. It cannot be denied that psychoanalysis is situated at the point where these two processes intersect."[1]

As Foucault's text takes psychoanalysis and medicalization as racially denuded procedures and as the taken-for-granted domains of sexuality's emergence,[2] the text has monopolized the conversations about sexual formations and steered them away from considerations of race. In an effort to drive the conversation about sexuality toward racial modernity, I located my own interrogation of the simultaneity of race and sexuality within and against the discursive maneuvers of canonical sociology. Attending specifically to African American sexuality, I argued, "The specific history of African Americans' constitution as the objects of racial and sexual knowledge through canonical sociology has produced modes of deployment that cohere with and diverge from those outlined by Foucault."[3] It is also important that we remember that the historical locations for women of color feminism and its theorizations for racialized sexuality were to be found in the interstices of academic fields like ethnic studies and women's studies and social movements like the women's movement, antiracist social movements among blacks, Chicano/Latinos, Asian Americans, Native Americans, and the labor movement. These historical circumstances mean that theorizations of racialized sexuality do not actually belong to any discipline, interdiscipline, or social movement. Indeed, the historicity of theoretical endeavors around racialized sexuality renders them eccentric to academic and political institutionality, an institutionality that often tries to force heterogeneous formations within singular pronouncements and deployments of "sexuality," "race," "class," and "gender." One way to summarize women of color feminism's contribution to the study of sexuality is to say that these particular feminist formations insist on the historical specificity and heterogeneity of "sexuality," a specificity and heterogeneity denoted as racial difference. As women of color feminist theorizations of racialized sexuality had many different locations, analyzing the intersectional maneuvers of race and sexuality means attending to the historical specificity and diversity of racialized sexuality's locations. This material specificity produces a tension between theorizations of racialized sexuality and efforts to capture those theorizations within universalist enunciations of sexuality. This attention to the specificity and diversity of racialized sexuality intersects with Foucault's own theorizations of the episteme as having specific and diverse domains. In a lecture titled "Politics and the Study of Discourse," he states

> [The] episteme is not a sort of grand underlying theory, it is a space of dispersion, it is an open and doubtless indefinitely describable field of relationships. They make it possible furthermore to describe not a universal history which sweeps along all the sciences in a single common trajectory, but the kinds of—that is to say, of remanences and transformation—characteristics of different discourses.[4]

If sexuality is an epistemological project characterized by dispersion, openness, and infinite descriptions, then we cannot assume that any one theory of sexuality can explain sexual formations regardless of how they are differentiated by race, gender, class, ethnicity, and nationality.

What is the status of sexuality if we resituate it as the epistemological effect of women of color feminism?

What is the status of sexuality if we resituate it as the epistemological effect of women of color feminism? In this discussion of women of color feminism, I have presumed that sexuality is not an object that belongs to one particular field of inquiry but is a network of relations that constitute knowledge and sociality. Indeed, we might observe this relation within several, if not all, disciplines and interdisciplines, queer studies only one among them. Taking sexuality to be one of the critical outcomes of women of color feminism cautions us against asking the question of sexuality and disciplinarity this way: "How can we make sexuality the *object* of African American studies or any other discipline for that matter?" Instead the history of women of color feminism begs us to ask the question this way, "In what ways has the racialized, classed, and gendered discourse known as sexuality dispersed itself to constitute this particular discipline or interdiscipline?" The former takes sexuality as an object that can be controlled and administered, an object characterized by a singularity. Sexuality is the gift presented to the discipline. Taking sexuality as propertied object actually lays the ground for the emergence of rational agents who control and administer sexuality's deployment, agents whose privileged access to and administration of the object is nothing less than a racial project in and of itself. In the latter formulation, however, sexuality undergoes a process of differentiation, hence it is racialized, classed, and gendered. The latter formulation emphasizes sexuality as a discourse to alienate sexuality from its presumed status as object. The history of women of color feminism, thus, necessitates a critique of the propertied status of sexuality and the rational status of its presumed proprietors.

As discourse, sexuality enjoys autonomy and self-direction and cannot therefore be reduced to disciplinary or interdisciplinary agents. Sexuality does not passively await a discipline or interdiscipline's attention. It is, in fact, constitutive of the disciplines *and* interdisciplines. It is active, having specific engagements with each epistemological context. By apprehending sexuality as the critical product of women of color feminism, we might offer the following postulates about sexuality:

- Sexuality is not an object of study that any one field can claim or an object that can be stolen from a discipline's grasp. Indeed, as we presume that sexuality is the property of this critical terrain or that one, we facilitate canonization rather than disrupt it.
- Sexuality is not extraneous to other modes of difference. Sexuality is intersectional. It is constitutive of and constituted by racialized gender and class formations. This formulation presumes genealogies of sexuality that collide with but steal away from articulations of sexuality in queer studies. Indeed, as queer studies insists that our analyses of sexuality withdraw from theorizations of racialized gender and class formations, queer studies proves inadequate for understanding sexuality's broad epistemic dispersions.
- Sexuality broadly defines sets of relations that traverse local antagonisms and divisions between discursive fields. Sexuality presumes a critical interdisciplinarity that has no trepidation about disciplinary, or for that matter interdisciplinary, constraints and boundaries. As interdisciplinary sites such as queer studies locate sexuality within one epistemic terrain (i.e., psychoanalysis) or attempt to arrogate sexuality to queer studies alone, those sites prove interdisciplinarity's complicity within disciplinarity rather than interdisciplinarity's rebellion against the disciplines.

This essay pursues one other deployment of sexuality. It does so by focusing on the emergence of African American intellectual and middle-class formations in the nineteenth century and by claiming that what we know today as African American intellectual history is one domain of sexuality and indeed is a discourse of sexuality itself. In fact, the genealogy of an inquiry of this type—one that presumes African American intellectual formations as sites for the production of discourses of sexuality and morality—arises from black feminist historiography, in particular. Evelyn Hammonds, for instance, thematizes the discursive components of black women's sexuality in this way: first, there was the eighteenth-century pathologization of black female sexuality as part of colonial and slave regimes as well as the shaping of biological sciences for that pathologization. Second, the nineteenth century saw the emergence of black women reformers, "U.S. black women reformers [who] began to develop strategies to counter negative stereotypes of their sexuality and their use as a justification for the rape, lynching, and other abuses of Black women by whites." As Hammonds states, those reformers relied on discourses of "Victorian morality to demonstrate the lie of the image of the sexually immoral Black women." Hammonds also notes that the strategies of silence and the culture of dissemblance around sexuality that black women reformers developed extends to present-day discussions of black women's sexuality. I would like to trouble this historical moment in particular—the one in which black middle-class and intellectual formations responded to pathologization by assuming gendered and sexual morality. I wish to extend Hammonds's considerations and the work by other black feminist theorists and historians of the nineteenth century by focusing not so much on how the moral discourses associated with reformers of the period produced a silence around sexuality but how the production of African American sexual normativity provided the grammar and logic for racialized strategies of governmentality within the United States.

As I try to illustrate in the body of the text, the overarching question of the epistemic dispersions of racialized sexuality has significance for how we might understand sexuality as a mode of racialized governmentality and power. By theorizing sexuality as a mode of racialized governmentality, I actually want to rekindle an aspect of *The History of Sexuality* that we seem to have drifted away from—that is, the consideration of sexuality as an operation of power. And by concentrating on the latter parts of the nineteenth century, I want to present what were the preconditions[5] for the formations that I discussed in *Aberrations*.

By theorizing sexuality as a mode of racialized governmentality, I actually want to rekindle an aspect of *The History of Sexuality* that we seem to have drifted away from—that is, the consideration of sexuality as an operation of power.

Sexuality and Governmentality

With the end of the Civil War in 1865, the United States faced the issue of how to manage a newly enfranchised population of black ex-slaves. Hence the U.S. government established the Bureau for the Relief of Freedmen and Refugees, popularly known as the Freedmen's Bureau. Part of the bureau's duties and responsibilities was to provide for education. To this end, the bureau founded one thousand schools for former slaves and also assisted with the founding of the major black colleges and universities. In *The Souls of Black Folk*, W. E. B. DuBois frames the founding of these schools within both the educational needs and economic possibilities of this population. He writes, "In the midst, then, of the larger problem of Negro education sprang up the more practical question of work, the inevitable economic quandary that faces a people in the transition from slavery to freedom, and especially those who make that change amid hate and prejudice, lawlessness and ruthless competition."[6] Within this moment—defined by such issues as the economic, intellectual, and moral management of a newly freed population—we can observe both a discourse of sexuality specific to African American racial formations and a genealogy of governmentality within the United States. This discourse and genealogy would seek to construct the African American middle class as the original model minority.

In the essay "Governmentality," Foucault argues,

> The art of government, as becomes apparent in this literature, is essentially concerned with answering the question of how to introduce economy—that is to say, the correct manner of managing individuals, goods and wealth within the family (which a good father is expected to do in relation to his wife, children, and servants) and of making the family fortunes prosper—how to introduce this meticulous attention of the father towards his family into the management of the state.[7]

Here, Foucault suggests that the tactics of governmentality have their genesis in the strategies needed to maintain the heteropatriarchal family. The management of state resources, therefore, comes from the gendered and sexualized management of familial resources. But Foucault goes on to say that the family ceases to be the model on which governmentality is based. Eventually family is replaced by population. He states,

> [Population] is the point around which is organized what in sixteenth-century texts came to be called the patience of the sovereign, in the sense that the population is the object that government must take into account in all its observations and *savoir*, in order to be able to govern effectively in a rational and conscious manner. The constitution of a savoir of government is absolutely inseparable from that of a knowledge of all the processes related to population in its larger sense: that is to say, what we now call economy.[8]

As population supplants family, governmentality ceases to be organized around the question of how to economize a household and is instead organized on how to economize a population. The transition from household to population, however, does not nullify the gendered and eroticized tactics associated with the domestic model of governmentality. Indeed, that transition begs the question of how those gendered and sexualized strategies associated with the family were inserted into the strategies appropriate to economizing a population.

We might, in fact, witness this insertion through the wider contexts surrounding African American enfranchisement in the nineteenth century—the disfranchisement of the white heteropatriarchal slave-owning home, the industrial revolution in the southern United States from 1885 to 1895, the establishment of black colleges and universities and with that establishment, the emergence of African American middle-class subjects and the rise of postbellum African American intellectual formations, and the project of U.S. imperial expansion toward the end of the nineteenth century. We might observe these elements in the writings of Booker T. Washington and in the context of industrial education for African Americans. Washington's speeches are significant here as they explicitly attempt to position black colleges and in particular industrial education as racialized, classed, gendered, and sexualized sites of governmentality. As an advocate for industrial education and in a speech titled "Industrial Training for Southern Women," Washington evokes domestic governmentality as necessary for the social and moral betterment of African American women, in particular, but Southern society in general. He writes,

Washington's speeches are significant here as they explicitly attempt to position black colleges and in particular industrial education as racialized, classed, gendered, and sexualized sites of governmentality.

> Here at the Tuskeegee Normal and Industrial Institute in Alabama, in connection with training three hundred girls in literary branches, sewing, cooking, laundering, millinerying, general household science, fruitcanning, etc. we are gradually moving into the fields of industry mentioned in the foregoing. Next year we are planning to give a large number of girls training in dairying, and the work will be pushed all along the line just as fast as we can secure funds with which to start and pay expenses of these departments.[9]

For Washington, industrial education for black girls did not simply have commercial benefits. As he states,

> There will be those who argue that such a course of training has much of the utilitarian idea in view, and does not lay enough stress on the mental and moral development. Right here is where the average man blunders. You cannot give a hungry man much moral training. To secure the highest moral and religious training among the poor white and colored women in the South, we have got to get them to the point where their stomachs can be regularly filled with good, well-cooked food.[10]

As the speech implies, the domestic sciences were not simply a means to produce proper female subjects but also to bring a recently enfranchised population into proper moral parameters. Industrial education and indeed industry were moral ventures that could rearticulate the meaning of black racial difference. For instance, Washington goes on to argue,

> Production and commerce are two of the great destroyers of race prejudice. In proportion as the black woman is able to produce something that the white or other races want, in the same proportion does prejudice disappear. Butter is going to be purchased from the individual who can produce the best butter and at the lowest price, and the purchaser cares not whether it was made by a black, white, brown, or yellow woman. The best butter is what is wanted. The American dollar has not an ounce of prejudice in it.[11]

Recognition and confirmation as moral subject could be secured through black women's participation in industry. Commodities like butter could be a metonym of black industry and morality. The commodity was neither the generic product of industry nor a discrete object separated from the social world of the emancipated. The commodity would represent the proof of industry's benevolence and tutelage and the evidence of the black female subject's moral status. In this logic, industry would play a crucial part in reforming the black subject from degenerate and immoral primitive to the normative citizen-subject of the United States.

We can understand Washington's address as forecasting and identifying a new and emergent moral and intellectual formation, that of the black middle class. The black middle class, as Washington avers, would inherit modernity by adhering to gender and sexual propriety. That is, the black middle class would be the first U.S. model minority, championing civic ideals around industry, citizenship, and morality. As a model minority, the black middle class would be at the vanguard of a new political economy, one based on free labor, industry, and the widening embrace of American citizenship.

I have not evoked Washington as a historical persona but as the shorthand for a discourse. So often, we assume the issue of industrial education to have begun and ended with Booker T. Washington. Other times we presume industrial education to be a debate between Washington and W. E. B. DuBois, with the latter as industrial education's radical antagonist. What does all of this assume? That industrial education simply issued out of one subject or one or two institutions (i.e., Tuskeegee and the Hampton Institute). It assumes that industrial education was something that you were either for or against, something that functioned at the level of consciousness and that operated very much as an identity. It assumes a dichotomy between industrial education and humanistic training, never knowing that this dichotomy might have been fictitious because of shared moral and normative investments. It assumes that industrial education is simply a political matter, not really appreciating industrial education as the name of alliance between sexual normativity and citizenship, a union that would refine and elaborate power through twin processes of nationalization and normalization.

Deployment and Perverse Implantations

Part of the moral function of this new model minority known as African American was to repair the damage that the Civil War did to the Confederate states, to the nation, and to the white heteropatriarchal family.

In a speech given on 21 March 1899 on behalf of the Tuskeegee Institute, Washington states,

> Then came the long years of war, then freedom, then the trying years of reconstruction. The master returned from the war to find the faithful slaves who had been the bulwark of his household in possession of their freedom. Then there began that social and industrial revolution in the South which it is hard for any one who was not really a part of it to appreciate or understand. Gradually day by day this ex-master began to realize, with a feeling almost indescribable, to what an extent he and his family had grown to be dependent upon the activity and faithfulness of their slaves; began to appreciate to what an extent slavery had sapped the sinews of strength and independence, how the dependence upon slave labor had deprived him and his offspring of the benefit of technical and industrial training, and worst of all had unconsciously led them to see in labor drudgery and degradation instead of beauty, dignity and civilizing power. . . . Lower and lower sank the industrial, financial and spiritual condition of the household. . . . Within a few months the whole mistake of slavery seemed to have concentrated itself upon this household. If there was proof wanting that slavery wrought almost as much . . . injury upon the Southern white man as upon the black man, it was furnished in the case of this family.[12]

The aftermath of the Civil War, for Washington, makes the white slave master aware of how the master's household and the plantation economy depended on the slaves. Returning to the plantation after the Civil War, the white slave master can see how the conditions of slavery had equipped the slave with industrial and technical knowledge and left the slaveholding family without this vital education. In the moment of industrial revolution within the South, the slave master patriarch had to confront his own terrible castration and his resultant inability to govern and manage the family.

For Washington the Tuskeegee Institute and industrial education facilitated not only the reformulation of African American subjectivity as the subject formation appropriate for an industrializing South but also repaired the white heteropatriarchal family as it was torn asunder by the civil war and caught unawares by industrialization. As Washington states, "And just here may I mention that one of the chief charms and compensations of the efforts put forth at Tuskeegee is in the abundant evidence that we are not assisting in lightening the burdens of one race but two—in helping to put that spirit into men that will make them forget race and color in efforts to lift up an unfortunate brother."[13]

Washington's narrative of uplift relates to Foucault's theorization of governmentality. Discussing governmentality as a discourse, Foucault

The appropriateness of African Americans for this recuperative task, according to Washington, could be demonstrated through the visibility of African American industry and deportment.

argues that "upwards continuity means that a person who wishes to govern the state well must first learn how to govern himself, his goods and his patrimony, after which he will be successful in governing the state." We might revise Foucault's argument in light of Washington's address by arguing that the specifically racialized circumstances for governmentality within the United States at the end of the nineteenth century meant that African American subjects seeking to embody the ideals of American citizenship had not only to govern themselves and their households but also to assist in the management and recuperation of white heteropatriarchy. Hence, in this context, upward continuity was not only composed of the government of self and household only to be followed by fitness for societal governance. In the context of African Americans, the recuperation of white heteropatriarchy was the intermediary step between governance at the microlevel and governance at the macrolevel. As Washington states,

> And so last of all did he [the white man] expect help or encouragement from an educated black man, but it was just from this source that help came. Soon after the process of decay began in this white man's estate, the education of a certain black man began—began on a logical sensible basis. It was an education that would fit him to see and appreciate the physical and moral conditions that existed in his own family and neighborhood and in the present generation, and would fit him to apply himself to their relief.[14]

Governmentality, in this instance, is about the racialized suppression of antagonisms that arise out of material and historic disparities. This suppression took as its goal the simultaneous nationalization and normalization of black subjects within the states and moreover attached these maneuvers to the recuperation of white heteropatriarchy. The appropriateness of African Americans for this recuperative task, according to Washington, could be demonstrated through the visibility of African American industry and deportment. Discussing this visibility as object lessons, Washington argued, "Object lessons that shall bring the Southern white man into daily, visible, tangible contact with the benefits of Negro education will go much further towards the solution of present problems than all the mere abstract argument and theories that can be evolved from the human brain."[15] Discourses of governmentality are far from being top-down theories of power, suggesting the passivity of those caught under regimes of governmentality. This theory of governmentality coheres with Foucault's description of power in the first volume of *The History of Sexuality*. In that text, power achieves itself not through interdiction, prevention, and prohibition but through encouragement, incitement, and exhortation: "What sustains our eagerness to speak of sex in terms of repression is doubtless this opportunity to speak out against powers that be, to utter truths and promise bliss, to link enlightenment, liberation, and manifold pleasures."[16] While the African American middle class were not eager to speak of sex in the ways that Foucault's constituency is in the above quote, Foucault's emancipated constituency and the African American middle class do indeed converge over their presumptions that agency—whether sexual or moral—is the overthrow of prior forms of power rather than a new circuitry for power. As the case of the African American middle class illustrates, governmentality actually describes power's activation through the constitution of agency rather than the abolition of it.

War and Sexual Governmentality

The domain of African American sexuality—a domain punctuated with notions of gender and sexual propriety, morality, domestic health and education, virile manhood, and genteel femininity—is an arena whose foundations are laid by African American intellectual discourse. We might say that object lessons not only refer to the production of literal objects but also to the production of normative gender and sexuality. The commodity and gender/sexual normativity had similar functions—both proved the black subject's fitness for an industrial order, all the while triangulating the normative imperatives of state, capital, and African American education. For Foucault, governmentality addresses the arrangement of things. In the gendered and sexualized context of nineteenth-century African American racial formations, governmentality was also about the production of things: here governmentality concerns not only the state but labor and industry as well. This new system of governmentality enlisted minoritized subjects as the new arrangers and producers of things. This new arrangement and production attempted to recuperate racialized heteropatriarchy in a general effort to restore the U.S. nation. It is important to note that this effort at restoration was much more than a national project but actually endeavored to contribute to the virility of the U.S. imperial project. The reunification of the South was hence part of the forcible unification of former Spanish territories. As Shelley Streeby notes in *American Sensations: Class, Empire, and the Production of Popular Culture*, "We might consider the South not just as the U.S. South but also as a transborder contact and conflict zone encompassing Mexico, Cuba, the Caribbean, and other parts of the old Spanish empire in Central and South America."[17] African American intellectual formations are, to a large degree, produced out of this genealogy of governmentality.

Indeed, Booker T. Washington's 1900 text *A New Negro for a New*

Governmentality becomes the system of power that drafts African Americans into war *and* regimes of sexual normativity.

Century: An Accurate and Up-to-Date Record of the Upward Struggles of the Negro Race connects the Civil War to the Spanish-American War. The text does so by arguing that the latter helped seal the rifts that the Civil War dramatized. As the introduction states, "Sectarianism, which threatened the disruption of the Union in 1861, has been banished forever. The cries of an enthralled and afflicted people have been answered and humanity has been redeemed."[18] In a chapter titled "Afro-American Volunteers," Washington states, "But the declaration of war with Spain was responded to with a fervor and enthusiasm in every State of the Union, among all the race elements of the population, that put at rest forever any lingering suspicion that the Republic would be divided in sentiment in the face of a foreign foe."[19]

The book in its discussion of war repeats a maneuver enacted in the speeches on industrial education as a moral imperative. In *A New Negro for a New Century* and in the speeches, governmentality becomes the system of power that drafts African Americans into war *and* regimes of sexual normativity. As the conscripted subjects of war, African Americans testify to the perfectability of the state as that system that can accommodate a previously inadmissible population whose naturalization as citizen is dubious at best. As the conscripted subjects of sexual normativity, African Americans swear on behalf of the capacious embrace of the nation as that moral ideal that can aid a group whose struggle against perversion is tenuous, to be sure. Both war and sexual normativity claimed to be able to draft African Americans into citizenship and humanity.

Indeed, the simultaneity of war as well as gender and sexual normativity means that we might regard the period between Reconstruction and the Spanish-American War as occasioning the emergence of a racialized network of power that speaks in anticipation of a humanity and citizenship that is secured by performing sexual and gender normativity. The genealogy of this network of power lies in the emergence of American nationality as well as in the specificities of African American citizenship, normativity, and intellectuality as they arose out of U.S. colonial expansion.

How might we apply this very preliminary hermeneutic about U.S. governmentality? Take, for example, an article by an anonymous proponent of industrial education, "The Future of the Race: Dependent Upon the Restrictions and Home-Training of the Unit of the Race," written circa 1910.

> There is a crying need in the city of Richmond for some method or means to put an end to youthful immorality—youthful obstreperousness. Boys at the age of twelve are men. Girls at the age of twelve are women, and grown

> up old men and women recognize these midgets as men and women. We were walking along the street the other day and saw a little girl coming up the street. The girl was of robust physique and in short skirts. She was, to appearance, a well-raised child and we considered her such. Coincidentally, she turned into the same street in which we turned. Before us, going in the opposite direction were two young men, apparently of good raising, well-dressed and comely lads they were. But their conduct belied their looks. This fact, their language to the child-woman attested. The conduct of the trio was such as would pain the heart of any *students of conditions as relate to our race.* Now possibly, all three of these children—for children they would have, in other days than these, been considered—may have been saved to the race if some means of restraint had been brought to bear to have impressed them of the folly of their way and the ultimate end of their cultivated methods.[20]

The article is found in the Tuskeegee Institute Records; we can assume that it is a justification of and advertisement for industrial education. It justifies and advertises industrial education by framing it as the moral antidote to the immorality of black youth, an immorality that arises out of urban conditions. It is a maturity inscribed on the girl's body. Her "physique" suggests full womanhood rather than youthful inexperience. Her dress issues invitations too grown for a girl to make. The boys share a language with the girl too ribald for the article to reveal. As the article suggests, industrial education might provide them with more appropriate languages and conducts. In the absence of industrial education, what we have is children who have come to sex too soon. The child also points to social conditions that undermine the normal progression from youth to adulthood, urbanization and industrialization principally among them. Industrial education could provide the restraints against the abominations that the city encouraged.

The article continues by presenting what is principally at stake for the author and for the race:

> Now, this is but one illustration of what really exists in this and other cities. It is a shame that should be publicly condemned by all decent people, that grown-up men hang around and "chin" little girls who, of a right should at the time be kneeling by the knees of their mothers saying their "Now I lay me down to sleep." But the men are not alone to be condemned. For the women, too, line up with the boys yet in their "teens" and allow them privileges that even men should not be allowed. They make of these boys men aforetime, and thus issue them into avenues which bring senility to youth and consequently—sterility of age—a fine process of murdering both the present and future generation or placing upon the latter the brand of imbecility and worthlessness. . . .

By adopting normative gender and sexuality, African American elites waged war against the state's racialized exclusions, teaching their children the same strategies.

> This should be a matter of grave concern to every Negro who has the future of the race at heart. Parents should place the "lid" down tighter upon their children. They should restrict their outgoings and their incomings. They should regulate the conduct of the youth with the old-time regulator. They should be careful of the company their children keep. This should be the point through which a social division should be drawn. Privilege should be based upon worth in morals and not upon color or creed. For that people will most effectually inherit the earth who, in protection of their virtue of their women and of their boys and girls, build the strongest fences. Therefore, put the boot to the idler, the "dude," the worthless plotter against the hearth and home around which and in which the jewels of the family circle—the comely girls and the manly boys, who are the future of the race and the perpetuators of our hope of the yet to be.[21]

Of course, one way to read this passage would be to suggest that these are regulations particular to this moment in Richmond, regulations that pertain only to the early years of the twentieth-century United States. In other words, we might use this archival document to claim the boundedness of the United States and to locate African American racial, gender, and sexual discourses firmly within those bounds. Another way to read the article would be to reframe the discourse of regulation, lifting it from presumptions that this discourse is discretely American or African American. If we place the article under a formulation of power defined as power's manifestation through the racialized compulsion to gender and sexual normativity, a normative compulsion that is part of the landmarks of war, then the regulations that the editorial calls for cease to be local but translocal. In the city what we see here is a partnership between an emerging indigenous black elite and state power over the regulation of a subaltern black population. In other words, the American city assumes the dangers and necessary regulations associated with the colonies. We might also conjecture that as African American normative and national formations arose out of U.S. imperialism, African American elites learned the tactics of sexual and gender regulation from the itineraries of imperialism, imposing those tactics onto black poor and working-class folks. That is, sexual and gender normativity repeated the strategies of normalization and nationalization that constituted Reconstruction and characterized the Spanish-American War. By adopting normative gender and sexuality, African American elites waged war against the state's racialized exclusions, teaching their children the same strategies. It was as if the good, industrious, and respectable black elites of Richmond scolded the youth because of their fast ways, in effect saying, "We didn't fight and die in those wars for you to act like this." This is the silence that whispers between the lines of this archival document, the battle cry of wars long passed and unceasing.

I ended *Aberrations in Black* by considering how women of color feminist and queer of color critical formations might provide and inspire critiques of revolutionary and cultural nationalisms and their residences in sociology and American studies. Now, we might ask ourselves how we might use queer of color and women of color formations to intervene in queer studies. To this end, I have tried to use this discussion of nineteenth-century black intellectual and middle-class formations as an occasion to demonstrate what is for me a vital and historic insight of women of color feminism. That insight goes somewhat like this: sexuality has a variety of deployments in which we might observe its constitution through discourses of race, gender, and class. Epistemologically, this means that we must embark on critical journeys to locate and explicate those deployments. Institutionally and politically, it involves assessing the racialized, gendered, and class forms of power that issue from sexuality's many extensive routes. To be sure, if there is any point to the study of sexuality at all, it is in the observation and clarification of this insight.

Notes

1. Michel Foucault, "The History of Sexuality," interview by Lucette Finas, in *Power/Knowledge: Selected Interviews and Other Writings, 1972–1977*, ed. Colin Gordon (New York: Pantheon, 1980), 191.

2. David L. Eng's wonderful text *Racial Castration: Managing Masculinity in Asian America* (Durham, NC: Duke University Press, 2001) provides an alternative to the deracination of psychoanalysis and sexuality, as does Siobahn Somerville's excellent *Queering the Color Line: Race and the Invention of Homosexuality in American Culture* (Durham, NC: Duke University Press, 2000).

3. Roderick A. Ferguson, *Aberrations in Black: Toward a Queer of Color Critique* (Minneapolis: University of Minnesota Press, 2004), 72.

4. Michel Foucault, "Politics and the Study of Discourse," in *The Foucault Effect: Studies in Governmentality*, ed. Graham Burchell, Colin Gordon, and Peter Miller (Chicago: University of Chicago Press, 1991), 55.

5. I thank George Lipsitz for this boilerplate statement.

6. W. E. B. DuBois, *The Souls of Black Folk* (Greenwich, CT: Fawcett, 1961), 77.

7. In Foucault, *Foucault Effect*, 92.

8. Ibid., 100.

9. Booker T. Washington, "Industrial Training for Southern Women," in Booker T. Washington Papers, Library of Congress, Box 541.

10. Ibid.

11. Ibid.

12. Booker T. Washington, "The Influence of Object-Lessons in the Solution of the Race Problem," in Booker T. Washington Papers, Library of Congress, Box 541.

13. Ibid.

14. Ibid.

15. Ibid.

16. Foucault, *The History of Sexuality*, vol. 1, *An Introduction*, trans. Robert Hurley (New York: Vintage, 1990), 7.

17. Shelley Streeby, *American Sensations: Class, Empire, and the Production of Popular Culture* (Berkeley: University of California, 2002), 247.

18. Booker T. Washington, *A New Negro for a New Century: An Accurate and Up-to-Date Record of the Upward Struggles of the Negro Race* (Miami: Mnemosyne, 1969), 3.

19. Ibid., 23–24.

20. Tuskeegee Institute News Clippings File, British Library (emphasis added).

21. Ibid.

Asian Diasporas, Neoliberalism, and Family

REVIEWING THE CASE FOR HOMOSEXUAL ASYLUM IN THE CONTEXT OF FAMILY RIGHTS

Chandan Reddy

> I came to the United States from Pakistan in 1991 as a student. I had come to the United States because I had a thought that coming out as a gay man would be safer for me in this country. After graduating in 1995, I moved to New York City and became a member of the South Asian Lesbian and Gay Association, SALGA. I had realized that going back to Pakistan was not an option for me anymore. I would not be able to do the kinds of work that I wanted to do with safety in Pakistan. There is no infrastructure in place in Pakistan where I could obtain legal recourse if threatened for being queer. As queer immigrants in this country are usually placed outside immigration law, applying for asylum seemed to be the only strategy where I did not feel that I was compromising myself as a gay man. Heterosexual marriage and working a job I did not like for years to get a green card did not seem like attractive choices. Choosing to apply for asylum instead of availing myself of other options also became a political choice. Furthermore, I strongly believed in my claim and felt that under U.S. immigration law I fit the categories of asylum. I did have a genuine fear that if I led life as an openly gay man in Pakistan, my life would be in danger.
>
> —Saeed Rahman, "Shifting Grounds for Asylum: Female Genital Surgery and Sexual Orientation," *Columbia Human Rights Law Review* (1998)

The sexual history of Asian diasporas is being written across nations, institutions, their publics. In this essay, I would like to speak about one privileged site and set of institutions in which the "sexual history" of the Asian diaspora is produced, organized, and subjected to regulation. That is, I would like to investigate the "history of sexuality" for Asian diasporas whose lines of dispersion cross U.S. space. What kind of "history of sexuality" is being written in this collision of diasporic groups and U.S. space?[1]

For nearly two centuries this collision has, in actuality, produced a genealogy of sex for both the U.S. nation-state and "modernized" diasporas. The "Chinese prostitute" consecrated by the Page Law of 1875 and the "Chinese bachelor" formed in the residue of successive Chinese Exclusion Acts from 1882 to 1943 are just some of the most famous figures to emerge from this collision. But I set my sights today on one of the newest figures to emerge from the annals of the sexual history of the

Social Text 84–85, Vol. 23, Nos. 3–4, Fall–Winter 2005. © 2005 by Duke University Press.

Asian diaspora.[2] This figure, like his counterparts in previous historical periods, is to be found in the legal text and its supplementary genres, such as public health, anthropology, and psychology. The figure is named the "gay Pakistani immigrant," and he is found in immigration proceedings, juridical cases, and legal journals. Though murmurs of his existence have been heard before, and debate as to whether he was real continued for a number of years, he crossed a certain threshold of reality in the mid-1990s and emerged onto the legal, cultural, and social scene in an attire and voice fully suited to claim equal personhood at the table. And like his predecessors, U.S. immigration law remains the defining apparatus for his juridical and discursive constitution.

The epigraph offers a representative instance of his speech as it has been produced by and deposited into the annals of law. It comes from the narrative testimony of Saeed Rahman, recorded in the pages of the *Columbia Human Rights Law Review* in 1998.[3] Rahman is a "gay" South Asian immigrant living in New York City who successfully petitioned the Immigration and Naturalization Service (INS) for "asylee" status based on his claim of "belonging to a persecuted social group." Rahman's experience is one of only a few hundred cases in which the applicant's "sexual orientation"—that is, his "homosexuality"—qualified him for membership in a "social group." But Rahman's discourse marks a certain liminality within both normative diasporic formations and the nation-state, each of which depends on the racialized institutions of kinship and family, a point to which I return later in this essay.

The very site in which Rahman's homosexuality is recorded and protected by the law is also a site partially deterritorialized from the nation-state. For while asylum law within the United States is governed by the Immigration and Nationality Act, the judges who preside over these administrative cases are generally understood as exempt from some of the mandates of national immigration law that otherwise define admission into the United States. Instead, these judges are bound to broadly defined "international human rights" standards and international humanitarian law as established by the 1951 Convention Relating to the Status of Refugees. Hence, as the globalization scholar Saskia Sassen has argued, asylum law is one instance by which nonnational or global forces are creating a de facto immigration policy, one that far from binding the universality of the nation begins to delink sovereignty and the nation-state in important ways.[4] In this way, asylum cases represent "anomalous states" from the perspective of national right, marking instead the emergence of supposedly new capitalist social formations that are parasitical of the modern institutions of the state and its forms of power. If Rahman, and the few hundred legal cases similar to his, enters the national record through the law and the institutions of the border, such as the INS courtroom, that entrance betrays a transformation of those very institutions. Indeed, his designation as a "homosexual" within the legal record is at once a symptom of the contemporary forms and forces of a capitalist globalization.

In this essay I argue that the juridical appearance of the "gay Pakistani immigrant" must be situated within the context of the neoliberal restructuring of state power. Examining the broader discursive and material reorganization of U.S. immigration policy in the 1990s through the Family Reunification Act, moreover, I claim that the reconstitution of state power through the deployment of "family" constitutes the conditions of possibility for the juridical recognition of the gay Pakistani immigrant. As a figure at the limit of national law, the gay Pakistani immigrant marks in fact an important and constitutive tension within the national record and the practice of governance it subtends. For the figure, like the Chinese prostitute and Chinese bachelor before it, is produced in the conflicts and contradictions expressed by the state. This critique requires us to situate that enfiguring statement, the gay Pakistani immigrant, within the context of neoliberalism, the name for the contemporary mode of capitalist accumulation and the logics, broadly speaking, that organize current political practice and social rule, enfolding the discursive practice of "family."[5]

As a figure at the limit of national law, the gay Pakistani immigrant marks in fact an important and constitutive tension within the national record and the practice of governance it subtends.

Neoliberalism and Its Citizens

While neoliberalism elaborates a world-historical context, it has articulated with the nation-state differently in the global North and the global South. In both cases neoliberal economic policies and programs, begun in the late 1970s, have stressed the opening of markets, the financialization of currency regimes, the privatization of the public services sector, and the commodification and capitalization of biological life. Composed of such practices and logics, neoliberalism has most powerfully affected the imagined relation between the state and civil society, disorganizing the fantasy structure if not the actual operation of the so-called closed welfare economies hegemonic during the period of neoliberalism's emergence. As Gayatri Chakravorty Spivak has written, in an essay on the politics of diasporic studies in our transnational times, "within the definition of an ideal civil society, if the state is a welfare state, it is directly the servant of the individual. When increasingly privatized, as in the New World Order [of neoliberalism], the priorities of the civil society are shifted from service to the citizen to capital maximization."[6] Yet, while "the undermining of the civil structures of society is now a global situation," Spivak suggests that

> a general contrast can be made: in the North, welfare structures long in place are being dismantled. The diasporic underclass is often the worst victim. In the South, welfare structures cannot emerge as a result of the priorities of the transnational agencies. . . . Political asylum, at first sight so different from economic migration, finally finds it much easier to re-code capitalism as democracy. It too, then, inscribes itself in the narrative of the manipulation of civil structures in the interest of the financialization of the globe.[7]

As Spivak argues, the particular structural economic constraints on global Southern countries (the postcolonial and decolonizing countries) continue to effect a dismantling of the state and the national economy as agencies and sites for social redistribution. Under such constraints, the national citizen as a figure of recent decolonization is by necessity disinterred from the state. This citizen then operates as the persistent reminder of the state's inability and failure to achieve security for its citizenry against the ravages that daily accompany neoliberal capitalism. Importantly, the seizure of citizenship discourse by the "new social movements" in the global South remains a compelling catachresis in the globalized fight for just life, in part because it necessarily foregrounds the splitting of nation and state from their modernist configuration as the "nation-state" because of the pressures of neoliberal capitalism.[8]

Yet, as Spivak reminds us, immigrant advocacy and social justice projects in the global North that make their appeals to the state are implicated in the very structure of global inequity that continues to separate nation from state in the global South. For in the global North, Spivak reveals, the citizen remains consonant with the state, not despite but precisely because of neoliberalism. We must therefore ask after how the promulgation of a politics of citizenship—most often expressed as the desire to partake in civil society and the social safety net designed by the welfare state—might only further the ends of neoliberalism rather than thwart it.

Indeed, this observation suggests that we respecify what has colloquially been understood as the contemporary "dismantling of the welfare state" in the United States. For, in actuality, neoliberalism has not precipitated entirely the state's dismemberment or the erosion of its social safety net. Rather, it has entailed the reorganization of the state through, first, the consolidation of a welfare state for lower-middle- through upper-class U.S. citizens and citizen clones (professional green-card holders). This consolidation promises not "social redistribution" but rather the *distribution of entitlements* and the security to wield and exercise those entitlements in a now "internationalized" civil society. In this process, the redistributive functions traditionally associated with the welfare state are indistinguishable from the social reproduction and growth of capital. Put otherwise, we can say that while the welfare state is organized to reproduce labor power and simultaneously regulate/capture labor, the current "postwelfare state" governmentality is organized to produce wealth through the extension and production of new domains and modes of valorization. The privatization and public investment of retirement funds and the growth of the 401(k) capital investment sector are a case in point.

Second, we have witnessed the state's revocation of this welfare structure and of social rights for the racialized poor and the noncitizen class, also in the name of citizen security. Since the mid-1990s, this has become a particularly salient phenomenon. The 1996 passage of three linked federal laws—the Welfare Reform Act, the Illegal Immigration Reform Act, and the Counterterrorism Act—together worked to politically and economically disenfranchise the noncitizen and simultaneously to redirect capital's surpluses back into the economy. In each instance, such acts were facilitated discursively through practices of security. Moreover, these acts specifically denied immigrants the basic rights of all workers at a time when the immigrant is a category primarily composed of Latino, Asian, and Caribbean people. Or take, for example, that the ending of affirmative action in major revenue states such as California and Texas coincided with the buildup of the "prison-industrial complex" in these very same states.[9]

We have witnessed the state's revocation of this welfare structure and of social rights for the racialized poor and the noncitizen class, also in the name of citizen security.

In both cases, the political and economic disenfranchisement of the racialized noncitizen immigrant and the racialized citizen poor is devised in the name of securitizing civil society for its entitled subject, the citizen-as-capitalist and its juridical clones. In addition, the current war, originally justified as protecting "American" lives, has extended this governmentality, clarifying that the so-called quality of life and standard of living that we attach to U.S. citizenship is, like CNN, embedded directly in the machinery of the neoliberal imperial state, in the occupation and the destruction of the fragile but still active infrastructures of Afghanistan, Iraq, Venezuela, North Korea, and any other non-European or non-Zionist country that challenges U.S. policies for their region. The current war has only magnified the conceit that to occupy the place and logic of the U.S. citizen is to situate oneself structurally, and willy-nilly, within an imperial neoliberal state and social formation.

If these latest acts of international war and violence by which the citizen becomes the subject of both neoliberal and imperial forms of power are retroactively coded as a defense of American life, that coding has facilitated the cementing of a discourse of security in which the "terrorist" is figured as the racialized and sexualized "other" of the citizen.[10] Within the binary that organizes this discourse, the "terrorist" is indistinguishable from any formation that seeks to contest the "welfare rights" of the U.S. citizen (as a bearer of capital) in whose name the state survives. Through preemptive defense, the practices that are metaleptically "founded" on national security, the state has relied on the logics of racial discourse to suture imperial and American multinational corporate endeavors. The U.S. citizen—even and especially as the liberal multicultural subject—is in fact a racial figure on the global scene.[11] Splitting the totality of populations for which the U.S. state operates as a tactic of rule into the bifurcated categories of the citizen or the "international" subject of civility and the varieties of nonnationals and noncitizens whose imperatives to redirect the state as a figure of redistribution and social difference designates them as "terroristic," the U.S. state has made "security" an aspect guaranteed almost exclusively to capital. Under such conditions, the keywords of modern political life, *democracy*, *citizenship*, *civil society*, and *rights*, become the very terms by which the liberal and now neoliberal representative state legitimates imperialism and racial exploitation as the socially good.

If the construct of the U.S. citizen, and more broadly the subject of international civility, ratifies the current mode of production, a mode for which the state is both a facilitator and decentered, that construct under the postwelfare state system inaugurates the very opposite of what it ideally represents: the citizen's freedom requires the reduction of the immigrant worker to the state of chance, democracy designates military order, and the protection of civil rights ratifies the torture of the enemy combatant. Or, as Marx wrote of the French Empire under Louis Bonaparte during the era of monopoly capitalist colonialism, "only *one thing* was needed to complete the true form of this republic . . . the [President's] motto, *liberté, égalité, fraternité* must be replaced with the unambiguous words *infantry, cavalry, artillery*!"[12]

We might say that the U.S. citizen-subject has become the twenty-first-century "conservative peasant" of which Marx spoke so scornfully in the Eighteenth Brumaire.[13] Petty in its interests, heterogeneous to the formation of social classes on the global scale, and resistant to being politically and socially represented by the global proletariat on whose back society prospers; under neoliberalism, the U.S. citizen is not a figure for reflexivity and enlightenment. Indeed, the regulative discourse of citizenship, which continues to operate as the bearer of capitalist rationality, deconstitutes the very positions and locations from which U.S.-based subjects might grasp the world-historical context of neoliberalism and the order by which they are both ruled and sustained.

Family Rights and the Reunification of the State

The current conditions suggest that it is imperative that we refuse the figure of the citizen as the subject of knowledge and as the trope of unity. Moreover, in the context of U.S. asylum cases, as Spivak argues, a narrative that promotes the racially and sexually excluded's desire to enter into U.S. civil society that also fails to situate that desire within the context of other "desires" (of the gendered subaltern, for example) that are structurally foreclosed, violently refused, or made impossible by the "fulfillment" of the former trajectory in neoliberal times risks producing current struggles as alibis for exploitation. It also risks foreclosing and "forgetting" the critical disruptions and radical possibilities these very struggles open up. In order, then, to develop a critical reading of Rahman's testimony, I suggest examining the conditions that produce that testimony but are not directly visible in the text in which that testimony appears. That is, I want to explore how "family" as a regulative formation in the current governmentality organizes the conditions for "gay asylum." Hence we can resituate that supplementary figure as the site for a critique of the regulative function of family.

In a recent article in the *Los Angeles Times*, as part of its daily reporting on the rush of gays and lesbians seeking marriage petitions from the San Francisco County bureaucracy, the reader is offered the following testimony:

> "We are already a family," said Mara McWilliams, a 34-year-old health worker from San Jose, as she waited in line for her turn [to receive a marriage certificate] in the clerk's office Sunday morning. Her 8-year-old daughter Serena, clutched her leg. . . . "This is to show the world we are already a family. We're normal professional people. We're not here with our freak on."[14]

In our contemporary moment in the United States we are witnessing a certain recrossing of what Foucault has named the "deployment of alliances" with the "deployment of sexuality" (HS, 106). These different historical currents have once again found their point of convergence and intersection in the space of "family." And, moreover, this domain of family, whose centrality to the current governmentality is as indisputable as it is unstable, is also the effect of new articulations of race and sexuality, articulations whose investigation poses specific challenges and critical opportunities for those of us working in the domain of queer studies.[15]

In *The History of Sexuality*, Foucault argues that the relations of sex organized by a "*deployment of alliance*: a system of marriage, of fixation and development of kinship ties, of transmission of names and possessions" (106) were gradually transformed, incorporated by the deployment of sexuality, into a new set of apparatuses whose object is the individual body. While both deployments have a constitutive relation to economy, the system of alliances arranged the relations of sex to definite statuses in order to direct the proper transmission and circulation of wealth. In contrast, the deployment of sexuality, Foucault argues, "is linked to the economy through numerous and subtle relays . . . proliferating, innovating, annexing, creating and penetrating bodies in an increasingly detailed way, and in controlling populations in an increasingly comprehensive way" (HS, 107). If the deployment of alliance waned in importance because of shifts in the mode of production by the late eighteenth century, Foucault argues that its main institution—the family—was preserved and even extended by the new deployment, which emerged from within the peripheralized apparatuses that subtended the previous system of sexual relations. Since then "the family," in the "West," has remained "the interchange of sexuality and alliance: it conveys the law and the juridical dimension in the deployment of sexuality; and it conveys the economy of pleasure and the intensity of sensations in the regime of alliances." This incorporation, in which alliance is sexualized and saturated by desire, is also the mode by which a new form of power links the "state" and the "family."

As our current moment attests, in which representations of same-sex marriage reconcile homosexuality with the family, the state has emerged as a central locus by which certain "nonnormative sexualities" have sought to make it a terrain of freedom, destigmatization, and normality. In doing so, sexuality has once again become, quite powerfully, organized around questions of legitimacy and illegitimacy, intensifying the libidinal attachments to legal figures and subjecthood, and displacing many of the diverse knowledges and practices of sexuality whose aims and modes of existence are in excess of or relatively autonomous from concerns about legal ratification.[16]

It would appear that the current moment would require us to think also about how the deployment of sexuality subtends and is anchored by the contemporary capitalist mode of production. In the United States, that mode of production continues to rely on nonnational differences (of gender, race, and sexuality) to expand the proletarian class. Diaspora and migration have increasingly come to define and restructure these differences, subtending new formations of nonnormative sexualities.[17] How might we enter the "focus on family," as the U.S. Christian Right names it, in order to pursue an inquiry into the functions of capital, the U.S. state, and contemporary strategies of accumulation? In particular, what might be the different functionings of family in the current elaboration of racial and neoliberal capitalism?

For the last three years the Audre Lorde Project (ALP), a queer people of color organizing center in New York City, has been involved in developing a report on queer immigrants of color and the politics of immigration.[18] The report reveals that since the 1980s the state has actively worked to produce a racialized and gendered labor migration through the rubric of family reunification. Designed to assess how current immigration policy creates the conditions for a certain "homophobia" within immigrant communities and yet remains unaddressed by both gay and lesbian and immigrant rights groups, the report and the broader organizing initiative sought to reveal how the depoliticization of certain social forms, such as the "family" deployed by the state at the current moment, became the very means by which the state racially stratified immigrant communities in relation to the broader citizenry and actively organized a social structure for global capital in the city while appearing to be pursuing facially "neutral," and even just, social policy—one that corrected historical exclusions.

The report reveals that since the 1980s the state has actively worked to produce a racialized and gendered labor migration through the rubric of family reunification.

Since 1986 a large quotient of low-wage immigrant workers came to New York City through the Family Reunification program. For example, though many scholars have suggested that the major pull factor for immigration in the 1990s was a shortage within the United States of workers, especially for those located within the domestic, low-end services, and "unskilled" labor markets, the Immigration Act of 1990 capped the number of immigrant visas for so-called unskilled workers at a paltry ten thousand while it increased family-based immigrant visas to 480,000 annually beginning in 1995. While family immigration obviously includes minors and seniors who are either legally or functionally unable to enter the labor market, family-based immigration offers by far the largest pool of immigrant visas for so-called unskilled workers.[19]

In other words, while immigrants are recruited by the persistence of entry-level jobs in the services, industrial, and informal sectors of New York, the federal government continues to recruit such workers through the language and networks of family reunification. The effect of creating economic pull factors that recruit immigrants to the United States while using bureaucratic categories like "family reunification" to code that migration as essentially produced by the petitioning activity of resident immigrants living in the United States is to enable the appeasement of capital's need for immigrant workers while projecting the state as either a benevolent actor reuniting broken families or an overburdened and effete agent unable to prevent immigrants' manipulations of its (mandatory) democratic and fair laws. In either case, the recruitment of low-wage workers—who compose the majorities of the immigrant of color populations in New York City—is displaced from the state's responsibility and relocated back onto immigrants themselves. In this manner, the state is absolved politically from having created and expanded the conditions of noncitizen life within the territorial parameters of the United States and, at the same time, distinguishes itself as the apotheosis of Western Democracy by achieving the status of depoliticized neutrality.

Indeed, since its original passage of the Family Reunification Act in 1986, the federal government has increasingly elected to attach the wardship of the welfare of all incoming immigrants to the petitioning families themselves.[20] In a rather stunning move that has effectively destroyed the state's redistributive function within a managed economy, the government's mandate that petitioning families must now absorb the state's welfare functions for immigrants, in the context of the government's continuing bid to dismantle the welfare economy, has meant that it is now the role of the poor to absorb the social costs of poverty and a "healthy" unemployment rate! The state has effectively managed to both increase the numbers of immigrants arriving into the United States, as the economy continues to demand low-wage noncitizen labor, and at the same time to use immigration as the vehicle to dismantle its welfare responsibilities.[21]

In addition to the benefits the state accrues through the recruitment of labor under family reunification, these governmental practices also engender conditions within which the family unit is now a site and apparatus (willy-nilly) of state regulatory and capitalist power. For immigrants recruited through family reunification, patriarchal and heterosexual mandates have often become prerequisites to gaining family or welfare support. With the effective dismantling of welfare benefits of noncitizen racialized workers, workers brought in through family reunification have increasingly been forced to depend on family ties for access to room and board, employment, and other services, such as (what amounts to) workplace injury insurance, health care, child care, etc. In other words, federal immigration policies such as Family Reunification extend and institute heteronormative community structures as a requirement for accessing welfare provisions for new immigrants by attaching those provisions to the family unit.

In sum, the new federal structure has increased immigrants' exposure and structural dependence on heteropatriarchal relations and regulatory structures. Many queer immigrant interviewees spoke about the impossibility of "being gay" in a context in which one's dependence on "family"—broadly defined—is definitional to living as an immigrant in the City.[22] While this is something spoken about commonly enough in progressive circles, the tendency is to immediately assume the supposedly more essential homophobic nature of immigrant cultures over "American" culture or to blame the extraordinary willingness of queer immigrants to accept homophobic silencing and closeting. However, such "culturalist" arguments only further mask the state's role (as I have described it) in exactly engendering and enforcing the very immigrant homophobias that many claim are brought over by immigrants from their home countries. Both the intensity and specificity of homophobia in queer immigrants of color's lives are founded on local conditions (and not because of the "culture" that they bring from abroad, as so many scholars are quick to suggest) and are produced at the intersection of state immigration policies and their fixation on the heteropatriarchal family unit. Rather, the category of "gay" presumes a particular liberal order of "family," "civil society," and the "state" discursively and ideologically impossible for queer immigrants, deferring the queer of color into the status of the nonnational, produced at the limit of civil society.[23] More pointedly, the liberal isomorphism of family, society, and state requires as its condition of possibility the "queer of color" immigrant as a nonindividuated, nonrights-bearing "subject," whose conditions of existence confounds that isomorphism.[24]

In addition to the state's official immigration policy, federal and state governments since the Clinton years also have been empowered to shift the delivery of services away from public and private nonprofit secular providers and toward religious organizations and groups. In New York City, rising numbers of church organizations petition for government money and an increasing number of immigrants access church services as their primary service provider. Again, it is the dislocating of the state's function as a welfare agent that has exposed queer immigrants of color in particular to remarkable heteropatriarchal coercion and that produces the disproportionate enforcement of heteropatriarchal relations within immigrant of color communities.

Some scholars have pointed to what they believe is a potential silver lining in the end of the traditional welfare state: the diminishing importance of the state in the private and social lives of citizens and residents.[25] However, as I have argued, the erosion of the welfare state has not only been manifested by the withdrawal of economic and social resources to working and poor people. In fact, and in addition, the continued deterioration of the welfare system will not result in the withdrawal of state power from the lives of immigrants of color, or queer immigrants of color in particular, but will instead foster the expansion of social regulation through a growing reliance on state-circumscribed or sponsored social forms, such as family and religion. Moreover, the state's dependence on these forms for social regulation and political economic reproduction suggests that these forms will increasingly be burdened by and restructured by the state's interest and demands, distancing them from their historical social forms, compelling them instead to conform to the state's representation of their limits, functions, and modalities.

Recruiting and socializing labor through the category of family reunification extended the state's regulatory power while disestablishing a welfare state for immigrant communities. Moreover, by posing the denial of family reunification as historically a racially restrictive and ascriptive state practice that denied equal citizenship to immigrant of color communities, the state was able to produce a racialized and gendered differentiated class of workers via its pursuit of equality and supposed "racial redress" of past discrimination in immigration policy. The state's recourse to "family" to recruit noncitizen racialized labor and simultaneously distance that labor from social rights, the ALP report suggests, also became the very conditions for a state-enforced heteronormativity that projected immigrant communities as antiliberal and sexually conservative. Lastly, the state began through asylum law—in which gender and sexuality were recognized as "membership in a social group"—in the very same decade to draft U.S. citizenship as a formally protective apparatus against patriarchy, homophobia, and supposed "illiberal" cultures. In other words, family reunification enabled state power to simultaneously create heteropatriachial relations for the recruitment and socialization of labor while justifying the exclusion of immigrant communities from state power through a liberal language of U.S. citizenship as the guarantor of individual liberty and sexual freedom.

Homosexual Asylum and the Critique of Law

Returning to Rahman's testimony, I would like to use the preceding discussion of neoliberal political economies of the family to pursue a "queer of color" critique of his petition for asylum. In *Aberrations in Black: Toward a Queer of Color Critique*, the theorist Roderick Ferguson argues that the "sexual," as the expression of "racially gendered relations," emerges in the United States in the conflict between capital and the political state, especially protracted since the twentieth century.[26] While industrial capital, Ferguson argues, seeks labor, regardless of its origins, the political state qualifies its body politic through a set of racialized and gender ideals that it narrates as fundamental. Ferguson writes, "Capital is based on a fundamentally amoral logic. Capital, without pressures from the state or citizenry, will assemble labor without regard for normative prescriptions of race and gender" (16). Yet "the modern nation-state has historically been organized around an illusory universality particularized in terms of race, gender, sexuality, and class, [and, as such,] state formations have worked to protect and guarantee this universality" (17).

Such imperatives come into conflict with one another as capital tends toward the accumulation of "heterogeneities," disrupting social hierarchies, while the state tends toward a "heteronormativity," multiplying racial, gender, and sexual differences and particularities as it seeks universality within the material conditions of heterogeneity. In this way, industrial capital also disrupts modern political ontologies of rule: "While capital can only reproduce itself by ultimately transgressing the boundaries of neighborhood, home, and region, the state positions itself as the protector of those boundaries" (17). Reading sociology as an archive of the arts of governance, Ferguson argues that this tense contradiction is expressed in the rise of certain stock figures in the sociological archive across the twentieth century, such as the "transgendered mulatto," the Negro as the "Lady among the Races," and the "out-of-wedlock mother." These figures (and others) constitute the genealogy and limit of "community," "family," and "nation."

The gay Pakistani immigrant extends that genealogy as industrial capitalism is reconstituted by transnationality, neoliberalism, and the dominance of finance capital in our contemporary moment. In particular, working through Ferguson's framework, we might suggest that the figure of the gay Pakistani immigrant offers a genealogy of "family" within the contemporary United States. Indeed, the gay Pakistani immigrant as produced by the law is a supplement within the discourse of family and kinship as the state seeks to survive in a "post-state class-system."[27] Hence I would like to take up a "queer of color" critique of the current U.S. social formation and place that critique in critical opposition to citizenship, particularly as that practice is organized by the discourse of security to "free" capital. Situated within the shift from the welfare to the postwelfare neoliberal governmentality, such a reading would eschew an interpretation of his petition as seeking the security of U.S. citizenship to protect gay liberty or sexual freedom or a reading that posed the emergence of the gay Pakistani immigrant within the legal text as a victory for gay visibility in the archive.

Rather, this reading would discover and name in the legal record the strategies of repressive management that seek to define for their own ends what is knowable and thinkable about the figures ensnared in its web. Such a reading would resist the national archive we call the law whose regime of truth demands the daily conquest of multiple pasts and of the historical differences irreconcilable with that regime. It would read the figure of the gay Pakistani immigrant as formed in the contradiction between heteronormative social relations mandated for immigrants of color by the state's policies and the liberal state's ideology of universal sexual freedom as a mask for growing these social relations. In the annals of the sexual

Indeed, the gay Pakistani immigrant as produced by the law is a supplement within the discourse of family and kinship as the state seeks to survive in a "post-state class-system."

history of the Asian diaspora, sexuality materializes the conflict between an emergent governmentality and the state's desire to perpetuate itself beyond its point of expiration, in which "family" is their site of intersection.

If, as Ethne Luibheid has argued, the U.S. nation-state has historically ascribed sexuality to its populace through the technologies of the border, then asylum law both extends and breaks with that historical practice.[28] For in this case, the set of logics, discourses, regimes of truth, and imperatives that establish and identify homosexuality as a "social group" and the gay Pakistani as a victimized member of that social group, available for the nation-state's protection, is paradoxically the expression of a transformation in contemporary governmentality. That is, the figure of the gay Pakistani immigrant is both a symptom of globalization and the transnationalization of U.S. capital, and a new formation developed in the interstices of the nation-state. This figure emerges in the breach between the nation-state and the political economy.

Returning, then, to Rahman's narrative we witness certain complexities. For, on the one hand, it names the legal and civil infrastructure of the United States as a protective space for freely conducting work or pursuing private enterprise, a work and enterprise that presumably connotes homosexuality or that subtends a homosexual existence. On the other hand, these very notions of freedom and security are negated or denied for Rahman by the same legal and civil infrastructure that denies "queer immigrants" through the apparatus of immigration permanent access to that civil and legal infrastructure of the U.S. nation-state. If his application of asylum "resolved" that contradiction, it also became a point of politicization, one whose trajectory, however, we are not given an account of here. In this way, Rahman's politicization is appropriable for a number of groups and interests. For example, it could be used by gay and lesbian "human rights" groups to claim the importance of sexuality as a human right and of human rights as incubators of political subjectivity, a presupposition of full personhood.[29] It could be used by U.S.-based gay and lesbian so-called civil rights groups such as the Human Rights Campaign (HRC) to expose the unfairness of immigration laws that deny gays and lesbians equal rights as citizens.[30] Alternatively, it might be appropriated by Asian American political and cultural groups to establish the authenticity and legitimacy of queer Asians.

Yet I want to ask how else we might read this statement, this racialized and sexualized "figure of speech." In doing so, I want to pose the law as more than a medium and terrain in which pressing social relations and the asymmetries and inequalities that subtend those relations are structured, adjudicated, and "resolved." Instead I situate the law, by which I mean more broadly the legal sphere, as an "archive," in this instance an archive of racialized sexuality. That is, the legal sphere might be approached as one site in which the nation's official records are maintained and reproduced, giving those who seek identity through the law a history of their kin.

By naming the law an "archive" I mean to observe how the law seeks to be the record of the confrontation of social groups with the universality of "community" and the "state" posited by liberal political theory and epistemologies. Not just the law of record, the law's textuality is also the expression of the law *as* record. And, as an archive or mode of record keeping, the law seeks to produce an account of social differences that preserves the conditions for universality. Put otherwise, historical and social differences (of gender, race, sexuality, etc.) are subjugated by the law, as a precondition of their entrance into the national record, forced to preserve the liberal narrative of universality on which the legal sphere bases its notion of justice and the nation is said to be founded. As an archive, the law organizes social and historical differences in ways that promise both knowledge (of difference) and membership. In this way the law as an archive is not a dispassionate or disinterested space of records. Rather, it is the privileged ledger by which knowledge, idealized as dispassionate and disinterested, is, paradoxically, made coincident with community, idealized as nonalienated experience, producing that peculiar epistemo-affect associated with the "citizen."

Like all archives, the law, and the broader textual legal sphere, as an archive is not simply an institutional site for the recording of the past and of historical and social difference. Rather, it is a framework that, ironically, promises its reader agency only through the perpetual subjugation of differences, a subjugation, then, that targets not only the past but also the future. Indeed the law as an archive addressed to the citizen or potential subject of "civility" seeks, above all, to be an archive of the future. If, as Foucault argues, the archive must be construed as "the law of what can be said," in a particular social formation, then that which we understand as the law in a more limited sense is an archive of how the state has come to be organized necessarily on and within that broader social and material formation.[31]

Hence the archive is not a passive domain in which differences, such as the gay Pakistani immigrant, can be found, extracted, and restored to their fullness, if necessary. It is the active technique by which sexual, racial, gendered, and national differences, both historical and futural, are suppressed, frozen, and redirected as the occasion for a universal knowledge. It is the technique by which the modern U.S. state promotes the citizen as a universal agent through that knowledge production—to women, queers, people of color, etc.—demanding that we take up its framework for difference (both historical and social) as a prerequisite for a validated agency.

U.S. capitalist society, as a differentiated social formation, is mediated by the law, which operates as the regulative structure and archive for that very differentiation. The legal archive subjugates pasts and futures in the name of recording supposedly both difference and community.

Contending with the law as an active archive, or technique of self-making and the making of selves, as I do here, requires that we not simply "take up" its narrative and framework. Instead, we need to ask how regulation marks its interest in difference. Asking after this regulation requires reading these figures against the grain of the archive, situating that archive within and against the social formation—the forces and relations that constitute it—which bourgeois law cites but which it, haplessly, cannot comprehend. In other words, we need to read the figure as the limit of the archive, the point at which the archive's own conditions for existence might be retraced.

Notes

This essay was supported by a grant from the Simpson Center for the Humanities at the University of Washington, Seattle, and a residency fellowship at the Humanities Research Institute at the University of California, Irvine. The author gratefully acknowledges their support.

1. By a "history of sexuality" I mean to reference Michel Foucault's argument that modern social power constitutes the very object "sex" that it then seeks to regulate. A historicist inspection of the repression of sexuality and its gradual emergence from repressive law, Foucault argues, naturalizes and disappears the diverse processes that affix "sex" as a unitary ideal. See Michel Foucault, *History of Sexuality*, vol. 1, *An Introduction*, trans. Robert Hurley (New York: Vintage Books, 1990), hereafter cited as HS in the text.

2. On the Chinese prostitute and Chinese bachelor as racialized and sexualized figures constituted by U.S. legal territory and its apparatuses, see Nayan Shah, *Contagious Divides: Epidemics and Race in San Francisco's Chinatown* (Berkeley: University of California Press, 2001). See also Lisa Lowe, *Immigrant Acts: On Asian American Cultural Politics* (Durham, NC: Duke University Press, 1996), 1–36.

3. See the symposium "Shifting Grounds for Asylum: Female Genital Surgery and Sexual Orientation," New York University School of Law, 16 October 1997. The proceedings have been transcribed, edited, and published in *Columbia Human Rights Law Review* 29 (1998).

4. See Saskia Sassen, *Losing Control? Sovereignty in an Age of Globalization* (New York: Columbia University Press, 1996), 33–62.

5. See David L. Eng, "Transnational Adoption and Queer Diasporas," *Social Text*, no. 76 (2003): 1–37.

6. See Gayatri Chakravorty Spivak, "Diasporas Old and New: Women in the Transnational World," *Textual Practice* 10 (1996): 248.

7. Ibid., 249.

8. On the differences between postcolonial and postimperial (or global Southern and global Northern) state formations under neoliberalism, see M. Jacqui Alexander, "Erotic Autonomy as a Politics of Decolonization: An Anatomy of Feminist and State Practice in the Bahamas Tourist Economy," in *Feminist Genealogies, Colonial Legacies, Democratic Futures*, ed. M. Jacqui Alexander and Chandra Talpade Mohanty (New York: Routledge, 1999), 63–100. On the splitting of nation and state in the compound abstraction "nation-state," see Spivak, "Diasporas Old and New," 249, 255–63. On the possibilities of postcolonial resignification of citizenship and more generally on the catechresis of Western regulative governmental terms in postcolonial space, see Spivak, "Postcoloniality, Marginality, Value," in *Outside the Teaching Machine* (New York: Routledge, 1993).

9. See Ruthie Gilmore, "Globalization and US Prison Growth: From Military Keynesianism to post-Keynesian Militarism," *Race and Class* 40 (1998–99): 171–87.

10. On the racialization of the "terrorist," the organization of the state through the discourse of security, and the rise of new "racial formations," see Leti Volpp, "The Citizen and the Terrorist," *UCLA Law Review* 49 (2002): 1575–600; and Muneer Ahmed, "Homeland Insecurities: Racial Violence the Day after September 11," *Social Text*, no. 72 (2002): 101–15. On the racialized sexualization of the figures of "terrorism," see Jasbir Puar and Amit Rai, "Monster, Terrorist, Fag: The War on Terrorism and the Production of Docile Patriots," *Social Text*, no. 72 (2002): 117–48.

11. Etienne Balibar, for example, pursues the allegorical reading of psychoanalysis in his theory of the nation-state and the citizen subject in his essay "Nation Form." Balibar disaggregates the nation and the state as naming different processes and, hence, different components of the subject's interpellation. While the nation figures as an "ideal-nation" and is responsible for the subject's patriotism, ensuring the collective promise to face death for the nation, it is the state, as a mythicized abstraction, that prefigures the unity between individuals and between an individual and the collectivity, cementing/casting individuality on the model of citizenship. This latter feature is named "fictive ethnicity" and is critical in fusing the individual with the national community. Recasting the notion of identification, Balibar argues that individuals are "interpellated" through the structures of language and race into citizens who share an "ethnicity." While whiteness has historically operated as the form of racialization that has secured the "fictive ethnicity" of the U.S. national citizen, in the contemporary period it is "multiculturalism" that secures the fictive ethnicity of the U.S. national citizen as multicultural citizen. The multicultural subject is the racial formation of the national citizen, prefiguring and promising the citizen's ability to claim universality, for which the state figures as a synecdoche of the universal. This is nowhere more powerfully articulated than in our current social formation, in which the U.S. *citizen* of Arab descent or person of "Muslim faith" is promoted as a figure of multiculturalism while the Arab citizen of an Arab state or a Muslim citizen of an Arab or Muslim state is promoted as a figure of a monstrous monoculturalism that threatens the universality represented by the U.S. "multicultural" state and must be repudiated, expelled, persistently violated, or "preemptively" assaulted or killed. The racialization of the Arab and Muslim U.S. citizen-subject as a U.S. multicultural subject (who has available the possibility of membership in univer-

sal culture) is constitutively linked to the "negative" racialization of the Arab or Muslim immigrant, nonimmigrant resident, and non-U.S. national as a social anachrony whose very presence invites violence and violation, a violation coded as violent humanization. Rewriting the seventeenth-century English jurist proclamation, "The king is dead, long live the king"—which distinguished between the crown and the king's body, killing the body when it did not conform to the sovereign subject of the crown—we can argue that as the multicultural citizen-subject is now installed as the sovereign, it is possible for George W. Bush to say, "The Arabs and Muslims are dead, long live our (U.S. multicultural) Arab and Muslim brothers and sisters." See Etienne Balibar, "The Nation Form: History and Ideology," in *Race, Nation, Class: Ambiguous Identities*, by Etienne Balibar and Immanuel Wallerstein (New York: Verso, 1991), 86–106. On the sovereign's two bodies, see Ernst H. Kantorowicz, *The King's Two Bodies* (Princeton, NJ: Princeton University Press, 1997). See also David Lloyd, "Ethnic Cultures, Minority Discourse, and the State," in *Colonial Discourse/Postcolonial Theory*, ed. Francis Barker, Peter Hulme, and Margaret Iverson (Manchester: University of Manchester Press, 1996), 221–38.

12. See Karl Marx, *The Eighteenth Brumaire of Louis Bonaparte*, trans. Ben Fowkes, in *Surveys from Exile: Political Writings: Vol. 2*, ed. David Ferbach (New York: Penguin Books, 1992), 184, emphasis in original.

13. Ibid., 240.

14. See Nicholas Riccarei, "Same-Sex Marriages Often a Family Affair," *Los Angeles Times*, 16 February 2004.

15. Judith Butler, characteristically prescient and perceptive, argued that the idea of gay marriage always already invokes the idea of kinship in the United States, France, and elsewhere. Family is the space of their intersection. See Judith Butler, "Is Kinship Always Already Heterosexual?" *Differences: A Journal of Feminist Cultural Studies* 13, no. 1 (2002): 14–44.

16. Ibid., 17–23.

17. See Roderick A. Ferguson, *Aberrations in Black: Toward a Queer of Color Critique* (Minneapolis: University of Minnesota Press, 2004), 1–29, 135–48.

18. This report is forthcoming from the Audre Lorde Project's Immigrant Rights Working Group. Lead investigators were Chandan Reddy and Natalie Bennett.

19. See Paul Wickham Schmidt, ed., *Understanding the Immigration Act of 1990: AILA's New Law Handbook* (Washington, DC: American Immigration Lawyers Association, 1991), 5–9. See also and in particular the essays "Family Sponsored Immigration (The Numbers Game)" by Harry Gee Jr. and "Overview of Employment-Based Immigration—The First Three Preferences" by Lenni B. Benson in this compilation. On the expansion of the labor market in low-end services and unskilled labor, see Saskia Sassen, *Globalization and Its Discontents* (New York: Free Press, 1998); see also her earlier book, *The Global City* (Princeton, NJ: Princeton University Press, 1991).

20. See the Immigration Reform Act of 1990 that stipulates that petitioning families must agree to shoulder the possible social cost of admitted immigrants.

21. Moreover, this was effected by ideologically centering a "middle-class" subject of migration within immigration law.

22. See the interviews with LGBT immigrants of color collected for this study; all archived at the Audre Lorde Project.

23. In pursuing this reading I have been aided by Wendy Brown's "Liberalism's Family Values," in *States of Injury* (Princeton, NJ: Princeton University Press, 1995), 135–65.

24. This has also been true of the figure of the "DL" (down low) as it is currently used by the Centers for Disease Control and Prevention and the news media for naming certain African American nonheteronormative formations that cannot "become" homosexual. See www.cdc.gov/hiv/pubs/faq/downlow.htm.

25. For a review of this literature, see "Introduction: Freedom and the Plastic Cage," in Brown, *States of Injury*, 3–29.

26. Ferguson, *Aberrations in Black*.

27. James Faubion writes of the supplement in relation to contemporary theories of kinship: "If the older anthropology of kinship is thus still with us, it has also had to endure the perturbations of an ever more unruly 'supplement' (a term I use in the Derridian sense, to denote the necessary and perhaps antithetical resolution of a primary, a hegemonic, an intellectually comfortable category)." See James Faubion, introduction to *The Ethics of Kinship: Ethnographic Inquiries*, ed. Faubion (Lanham, MD: Rowman and Littlefield, 2001), 1–28. See also John Borneman's contribution to this anthology, titled "Caring and Being Cared For: Displacing Marriage, Kinship, Gender, and Sexuality." As a "supplement," the gay Pakistani immigrant must be distinguished from the Chinese prostitute and Chinese bachelor of the nineteenth and early twentieth century, which were produced both materially and discursively in the United States as constitutive exclusions and hence as constitutively excluded. On the post-state class system, see Spivak, "Diasporas Old and New," 245–69; see also Michael Hardt and Antonio Negri's use of the term *empire* to describe this formation in *Empire* (Cambridge, MA: Harvard University Press, 2000).

28. See Ethne Luibheid, *Entry Denied: Controlling Sexuality at the Border* (Minneapolis: University of Minnesota Press, 2002).

29. See, for example, the "Asylum Project" at the International Gay and Lesbian Human Rights Commission, www.iglhrc.org/site/iglhrc/.

30. This is, in fact, how the HRC has "addressed" queer immigrant formations and politics, seeking to pass the Permanent Partners Immigration Act of 2003 through U.S. legislators' offices. The act would extend the same legal rights to gays and lesbians as heterosexual citizens possess in immigration matters. See David Crary, "U.S. Immigration Law Not Friendly to Gay Couples," *Seattle Times*, 24 November 2003; see also www.hrc.org/Template.cfm?Section=Permanent_Partners_Immigration_Act.

31. See Michel Foucault, "The Statement and the Archive," in *The Archaeology of Knowledge and the Discourse on Language*, trans. A. M. Sheridan Smith (New York: Pantheon, 1972), 129.

Queer Times, Queer Assemblages

Jasbir K. Puar

These are queer times indeed. The war on terror is an assemblage hooked into an array of enduring modernist paradigms (civilizing teleologies, orientalisms, xenophobia, militarization, border anxieties) and postmodernist eruptions (suicide bombers, biometric surveillance strategies, emergent corporealities, counterterrorism gone overboard). With its emphases on bodies, desires, pleasures, tactility, rhythms, echoes, textures, deaths, morbidity, torture, pain, sensation, and punishment, our necropolitical present-future deems it imperative to rearticulate what queer theory and studies of sexuality have to say about the metatheories and the "realpolitiks" of Empire, often understood, as Joan Scott observes, as "the real business of politics."[1] Queer times require even queerer modalities of thought, analysis, creativity, and expression in order to elaborate on nationalist, patriotic, and terrorist formations and their intertwined forms of racialized perverse sexualities and gender dysphorias. What about the war on terrorism, and its attendant assemblages of racism, nationalism, patriotism, and terrorism, is already profoundly queer? Through an examination of queerness in various terrorist corporealities, I contend that queernesses proliferate even, or especially, as they remain denied or unacknowledged. I take up these types of inquiries not only to argue that discourses of counterterrorism are intrinsically gendered, raced, sexualized, and nationalized but also to demonstrate the production of normative patriot bodies that cohere against and through queer terrorist corporealities. In the speculative, exploratory endeavor that follows, I foreground three manifestations of this imbrication. One, I examine discourses of queerness where problematic conceptualizations of queer corporealities, especially via Muslim sexualities, are reproduced in the service of discourses of U.S. exceptionalisms. Two, I rearticulate a terrorist body, in this case the suicide bomber, as a queer assemblage that resists queerness-as-sexual-identity (or anti-identity)—in other words, intersectional and identitarian paradigms—in favor of spatial, temporal, and corporeal convergences, implosions, and rearrangements. Queerness as an assemblage moves away from excavation work, deprivileges a binary opposition between queer and not-queer subjects, and, instead of

Social Text 84–85, Vol. 23, Nos. 3–4, Fall–Winter 2005.

retaining queerness exclusively as dissenting, resistant, and alternative (all of which queerness importantly is and does), it underscores contingency and complicity with dominant formations. Finally, I argue that a focus on queerness as assemblage enables attention to ontology in tandem with epistemology, affect in conjunction with representational economies, within which bodies, such as the turbaned Sikh terrorist, interpenetrate, swirl together, and transmit affects to each other. Through affect and ontology, the turbaned Sikh terrorist in particular, I argue, as a queer assemblage, is reshaping the terrain of South Asian queer diasporas.

Queer Narratives of U.S. Exceptionalism

As a critique, "queer liberalism" notes an unsettling but not entirely unexpected reconciliation of the radical convictions of queerness as a post-structuralist anti- and transidentity critique with the liberal demands of national subject formation. We can map out a couple of different yet overlapping genealogies of queer liberal subjects. The first is the rise of the queer consumer-citizen, hailed with force in the late 1980s and early 1990s, fueled by the fantasy of enormous disposable incomes for unburdened-by-kinship gays and lesbians. The second genealogy, of the queer liberal subject before the law, culminates with the 2003 decriminalizing of sodomy through *Lawrence and Garner v. Texas*. While both consumptive and juridical lineages reflect heavily on the status of the nation, I argue that one very concise way queer liberalism is inhabited is through stagings of U.S. nationalism via a praxis of sexual othering that unwittingly exceptionalizes the identities of U.S. queernesses vis-à-vis Islamophobic constructions of sexuality in the Middle East. This is not a critique of the racisms and other constitutive exclusions of conservative lesbian, gay, bisexual, transgender, queer, and questioning (LGBTQ) discourses. Rather, I am taking issue with queer theorizing that, despite (and perhaps because of) a commitment to an intersectional analytic, fails to interrogate the epistemological will to knowledge that invariably reproduces the disciplinary interests of the U.S. nation-state. Forms of U.S. sexual exceptionalism from purportedly progressive spaces have historically surfaced through feminist constructions of "third world" women; what we have now, however, is the production of a sexual exceptionalism through normative as well as nonnormative (queer) bodies. That is, queerness is proffered as a sexually exceptional form of American national sexuality through a rhetoric of sexual modernization that is simultaneously able to castigate the other as homophobic *and* perverse, and construct the imperialist center as "tolerant" but sexually, racially, and gendered normal.

Queerness colludes with U.S. exceptionalisms embedded in nationalist foreign policy via the articulation and production of whiteness as a queer norm and the tacit acceptance of U.S. imperialist expansion. For example, national LGBTQ organizations such as the National Gay and Lesbian Task Force (NGLTF) and the Human Rights Commission (HRC) have been far more preoccupied with gay marriage and gays in the military than the war on terrorism or even the "homosexual sex" torture scandal at Abu Ghraib.[2] In fact, Mubarak Dahir suggests that some organizations have actually harnessed the oppression of LGBTQ Arabs to justify the war, and calls on gays and lesbians who support the war in Iraq to "stop using the guise of caring about the plight of gay Arabs to rationalize their support."[3] For Queer Left organizing not to center people of color borders dangerously on eliding a critique of the racist, imperialist war, or conversely reenacting forms of colonial and multiculturalist fetishisms, for example, in relation to queer Filipino war resister Stephen Funk, who has become the poster queer for LGBTQ antiwar sloganeering. Are LGBTQ communities addressing the war on terrorism as a "gay issue"?[4] If so, are they articulating a politics of race, empire, and globalization?

The most explicit production of this queer exceptionalism can be found in numerous instances of the responsive commentary to the Abu Ghraib "sexual torture scandal." The Abu Ghraib saga demonstrates that sexuality is at once absolutely crucial to the production of the geopolitics of American exceptionalism, and despite this critical role, or perhaps because of it, it is an undertheorized, underrated, and often avoided aspect of the debate on the war on terror. Very shortly after the first release of the photos in May 2004, the descriptions of the torture cathected within the specter of "homosexual acts," prompting a flurry of interviews with queer theorists, organizational press releases from LGBTQ associations, and articles within the gay press, all of which, incredibly enough, demonstrated no hesitations about speaking knowledgeably of "Muslim sexuality." In the gay press, the Abu Ghraib photos were hailed as "evidence of rampant homophobia in the armed forces,"[5] with scarce mention of the linked processes of racism and sexism. Even more troubling was the reason given for the particular efficacy of the torture: the taboo, outlawed, banned, disavowed status of homosexuality in Iraq and the Middle East, complemented by an aversion to nudity, male-on-male contact, and sexual modesty with the rarely seen opposite sex. It is exactly this unsophisticated notion of Arab/Muslim/Islamic (does it matter which one?) cultural difference that military intelligence capitalized on to create what they believed to be a culturally specific "effective" matrix of torture techniques. What we have here, then, is the paralleling of the Pentagon's strategies, which used among other materials an anthropology study, *The Arab Mind*,

The most explicit production of this queer exceptionalism can be found in numerous instances of the responsive commentary to the Abu Ghraib "sexual torture scandal."

and the discourses that emanate from progressive queers. For example, Faisal Alam, founder and director of the international Muslim lesbian, gay, bisexual, transgender, intersex, queer, and questioning (LGBTIQ) organization Al-Fatiha, states that "sexual humiliation is perhaps the worst form of torture for any Muslim." The press release from Al-Fatiha continues: "Islam places a high emphasis on modesty and sexual privacy. Iraq, much like the rest of the Arab world, places great importance on notions of masculinity. Forcing men to masturbate in front of each other and to mock same-sex acts or homosexual sex, is perverse and sadistic, in the eyes of many Muslims." In another interview Alam reiterates the focus on the violation of proper gender norms, maintaining that the torture is an "affront to their masculinity."[6]

I take issue with Al-Fatiha's statements, as they along with many other statements relied on an orientalist notion of "Muslim sexuality" that foregrounded sexual repression and upheld versions of normative masculinity—that is, the feminized *passivo* positioning is naturalized as humiliating, producing a muscular nationalism of sorts. In displays of solidarity, Al-Fatiha's comments were uncritically embraced by various queer sectors: the Center for Lesbian and Gay Studies newsletter used them to authenticate its perspective through that of the native informant, while the gay press endlessly reproduced the appropriate masculinity and sexual conservatism lines. I want to underscore the complex dance of positionality that Muslim and Arab groups such as Al-Fatiha must perform in these times, whereby a defense of "Muslim sexuality" through the lens of culture is easily co-opted into racist agendas.[7] Given their place at the crossroads of queerness and Arabness, Al-Fatiha was, and still is, under the most duress to authenticate orientalist paradigms of Muslim sexuality, thus reproducing narratives of U.S. sexual exceptionalism. Reinforcing a homogenous notion of Muslim sexual repression vis-à-vis homosexuality and the notion of "modesty" works to resituate the United States, in contrast, as a place free of such sexual constraints. For Al-Fatiha to have elaborated on the issues of Islam and sexuality more complexly would have not only missed the orientalist resonance so eagerly awaited by the mass media—that is, there is almost no way to get media attention unless this resonance is met—it would have also considerably endangered a population already navigating the pernicious racist effects of the Patriot Act: surveillance, deportations, detentions, registrations, preemptive migrations, and departures. Thus Al-Fatiha's performance of a particular allegiance with American sexual exceptionalism is the result of a demand, not a suggestion. The proliferation of diverse U.S. subjects, such as the Muslim American, and their epistemological conditions of existence, are mandates of homeland security.

The point to be argued is not how to qualify the status of homosexuality across the broad historical and geographic, not to mention religious, regional, class, national, and political variances, of the Middle East (a term I hesitate to use, given its area studies implications). We must consider instead how the production of "homosexuality as taboo" is situated within the history of encounter with the Western gaze. The Orient, once conceived in Foucault's *ars erotica* and Said's deconstructive work as the place of original release, unfettered sin, and acts with no attendant identities or consequences, now symbolizes the space of repression *and* perversion, and the site of freedom has been relocated to Western identity. For example, the queer theorist Patrick Moore, author of *Beyond Shame: Reclaiming the Abandoned History of Radical Gay Sex*, opines:

> Because "gay" implies an identity and a culture, in addition to describing a sexual act, it is difficult for a gay man in the West to completely understand the level of disgrace endured by the Iraqi prisoners. But in the Arab world, the humiliating techniques now on display are particularly effective because of Islam's troubled relationship with homosexuality. This is not to say that sex between men does not occur in Islamic society—the shame lies in the gay identity rather than the act itself. As long as a man does not accept the supposedly female (passive) role in sex with another man, there is no shame in the behavior. Reports indicate that the prisoners were not only physically abused but also accused of actually being homosexuals, which is a far greater degradation to them.[8]

The act to identity telos spun out by Moore delineates the West as the space of identity (disregarding the confusion of act-identity relations at the heart of U.S. homosexualities), while the Arab world is relegated, apparently because of "Islam's troubled relationship to homosexuality," to the backward realm of acts. The presence of gay- and lesbian-identified Muslims in the "Arab world" is inconceivable. Given the lack of any evidence that being called a homosexual is much more degrading than being tortured, Moore's rationalization reads as an orientalist projection that conveys much more about the constraints and imaginaries of identity in the "West" than anything else. Furthermore, in the uncritical face-value acceptance of the notion of Islamic sexual repression, we see the trenchant replay of what Foucault termed the "repressive hypothesis": the notion that a lack of discussion or openness about sexuality reflects a repressive, censorship-driven apparatus of deflated sexual desire.[9] While in Said's *Orientalism* the illicit sex found in the Orient was sought out in order to liberate the Occident from its own performance of the repressive hypothesis, in the case of Abu Ghraib, conversely, it is the repression of the Arab prisoners that is highlighted in order to efface the rampant hypersexual excesses of the U.S. prison guards.

Given the unbridled homophobia, racism, and misogyny demonstrated by the U.S. guards, it is indeed ironic, yet predictable, that the United States nonetheless emerges exceptionally, as more tolerant of homosexuality (and less tainted by misogyny and fundamentalism) than the repressed, modest, nudity-shy "Middle East." We have a clear view of the performative privileges of Foucault's "speaker's benefit": those who are able to articulate sexual knowledge (especially of oneself, but in this case, also of others) then appear to be freed, through the act of speech, from the space of repression.[10] Through the insistent and frantic manufacturing of "homosexuality" and "Muslim" as mutually exclusive discrete categories, queerness colludes with the delineation of exceptional U.S. sexual norms, produced against the intolerable forms of the sexualities of "terrorist" bodies. Furthermore, queer exceptionalism works to suture U.S. nationalism through the perpetual fissuring of race from sexuality—the race of the (presumptively sexually repressed, perverse, or both) terrorist and the sexuality of the national (presumptively white, gender normative) queer: the two dare not converge.

Terrorist Corporealities

José Esteban Muñoz's writing on the "terrorist drag" of the Los Angeles–based performance artist Vaginal Davis harks back to another political era—bizarrely as if it were long ago, although in measured time we are talking about the mid-1990s—when the notion of the terrorist had a trenchant but distant quality to it.[11] Muñoz argues that Davis's drag performances, encompassing "cross-sex, cross-race minstrelsy," is terrorist on two levels. Aesthetically, Davis rejects glamour-girl feminine drag in favor of "ground level guerrilla representational strategies" such as white supremacist militiamen and black welfare queen hookers, what Muñoz calls "the nation's most dangerous citizens." This alludes to the second plane of meaning, the reenactment of the "nation's internal terrors around race, gender, and sexuality." It is imperative in a post-9/11 climate of counterterrorism to note that guerrillas and terrorists have vastly different racial valences, the former bringing to mind the phantasmic landscapes of Central and South America, while the latter, the enduring legacy of orientalist imaginaries. In the context of these geographies it is notable that Davis as the white militiaman astutely brings terrorism home—to Oklahoma City, in fact—and in doing so dislodges, at least momentarily, this orientalist legacy.

Muñoz's description of this terrorist drag points to the historical convergences between queers and terror—homosexuals have been the traitors to the nation, figures of espionage and double agents, associated with Communists during the McCarthy era, and, as with suicide bombers, bring on and desire death (both are figured as always already dying, although for homosexuals it is through the AIDS pandemic). More recent exhortations place gay marriage as "the worst form of terrorism" and gay couples as "domestic terrorists."[12] Clearly, one can already ask, what is terrorist about the queer? But the more salient and urgent question is what is queer about the terrorist? And what is queer about terrorist corporealities? The depictions of masculinity most rapidly disseminated and globalized through the war on terrorism are terrorist masculinities: failed and perverse, these emasculated bodies always have femininity as their reference point of malfunction and are metonymically tied to all sorts of pathologies of the mind and body—homosexuality, incest, pedophilia, madness, and disease. We see, for example, the queer physicality of terrorist monsters haunting the U.S. State Department counterterrorism Web site.[13] With the unfurling, viruslike, explosive mass of the terrorist network, tentacles ever regenerating despite efforts to truncate them, the terrorist is concurrently an unfathomable, unknowable, and hysterical monstrosity, and yet one that only the exceptional capacities of U.S. intelligence and security systems can quell. This unknowable monstrosity is not a casual bystander or parasite; the nation assimilates this effusive discomfort with the unknowability of these bodies, thus affectively producing new normativities and exceptionalisms through the cataloging of unknowables. It is not, then, that we must engage in the practice of excavating the queer terrorist or queering the terrorist; rather, queerness is always already installed in the project of naming the terrorist; the terrorist does not appear as such without the concurrent entrance of perversion, deviance, deformity. The strategy of encouraging subjects of study to appear in all their queernesses, rather than primarily to queer the subjects of study, provides a subject-driven temporality in tandem with a method-driven temporality. Playing on this difference, between the subject being queered versus queerness already existing within the subject (and thus dissipating the subject as such) allows for both the temporality of being and the temporality of always becoming.

Homosexuals have been the traitors to the nation, figures of espionage and double agents, associated with Communists during the McCarthy era, and, as with suicide bombers, bring on and desire death.

As there is no entity, no identity to queer, rather queerness coming forth at us from all directions, screaming its defiance, suggests to me a move from intersectionality to assemblage. The Deleuzian assemblage, as a series of dispersed but mutually implicated networks, draws together enunciation and dissolution, causality and effect. As opposed to an intersectional model of identity, which presumes components—race, class, gender, sexuality, nation, age, religion—are separable analytics and can be thus disassembled, an assemblage is more attuned to interwoven forces that merge and dissipate time, space, and body against linearity, coherency, and permanency. Intersectionality demands the knowing, naming, and thus stabilizing of identity across space and time, generating narratives of progress that deny the fictive and performative of identification: you become an identity, yes, but also timelessness works to consolidate the fiction of a seamless stable identity in every space. As a tool of diversity management, and a mantra of liberal multiculturalism, intersectionality colludes with the disciplinary apparatus of the state—census, demography, racial profiling, surveillance—in that "difference" is encased within a structural container that simply wishes the messiness of identity into a formulaic grid. Displacing queerness as an identity or modality that is visibly, audibly, legibly, or tangibly evident, assemblages allow us to attune to intensities, emotions, energies, affectivities, textures as they inhabit events, spatiality, and corporealities. Intersectionality privileges naming, visuality, epistemology, representation, and meaning, while assemblage underscores feeling, tactility, ontology, affect, and information. Most important, given the heightened death-machine aspect of nationalism in our contemporary political terrain—a heightened sensorial and anatomical domination described by Achille Mbembe as "necropolitics"—assemblages work against narratives of U.S. exceptionalism that secure empire, challenging the fixity of racial and sexual taxonomies that inform practices of state surveillance and control, and befuddling the "us versus them" of the war on terror. For while intersectionality and its underpinnings—an unrelenting epistemological will to truth—presupposes identity and thus disavows futurity, assemblage, in its debt to ontology and its espousal of what cannot be known, seen, or heard, or has yet to be known, seen, or heard, allows for becoming/s beyond being/s.[14]

Queer assemblages appear in Mbembe's devastating and brilliant meditation on the necropolitics of our current infinite war positioning. Mbembe argues for a shift from biopower to necropolitics (the subjugation of life to the power of death), noting that the historical basis of sovereignty that is reliant on a notion of (Western) political rationality begs for a more accurate framing: that of life and death.[15] He asks, "What place is given to life, death, and the human body (especially the wounded or slain body)?" Mbembe attends to the informational productivity of the (Palestinian) suicide bomber. In pondering the queer modalities of this kind of terrorist, one notes a pastiche of oddities: a body machined together through metal and flesh, an assemblage of the organic and the inorganic; a death not of the self or of the other, but both simultaneously; self-annihilation as the ultimate form of resistance and self-preservation. This body forces a reconciliation of opposites through their inevitable collapse—a perverse habitation of contradiction. As a figure in the midst of always already dying even as it is in the midst of becoming, like the homosexual afflicted with HIV, the suicide bomber sutures his or her status as sexually perverse.[16] Mbembe also points to the queer becomings of a suicide bomber—a corporeal experiential of "ballistics." The dynamite strapped onto the body of a suicide bomber is not merely an appendage; the "intimacy" of weapon with body reorients the assumed spatial integrity (coherence and concreteness) and individuality of the body that is the mandate of intersectional identities: instead we have the body-weapon. The ontological affect of the body renders it a newly becoming body, queerly:

As a figure in the midst of always already dying even as it is in the midst of becoming, like the homosexual afflicted with HIV, the suicide bomber sutures his or her status as sexually perverse.

> The candidate for martyrdom transforms his or her body into a mask that hides the soon-to-be-detonated weapon. Unlike the tank or the missile that is clearly visible, the weapon carried in the shape of the body is invisible. Thus concealed, it forms part of the body. It is so intimately part of the body that at the time of its detonation it annihilates the body of its bearer, who carries with it the bodies of others when it does not reduce them to pieces. The body does not simply conceal a weapon. The body is transformed into a weapon, not in a metaphorical sense but in a truly ballistic sense.[17]

Temporal narratives of progression are upturned as death and becoming fuse into one: as one's body dies, one's body becomes the mask, the weapon, the suicide bomber, not before. Not only does the ballistic body come into being without the aid of visual cues marking its transformation, it also "carries with it the bodies of others." Its own penetrative energy sends shards of metal and torn flesh spinning off into the ether. The body-weapon does not play as metaphor, or in the realm of meaning and epistemology, but rather forces us ontologically anew to ask: what kinds of information does the ballistic body impart? These bodies, being in the midst of becoming, blur the insides and the outsides, infecting transformation through sensation, echoing knowledge via reverberation and vibration. The echo is a queer temporality; in the relay of affective information between and amid beings, the sequence of reflection, repetition, resound, and return (but with a difference, as in mimicry), and brings forth waves of the future breaking into the present. Gayatri Spivak, prescient in drawing our attention to the multivalent textuality of suicide in "Can the Subaltern Speak?" reminds us in her latest ruminations that suicide terrorism, as a relay of affective information, is a modality of expression and communication for the subaltern:

> Suicidal resistance is a message inscribed on the body when no other means will get through. It is both execution and mourning, for both self and other. For you die with me for the same cause, no matter which side you are on.

> Because no matter who you are, there are no designated killees in suicide bombing. No matter what side you are on, because I cannot talk to you, you won't respond to me, with the implication that there is no dishonor in such shared and innocent death.[18]

We have the proposal that there are no sides, and that the sides are forever shifting, crumpling, and multiplying, disappearing and reappearing—unable to satisfactorily delineate between here and there. The spatial collapse of sides is due to the queer temporal interruption of the suicide bomber, projectiles spewing every which way. As a queer assemblage—distinct from the "queering" of an entity or identity—race and sexuality are denaturalized through the impermanence, the transience of the suicide bomber; the fleeting identity replayed backward through its dissolution. This dissolution of self into other/s and other/s into self not only effaces the absolute mark of self and other/s in the war on terror, it produces a systemic challenge to the entire order of Manichaean rationality that organizes the rubric of good versus evil. Delivering "a message inscribed on the body when no other means will get through," suicide bombers do not transcend or claim the rational or accept the demarcation of the irrational. Rather, they foreground the flawed temporal, spatial, and ontological presumptions on which such distinctions flourish.

The body of Mbembe's suicide bomber is still, however, a male one and, in that universalized masculinity, ontologically pure regardless of location, history, and context. Whereas, for Mbembe, sexuality—as the dissolution of bodily boundaries—is elaborated through the ballistic event of death, for female suicide bombers, sexuality is always announced in advance: the petite manicured hands, mystical beauty ("beauty mixed with violence"), and features of her face and body are commented on in a manner not requisite for male suicide bombers; the political import of the female suicide bomber's actions are gendered out or into delusions about her purported irrational emotional and mental distress.[19] Female suicide bombers disrupt the prosaic proposition that terrorism is bred directly of patriarchy and that women are intrinsically manifesting peace. This rationale is reinscribed, however, when observers proclaim that women cast out of or shunned by traditional compositions of gender and sexuality (often accused of being lesbians) are most likely predisposed toward violence. These discursive and bodily identity markers reflect the enduring capacities of intersectionality—we cannot leave it completely behind—but also its limitations.

Mbembe and Spivak each articulate, implicitly, how queerness is constitutive of the suicide bomber: delinked from sexual identity to signal instead temporal, spatial, and corporeal schisms, queerness is installed within as a prerequisite for the body to function symbolically, pedagogically, and performatively as it does. The dispersion of the boundaries of bodies forces a completely chaotic challenge to normative conventions of gender, sexuality, and race, disobeying normative conventions of "appropriate" bodily practices and the sanctity of the able body. Here then is a possible rereading of these terrorist bodies, typically understood as culturally, ethnically, and religiously nationalist, fundamentalist, patriarchal, and, often even homophobic, as queer corporealities. The political import of this queer rereading should not be underestimated: in the upheaval of the "with us or against us" rhetoric of the war on terror, queer praxis of assemblage allows for a scrambling of sides that is illegible to state practices of surveillance, control, banishment, and extermination. These nonexceptional, terrorist bodies are nonheteronormative, if we consider nation and citizenship to be implicit in the privilege of heteronormativity, as we should. Following from Cathy Cohen's argument that heteronormativity is as much about (white) racial and (middle- to upper-) class privilege as it is about sexual identities, identifications, and acts,[20] the (American imperialist) nation also figures as an important axis of psychic and material identification, repeatedly casting these bodies into the spotlight of sexual perversity. Through the reclamation of the nation's perverse beings across homo-hetero divides, the tenor of queerness is intrinsically antinationalist. In attending to affective corporeal queernesses, ones that foreground normativizing and resistant bodily practices beyond sex, gender, and sexual object choice, queerness is expanded as a field, a vector, a terrain, one that must consistently, not sporadically, account for nationalism and race within its purview, as well as insistently disentangle the relations between queer representation and queer affectivity. What does this rereading and rearticulation do to Cohen's already expansive notion of queer coalitional politics? What types of affiliative networks could be imagined and spawned if we embrace the already queer mechanics and assemblages—threats to nation, to race, to sanctioned bodily practices—of terrorist bodies?

Affective Queerness

These bodies are old, no doubt, but their queernesses are suggested by the intense anxieties they provoke; they trouble the nation's perimeters, from within and also from the outside, and appear to be rife with, as well as generative of, fear and danger. Why, in the name of a secular state, ban the use of head scarves for Muslim women in France, with allusions to the next targets: turbans and beards?[21] What kinds of monstrous bodies are visualized when daily the papers are plastered with turbaned al-Qaeda operatives? Why scream, "Take that turban off, you fucking terrorist"?[22] What is lost, gained, and retained in the act of shaving Saddam Hussein's beard off just hours after his purported capture? (See also the picture "Saddam's Queer Eye Makeover" and "Queer Eye for Saddam," aka "Queer Eye for the Hopeless Guy.")[23] Who is appeased through the motions of shaving the facial and head hair of prisoners before they are taken to Guantánamo Bay? These bodies are not only being commanded to the restoration of the properly visible. (The name of the detention site, Camp X-Ray, suggests in itself a profound yearning for the transparency of these bodies, the capacity to see through them and render them known, taciturn, disembodied.) In the act of removing Hussein's battered, overgrown beard, Hussein's monstrosity is renewed. We do not recognize in him the decrepit, worn, tired man found in a hole, a man whose capture has more symbolic than material utility and entails the erasure of decades of U.S. imperialist violence in the "Middle East." But do not look too closely at his eyes, for his familiarity may be lost. And it is the reterritorialization of the body that must be performed through the ritual of cutting and shaving hair, the prodding medical examinations, the prayer quarters proximate to arrows pointing to Mecca, and other forms of apparently "humane" incarceration tactics that supplement those of torture. The "detained body" is thus a machination of ceremonial scrutiny and sheer domination.

Terrorist look-alike bodies may allude to the illegible and incommensurable affect of queerness—bodies that are in some sense machined together, remarkable beyond identity, visuality, and visibility, to the realms of affect and ontology, the tactile and the sensorial. Brian Massumi concisely pinpoints the effect of affect: "The primacy of the affective is marked by a gap between content and effect: it would appear that the strength or duration of an image's effect is not logically connected to the content in any straightforward way. This is not to say there is no connection and no logic."[24] Beyond what the body looks like, then, this is also about what the queer body feels like, for the embodied and for the spectator. Reworking Michael Taussig's notion of "tactile knowing,"[25] May Joseph eloquently asserts,

> For cultures whose forms of social knowledge have been fragmented and mutated by multiple experiences of conquest and cultural contact . . . tactile practices are difficult to read and contain multiple meanings. Such exchanges are frequently informal events intrinsic to everyday life through which cultural knowledge gets cited, transmitted or re-appropriated. The senses acquire texture.[26]

As that which "immerses the senses beyond the structuring logic of vision and dislodges memory as the fascia of history,"[27] tactile knowledges install normativizing traces of danger, fear, and melancholia into the bodies of racialized terrorist look-alikes. The turban, for example, is not merely an appendage to the body. It is always in the state of becoming, the becoming of a turbaned body, the turban becoming part of the body. The head scarf, similarly (along with the burka and the hijab, often decried as masks), has become a perverse fetish object—a point of fixation—a kind of centripetal force, a strange attractor through which the density of anxiety accrues and accumulates. For the wearer, the rituals and sensations attached to these parts of the body—the smells during the weekly starching of the linens, the stretching of yards of coarse fabric to induce some softening, the wrapping and pinning of the turban into place—these are experiences in the midst of becoming qualitatively different than before.

Through queerly affective and tactile realms, the Sikh *pagri*, or turban, is acquiring the inscriptions of a (terrorist) masculinity, much in the way that veiling has been read as indicative of an other femininity. The turbaned man, no longer merely the mark of a durable and misguided tradition, a resistant antiassimilationist (albeit patriarchal) stance, now inhabits the space and history of monstrosity, that which can never become civilized. The turban is not only imbued with the nationalist, religious, and cultural symbolics of the other. The turban both reveals and hides the terrorist. Despite the taxonomies of turbans, their specific regional and locational genealogies, their placement in time and space, their singularity and their multiplicity, the turban as monolith profoundly troubles and disturbs the nation and its notions of security. Since 9/11, Sikh men wearing turbans, and mistaken for kin of Osama bin Laden, have been disproportionately affected by backlash racist hate crimes targeting Muslims and other South Asians. As a sign of guilt and also the potential redemption of that guilt, the elusive, dubious character of the turbaned man or woman could drive the onlooker crazy. It is not for nothing that in one hate crime incident after another, turbans are clawed at viciously, and hair is pulled, occasionally even cut off. The intimacy of such violence cannot be overstated. The attack functions as a double emasculation: the disrobing is an insult to the (usually) male representative (Sikh or Muslim) of the community, while the removal of hair entails submission by and to normative patriotic masculinities. The turban insinuates the constant sliding between that which can be disciplined and that which must be outlawed. Sometimes death ensues.

Through queerly affective and tactile realms, the Sikh *pagri*, or turban, is acquiring the inscriptions of a (terrorist) masculinity, much in the way that veiling has been read as indicative of an other femininity.

In relation to Sikhs, misnamed "Hindoo" during the first migrations of Sikhs to the Northwest and California in the early 1900s and now mistaken as Muslim, the hypothesis of mistaken identity as the main causal factor for post-9/11 hate crimes has been embraced by conservative and progressive factions alike. The Bush administration and progressive Sikh advocacy groups have promoted education as the primary vehicle through which to ameliorate this situation. The notion of mistaken identity relies on multiple premises: that the viewer is open to and willing to discern the visual differences between Sikh turbans and Muslim turbans; that the ideals of multiculturalism as promulgated by liberal education acknowledges that differences within difference matter. The focus on mistaken identity favors the visual experience of the turban over its affective experience, one that hails historical formations of orientalism and elicits fear, loathing, and disgust. Tactile economies reassert ontological rather than epistemological knowing and highlight touch, texture, sensation, smell, feeling, and affect over what is assumed to be legible through the visible. Furthermore, the turban wearer, usually male, bears the typically female burden of safeguarding and transmitting culture and of symbolizing the purity of nation. But this does not automatically or only feminize him; instead, the fusion of hair, oil, cloth, skin, the organic with the nonorganic, renders the turban a queer part of the body. It is this assemblage of visuality, affect, feminized position, and bodily nonorganicity that accounts for its queer figuration in the execution of a hate crime.

This queer assemblage of the turbaned terrorist speaks to the prolific fertilization and crosshatching of terrorist corporealities amid queer South Asian diasporas, bodies that must be reclaimed as queer. South Asian queer diasporas may mimic forms of (U.S.) model minority exceptionalism that posit queerness as an exemplary or libratory site devoid of nationalist impulses, an exceptionalism that narrates queerness as emulating the highest transgressive potential of diaspora. But the tensions—and overlaps—between the now-fetishized desi drag queen and the turbaned or otherwise Sikh or Muslim terrorist temper this exceptionalism. Brian Keith Axel, in his ground-clearing essay "The Diasporic Imaginary," poses two radical modifications to the study of diaspora as it has been conceived in anthropology, cultural studies, and interdisciplinary forums. Referencing his study of Sikh diasporas, he argues that "rather than conceiving of the homeland as something that creates the diaspora, it may be more productive to consider the diaspora as something that creates the homeland."[28] Axel is gesturing beyond the material locational pragmatics of the myth of return, the economic and symbolic importance of the NRI (nonresident Indian), Khalistan and Hindutva nationalist movements funded by disaporic money, or the modalities of homeland that are re-created in the diaspora. The homeland, he proposes, "must be understood as an affective and temporal process rather than a place."[29] But if not the fact of place, what impels a diasporic sensibility or collectivity?

In situating "different bodies or corporeal images and historical formations of sexuality, gender and violence" as deeply and equally constitutive of the diasporic imaginary as the place of the homeland, Axel's formulation can be productively reworked to further queer the habitus of nation and its geographic coordinates. The notion of queer diaspora retools diaspora to account for connectivity beyond or different from sharing a common ancestral homeland.[30] That is, to shift away from origin for a moment allows other forms of diasporic affiliative and cathartic entities, for Axel (and also Mbembe) primarily that of bodies and the traumas that haunt them, to show their affiliative powers. Furthermore, an unsettling of the site of origin, that is, nation as one of the two binding terms of diaspora, de facto punctures the homeland-to-diaspora telos and wrenches ancestral progression out of the automatic purview of diaspora, allowing for queer narratives of kinship, belonging, and home. The sensation of place is thus one of manifold intensities cathected through distance. The diaspora, then, for Axel, is not represented only as a demographic, a geographic place, or primarily through history, memory, or even trauma. It is cohered through sensation, vibrations, echoes, speed, feedback loops, and recursive folds and feelings, coalescing through corporealities, affectivities, and, I would add, multiple and contingent temporalities: not through an identity but an assemblage.

The corporeal images in question for Axel are the tortured bodies, not unlike those of Abu Ghraib, of Sikh male Amritdharies, those caught in civil unrest in Punjab in the mid-1980s to early 1990s and arbitrarily incarcerated by the Indian government. Again we have the appearance of the turbaned Sikh male. Axel details the mechanics of the torture:

> Often the first act is to cast off the detainee's turban. . . . For many victims, the displacement of the turban, along with the use of the hair to tie the victim down, is one of the deepest gestures of dishonor (beizatti). But after surrender and dishonor are enacted on the head, focus shifts to the genitals and anus, which become the objects of taunts and violation.[31]

Collectively, the turban, genitals, and anus take on the force of the phallus: the sexual shaming begins with the nakedness of the head and use of the otherwise pride-engendering hair to subjugate, then continues on to the habitual objects of sex. In particular, torture of the anus seeks to simulate anal sex and, thus, arouse the specter of homosexuality. The turbaned male body, now the tortured deturbaned body, is effectively rendered religiously impotent and unable to repeat its threat to national boundaries:

> National-normative sexuality provides the sanctioned heterosexual means for reproducing the nation's community, whereas antinational sexuality interrupts and threatens that community. Torture casts national-normative

The turbaned male body, now the tortured deturbaned body, is effectively rendered religiously impotent and unable to repeat its threat to national boundaries.

sexuality as a fundamental modality of citizen production in relation to an antinational sexuality that postulates sex as a "cause" of not only sexual experience but also of subversive behavior and extraterritorial desire ("now you can't be married, you can't produce any more terrorists").[32]

Sexual violence, not place, is the dominant constitutive factor of Axel's diasporic imaginary. This violence is performative in that queerness of the body is confirmed on several fronts: first, there is the queer inversion of reproductive capacity to the male terrorist body, away from the normative focus on women as reproducers of nation and culture; second, the body is symbolically stripped of its reproductive capacities, propelled into the queer realm of an antinational sexuality; temporality is re-planed because the assumption of normative familial kinship forms as engendered by generational continuity is ruptured. But, third, in line with the queer figuration of the turbaned Sikh body, this body already appears as queer, and thus the torture performs, in the citational sense, the very queer assemblage that instantiates it. The assemblage is possible not through the identity markers that encapsulate this body—Sikh, male, turbaned, heterosexual but perverse—but, rather, the temporal and spatial reorderings that the body reiterates as it is tortured. There is the doubling of time and space as the body is simultaneously refashioned for normative (Indian) national aesthetics yet cast from the nation as its reproductive capacity is castrated. Spatially situated both within and outside nation, temporally always becoming both national and its antithesis, the assemblage is momentary, fleeting even, and gives way to normative identity markers even in the midst of its newly becoming state.

It is this shift from national and regional origin to corporeal affectivity—from South Asia as unifying homeland to the assemblage of the monster-terrorist-fag[33]—in South Asia and in the diasporas, as they work together, that dislodges identity-based notions of queerness, thus problematizing queer diasporic exceptionalisms but also motivating their exponential fortification and proliferation in the first place. Queer occupation of the turbaned Sikh male and other terrorist assemblages not only counters sexual exceptionalisms by reclaiming perversion—the nonexceptional—within the gaze of national security. In the comingling of queer monstrosity and queer modernity, it also creatively, powerfully, and unexpectedly scrambles the terrain of the political within organizing and intellectual projects. These terrorist assemblages, a cacophony of informational flows, energetic intensities, bodies, and practices that undermine coherent identity and even queer anti-identity narratives, bypass entirely the Foucauldian "act to identity" continuum that informs much global LGBTIQ organizing, a continuum that privileges the pole of identity as the evolved form of Western modernity. Yet reclaiming the nonexceptional is only partially the point, for assemblages allow for complicities of privilege and the production of new normativities even as they cannot anticipate spaces and moments of resistance. Opening up to the fantastical wonders of futurity is the most powerful of political and critical strategies, whether it be through assemblage or to something as yet unknown, perhaps even forever unknowable.

Notes

Many thanks to Patricia Clough for her inspirational thinking on affect and assemblages, to Julie Rajan for her research assistance, and to Amit Rai, Katherine Sugg, David Eng, and Kelly Coogan for their feedback on earlier drafts. In memory of my brother, Sandeep.

1. Joan Scott, "Gender: A Useful Category of Historical Analysis," in *Gender and the Politics of History* (New York: Columbia University Press, 1988), 28–52.

2. In an article titled "Highlighting the Q in Iraq" ("Letters from Camp Rehoboth," 18 October 2002, www.camprehoboth.com/issue10_18_02/capitalletters.htm), Hastings Wyman argues that "for gay groups such as HRC, NGLTF, and others to take a position on a major issue that affects gay people no differently from the rest of society ultimately divides our community, dilutes our resources, and risks undermining our standing with the public."

3. Mubarak Dahir, "Stop Using Gay 'Liberation' as a War Guise," *Windy City Times*, 23 April 2003. Noting that the "forces that are supposedly emancipating our downtrodden GLBT brethren are themselves hyper-homophobic," Dahir asks, "How can anyone seriously argue that the United States military is an instrument for glbt liberation?" According to Dahir, "gay hawks" have pointed out the oppressiveness toward homosexuality of regimes in Syria and Iraq while conveniently forgetting those in Saudi Arabia and Egypt. Claiming that the lives of gays and lesbians in Iraq will change very little regardless of the ousting of Hussein, Dahir writes: "The final and perhaps most personally infuriating aspect of the hypocrisy around the argument that we are invading foreign countries in the interest of freeing gay people is the way we treat gay Arabs and gay Muslims here in the United States."

4. On gay issue versus not-gay issue organizing, see Michael Bronski, "Gay Goes Mainstream," *Boston Phoenix*, 16–23 January 2003, www.bostonphoenix.com/boston/news_features/other_stories/documents/02653048.htm.

5. Joe Crea, "Gay Sex Used to Humiliate Iraqis," *Washington Blade*, 7 May 2004.

6. Ibid.

7. Andrew Sullivan, "Daily Dish," www.andrewsullivan.com (accessed 4 May 2004).

8. Patrick Moore, "Gay Sexuality," *Newsday*, 7 May 2004.

9. In the face of the centrality of Foucault's *History of Sexuality* to the field of queer studies, it is somewhat baffling that some queer theorists have accepted

at face value the discourse of Islamic sexual repression. That is not to imply that Foucault's work should be transparently applied to other cultural and historical contexts, especially as he himself perpetuates a pernicious form of orientalism in his formulation of the *ars erotica*. Rather, Foucault's insights deserve evaluation as a methodological hypothesis about discourse.

10. But are the acts specifically and only referential of gay sex (and here, gay means sex between men)? Certainly this rendition evades a conversation about what exactly constitutes the distinction between gay sex and straight sex, and also presumes some static normativity about gender roles as well. Amnesty International is among the few that did not mention homosexuality, homosexual acts, or same-sex sexuality in its press release condemning the torture. See "USA: Pattern of Brutality and Cruelty—War Crimes at Abu Ghraib," web.amnesty.org/library/index/ENGAMR510772004.

11. José Esteban Muñoz, *Disidentifications: Queers of Color and the Performance of Politics* (Minneapolis: University of Minnesota Press, 1999), 108.

12. "Bauer Compares Vermont Gay Rights Decision to Terrorism," 27 December 1999, www.cnn.com/1999/ALLPOLITICS/storeis/12/27/campaign.wrap/Concerned Women of America (accessed 2 April 2003; this site is no longer available).

13. See usinfo.state.gov/topical/pol/terror/. For a detailed analysis of this Web site, see Jasbir K. Puar and Amit S. Rai, "The Remaking of a Model Minority: Perverse Projectiles under the Spectre of (Counter)Terrorism," *Social Text*, no. 80 (2004): 75–104.

14. This is not to disavow or minimize the important interventions that intersectional theorizing makes possible and continues to stage, or the feminist critical spaces that gave rise to intersectional analyses.

15. Achille Mbembe, "Necropolitics," *Public Culture* 15 (2003): 11–40.

16. Judith Butler, in "Sexual Inversions," writes: "The male homosexual is figured time and time again as one whose desire is somehow structured by death, either as the desire to die, or as one whose desire is inherently punishable by death" (Butler, "Sexual Inversions," in *Discourses of Sexuality: From Aristotle to AIDS*, ed. Donna Stanon [Ann Arbor: University of Michigan Press, 1992], 83).

17. Mbembe, "Necropolitics," 36.

18. Gayatri Spivak, "Class and Culture in Diaspora" (conference keynote address, "Translating Class, Altering Hospitality," Leeds University, England, June 2002).

19. Sudha Ramachandran, "Women Suicide Bombers Defy Israel," *Asia Times*, 25 October 2003, www.atimes.com/atimes/Middle_East/EJ25Ak02.html; www.guardian.co.uk/israel/Story/0,2763,428563,00.html.

20. Cathy J. Cohen, "Punks, Bulldaggers, and Welfare Queens: The Radical Potential of Queer Politics?" *GLQ* 3 (1997): 437–65.

21. *Times of India*, 23 January 2004.

22. From *Targeting the Turban: Sikh Americans and the Aversion Spiral after September 11* (2002), a documentary about hate crimes against Sikh Americans since 9/11, directed by Valarie Kaur Brar.

23. See politicalhumor.about.com/library/images/blsaddamqueereye.htm.

24. Brian Massumi, *Parables for the Virtual: Movement, Affect, Sensation* (Durham, NC: Duke University Press, 2002), 24.

25. Michael Taussig, *Mimesis and Alterity* (New York: Routledge, 1993).

26. May Joseph, "Old Routes, Mnemonic Traces," *UTS Review* 6, no. 2 (2000): 46.

27. Ibid.

28. Brian Keith Axel, "The Diasporic Imaginary," *Public Culture* 14 (2002): 426.

29. Ibid.

30. Ibid.

31. Ibid., 420.

32. Cynthia Keppley Mahmood, *Fighting for Faith and Nation: Dialogues With Sikh Militants* (Philadelphia: University of Pennsylvania Press, 1996), 40, quoted in Axel, "The Diasporic Imaginary," 420.

33. See Jasbir K. Puar and Amit Rai, "Monster-Terrorist-Fag: The War on Terrorism and the Production of Docile Patriots," *Social Text*, no. 72 (2002): 117–48.

Race, Violence, and Neoliberal Spatial Politics in the Global City

Martin F. Manalansan IV

> The city has become the sign of desire.
> —Pat Califia, "San Francisco: Revisiting the 'The City of Desire'"

What does it mean to claim a space for queers of color in the global city of New York?[1] How do queer communities of color stake out a territory beyond ghettos and enclaves and beyond demarcated moments such as Pride Days and ethnic celebrations? These questions haunt the struggles, rituals, and practices of African American, Latino, and Asian American queers as they engage with the travails of urban life today.[2] Yet, despite the centrality of the city as the site of queer cultural settlement, imagination, and evolution in the late twentieth and early twenty-first centuries, larger economic and political forces have increasingly and vociferously shaped, fragmented, dispersed, and altered many queers of color's dreams and desires.[3] These forces can be traced to the emergence of post-Fordist capitalism and its concomitant neoliberal policies and are most palpable in cities worldwide.

In the past few decades, new forms of urban governance have taken root in many cities and, in particular, global cities like New York.[4] Neoliberal policies seek to delimit governmental intervention, increase privatization, and remove the safeguards of welfare services, creating a virtual free-for-all arena for economic market competition.[5] Such policies have redrawn boundaries, neighborhoods, and lives and given rise to insidious forms of surveillance of and violence in communities of color.[6]

This essay critically examines and documents the violent remapping of lives, bodies, and desires of queers of color in contemporary New York caused by neoliberal practices. This remapping is the result of expansion of private businesses as well as city, state, and federal efforts not only in so-called crime prevention efforts and "quality of life" campaigns since the early nineties but also in what has come to be called homeland security after September 11. Using two New York City spaces, the Christopher Street piers in Manhattan's Greenwich Village and the Jackson Heights neighborhoods in Queens, I assess how various neoliberal agents and institutions such as mass media, private businesses, and the state (including the police) mediate discourses about changing urban space. By mass

Social Text 84–85, Vol. 23, Nos. 3–4, Fall–Winter 2005.

media, I include not only mainstream ones but also various publications that purport to serve the "gay community." Examples from recent gay print media show that a significant number of gay journalists and scholars are in fact complicit with neoliberal interests.

To further elucidate this contention, it important to note that neoliberal processes are partly constituted by a particular kind of sexual politics that Lisa Duggan has rightly called homonormativity.[7] Homonormativity is a chameleon-like ideology that purports to push for progressive causes such as rights to gay marriage and other "activisms," but at the same time it creates a depoliticizing effect on queer communities as it rhetorically remaps and recodes freedom and liberation in terms of privacy, domesticity, and consumption.[8] In other words, homonormativity anesthetizes queer communities into passively accepting alternative forms of inequality in return for domestic privacy and the freedom to consume.

Through ethnographic observations and analysis of everyday lives and public spaces in the two neighborhoods, I describe how homonormativity creates violent struggles around urban space by queers of color. These forms of violence are characterized by their structural character spawned by neoliberal economic, political, and cultural policies and practices. By structural violence, I mean the informal and formal processes by which institutions promote what the social theorist Roderick Ferguson has called "ideologies of discreteness,"[9] or practices that seek to demarcate and police racial, ethnic, class, and sexual spaces and boundaries, while creating physical, emotional, and symbolic brutalities and cruelties toward marginalized peoples.

This kind of violence transforms the built environment, eradicating spaces imbued with meanings that coalesce around marginalized identities. For example, Samuel Delany eloquently chronicled how new urban policies around Times Square have created new forms of policing that not only transformed the architectural landscape or built environment but also altered the lifeways of numerous groups of people of color who used to hang out on the sidewalks and corners of the area for sex, leisure, and other forms of commerce. Not only are these groups visibly disciplined, they are also sequestered at a safe distance and are typically dispersed when they are seen to be a "nuisance" or are suspected of causing public annoyance or disturbance particularly to patrons and owners of new swank businesses.[10]

To underscore the insidious ways in which homonormativity is inscribed in hegemonic discourses and participates in these ideologies of discreteness, I suggest that established authorities and institutions such as police and city government are not the only perpetrators of this form of neoliberal violence; they also include a motley of mostly white gay scholars from both sides of the political spectrum. For example, in the much-lauded book *The World Turned*, John D'Emilio, the eminent gay historian, encapsulates the contemporary queer moment as a celebratory one and goes on to enumerate the important social gains gays and lesbians have garnered in the past twenty years. By doing so, he can comment on the issue of inequality among gays and lesbians. D'Emilio, by no means a conservative, argues that the idea of racial differences and differential privilege should not be considered when coming to terms with gay oppression. At this moment of gay triumph, he posits that differences between white gays and gays of color are immaterial. He suggests that, in fact, all gays are oppressed and any move that attempts to delineate or complicate intragroup differences is an impolitic act.

> The assumption that privilege makes one politically suspect or somehow inadequate as an agent of social change also threatens to obscure the truth at the heart of our movement: *All* homosexuals are oppressed; gay oppression is real and vicious. It isn't necessary to shed extra tears for the plight of prosperous white gay men in order to acknowledge that if one scratches below the surface of any gay life, one will find a bottomless well of pain whose source is oppression. And gays with privilege risk their status and expose themselves to penalties when they make the leap to activism.[11]

On the one hand, the preceding quotation may seem to be a surprising statement coming from one of the most admired and respected progressive gay scholars and activists. However, I do not take this statement as occasion for a personal indictment against D'Emilio, whose works are to be admired, but rather as symptomatic of the insidious forces of homonormativity that encompasses political affiliations of all sorts. In her critique of gay pundits like Andrew Sullivan, Duggan argues for not dividing homonormative ideas in terms of conservative and progressive camps but rather framing these seeming political extremes as part of a continuum of ideas whose proponents are complicit with the stabilizing and normalizing of specific forms of capitalist inequalities. D'Emilio's statement is indicative of the now-emerging call for "color-blindness" within the gay community and in the larger community. This call is based on the increasing privatization of gay struggles. For example, shows like *Will and Grace* and *Queer Eye for the Straight Guy* enable the parsing of identity wherein freedom to be gay is mobilized through niche marketing. Taking this logic to the extreme, to be gay and to be free therefore means to wear Prada. In other words, identity follows consumption.

The market is constructed to be the filter of gay freedom and progress so much so that dominant discourses in the gay community disregard how this kind of freedom is predicated on the abjection of other groups of people

Taking this logic to the extreme, to be gay and to be free therefore means to wear Prada. In other words, identity follows consumption.

who are not free to consume and do not have access to these symbolic and material forms of capital. Therefore, if one were to construe the free market as a kind of competitive arena or war zone, then the unnamed enemy in neoliberal warfare is not as varied as the proclivities and activities of these diverse groups of activists and politicians. Rather, on closer inspection what is seemingly a chaotic assemblage of political culprits fuses into the figure of the female and the feminized, the foreigner, the colored, the sexually deviant and the poor. In other words, queers of color are located at the crux of veiled homonormative rhetorical machinations of mostly white gay commentators and scholars.

To better understand these rhetorical strategies, I deploy a triangulated exploration of space, race, and queerness. However, while studies of space, race, and queerness and queer identities have proliferated since the mid- to late nineties,[12] these works have largely focused on the emergent qualities and valiant struggles to claim spaces by various gays, lesbians, and other queers. Such queer spatial narratives are notably lacking in their analyses of the relationships between queer cultural production and struggles with race and political-economic processes.

The axes and intersections that provide the framework for my analysis of queers of color struggles and narratives include the redrawing of boundaries between public and private, the creation of new forms of exclusions and access, consumption and citizenship. I pose the following questions that transform the concerns I outlined above into guiding frames of analysis. How does homonormativity operate on the ground (the ethnographic question)? How does the operation of homonormativity as a body of discourses inflect and shape narratives about space and race among queers of color? Also, what other kinds of narratives about various physical and symbolic topographies are imagined and enabled by homonormative practices?

Jackson Heights: Disappearance and Emergence

Jackson Heights, like many other neighborhoods in the New York City borough of Queens, presents a kaleidoscope of communities that can be gleaned from the business signs and billboard ads along the main roads and the pedestrians who walk the streets. Sights and sounds of Spanish, Korean, Hindi, and many other languages declare the panoply of peoples and cultures that crisscross and overlap each other. Jackson Heights and Queens occupy a peculiar location in popular cartography of the city. For many people, including its own inhabitants, Jackson Heights is outside "the city" that is Manhattan. As such, it also occupies a relative outsider status in relation to the mainstream gay neighborhoods of Manhattan like the Village, Chelsea, and, recently, Hell's Kitchen. As *HX*, a popular gay magazine, puts it, Jackson Heights and the non-Manhattan neighborhoods are all "Out There," which is the category the magazine uses to catalog all the gay activities that happen beyond the glare of mainstream limelight.[13]

Jackson Heights's gay bars and other queer spaces coexist with the multiethnic enclave economies that inhabit the same geographic location. At the same time, residences of various kinds from buildings to brick townhouses or row houses span out from the main thoroughfares, particularly Roosevelt Avenue where the main arteries of the New York City subway system converge around 73rd and 74th streets.

The recent history of the neighborhood as told by my informants of queers of color, many of whom have lived in the area for more than ten years, is typically constructed not through a linear chronology but in somewhat aberrant cycles of disintegration and reconstitution of spaces. For example, as one Colombian informant told me,[14] the gay bars on Roosevelt Avenue have come and gone, including a couple of really "private" bars or hangouts one needed a password or someone from the neighborhood to gain access to. These aberrant cycles are apparent in how spaces in the neighborhood have been subject to the conflicting processes of disappearances, disintegration, disciplining as well as emergence and so-called renaissance of places and venues.

One popular narrative about the transformation of the streets in the past five to ten years is through what most informants term as a "cleaning up," not in the sense of physical hygiene but in terms of routing out queer public-sex spaces. In particular, most people would talk about Vaseline Alley, which is an area not too far away from the main thoroughfare where cruising and some form of public sex were performed. But unlike most mainstream gay narratives of urban public-sex spaces where nostalgia and sense of privilege permeate the stories, narratives around Vaseline Alley are quite different. While the Alley, according to some informants, may still be a location where illicit activities may still take place depending on the time of year and hour of the day, the place has quieted down. As one informant framed it, "the nervous energy" of lust and desire has been shunted away or, in the words of an astute queer observer, "muffled" from public view. It is now more than ever just an ordinary street in an immigrant neighborhood. At least, that is what it presents at first glance.

As one informant framed it, "the nervous energy" of lust and desire has been shunted away or, in the words of an astute queer observer, "muffled" from public view.

Nowadays, the narratives are punctuated not only by some nostalgic longing but are strongly marked by fear and some kind of disbelief and even puzzlement. Some informants were especially cognizant of the changes after September 11. While many informants who were neither South Asian nor Muslim did not readily feel any negative response immediately, after several months, they reported sightings of immigration, FBI, and CIA officials in the neighborhood, and these figured in many fearful gossip and informal accounts.

A Puerto Rican informant told me that while he initially did not see himself implicated in the imagined terrorist havens supposedly embedded in Middle Eastern and South Asian immigrant communities, he nevertheless noticed that there were more arrests and rounding up of Mexican and other Latino men, most if not all of whom were undocumented. These men typically stood around or sat on the sidewalks of Roosevelt Avenue waiting for someone in a car or van looking for cheap labor in construction, food service, and other industries to hire them. He noted that there seemed to be more surveillance of the neighborhood as evident from the increased presence of uniformed police around the public areas. He also mentioned that he has increasingly noticed individual or groups of mostly white men hanging around who clearly did not belong to the neighborhood. At the same time, he said that while the Latino men waiting and looking for work still occupy the sidewalks and are still hungry for work, he and other Latinos who are otherwise employed or who seek employment in other ways have started to not hang out in these public areas for sexual or economic purposes.

A Filipino gay man I interviewed also talked about what he perceived to be the disappearance of the groups of men that he labeled as Arabo for "Arab," for the Middle Eastern and South Asian men who used to hang out in a couple of corners and would whistle at him every time he passed by.[15] They were nowhere to be seen, and, as he said, they disappeared "like smoke" or were "in hiding." "From what?" I asked. He could only guess, "the government" or "Mister Bush."

These narratives point to how the various styles of occupying everyday public spaces have been radically altered so that an innocent staking out of public space for whatever reason can easily be couched as "loitering," "vagrancy," or a suspicious congregation of people. Thus these public spaces are subject to intense monitoring that once started with former mayor Rudolph Giuliani's "quality of life" program and now blur into questions of "national security." This is evident in my informants' lingering suspicions that the police and "other authorities" have equated the brown, black, and yellow bodies to be possible dangerous entities, purveyors of terror by reason of their color and in some instances of their so-called suspicious maleness. I coined this phrase to capture the various ways in which queers of color have taken the official state terrorist profile of a Middle Eastern or South Asian male in their teens to late forties. But while it may seem that such a profile releases "other" racial and ethnic groups such as Latino and East or Southeast Asian from being implicated in this tawdry and messy affair, several informants insists that in the gritty light of everyday life, difference is always and already suspect. As one Puerto Rican informant said, "If you are not a white man, it does not matter, you will be scrutinized. You are not an ordinary citizen. If you are a little dark, then you better watch how you walk in front of them [the police]." Therefore quotidian images of citizenship and safety in the neighborhood are encased in racialized terms and colored by fear and trepidation.

Narratives about public spaces by gay Latino and Asian men have been transformed into what Teresa Caldeira calls the "talk of crime."[16] These discourses involves a "symbolic re-ordering of the world" through "everyday narratives, commentaries, conversation and jokes that have crime and fear as their subject." While at first glance these "talks of fear and crime" might reproduce and "naturalize" stereotypes,[17] they also talk about a commonality of experience. This is not to suggest an emergence of an organic solidarity across racial lines. Rather, there is a collective acknowledgment of how these queers of color who are neither South Asian nor Middle Eastern are not free from profiling, from the racist and racializing practices of state authorities, and how they are, to some extent, in the same predicament. I suggest that this situation may become the impetus or basis for political action to which I turn in the final section.

Interestingly, the reported evacuation of particular scenes and the alleged disappearance of groups of people coincided with other discourses around Jackson Heights as the new exotic gay mecca. The Manhattan-based mainstream gay press has created travelogue-like essays about the gay attractions in the neighborhood for adventurous outsiders and Manhattanites willing to "risk" the foray into uncharted territories. Consider this passage from the recent issue of *NEXT*, a weekly guide to the city's gay activities and hangouts: "Might there be something that Manhattan snobs (like myself) are missing out on in those other boroughs? . . . To find out, a few friends and I got Metrocards, brushed up on our Spanish, prepared ourselves for the unknown, and ventured out to Jackson Heights, a racially diverse neighborhood in Queens which hosts a thriving gay scene and sublime Mexican food."[18]

Indeed, this initial passage combines the culinary and the sexual quite purposively. The main idea is that Jackson Heights is not a space but a commodity to be consumed and literally eaten up for people who will spend a few hours being temporary gay tourists. Consider the next passage from the same article:

> But don't label us Christopher Columbus just yet. It's not like we found a brand new gay scene. Jackson Heights has had a queer vibe since the 1940s.

> Local nightlife impresario, Eddie Valentine informed us that "Jackson Heights had always been a predominately [*sic*] gay neighborhood, but it's always been very quiet." The bars have been subdued, they didn't scream 'gay' because two more bars are opening up this month. I envison [*sic*] Jackson Heights becoming Chelsea with a Latin bite. And bite we did.[19]

Here are two seemingly paradoxically opposed or unrelated processes of the disintegrating and fear-laden neighborhood landscapes and an emergent and vibrant gay nightlife. But the scenarios are not of two Jackson Heights—the insider, or resident's point of view, and the outsider—but rather of a neighborhood in the throes of two interrelated and intersecting forms of violence. The narrative of emergent gay life in this "Latino version of Chelsea" is premised on the performance of consumption. Indeed, like many contemporary narratives of gay mainstreaming, the practices of touristic consumption constitute the central performative scripts of good gay citizens.

As the article suggests, Jackson Heights is something that one "bites" into. It is not a habitat or dwelling but a temporary site for leisure and space for sociality to be eaten and quickly swallowed. At the same time, the neighborhood's considerable marketing allure is its relative exoticness. Like a gay Columbus, the author of the travel guide performs the role of being able to conquer and hold at bay the other less palatable side of this location. The unsavory side includes the criminalization of South Asian and Middle Eastern people who have been gendered male and marked as sexually deviant. This situation has caused a veritable conjunction of conflicting identities and practices.

Jasbir Puar and Amit Rai powerfully recorded and analyzed the ambivalent and rather violent confrontation of immigrant heteronormativity and national xenophobia after September 11.[20] In their study, the coalescing of the images of the terrorist monster, the foreigner, and the sexually deviant into the figure of the South Asian immigrant has become evident not only in mainstream media images but also in the everyday practices of South Asian individuals and organizations—a good number of these were situated in Jackson Heights. The fear and suspicion that abound in the community have lead to extreme displays of patriotism such as the profusion of American flags on all the South Asian businesses immediately after the World Trade Center bombings and the removal of turbans as everyday wear for Sikh men. These fearful measures were performed under the duress of being questioned and surveilled for possible unpatriotic political leanings and desires. And yet, as I have suggested above, this is not the complete picture.

The narratives of fear told by a racialized, sexualized, and criminalized group of gay immigrants and the exuberant tale of an emerging gay mostly Latino culture are mutually constitutive elements of a neoliberal portrait of Jackson Heights. Such a portrait is founded on the artificial bounding of identities into discrete elements. A Latino is not an Arab or a Filipino is not the same as a Pakistani, or an immigrant is not the same as an American. Such concatenation of negations and affirmations promote facile separations of political agendas. Mainstream gay culture has been calcified into the enactments of consumption rituals—buying, eating, dancing, wearing, and, yes, even fucking. Indeed, there is rarely any mention in the gay media of these kinds of tensions between other forms of gay cultures or other communities as well as the stepped-up policing of communities of color. The connections between the common narratives of fear and the intrusions of private gay enterprise are blissfully ignored. Jackson Heights's predicament is made clearer by parallel kinds of developments in Christopher Street in Manhattan's Greenwich Village.

The Village and Christopher Street: Fenced-Out Lives

The Christopher Street piers no longer exist. As cruising and socializing areas in the seventies and eighties, they occupy an important place in the memories and imaginaries of queers, particularly queers of color. The piers were also the sites for Latino and African American queer youth who would prance around and practice their vogueing moves and conduct informal competitions and runway shows. These piers and the surrounding environs were places for queers of color to congregate and to commune. But far from being a utopic space, the piers nevertheless signify the days when queers felt they owned the sites.

Located at the intersection of Christopher Street and the West Side Highway, several of these piers jutted out into the Hudson River. Today, the spaces have been dismantled and given way to a manicured park that runs the length of the highway beyond the confines of the Village. Near its edge, instead of the rundown warehouses, you find new buildings—mostly apartment and condominium complexes rising up along the water. A fountain and several meters of wire fences mark the intersection, and a jogging, biking, or skating path threads through several blocks of the pier. While this may seem to invite more leisure activities, many of my queer of color informants said that this was not built for them. One Latino gay man said, "We don't come here to rollerblade or jog. We come here to practice our [vogueing] moves. But we are told [by the police] not to play any loud music or to carry on. How can you have a bunch of queens and not carry on?"

The Christopher Street piers no longer exist. As cruising and socializing areas in the seventies and eighties, they occupy an important place in the memories and imaginaries of queers, particularly queers of color.

Surrounding the walkways are concrete plant holders punctuated by what many queer African American and Latinos have reported as increased visible police presence. While the queers of color still try to hold court in these spaces, they can do so only at certain times, and they are definitely discouraged and disciplined from congregating in the early hours of the morning and from being too rowdy. Between 2 and 5 a.m., the police show up in full force to make sure that no trouble occurs when the bars start closing. As one African American informant said, "They want to make sure to point us to the right direction—right to the Path Train [to New Jersey] station or to the number one subway. Girl, they make sure we don't hang around and we go on right home after we have spent all our money in the bars here [in the Village]."

The present environment has led several African American and Latino queers I interviewed to remark that while many people have marveled at the area's transformation—particularly around the literal and metaphoric "cleaning up" of the piers and the surrounding streets from vagrants, "gangs," and other "unwanted" groups—they have lost something that could never be replaced: a sense of ownership of the area. Moreover, they complained that not only has the place become too expensive but it has also become hostile toward them.

One African American narrated how he and several of his friends were prevented from congregating in front of a new condominium on the West Side Highway. The building guard told them that they were scaring unit owners. The informant said, "You think we were garbage or something. So just to spite him [the guard], we turned on the boom box and strutted to Chaka and worked the sidewalk. The guard was so pissed but we didn't care."

Many of them also talked about the many ways in which they have been sequestered into particular areas. Despite the crowds of queers of color traipsing the sidewalks of Christopher Street, many still confided their feelings of being slowly eased out of the neighborhood. While queers of color frequent most of the bars on the street west of Seventh Avenue, for the past twenty years white upper-class people populated most of the surrounding residential areas. As one queer said, "We can only own Christopher Street for a few hours of the day—and for a couple of days of the week. But this is our street! How can we manage to stay here?"

No one quite knows the answer. However, these narratives can be counterposed with another emergent narrative, this time of the opulence and glamour that are part of the area's new spatial narratives. These narratives are found not only in feature articles but in real estate ads. One prime piece of real estate in particular, advertised in the *Gay City*, a mainstream gay newspaper, is actually on the other side of the Hudson and overlooks this fabled waterfront. Not surprisingly, the building is called "The Pier."

> The Pier—Rising from the Hudson, The Pier stands as the newest landmark to living on the water. Reserved for the few . . . the resident's view is majestic. . . . the Manhattan skyline seems within reach and beckons to be touched. A statement of status and choice, The Pier offers a variety of luxuries and homes melded in contemporary architecture the essence of function. The Pier is a concept of living and a measurement of worth and style. The Pier . . . like no other.[21]

The play on the word *pier* against the meaning of *peer* is quite informative. The ad's subtle use of gay lore about the piers is utilized to ironically magnify the condominium's exclusivity. It seems to suggest, "This is 'ours' yet only a select group of 'us' get to live in it." The rhetorical play parallels a neoliberal tactic that purveys inequality in the guise of similitude. In other words, much like the rhetoric of neoliberal gay pundits like John D'Emilio, the stabilization of difference is enacted to justify inequality. Indeed, the pier—both the renovated docks and the new condominiums—is about fencing off unwanted colored bodies, yet these elements of the built environment are rhetorically rendered as positive outcomes and developments for all queers. At the same time, such a declaration is possible only by symbolically and physically sequestering colored queer bodies. Colored queer bodies, if one were to dismantle the rhetoric, muddle if not muddy the "gay waters." If one were to follow D'Emilio's arguments, then, queers of color issues are rendered merely as "grievances" irrelevant to and in fact inimical to the understanding of the queer moment.

Colored queer bodies, if one were to dismantle the rhetoric, muddle if not muddy the "gay waters."

Presently, the mainstream gay agenda is preoccupied with privatized desires and issues, one of which is gay marriage. Gay marriage, according to many scholars and activists, cannot be muddied by and muddled with these other "external" issues. Marriage, like all of the other important gay agenda items, is really about keeping and maintaining the rights to privacy. Privacy was also the linchpin in the striking down of sodomy laws by the U.S. Supreme Court. Privacy and its propelling energies can uplift capitalist markets free from government intervention. Privacy is also about the needs and desires of the moneyed few who can fulfill them by indulging in the right brand of cosmetics and blue jeans and the correct exclusive home address. It is privacy, as Lisa Duggan tells us, in all its modulations and inflections, that shapes the very ethos of neoliberal homonormative conceptions of freedom—free to consume and to possess despite the hordes of lives and bodies fenced out of these extremely private and privatized domains.[22] Finally, it is privacy that induces some activists and contemporary scholars alike to parse out identities and social locations like race and sexuality as distinct stable categories and entities. Based on Roderick Ferguson's ideas, we can see that this practice of focusing on the discreteness of categories leads to the violent homonormative order of gay things, spaces, and bodies.[23]

Hopes for an Urban Democratic Future

Based on my charting of the narratives of Jackson Heights and the Greenwich Village piers, I suggest that the increasing visibility of elegant condominiums, gay bars, and gay-friendly restaurants and other businesses go hand in hand with the other narratives of decreased visibility if not obliteration of queerness and race in the city's streets and other public venues. The seeming antipodal narratives of emergence and disappearance actually mutually constitute a form of structural violence. The rise of a vibrant exclusive real estate, gay commodified businesses, and other signs of the new gentrified New York are based on the very process of eradication and disappearance of the unsightly, the vagrant, the alien, the colored, and the queer.

While these narratives of fear and of structural violence need not involve actual physical violence, reports of increased frequency of actual beatings, harassments, and assaults of queers of color actually amplify the urgency of these stories. I submit that physical violence is a more overt manifestation of structural violence. A recent report from the Anti-Violence Project,[24] a lesbian and gay agency that aims to document and fight violence against queers, has presented evidence that while the number of cases involving violence against white queers have remained constant, the number of cases against queers of colors—particularly blacks, Latinos, and, most recently, Middle Eastern and South Asian queers—have doubled if not quadrupled. The dramatic and ruthless physical violence needs to be interpreted beyond the sheer number of those actually reported and understood in terms of the thousands more cases that have gone unreported or unmarked because of fear of the police and other figures of authority. Most important, these ghastly reports also need to be read with and against the highly muted if not muffled sights and sounds of structural violence that have been steadily aimed at effacing queers of color spaces and silencing their voices.

Now the question is, what is to be done? Here again, I follow the example set out by Lisa Duggan, who looks to coalition work across identities, causes, and politics as alternative tactics to the traditional activist practices.[25] The kinds of expansive coalition work she briefly outlined in her latest book calls for dismantling the neoliberal programs that mystify and constitute inequalities and moving beyond the culture/economy split.[26] At this juncture, I go back to my initial suggestion above that the narratives of fear of queers of color need not be construed as either hysterical unfounded stories or empty useless talk. Rather, these stories can be the foundation for politicizing the citizenry and can be used as a wake-up call from the stupor of single-issue activism. As these narratives symbolically reorder the social environment, they can also serve as the pivot for mobilizing groups and constituencies to spearhead multilateral changes. Queers of color can potentially harness the fear and trepidation through a systematic and consistent organizing around cross-ethnic/racial and multisectoral issues by organizations equipped for such purposes. As possible models, Duggan points to exemplary organizations like the Audre Lorde Project, which "organizes queers of color . . . to address issues from immigration and HIV prevention, to violence and employment."[27] Drawing a partial map of the way out of the debacle, she eloquently proffers the following words: "Calls for expansive democratic publicness, *combined* with arguments for forms of individual and group autonomy, attempts to redefine *equality*, *freedom*, *justice* and *democracy* in ways that exceed their limited (neo)liberal meanings. They gesture away from *privatization* as an alibi for stark inequalities, and away from personal responsibility as an abdication of public, collective caretaking."[28]

Despite the battles and struggles that queers of color are currently waging, cities still hold the promise of redemption. For many queers, urban space offers some semblance of a possible democratic future.[29] Amid their hopes and disintegrating dreams, queers of color forge on. If, as Pat Califia has suggested, the city has become the sign of desire,[30] then New York City in the twenty-first century has become the sign and the site for the violent contestation of desire as queers of color resist and refuse the onslaught of urban neoliberal oblivion.

Notes

This article was originally presented in the annual meeting of the American Studies Association. Special thanks to Lisa Lowe for convening the panel—together with Nayan Shah, David Eng, and Rod Ferguson—and for her comments and continued support. A revised version was presented in a lecture sponsored by the Center for the Study of Sexual Cultures and the Department of Anthropology at the University of California, Berkeley. I would like to thank Lawrence Cohen, Michael Lucey, and Aihwa Ong for their insights and questions. Siobhan Somerville provided a sensitive and encouraging reading of the first draft. I thank her for her incisive comments, collegiality, and friendship. Urbana-Champaign will be bleak without her presence.

1. I am cognizant of the fact that New York has a unique function as a global city and, as such, is subject to specific if not amplified operations of neoliberalist economic, political, and cultural processes that may diverge from other urban neoliberal experiences across the world. As an anthropologist, I believe that my role is to demonstrate the particularities of neoliberalism in specific global/local spaces. See Saskia Sassen, *The Global City* (Princeton, NJ: Princeton University Press, 2001).

2. I am aware of the problems of cross-racial groupings, but I use "queers of color" here as a provisional and strategic mode of understanding commonality experiences that can become a basis for broad-based coalition while recognizing numerous forms of difference.

3. Kath Weston, "'Get Thee to a Big City': Sexual Imaginary and the Great Gay Migration," *GLQ* 2 (1995): 254–77.

4. I used neoliberal urban governance and not "gentrification" to move away from the popular notion of the latter as an organic, natural supplanting of on-site inhabitants by outside forces and agents. I wanted to highlight how New York City's neoliberal policies are not like many cities, particularly those of the third world, that are mediated by institutions like the World Bank or the International Monetary Fund; instead, the very forces at work are situated within the city itself as a global financial center.

5. For a schema of new forms of urban politics, see Margit Mayer, "Post Fordist City Politics," in *Post Fordism: A Reader*, ed. Ash Amin (Oxford: Blackwell, 1994).

6. See Andrea McArdle and Tanya Erzen, eds., *Zero Tolerance: Quality of Life and the New Police Brutality in New York City* (New York: New York University Press, 2001).

7. Lisa Duggan, "The New Homonormativity: The Sexual Politics of Neoliberalism," in *Materializing Democracy*, ed. Russ Castronovo and Dana D. Nelson (Durham, NC: Duke University Press, 2002), 173–94. See also Lisa Duggan, *Twilight of Equality? Neoliberalism, Cultural Politics, and the Attack on Democracy* (Boston: Beacon, 2003).

8. Ibid., 179.

9. Roderick Ferguson, *Aberrations in Black: Toward a Queer of Color Critique* (Minneapolis: University of Minnesota Press, 2004).

10. Samuel Delany, *Times Square Red, Times Square Blue* (New York: New York University Press, 1999).

11. John D'Emilio, *The World Turned: Essays on Gay History, Politics, and Culture* (Durham, NC: Duke University Press, 2002), 152.

12. See, for example, Gordon Brent Ingram, Anne-Marie Bouthillette, and Yolanda Retter, eds., *Queers in Space: Communities, Public Places, Sites of Resistance* (Seattle: Bay, 1997).

13. See "'Out There': The Topography of Race and Desire in the Global City," chapter 3 of my book *Global Divas: Filipino Gay Men in the Diaspora* (Durham, NC: Duke University Press, 2003). In this chapter, I argue for the intersecting "grids of difference that both fragment the queer spaces in New York City and at the same time create and constitute a unitary narrative of inside/outside and colored/white.

14. I use the term *Latino* for Spanish-speaking men for whom I was unable to get their specific ethnic identities; I use Colombian, Puerto Rican, and Mexican categories for men who self-identified as such.

15. This observation about "Arabos" has been eerily echoed by other queer Filipinos in other parts of the greater New York metropolitan area. See my essay "A Gay World Make-Over: An Asian American Queer Critique," in *Asian American Studies after Critical Mass*, ed. Kent Ono (Malden, MA: Blackwell, 2005), 104–5.

16. Teresa Caldeira, *City of Walls: Crime, Segregation, and Citizenship in Sao Paulo* (Berkeley: University of California Press, 2000), 4.

17. Ibid.

18. Art Dias, "Hitting the Jackson Heights: Chelsea with a Latin Bite. Grrrr . . . ," *NEXT*, 26 September 2003, 25.

19. Ibid.

20. Jasbir Puar and Amit Rai, "Monster, Terrorist, Fag: The War on Terrorism and the Production of Docile Patriots," *Social Text*, no. 72 (2002): 117–48.

21. *Gay City News*, 26 September–2 October 2003.

22. Duggan, "New Homonormativity," 190.

23. Ferguson, *Aberrations in Black*.

24. See www.avp.org.

25. Duggan, *Twilight of Equality*, 67–88.

26. Ibid.

27. Ibid., 87.

28. Ibid.

29. See David Bell and Jon Binnie, *The Sexual Citizen: Queer Politics and Beyond* (Cambridge: Polity, 2000), 82–95.

30. Pat Califia, "San Francisco: Revisiting the 'The City of Desire,'" in Ingram, Bouthillette, and Retter, *Queers in Space*, 177–96.

Bollywood Spectacles

QUEER DIASPORIC CRITIQUE IN THE AFTERMATH OF 9/11

Gayatri Gopinath

Since 9/11, South Asian racialization in the United States has taken place through curious and contradictory processes. Even as the "indefinite detentions" and deportations of Arabs, Muslims, and South Asians continued unabated, the last three years saw an explosion of interest in Bollywood cinema among non–South Asian audiences.[1] In March and April 2004 alone, major stories about Bollywood's moment of "arrival" in the West appeared in quick succession in *Time Out*, the *New York Times*, and the *Los Angeles Times*, to name just a few of the most visible instances of media coverage.[2] How can we account for this heightened visibility and "discovery" of Bollywood cinema at precisely the moment when South Asian communities in the United States are being more intensely surveilled, policed, and terrorized by the state than ever before? The stark contradiction between representational excess and material violence became particularly apparent to me during the 2004 Republican National Convention, as I found myself flipping through television channels hoping for some coverage of the massive protests in New York City. I came across the incongruous sight of protesters confronting a rather befuddled group of North Carolina delegates as they emerged from the latest Broadway show, none other than Andrew Lloyd Webber's Bollywood extravaganza, *Bombay Dreams*. The show was apparently a hot ticket among the RNC delegates, and its tag line—"Somewhere You've Never Been Before"—provided a colorful backdrop as the camera captured delegates admonishing protesters for preventing the police from doing their job of "keeping America safe." It seemed particularly ironic to me that the delegates occupied themselves inside Madison Square Garden with xenophobic calls for a never-ending "war on terror" while they diverted themselves outside the Garden with a brief foray into Bollywood glamour. The juxtaposition of nationalist spectacle and Bollywood spectacle may initially appear unremarkable, in the sense that *Bombay Dreams* can be seen as simply another safely multicultural, "ethnic" musical aimed at middle American consumers. One of the show's producers, in fact, stated that she "views the show as a descendant of *Fiddler on the Roof* or *The King and I*, musicals with an ethnic milieu that have universal appeal."[3] Yet I would argue that

Social Text 84–85, Vol. 23, Nos. 3–4, Fall–Winter 2005.

the ubiquity and popularity of Bollywood at this particular moment of U.S. imperialist aggression and global hegemony bears closer scrutiny, as it reveals a great deal about the complex interrelation of multiple nationalisms and diasporic formations in the context of globalization.

To fully unpack these connections, I want to suggest the necessity of what we can term a queer diasporic frame of analysis. The concept of diaspora, as we know well from Stuart Hall and other theorists of diaspora, is double-edged in that it can undercut and reify various forms of ethnic, religious, and state nationalisms simultaneously.[4] Its potential has always been that it can work to foreground notions of impurity and inauthenticity that resoundingly reject the ethnic and religious absolutism at the center of nationalist ideologies. But the danger of diaspora as a concept, ironically, is its adherence to precisely those same myths of purity and origin that seamlessly lend themselves to nationalist projects. Indeed, while the diaspora within nationalist discourse is often positioned as the abjected other to the nation, the nation also simultaneously recruits the diaspora into its absolutist logic. The millions of dollars funneled from Indian American business, religious, and political groups in the United States to support Hindu Right governments and organizations in India is but one example of how diaspora and nation can function together in the interests of corporate capital and globalization, as well as ideologies of religious, cultural, and national purity.[5]

While Hindu nationalist forces in India acknowledge the diaspora solely in the form of the prosperous, Hindu, heterosexual nonresident Indian (NRI) businessman, there exists an alternative embodiment of diaspora that remains unthinkable within this Hindu nationalist imaginary. The category of "queer" works to name this alternative rendering of diaspora and to dislodge diaspora from its adherence and loyalty to nationalist ideologies. Suturing "queer" to "diaspora" points to those desires, practices, and subjectivities that are rendered impossible and unimaginable within conventional diasporic and nationalist imaginaries. A consideration of queerness, in other words, becomes a way to challenge nationalist ideologies by insisting on the impure, inauthentic, nonreproductive potential of the notion of diaspora. Queer diasporic cultural forms suggest alternative forms of collectivity and communal belonging that redefine "home" as national, communal, or domestic space outside a logic of blood, purity, authenticity, and patrilineal descent.

The notion of a queer diaspora resonates with Roderick Ferguson's framing of a "queer of color critique." While both queer of color and queer diasporic analysis are part of a collective endeavor to reshape queer studies through a thorough engagement with questions of race, nationalism, and transnationalism, it may also be useful to explore some of the points at which the interventions and emphases of each project both intersect and diverge. In *Aberrations in Black: Toward a Queer of Color Critique*, Ferguson writes: "As the site of identification, culture becomes the terrain in which formations seemingly antagonistic to liberalism, like Marxism and revolutionary nationalism, converge with liberal ideology, precisely through their identification with gender and sexual norms and ideals. Queer of color analysis must examine how culture as a site of identification produces such odd bedfellows and how it . . . fosters unimagined alliances."[6] Ferguson suggests here how queer of color analysis can be seen as a particular reading practice that enables us to trace the convergence of what seem to be radically distinct and disparate ideologies as they shore up heteronormativity. A queer diasporic framework similarly challenges what Ferguson terms "ideologies of discreteness"[7] by identifying and unraveling those peculiar alliances, the "odd bedfellows," that emerge in the global restructuring of capital and its attendant gender and sexual hierarchies. It also names a mode of reading, of rendering intelligible that which is unintelligible and indeed impossible within dominant diasporic and nationalist logic.

While queer of color analysis identifies the U.S. nation-state and its particular mapping of racialized, gendered, and sexualized citizenship and belonging as a primary site of reference and critique, a queer diasporic analysis pays greater attention to the intimate connections between disparate diasporic and national locations as they converge in the production of "home" space. This is a particularly urgent and necessary project in the context of the Indian diaspora, given the centrality of the diaspora to the material and ideological maintenance of Hindu nationalism in India, and in light of the unholy alliance between the Hindu Right in India and the current Bush regime in the United States.[8] I do not mean to suggest here that queer of color critique and queer diasporic critique exist in a binary relation to each other, where the former is narrow, local, and national, as opposed to the latter's apparent cosmopolitanism and expansiveness. On the contrary, queer of color critique, as Ferguson articulates it, explicitly rejects the parochialism of American studies as well as the underlying heteronormativity of even its postnationalist versions. In attending to the particularities of African American racial formation, Ferguson's framing of queer of color critique allows for a wide-ranging inquiry into the racial, sexual, and gendered underpinnings of modernity and posits nonheteronormative racialized subjects as sites of knowledge that challenge the disarticulation of racial formation from national, class, gender, and sexual formations. Ferguson's analysis foregrounds the sexual and racial normativity at the heart of the liberal nation-state while pointing to the inadequacy of nation-based, conventional area-studies approaches to theorizing the production of modern racial and sexual formations.[9]

The necessity of a queer diasporic critique that unravels the relation between diaspora and dual nationalisms (both U.S. and Indian) becomes apparent when considering the current global circulation of Bollywood cinema.

Queer diasporic critique can be seen as extending this project and as its necessary complement. In the context of South Asia, the framework of a queer diaspora is crucial if we are to challenge area studies models that fail to account for the ongoing interplay between diaspora and nation, and for how heteronormativity has historically functioned as a structuring mechanism of both colonialism and nationalism in the region. Queer diasporic critique shares with queer of color critique an interest in tracing how particular racial, sexual, and gender formations engender practices and subjectivities that exceed the nation's boundaries and contest its absolutist logic. If queer of color and queer diasporic critique take to task the implicit heteronormativity within some strands of area studies, they also powerfully challenge the parochialism of some strands of queer studies by making the study of sexuality central to an anti-imperialist, antiracist project. Together queer of color and queer diasporic critique reveal the gendered and sexualized dimensions of imperial projects both domestically (in relation to U.S. communities of color) and internationally. Indeed, at this current moment of U.S. imperial aggression, the indispensability of this new formulation of queer studies has never been clearer.

The necessity of a queer diasporic critique that unravels the relation between diaspora and dual nationalisms (both U.S. and Indian) becomes apparent when considering the current global circulation of Bollywood cinema. Bollywood has, of course, always been a global cinema,[10] but what is new, as I have suggested, is its popularity and visibility in the West, outside the South Asian diasporic audiences that have historically formed its largest viewership. This newfound popularity can be traced to how the genre and idiom of Bollywood cinema are being rapidly translated into terms more in keeping with the narrative and representational conventions of Hollywood cinema. We can identify three distinct but interconnected ideological projects where this appropriation and translation of Bollywood cinema is taking place: first, in a U.S. nationalist project; second, in an Indian diasporic liberal feminist project; and third, in an Indian nationalist project. Scrutinizing the deployment of Bollywood in each project reveals how popular culture becomes the contested terrain for consolidating ideologies of nation, race, gender, and sexuality. Crucially, the effacement of queer female desire and subjectivity marks each discursive site. This effacement, I would argue, is hardly incidental; rather, it must be understood as a constitutive absence in that it indexes the successful translation of Bollywood to Hollywood and is precisely what enables each of these ideological projects to function seamlessly.

The anecdote with which I began this essay is a telling instance of how the translation of a Bollywood genre and idiom operates within the context of a U.S. nationalist project. The move to make Bollywood intelligible to non–South Asian audiences is nowhere more apparent than in the transfer of *Bombay Dreams*, originally a British product, to Broadway. The *New York Times* reported how the show had to be completely overhauled in terms of narrative, score, and design as it moved from targeting a primarily British Asian audience in London to a predominantly white one on Broadway. A cover story in the *Los Angeles Times* on both the show and Bollywood in general sums up much of the media coverage on Bollywood's "emergence" in the West. The author writes, "The golden age of Hollywood has moved to India. . . . These Bollywood films will bring you back to an era, long gone in our culture, when audiences demanded a lot of entertainment and had the wherewithal to enjoy it when it arrived. In our super-stressed age, it's positive tonic to act as if we have that kind of time, even if we really don't."[11] A subsequent *New York Times* article echoes these sentiments, stating, "Bollywood has kept alive the vibrant, sumptuous spectacle that Hollywood has all but abandoned."[12] Such statements reassert a familiar colonial, teleological narrative of modernity, where Bollywood embodies the past of Western cinematic history, and of the West as a whole, in that it is temporally anterior to Western representational regimes. The "we" in these comments interpellates an implicitly white Western viewer, where Bollywood enables "us" to come face to face with an exotic other that is uncannily familiar: "we" confront an earlier version of ourselves, one that is faintly recognizable while retaining a pleasurable frisson of otherness. The oscillation between sameness and difference, as Homi Bhabha has shown,[13] is the very structure of colonial subjectification that we find today reanimated in a post-9/11 racial landscape.

This strategy of containment of the racial/religious/cultural other through the consumption of Bollywood spectacle is one that is, not surprisingly, clearly gendered and heterosexualized. What is particularly striking in much of the media coverage of Bollywood is the hypervisibility and fetishization of South Asian women's bodies, framed as infinitely available to a heterosexual white Western gaze.[14] This discursive hypervisibility of South Asian women's bodies starkly contrasts with the literal effacement and invisibilization of South Asian men's bodies as they are increasingly being "disappeared" by the state. Martin Manalansan's recent study of the changing racial, sexual, and class landscape of Queens, New York, details how the months following 9/11 saw the ominous disappearance of South Asian men who used to populate the storefronts and street corners of Jackson Heights, a predominantly immigrant neighborhood in Queens. As one of Manalansan's Filipino informants commented about the men, "Suddenly they were just gone, they vanished like smoke."[15] In the context of this erasure of large numbers of Muslim men from the city's public space, as they are banished to a no-man's-land of infinite detentions and deportation proceedings, it would be a mistake to dismiss the media blitz on Bollywood as simply another benign popular cultural fad. Rather, the recent fascination with Bollywood cinema is inseparable from the material and representational violences currently being enacted on South Asian communities in the United States.

Chandan Reddy has noted that "as an imperial state . . . the U.S. government has expanded its governance of racialized non-nationals in the name of guaranteeing the citizen's liberty: the racialized immigrant, the black incarcerated, the enemy combatant, the Afghani, and the Iraqi are just some of the legally created categories against which the national citizen is both defined and materially supported."[16] Similarly, Jasbir Puar and Amit Rai detail how racial discourses after 9/11 have produced "hypervisible icons" such as the "monster-terrorist-fag" that serve to both quarantine racial and sexual others and transform them into docile patriots.[17] In light of these observations by Reddy and Puar and Rai, the fetishization of Bollywood as sexualized and gendered spectacle must be understood as yet another discursive mechanism that regulates and disciplines South Asian populations in the United States. The Bollywood boom, in this context, incorporates South Asians into the U.S. national imaginary as pure spectacle to be safely consumed while keeping intact their essential alienness and difference; such an incorporation holds safely at bay those marginalized noncitizens who function under the sign of terrorist and "enemy within." We can mobilize queer diasporic critique as it intersects with queer of color critique here to name an oppositional subject position to the neoliberal citizen subject that provides a space from which to challenge the construction of South Asian bodies as either inherently criminal and antinational or multicultural and assimilationist.

The translation of Bollywood into terms that are intelligible and familiar to audiences steeped in Hollywood conventions invariably entails the erasure of queer female bodies, desires, and pleasures. This erasure is apparent not only in the mainstream manifestations of the Bollywood boom that I have referenced thus far but perhaps more surprisingly in the work of a new crop of Indian diasporic feminist filmmakers such as Mira Nair, Deepa Mehta, and Gurinder Chadha. As I argue in greater detail elsewhere,[18] these filmmakers are in no small part responsible for this translation of Bollywood into Hollywood,[19] in that they act as modern-day tour guides that in effect "modernize" Bollywood form and content for non–South Asian audiences.[20] We can read Mira Nair's *Monsoon Wedding*, for instance, as a diasporic feminist rescripting of the Bollywood genre of the wedding movie; Nair's film specifically references the 1994 Bollywood megahit *Hum Aapke Hain Koun . . . !* (*Who Am I to You!*), directed by Sooraj R. Barjatya. For all its religious and political conservatism, I argue that this earlier film opened up the possibility of queer female desire in a way that *Monsoon Wedding* quite categorically shuts down. Indeed, the possibilities of female homoeroticism that we see in *Hum Aapke Hain Koun . . . !* are sacrificed in *Monsoon Wedding* in order for a modern, heterosexual, liberal feminist subject to emerge. We can trace a similar dynamic in other films by South Asian diasporic feminist filmmakers that purport to "update" the Bollywood genre; in each case, it is precisely the evacuation of queer female desire that enables a heterosexual feminist subject to come into being.[21]

The translation and transformation of a Bollywood idiom is also evident in films emerging out of the Bollywood film industry itself. Just as *Monsoon Wedding* "updates" the Bollywood genre of the wedding movie, a recent Bollywood hit such as Nikhil Advani's *Kal Ho Naa Ho* (*Tomorrow May Never Come*, 2003), modernizes the classic Bollywood genre of the buddy movie. *Kal Ho Naa Ho*, which is set in New York City, shares with *Monsoon Wedding* an anxiety around representing a particularly "modern" Indian transnational subject. As such, both films attempt to reverse the colonial telos so evident in mainstream appropriations of Bollywood that situates it (and South Asia in general) in terms of a prehistory of Hollywood cinema and the West. In Nair's film, it is a liberal feminist narrative of female self-empowerment that confers modernity onto its characters; in *Kal Ho Naa Ho*, curiously, it is male homosexuality that marks and consolidates this newly emergent transnational Indian subject as fully modern. The film in effect "outs" the representational conventions of the Bollywood buddy movie by making explicit the genre's latent homoeroticism. *Kal Ho Naa Ho*'s pointed references to male homosexuality serve to mark the increasing modernity and cosmopolitanism of Bollywood cinema itself, as it comes to more closely approximate some of mainstream Hollywood's strategies of gender and sexual representation.

In one telling scene, for instance, the film's male hero, Amman, is found in bed with his male best friend by the friend's housekeeper, a sari-clad, bindi-wearing elderly Indian woman named Kanthabehn. Kanthabehn is horrified by what looks like illicit sexual activity between the two men. The scene is predictably played for laughs, at Kanthabehn's expense, as Amman proceeds to deliberately heighten the misrecognition by caressing his friend and making salacious double entendres. This misrecognition of the two men as "gay," and Amman's willingness to perform this identity, serves to underscore the modernity and mobility of the two men over and against Kanthabehn's fixity, recalcitrance, and untranslatability. She remains an anachronistic figure quite literally out of time and out of place in the newly globalized landscape that the film maps out. Hopelessly mired in "tradition" and as the apparent marker of normative gender and sexual ideologies, she functions purely instrumentally, as it is her gaze

Within the frame of U.S. nationalism, the spectacular hetero- sexualization of South Asian women's bodies conceals the simultaneous disappearance of South Asian men and transforms South Asians into an eminently consumable multicultural commodity.

that allows the men to be read as modern, transnational, cosmopolitan, and mobile subjects.

Thus in all three sites where we see a Bollywood idiom being evoked and transformed, the concomitant absence of queer female desire and subjectivity is crucial to each project's ideological coherence. Within the frame of U.S. nationalism, the spectacular heterosexualization of South Asian women's bodies conceals the simultaneous disappearance of South Asian men and transforms South Asians into an eminently consumable multicultural commodity. In a diasporic feminist project such as *Monsoon Wedding*, or in a film that betrays the anxieties of Indian nationalism such as *Kal Ho Naa Ho*, the evacuation of queer female desire purchases the modernity of the emergent transnational Indian subject, one that is newly coded as "feminist" or "gay." It is only by deploying a queer diasporic framework that we can read the ways in which these seemingly disparate and disconnected projects converge around the rendering of queer female desire and subjectivity as impossible and unimaginable.

If the absence of queer female desires, bodies, and subjectivities is indeed constitutive of these various ideological projects, I want to end by pointing to queer diasporic culture's powerful alternative narratives to such literal and discursive effacements. The work of the British Asian photographer Parminder Sekhon, for instance, removes queer female desire from a logic of impossibility by installing it at the very heart of the "home" as both national and diasporic space. In so doing, queer feminist work such as Sekhon's fulfills the radical potential of the notion of a queer diaspora, a potential foreclosed by the availability of gay male desire to recuperation within patriarchal narratives of "home," diaspora, and nation in a globalized landscape. By shifting from a focus on the routes traveled by Bollywood cinema to the work of an individual artist such as Sekhon, I do not mean to reinstate a familiar opposition between the industrial dominant versus the subversive alternative.[22] Indeed, this essay has turned a critical eye not so much on the genre and idiom of Bollywood cinema itself but on its evocation, translation, and transformation in different ideological projects—even those (such as that of liberal feminism) that proclaim their ostensibly liberatory, progressive politics. Similarly, Sekhon's work is not purely redemptive but rather bears the marks of the same teleological narratives of modernity and progress that structure hegemonic nationalist and diasporic ideologies. At the same time, however, her images critique and lay bare the very production of South Asian bodies—particularly female bodies—as pure spectacle that we see in the various uses of a Bollywood idiom. By moving from the United States to the UK, I am pointing to the need to produce an analytic framework supple enough to engage multiple national sites simultaneously and to track the transnational traffic of cultural and political influences between these diasporic locations.

Sekhon is well known in the black British arts scene because of her work in the 1990s on a series of public service posters on HIV/AIDS targeted to South Asian communities in the UK. Similar to the interventionist graphics of Women's Health Action and Mobilization (WHAM!) and other activist arts collectives in the United States in the early 1990s, many of Sekhon's images used the idiom of glossy Benetton or Gap ads to insert into public space those lives and bodies—queer, brown, HIV+—studiously effaced within a dominant nationalist and diasporic imaginary. The collapse of public and private that characterizes her work is particularly apparent in her documentation of queer South Asian life in London: her photographs are populated by glamorous South Asian butch-femme couples, the drag queens of Club Kali (London's queer South Asian night club), and drag kings who nostalgically evoke the masculinity of Bollywood film stars of the 1940s and 1950s. These images do the crucial work of providing a rich, material archive of queer South Asian public culture and attest to the unceasingly imaginative ways in which queer diasporic communities carve out literal and symbolic spaces of collectivity in inhospitable and hostile landscapes.

In one of her most compelling series of photographs, titled "Urban Lives," Sekhon uses the streets of predominantly South Asian neighborhoods in London as a backdrop for portraits of paired figures, one nude and one clothed. The images are named for the streets and neighborhoods in which the figures are situated—Tooting, Bethnal Green, Whitechapel, Southall—and provide a litany of geographic locales that evoke a history of working-class, South Asian settlement in London. The queer art critic Cherry Smyth writes of her initial reaction to the images as follows: "For me, they have something of the arousal and alarm of seeing my first nude photograph: here are Asian queers naked in the streets. Here are queer Muslims, naked in the streets. Nothing is happening to them. Nothing is said or done to them."[23] Smyth succinctly captures how Sekhon's images cull their power from simultaneously evoking both the extreme vulnerability and the defiance of queer racialized bodies as they lay claim to public space. As such, they force the viewer to read them not simply as static visual artifacts but rather as archival evidence of a live performance, with the threat of physical violence that such a performance evokes.

The interplay between bodily vulnerability and defiance is most notable in a particularly startling and moving photograph titled "Southall Market," where Sekhon pairs her own nude, pierced body with that of her elderly mother, in a *salwar kameez* and woolen sweater, as they stand in front of a market in Southall, the South Asian neighborhood where Sekhon grew up and her mother still lives. The mother grips the handle of a battered shopping cart as she, like Sekhon, gazes directly into the camera. Behind them is the detritus of the market—empty stalls, discarded cardboard boxes, and packing crates. The light is indeterminate: it could be early morning or twilight, the low clouds and uniform grayness of the sky reflected in the rain-slicked pavement on which the two women stand. As a visual artifact, "Southall Market" is immediately intelligible within a number of "ready-made interpretive frames":[24] if read through the lens of a conventional liberal feminist or "GLBT" framework, the photograph seems to suggest an easy equation of queerness (embodied by Sekhon) with modernity, visibility, sexual liberation, and revelation, which is set over and against the tropes of "tradition," concealment, secrecy, and modesty (embodied by her mother). Indeed, the positioning of Sekhon, slightly in front of her mother, supports such a reading. In staging this series of binary oppositions—tradition/modernity, secrecy/disclosure, invisibility/visibility, queer/straight, first generation/second generation—the photograph evokes what Lisa Lowe terms "the master narratives of generational conflict and filial relation" that characterize dominant representations of South Asian immigrant existence in the UK. As such, the image can be seen to "displac[e] social differences into privatized familial opposition"[25] in a way that fits squarely into British nationalist discourse around unassimilable Asian immigrants, a discourse that occludes the British state's central role in naturalizing and indeed legislating patriarchal familial relations in its production of the "Asian family."[26]

"Southall Market," then, cannot be understood as purely resistant to hegemonic structures of race, sexuality, nation, or gender any more so than Bollywood cinema can be understood as purely complicit with these structures. Rather, it is the uses to which these cultural texts are put and the circuits of their reception that determine their meanings. This is where the necessity of a queer diasporic analysis becomes most apparent. As Stephen Wright, in his discussion of colonial-era, anthropological photographs of young girls in Papua New Guinea, reminds us, "Photographs trace multiple trajectories: for all their superficial fixity and their inclusion in structures like the archive that seek to contain them, they are processual and constantly in motion. What brings meanings to photographs are performances of them, specific readings and enactments. What is important is not so much what the image contains, a meaning that resides within it, but what is brought to it, how it is used, and how it is connected to various trajectories."[27] Following Wright, we can understand a queer diasporic reading practice as a kind of critical performance, one that restores a multivocality to Sekhon's photograph that a conventional liberal feminist or queer reading would deny. Reading the image through a queer diasporic frame renders it intelligible outside a teleological narrative of modernity and instead allows different historical and social contexts to come into view. "Southall Market," as well as Sekhon's other images of naked Asian bodies on London streets, places the viewer in the uncomfortable position of voyeur, in that it conjures forth a history of colonial (and specifically orientalist) practices of photography that fix "native" women as pure spectacle. But if colonial photography decontextualizes its objects and cuts them off from all meaningful social relations, Sekhon's photographs radically recontextualize them, transforming objects into subjects by situating them within the banal details of the everyday—shopping for groceries on a Sunday morning, for instance—and in a paired relation to each other. Thus while "Southall Market" certainly evokes the ambivalent relation of undutiful queer daughters to immigrant mothers who seek to inculcate them into heteronormative domesticity, the image also suggests a more complex relay of desire and identification between the bodies of mother and daughter. Sekhon's queerness is formed in and through her relation to "home" space, even as it radically disrupts and reterritorializes this space. Her nude body places queer female subjectivity at the very heart of diasporic public cultural space. We glimpse here an alternative construction of diaspora organized around queer, female lives, desires, bodies, cultures, and collectivities that remains utterly unintelligible and unimaginable within dominant state and diasporic nationalist frameworks, as well as within more conventional feminist or queer readings of the image.

I close with this evocation of Sekhon's work because it suggests how queer diasporic cultural forms contest the modes of hypervisibility, spectacularization, and effacement through which South Asian bodies appear or disappear in the dominant representational regimes of this particular historical juncture. But her work does not simply provide a corrective to the deployments of gender and sexuality in the various ideological projects I have examined here. Rather, it underscores how a queer diasporic framework offers us a reading practice that enables us to "see" differently, to identify the places where seemingly discrete ideological projects intersect, and to suggest, to borrow a phrase from Dipesh Chakravarty, "other ways of being in the world."[28]

Notes

I am grateful to David Eng and the anonymous readers from the *Social Text* collective for their invaluable suggestions on an earlier version of this essay.

1. The phrase *Bollywood cinema* refers to Hindi-language films from the Bombay film industry, the largest and most influential sector of Indian commercial cinema. For recent book-length analyses of Bollywood cinema, see Lalitha Gopalan, *Cinema of Interruptions: Action Genres in Contemporary Cinema* (London: BFI, 2003); Vijay Mishra, *Bollywood Cinema: Temples of Desire* (New York: Routledge, 2002); and Madhava Prasad, *Ideology of the Hindi Film: A Historical Construction* (New Delhi: Oxford University Press, 1998).

2. With titles like "Salaam New York!" (in *Time Out*) and "Salaam L.A.!" (in the *Los Angeles Times*), these articles betray a numbing sameness in their recycling of a limited number of orientalist tropes and imagery. See Tanuja Desai Hidier, "Salaam New York!" *Time Out New York*, 25 March–1 April 2004, 12–29; Kenneth Turan and Susan Carpenter, "Salaam L.A.!" *Los Angeles Times Weekend Calendar*, 15 April 2004.

3. Zachary Pincus-Roth, "The Extreme Makeover of 'Bombay Dreams,'" *New York Times*, 18 April 2004.

4. Stuart Hall, "Cultural Identity and Diaspora," in *Theorizing Diaspora*, ed. Jana Evans Braziel and Anita Mannur (Malden, MA: Blackwell, 2003), 245.

5. Another stark illustration of diaspora's double-sided character was apparent during the savage state-sponsored violence against Muslims in Gujarat, India, in February 2002. The Hindu nationalist state government in Gujarat received the support of NRIs even while other anticommunalist NRI organizations in New York and San Francisco mobilized against the violence and the government's complicity in the killing and displacement of thousands of Indian Muslims. For an analysis of diasporic support for the Hindu Right in India, see Vijay Prashad, "Suburban Whites and Pogroms in India," www.zmag.org/sustainers/content/2002–07/14prashad.cfm (accessed 15 September 2004; this site is no longer active).

6. Roderick Ferguson, *Aberrations in Black: Toward a Queer of Color Critique* (Minneapolis: University of Minnesota Press, 2004), 3.

7. *Ibid.*, 4.

8. For a persuasive analysis of how the alliance between the Bush regime, the Hindu nationalist Bharatiya Janata Party in India, and the Sharon government in Israel constitutes a new "global Right," see Vijay Prashad, *Namaste Sharon: Hindutva and Sharonism under U.S. Hegemony* (New Delhi: LeftWord, 2003).

9. Rod Ferguson, e-mail message to author, 23 September 2004. My gratitude to Rod Ferguson for helping me begin articulating the differences and similarities between queer of color and queer diasporic critique.

10. For various accounts of its circulation outside India, see Brian Larkin, "Indian Films and Nigerian Lovers: Media and the Creation of Parallel Modernities," *Africa* 67 (1997): 406–39; Mark Liechty, "Media, Markets, and Modernization: Youth Identities and the Experience of Modernity in Kathmandu, Nepal," in *Youth Cultures: A Cross-Cultural Perspective*, ed. Vered Amit-Talai and Helena Wulff (London: Routledge, 1994), 166–201; Minou Fuglesang, *Veils and Videos: Female Youth Culture on the Kenyan Coast* (Stockholm: Studies in Anthropology, 1994).

11. Turan and Carpenter, "Salaam L.A.!"

12. A. O. Scott, "From Breezy Bollywood, Film Anything but Vérité," *New York Times*, 16 April 2004.

13. Homi Bhabha, *The Location of Culture* (New York: Routledge, 1994), 85–92.

14. The cover image of *Time Out*, for instance, features the curvaceous stars of *Bombay Dreams*, supplemented by the tagline "Spice Girls," while the *Los Angeles Times* cover depicts women in blue body paint and gold headdresses.

15. Martin Manalansan, "Race, Violence, and Queer Citizenship in the Global City" (paper presented at the American Studies Association Conference, Hartford, CT, 17 October 2003).

16. Chandan Reddy, "They Cannot Represent Themselves, They Must Be Represented: A Queer of Color Critique of Neo-liberal Citizenship" (paper presented at the Association of Asian American Studies Conference, San Francisco, 10 May 2003).

17. Jasbir Puar and Amit Rai, "Monster, Terrorist, Fag: The War on Terrorism and the Production of Docile Patriots," *Social Text*, no. 72 (2002): 118–48.

18. Gayatri Gopinath, *Impossible Desires: Queer Diasporas and South Asian Public Cultures* (Durham, NC: Duke University Press, 2005).

19. Indeed, Gurinder Chadha's latest feature is titled *Bride and Prejudice*, a Bollywood-influenced adaptation of Jane Austen's *Pride and Prejudice*.

20. For a much more detailed analysis of these films than is possible here, see Gopinath, *Impossible Desires*.

21. In Deepa Mehta's *Bollywood/Hollywood*, queerness conveniently resides on the body of the loyal male servant, who has a double life as a drag queen in a local gay bar. Similarly in Gurinder Chadha's *Bend It Like Beckham*, queerness resides not on the body of the football-loving female protagonist but rather on her best male friend. Both films once again use the gay male figure as the "real" queer character in the film.

22. I thank an anonymous reader from the *Social Text* collective for bringing this point to my attention.

23. Cherry Smyth, "Out of the Gaps: The Work of Parminder Sekhon," in *Red Threads: The South Asian Queer Connection in Photographs*, ed. Poulomi Desai and Parminder Sekhon (London: Diva, 2003), 108.

24. Christopher Wright, "Supple Bodies: The Papua New Guinea Photographs of Captain Francis R. Barton, 1899–1907," in *Photography's Other Histories*, ed. Christopher Pinney and Nicolas Peterson (Durham, NC: Duke University Press, 2003), 150.

25. Lisa Lowe, *Immigrant Acts: On Asian American Cultural Politics* (Durham, NC: Duke University Press, 1996), 63.

26. For an analysis of how British immigration laws in the 1960s and 1970s legislated heteronormative familial arrangements within immigrant communities, see Anna Marie Smith, *New Right Discourse on Race and Sexuality: Britain 1968–1990* (Cambridge: Cambridge University Press, 1994), 181.

27. Wright, "Supple Bodies," 166.

28. Dipesh Chakravarty, *Provincializing Europe: Postcolonial Thought and Historical Difference* (Princeton, NJ: Princeton University Press, 2000), 66.

You Can Have My Brown Body and Eat It, Too!

Hiram Perez

> They say when trouble comes close ranks, and so the white people did.
> —Jean Rhys, *Wide Sargasso Sea*

Queer theory is very particular about the kinds of trouble with which it troubles itself. The problem of race in particular presents queer theory with dilemmas over which it actively untroubles itself. I speculate in this essay on the resistance within establishmentarian queer theory to thinking race critically, a resistance that habitually classifies almost any form of race studies as a retreat into identity politics. This defensive posture helps entrench institutionally the transparent white subject characteristic of so much queer theorizing. Queer theorists who can invoke that transparent subject, and choose to do so, reap the dividends of whiteness.[1]

In addition to plotting an inside and out of queer theory, I begin to set down with this essay a demystification of the primitive, exotic, or "brown" body commodified by dominant gay male culture. I propose regarding that brown body as an axis in the formation of a cosmopolitan gay male identity and community. More specifically, I argue that this brown body mediates gay male shame. These preliminary speculations are prompted by my confrontation with queer theory at the "Gay Shame" conference at the University of Michigan, 27–29 March 2003. The location and date are significant to situating this conference historically, especially for a discussion of identity politics in higher education. Gay Shame occurred within a week of the U.S. invasion of Iraq and in the midst of the *Grutter v. Bollinger* (2003) and *Gratz v. Bollinger* (2003) affirmative action cases involving the University of Michigan.

I was invited to participate at the conference after contacting its organizers and expressing my interest as someone working on the relationship between shame and racial embodiment. Upon arriving at Ann Arbor, I was startled to learn that of the approximately forty guests, I was the only invited queer person of color present. (Samuel Delany had been invited but canceled.) Although women of color students, faculty, and staff attended the proceedings, none from outside the university were invited as guest speakers. The schedule included some of the most prominent names in queer theory, making the absence of the many scholars of color publish-

Social Text 84–85, Vol. 23, Nos. 3–4, Fall–Winter 2005.

A distressing racialized division of labor resulted at Gay Shame. White folks performed the intellectual labor while black and brown folks just plain performed, evidently constituting the spectacle of gay shame.

ing important work on race and sexuality that much more striking. Events included a screening of Andy Warhol's *Screen Test #2* (starring Mario Montez); a performance by Vaginal Davis, "Intimacy & Tomorrow"; remarks on the topic of gay shame by the conference's organizers, David Halperin and Valerie Traub; and a discussion with Douglas Crimp about his reading of the Warhol film. Mario Montez, a Puerto Rican drag queen also featured in films by Jack Smith, and Davis, a black performance/conceptual artist and self-proclaimed "ghetto androgenue," provided the conference with what I argue constitute the prerequisite "brown" bodies for prevailing recuperations of gay shame.[2] They embodied Gay Shame's imagined prehistory. While Davis's performances may disrupt such objectifications, I do not include her as one of the queer of color invited speakers theorizing gay shame because she was not presented as such. "Intimacy & Tomorrow" was scheduled at 9 p.m. on 27 March, following a champagne reception and the Warhol screening. Since the conference was billed as a two-day event, it is safe to presume that *Screen Test #2* and "Intimacy & Tomorrow" were not scheduled as part of the conference proceedings proper, occurring over 28–29 March. Warhol's work was attended to by Douglas Crimp during the opening discussion on Friday, 28 March. No such discussion was scheduled to address Davis's performance, despite the prominent critical attention to her work by José Muñoz.

A distressing racialized division of labor resulted at Gay Shame. White folks performed the intellectual labor while black and brown folks just plain performed, evidently constituting the spectacle of gay shame. While race consciousness continues to function as the false consciousness of establishmentarian queer theory, I argue in this essay that race makes all the difference for Gay Shame—its eponymous first international conference, its prevailing theoretical formulations, its primal scenes. A great deal of queer theorizing has sought to displace identity politics with an alternative anti-identitarian model, often—and perhaps disingenuously—christened "the politics of difference." This model accommodates familiar habits of the university's ideal bourgeois subject, among them, his imperial gaze, his universalism, and his claims to a race-neutral objectivity. It is not surprising then to find buried underneath the boot of this establishmentarian anti-identity all sorts of dissident bodies.

In her article "Against Proper Objects" (1997), Judith Butler revisits an earlier collaboration with Biddy Martin. Asked to edit a special issue of the journal *Diacritics* dedicated to gay and lesbian studies, Butler and Martin "broadened the scope of that request to include work that interrogates the problem of cross-identification within and across race and postcolonial studies, gender theory, and theories of sexuality."[3] Assessing three years later this critical challenge, Butler determines that queer theory has resisted the call for boundary crossings that she and Martin first put forth in 1994. Echoing the concerns originally voiced in Martin's essay, "Sexualities without Gender," Butler expresses alarm over queer theory's wholesale transition from gender to sexuality as the proper object of its analysis. The shift from gender to sexuality does not effectively anticipate how institutionalized patriarchy and racism might be retrenched precisely as a result of this transition.

Informed at Gay Shame—and reminded several times since then—that criticisms identical to mine have recurred for over a decade, I find it instructive to revisit this earlier writing on queer theory's negotiations of identity. The interrogation into cross-identifications proposed by Martin and Butler remained unrealized nearly a decade later at Gay Shame; the resistance to such interrogations strikes me as fairly symptomatic of the present state of queer theorizing in its institutionalized forms. I share Biddy Martin's faith in the potential of queer theory to complicate questions of identity and power, but I also wish to pursue her argument that queer theorizing derails that potential by conceiving both gender and race in terms of a "fixity and miring" that provide the ground for a figural and performative sexuality.[4]

I interrogate in this essay the cross-identifications specifically occasioned by Gay Shame to set in relief the often transparent alignments of queer theory with systemic racial domination and violence. However, I also revisit queer theory's promise to "complicate assumptions about routes of identification and desire,"[5] inspired by Butler's and Martin's still-pressing, even if long-expired, solicitation. The brown body's mediations of shame, queer theorizing, and gay male cosmopolitanism provide the cross-identifications on which I focus. My own body included, the brownness contested at Gay Shame comprised a further episode in the overdetermined black/white opposition that characterizes U.S. histories of racialization. The work of critical race theory, and in particular Cheryl Harris's essay, "Whiteness as Property," charts the convergence of U.S. racial formation with property rights and the doctrines of liberalism. Harris argues that an unacknowledged "property interest in whiteness . . . forms the background against which legal disputes are framed. . . . Through this entangled relationship between race and property, historical forms of domination have evolved to reproduce subordination in the present."[6] I examine in this essay how the brown body marks yet another evolution of this entanglement. At Gay Shame, brown bodies were allowed "access"—if it can be called that—only as spectacle for the consumption of gay cosmopolitanism.

Those stakes not only include whiteness, masculinity, and even heteronormativity but perhaps also do so in uniquely American formations. The queer establishment's desires and identifications align not-so-queerly with those of U.S. nationalism.

Queer Patriot Acts

In the weeks following the Michigan fiasco, a number of allies reported to me hearing complaints that Gay Shame had been "hijacked by identitarian politics"—that Gay Shame in fact had been a great conference until its hijacking. Needless to say, I found this language staggering, especially so the use of the word *hijacked*. My anger at the conference resurfaced. But I was grateful, too, for how perfectly the phrase "hijacked by identitarian politics" condensed for me the political dynamics of establishmentarian queer theory. In the era of the "war on terrorism" and the USA PATRIOT Act,[7] the word *hijacked* invokes the rhetoric of national belonging—and not belonging. The restriction of brown bodies from queer theory's institutional spaces shares ideological underpinnings with the expulsion of brown bodies from the nation-state.

The Patriot Act demonstrates how dissidence is stigmatized onto bodies. The very presence of dissident bodies—or rather the unacceptable metaphysics of this presence as distinguished from objectification as spectacle—also constitutes a hijacking. Brown bodies must never improvise on their brownness. Whiteness experiences such improvisations as the theft of something very dear: its universal property claim to the uniqueness of being. Queer theorizing, as it has been institutionalized, is proper to—and property to—white bodies. Colored folk perform affect but can never theorize it. Actually, shame seemed strangely *dis*affected at the conference; U.S. race discourse stipulates that gay shame, as an experience both visceral and self-reflexive, be recuperated for whiteness. The charge of "hijacking" contains my dissent as fanaticism. But it also foregrounds queer theory's own indivisibilities—its own unacknowledged stakes in identity. Those stakes not only include whiteness, masculinity, and even heteronormativity but perhaps also do so in uniquely American formations. The queer establishment's desires and identifications align not-so-queerly with those of U.S. nationalism.

The queer theorizing of shame has invoked gay cosmopolitanism. In denaturalizing the relationship of sexuality to gender and sex, queer theory consistently locates the constitutive scenes of this disjuncture in the past. The function of shame in the formation of queer identities, for instance, is restricted primarily to childhood or to an era before Pride. In so doing, queer theory also predominantly situates shame as a resistance and in opposition to normalization. At Gay Shame, for example, this primal past included the "New York City queer culture of the 1960s." This designated period of prenormalization is idealized as precivilized, but queer theory must then recruit the brown body to authenticate the scene as primitive. Gay cosmopolitanism and a complementary species of queer theorizing evolve from this shared ground. The relationship of shame to identity formation is not theorized as an ongoing, dynamic process. In fact, much queer theorizing of shame is oddly nostalgic without consideration of the dynamic, affective quality of that nostalgia. The accordingly *dis*affective character of gay shame reveals a formulation of "queer" indivisible from dominant white masculinity.

The abolition of the draft in 1973, despite ongoing U.S. militarism, saved the nation's white elite by sacrificing its black, brown, and poor white populations. Gay Shame's absent black and brown bodies constitute queer theory's missing in action—quite literally. The white presence at Gay Shame was conditioned literally on black and brown absence. The intellectual capacity of whiteness required the both literal and figurative presence-in-absence of the brown body as spectacle. Gay Shame's resistance, then, to thinking race needs to be understood within the context of the military's ever-browning warrior caste and the continuing siege on affirmative action.[8] Queer theorizing also needs to more critically regard historical criminalizations of race.[9]

In its institutionalization as an academic discipline, queer theory took the question of its political viability off the table. But if queer is to remain an effective troubling of the normative and its attendant regimes, it must painstakingly excavate its own entrenchments in normativity. Establishmentarian queer theory houses itself not only in the academy but also within the identificatory boundaries of U.S. nationalism. The shaming of brown bodies is fundamental to dominant U.S. cultures, among them now a dominant queer culture.

Why the Boys Are Always Browner on the Other Side of the Fence

What color is brown? In regard to race classification, brown is no more a natural color than black or white or yellow or red; brown is a verb.[10] "Brown" designates a kind of constitutive ambiguity within U.S. racial formations—an identity that both complicates and preserves the binary opposition white/other.[11] I use the category here to mark a position of essential itinerancy relative to naturalized, positivist classes such as white, black, Asian. Itself provisional as an identity category (a waiting station of sorts between white and black, or white and Asian, for example), I make use of "brown" provisionally myself—and tactically—to demystify how bodies are situated outside white/black or white/Asian binaries to consolidate cosmopolitan, first world identities. As a repository for the disowned, projected desires of a cosmopolitan subject, it is alternately (or simultaneously) primitive, exotic, savage, pansexual, and abject. It is black and not black, Asian and not Asian, white and not white. In an age of weak multiculturalism, it is what it needs to be to maintain existing racial hierarchies, a race discourse morally divested from politics and social redistribution. That ambiguity designated here as "brown" is opportunistically and systemically deployed at times of crisis—as instanced by the intensified race profiling authorized by 9/11.[12]

Examining how "brown" circulates within a cosmopolitan gay male sexual economy proves worthwhile critically for reconstructing the racialized character of all sexuality and for chipping away at the curiously harmonious race discourses of Right and Left, namely, color blindness and anti-identity. These approaches to thinking and, more significantly, delegislating race constitute perhaps a common discourse rather than analogous ones. I use "brown" to trouble the post-structuralist critiques of identity politics that participate in retrenching white patriarchal order and dismantling the hugely significant yet still-inadequate gains made since, ironically, *Brown v. Board of Education* (1954). Having just celebrated its fiftieth anniversary, the *Brown* decision—located historically as an inauguration of the civil rights era—looms large over this project in the wake of the *Bollinger* cases, the demographic transformation of the military witnessed by the brown warrior caste dispatched onto (or sacrificed in) Iraq, and state actions punitively directed at expelling immigrants from the domain of civil society and its nominal protections.

I use the word *cosmopolitan* to identify a subject position originating with a white, urban, leisure-class gay male whose desire is cast materially onto the globe at the close of the nineteenth century. A range of mobilities, transformed or generated by industrialization (i.e., class privilege, whiteness, transportation technology, mass media, tourism) and eventually postindustrial society (i.e., communications and information technologies), provide conditions for a cosmopolitan gay male subject. However, that subject need not materially possess the full range of these mobilities. He can occupy an ambivalent position as both exoticizing/exotic and subject/object in relation to a cosmopolitan gay male desire. His experience of this subjectification can be simultaneously resistant and ecstatic.

Although originating with a white leisure class, this gay cosmopolitanism is by no means in its contemporary manifestations limited to white or urban or affluent subjects. It constitutes a major rite of gay male acculturation. Gay men of color participate in these contradictions but do not emerge unscathed. The desires comprising the cosmopolitan gay male subject in fact reinscribe oppressive racial hierarchies while enjoining gay men of color to both authenticate and celebrate those desires and the sexual cultures they organize. After all, the culture of the gay male cosmopolitan follows his desire and necessarily embroils the objects of that desire. If his desire is cast materially onto the world, so too is the culture that accommodates that desire. The development of an Anglo-American tourism industry to service a growing leisure class contributed to the formation of a cosmopolitan gay male identity, making available for consumption both spaces and bodies imagined as precivilized. The very notion of civilization requires a fantasied, primitive space onto which repressed desires are projected and disavowed. This idyllic space, populated by pansexual, uninhibited brown bodies—bodies without shame—promised liberation from Victorian restrictions on same-sex desires. These characteristics—mobility and shame and fantasies about the primitive—continue to shape dominant Anglo-American gay male culture.

The very notion of civilization requires a fantasied, primitive space onto which repressed desires are projected and disavowed.

The tourism scholar Howard Hughes's observation that "tourism and being gay are inextricably linked" functions for me here as a kind of axiom.[13] Being gay always involves, to some extent, being someplace else. Just to be clear, I am not talking about same-sex desire or even practices, which can be satisfied even in the most fixed and isolated of conditions and which do not in themselves necessarily signal any kind of group identification. Neither am I using "gay" as an ahistorical, universal category. In reference to Hughes's formulation, I understand "gay" as an already universalizing agent or its trace subject. Identification as "gay" is premised on mobility. Whether it is the South Seas of William Stoddard's Victorian travel writing or New York City's Chelsea or anywhere other than the heteronormative confines of the traditionally defined "home" and "family," being "gay" requires some kind of travel, actual or imagined. The most canonical expression of being gay, "coming out of the closet," is a quintessential articulation of the link between identity and travel. Needless to say, the mobility that modern gay identity requires is not universally available. Here we encounter trouble in the form of noncanonical bodies (not surprisingly, also quite often brown bodies) nonetheless interpellated as gay. Gays who cannot properly be gay.

The closet, as the primary cultural canon of mainstream gay and lesbian politics, is a spatial metaphor, yet there is insufficient consideration of how that figurative space presupposes specific material conditions. The closet metaphor spatially and temporally suggests access to privacy not collectively experienced by all sexual minorities. The privacy this metaphor takes for granted requires specific economic, cultural, and familial circumstances. Likewise, the "coming out" metaphor suggests a kind of mobility not universally available. These canonized metaphors for gay and lesbian experience crystallize homosexual identity within a tradition of possessive individualism. Coming out promises liberation and celebrates a species of individualism in the form of self-determination. Conceptually and materially, that freedom and self-determination are premised on the property of whiteness. The closet narrativizes gay and lesbian identity in a manner that violently excludes or includes the subjects it names according to their access to specific kinds of privacy, property, and mobility.

For Jasbir Kaur Puar, as well as Hughes, the link between travel and a specifically gay identity is also determined by homophobia. Much of the writing on gay and lesbian travel narrativizes this movement primarily as a kind of dislocation (a flight from oppression to freedom) without adequately examining how such movement also constitutes an exercise in mobility and privilege. In her article on queer mobility, Puar departs from the dominant paradigms in tourism studies, shifting her focus onto a theorization of gay and lesbian consumption. As an example of the traditional approach to understanding gay and lesbian travel, she quotes Thomas Roth, a marketing strategist whose surveys are used by the gay and lesbian tourism industry: "Many [tourists] are closeted, or come from repressive families, communities or societies. At least during our vacations, we should be free to be ourselves in a welcoming environment."[14]

What kinds of violences are necessary to consolidate the constituency designated by the pronoun "we"? Roth makes it clear that the freedom "to be ourselves" requires the securing of a space. His use of the pronoun "ourselves" signals the possessiveness of his subject, but the grammar suppresses the acquisitiveness that the subject "we" must exercise to obtain and safeguard the possessive individuality coordinated by the infinitive phrase "to be ourselves." The mobility of Roth's touristing subject is enabled by privileges of class, race, citizenship, and quite often also gender (hence the need to also distinguish between cosmopolitan gay and lesbian mobilities). Roth's gay travelers move not only from the domestic/repressive to the foreign/liberating but also from isolation to publicity and, arguably, from obscurity to identity. "We" exist so long as "we" can freely consume abroad the pleasure that both defines and defiles us at home. Coming out of the closet, the canonized narrative for gay and lesbian identity, hinges on mobility, a globalized consumerism, and imperialism.

Before they can be deemed "welcoming," the "environments" Roth so vaguely references must be properly colonized to satisfy the desires of gay and lesbian cosmopolitans. This is true not only for the international locations of gay and lesbian tourism but also for the domestic locations of gay and lesbian gentrification. The formation of these identities, and I focus here on the gay male cosmopolitan, demands spaces imagined as precivilized. The cosmopolitan calls upon the native bodies to authenticate the underdevelopment (in every sense) and innocence of these "welcoming" destinations. Puar points out that "on the one hand, there is the disruption of heterosexual space and, on the other, the use of the exotic to transgress;

in this case, the exotic is signaled by discourses of homophobia."[15] This fantasy of the exotic is necessary to the formation of a modern gay male cosmopolitan identity. Queer theorizing more resolutely needs to investigate how dominant Euro-American formations of gay, lesbian, and queer cultures (not only during this era of normalization but also historically) collude with a hegemonic white masculinity.

Speaking in Tongues without Even Trying

Speaking as a member of the conference's "final discussion," stationed before an assembled vanguard of queer theorizing (which I identified at the time, vis-à-vis my own generically brown condition, as a Queer Illuminati), I could not help but realize that I too was obliging Gay Shame's desire for brown spectacle. The circumstance was a familiar one: a scholarly presentation deteriorates into what feels like a cake walk, and I am left pondering the futility of any intervention on my part. I was there neither to comprise nor to interrogate the category "queer"; I was there to bind its community. For a conference devoted to theorizing shame, there was curiously little scholarship specifically addressing affect. Despite the conference theme, the proceedings reproduced an opposition between theory and affect, particularly in its gendered and raced foundations, characteristic of Enlightenment thought: theory is to affect as masculine is to feminine; civilized to primitive; rational to paranoid; white to other. The brown thug and the sentimental feminine find themselves unlikely compatriots in this opposition. The identities "gay" or "queer" or "lesbian" do not preempt queer theorists from reinstituting masculinist biases and patriarchal privileges. The most elitist manifestations of theorizing, even when articulated by queer subjects, also often evidence the most vulgar masculinisms.[16]

Having been accused at the conference of practicing "paranoid criticism" and being too literal,[17] I provisionally maintain my guilt on both counts and inhabit that paranoia to license here the following rhetorical indulgence: *Everything I am about to say in this essay has already been said.* I make this concession on behalf of a particular kind of resistant reader. Namely, I have in mind readers who might feel disgruntled about hearing "the same thing" for the past "ten years," a protest voiced by conference participants at Ann Arbor.

Rather than focusing on a critique's "originality," queer theory is better served by interrogating its own capacity to listen imaginatively. The professional pressure to produce "originality" is really a call to make property claims demarcating intellectual territory and thus an appeal to privatism and individualism. It is entirely possible that I am revisiting already exhausted arguments, but it is also possible that queer theory quite opportunely resists engaging particular types of inquiry. The field needs to ascertain how any such resistance is rewarded. After a decade (or longer) of hearing "the same thing," it might be time for queer theory to start listening. The chronic failure of establishmentarian queer theory to revisit its fundamental collusions with American liberalism consolidates indivisibilities—white, patriarchal, heteronormative—contrary to any professed anti-identity. This refusal to engage race-consciousness corresponds exactly to the historical contingency of property rights to U.S. racial oppression.

The chronic failure of establishmentarian queer theory to revisit its fundamental collusions with American liberalism consolidates indivisibilities—white, patriarchal, heteronormative—contrary to any professed anti-identity.

There is little consideration within establishmentarian queer theory as to whether it has at all toppled the exclusionary infrastructures of the spaces it inherits. Indeed, the space queer theory occupies within the academy, it has inherited from liberal humanism and its contemporary multiculturalist traditions. It is neither defeatist nor simplistically nihilistic to concede that queer theory is necessarily compromised at the junctures of institutionalization, nationalism, and citizenship; queer theorists might in fact approach this bind productively. By interrogating the complicity demanded by institutionalization, we can more effectively resist such collusion and attempt to reinvent our relationships to the academy and perhaps even transform the institution itself.

How Do You Solve a Problem Like "Poor Mario"?

Douglas Crimp's "Mario Montez, For Shame," originally published in a collection of critical revaluations of Eve Sedgwick's contributions to critical theory, provided a critical foundation for the conference. In arguing for a productive (or ethical) mobilization of gay shame, Crimp invokes Sedgwick's oft-reiterated axiom: "People are different from each other." He gleans from this axiom "the ethical necessity of developing ever finer tools for encountering, upholding, and valuing other's differences—or better, differences and singularities—nonce-taxonomies, as she wonderfully names such tools."[18] However, both Crimp's essay and the conference proceedings demonstrate a resistance within queer theory to appreciating how racial differences contribute to queer singularities. Such resistance, hardly ethical or productive, secures both white privilege and its transparency, and forecloses the rigorous examinations of desire and fantasy and pleasure that we should expect from queer theory.

Crimp's essay focuses on what he reads as Andy Warhol's and Ronnie Tavel's humiliation of Mario Montez, a Puerto Rican drag queen starring in Warhol's *Screen Test #2*. Trusting Warhol to speak for Montez, who remains entirely passive in relationship to both queer and U.S. cultures, Crimp renders Montez supplemental to the "New York City queer culture of the 1960s" that Crimp's project seeks to reclaim. Montez forms a surface for the inscription of that culture but is never a participant. His presence at the scene of the crime—whether that be the 1960s experimentation of Warhol's Factory or the 2003 Gay Shame of Ann Arbor—is incidental. The categories "Puerto Rican" and "Catholic," deployed monolithically, comprise for Crimp the totality of Montez's difference. Crimp interrogates neither Warhol's nor his own investments in the particularities of this representation of difference. His unqualified confidence in a secondhand account of Montez's Catholicism together with generalizations about Puerto Rican national culture provide Crimp with the only tools he needs to construct a narrative for Montez's shame. The absence, for example, of any examination of Warhol's Catholicism is only one of several telling omissions in Crimp's project.

For Crimp, only Warhol and Tavel can exercise agency. Crimp's reading of *Screen Test #2* elides any possible authority and oppositionality on the part of Montez: "Poor Mario looks alternately bewildered and terrified" (62). Montez is always authentically authentic. In response to Tavel's mocking, according to Crimp, Montez is "so delighted as to make it obvious he's still hoodwinked" (61). Conversely, Warhol's and Tavel's insight and irony become authentic qualities. Warhol, for example, demonstrates an "uncanny ability to conceal dead-on insight in the bland, unknowing remark" (59). Unknowing *and* insightful. Mindful even when unmindful in opposition to Montez's alternate bewilderment and terror in the face of authority.

Crimp identifies "exposure" as the subject of *Screen Test #2*. He cites Stephan Brecht's celebration of Warhol's genius: "Here again Warhol's true genius for abstraction paid off: he invented a camera-technique that was nothing but exposure" (59). I concur with Crimp that "exposure" is a subject of the film. The object of that exposure, however, is not fixed; as Crimp acknowledges, the film's deployment of shame exposes him, too. Exposure can never be equivalent to just one thing; it requires at least two actors (curator and spectator) and an object. Perhaps what is masterful about *Screen Test #2* is its unfixing of the components of exposure. In other words, what is masterful about the film is its undetermined mastery. Crimp imagines Montez only as the object of exposure. But what if authority in the film is reassigned? The moments that Crimp reads as "bewilderment and terror" might also comprise Montez's pirating (hijacking?) of authority. Montez shifts the film's scrutiny (its defining quality according to Crimp and Brecht) alternately onto Warhol, Tavel, the spectator.

For Crimp the important questions are as follows: "How might we square these scenes of violation and shaming with what I'm describing as an ethical project of giving visibility—and I want also to say dignity—to a queer world of differences and singularities in the 1960s? What does the viewer's discomfiture at Warhol's techniques of exposure do to the usual processes of spectator identifications?" (63). Crimp's questions generate several of my own: What violences are imposed on Mario Montez and similarly situated subjects by the visibility Crimp seeks to confer? What does it mean for Montez (or a subject similarly situated) that his exposure is a necessary condition for conferring dignity to others? (What of Montez's dignity?) Who is this isolated viewer by whose discomfiture all other spectator identifications are measured?

The ethico-political possibilities inherent in shame emerge from the urgent yet impossible dissociation upon which it insists. Crimp explains: "In the act of taking on the shame that is properly someone else's, I simultaneously feel my utter separateness from even that person. . . . I do not share the other's identity. I simply adopt the other's vulnerability to being shamed. . . . the other's difference is preserved; it is not claimed as my own" (65). The problem with Crimp's formulation is that the other's shame is already always his own before it can be "properly someone else's." The only shame Crimp takes on is the shame he projects onto Montez. The urgency to dissociate from the other's shamed body arises subsequent to his vexed assimilation of that body. Montez's body is a palate for Crimp's shame (as it is in different contexts for my own).

Perhaps the clearest evidence of Crimp's identification with (and incorporation of) Montez is his continued reference to the actor by his first name, while he refers to Tavel and Warhol exclusively by their surnames. He forecloses any possibility that Montez might also actively coauthor the text rather than merely serve as its passive object. Crimp cites an anecdote from *Popism* in which Warhol describes how "poor Mario Montez got his feelings hurt for real in his scene" while shooting "Chelsea Girls" (58). This description defines for Crimp Montez's relationship to exposition and ultimately to (gay white male) shame. Montez *feels for real* while Warhol fictionalizes, experiments, creates, and Crimp expounds. As Biddy Martin forecast a decade ago, the "fixity and miring" of race and gender provides the ground for queer theory's performative sexuality.[19]

If You White, You Right; If You Black, Get Back; If You Brown . . . Prepare to Get Your Spectacle On!

It is useful to think about the experience of racial oppression as a kind of trauma, to think about how shame and trauma might somehow be constitutive of race.

The reduction to spectacle, a reduction to the body, was most devastatingly realized in a presentation on Plato's *Symposium* late in the conference's first day. As Ellis Hanson addressed Plato, Derrida, the "cadaverization" of the teacher's body, and hypothesized that love is a victimless crime, images of a model named Kiko, featured in *Latin Inches* magazine, flashed behind him. These publicity photos for the video *Learning Latin* (1996) show Kiko, costumed in something akin to a colonial schoolboy uniform (khaki shorts, white polo shirt), posing in a classroom. He appears in various states of undress, at first his dick hanging out of his unzipped fly, eventually bent naked over a stool. On the blackboard behind him, the sentence "I love sex" has been written over and over, as Kiko has apparently been kept after class and this is his punishment. During his presentation, Hanson wore a uniform identical to the one worn by Kiko, suggesting a kind of mimetic annihilation, the nostalgia characteristic of the queer theorizing of shame, in this instance a colonial nostalgia. At no point did Hanson offer a substantive reading of the images flashing behind him.[20]

The presentation rendered me speechless. Initially I attributed that speechlessness to exhaustion. Later I determined that my speechlessness might be more productively understood as a quality of collective trauma.[21] It is useful to think about the experience of racial oppression as a kind of trauma, to think about how shame and trauma might somehow be constitutive of race. Trauma results not only from a "discrete happening" but also, as Kai Erikson argues, from a "*constellation of life's experiences* . . . from a *persisting condition* as well as from an acute event."[22] This definition broadens the understanding of trauma so that it is not isolated to discrete experiences and personalities; trauma can also function as a constitutive social force in relation to group identity. Erikson clarifies how trauma might generate communality: "Traumatic wounds inflicted on individuals can combine to create a mood, an ethos—a group culture, almost—that is different from (and more than) the sum of the private wounds that make it up. Trauma, that is, has a social dimension" (185).

I experienced the Kiko presentation (and ultimately the Gay Shame conference in its entirety) as a kind of assault. Not an assault in the sense that Ellis Hanson intended to hurt me or anybody else (although neither would I categorize his presentation, or his desire, or any desire, as innocent), but an assault in the sense that the images displayed have a context and a history that are meaningful to me in ways very different from how they are meaningful, I suspect, for Hanson. These images, or more precisely the politics of their display, belong for me to an already existing "constellation of life's experiences." My hope that queer theory might learn to listen more imaginatively finds a prescription in the questions Erikson introduces to trauma theory: "To what extent may one conclude that the communal dimension of trauma is one of its distinctive clinical signatures? And to what extent does it make sense to conclude that the traumatized view of the world conveys a wisdom that ought to be heard?" (198), an affect requiring recognition?

The first comment after Hanson's presentation came from Tobin Siebers, seated next to me. Siebers, a disability studies theorist, jokingly announced that Kiko's was the most "able-bodied dick" he'd ever seen. I felt kicked in the gut. Can the reduction—not just to body, but to dick—find any more unequivocal articulation? Yet if I cannot convey to fellow queer theorists how this whole scene constituted for me an assault, and if they cannot hear my criticism, how can I be sure that I am ever intelligible to them as human? Following Siebers's remark, the next few comments also joked, albeit nervously, about the photos. I listened dumbfounded as Hanson was teased about him and Plato having to compete with the big, "purple" dick (the biggest anyone had ever seen, it turns out) for the audience's attention. There occurred no substantive discussion about the representation of Kiko, about fantasy, about racialized desire, or even about Hanson's reading of Plato. Kiko's dick assumed its historical place as the focal point of white fantasy.

That night and into the next day I heard several queer theorists, white men and women, proclaim that Kiko's was indeed the biggest dick they had ever seen—an astonishing declaration from queer theorists, many of whom write on gay male pornography. I guarantee that this was *not* the biggest dick conference participants had ever seen; a few seconds on the Internet would turn up innumerable dicks, fatter and longer. The need even to explain this is demeaning. But the circumstance is indicative also of dominant culture fantasies about black male sexuality. Kiko is both Latino and black. I cannot be certain that he would identify himself as black. Maybe he would; maybe he would not. (The complications of the classification "Latino" are a topic for another essay.)

This incident demonstrates, however, how the brown body signifies ambiguities that ultimately reinforce contemporary white hegemony through its intersection with a spectralized blackness. Kiko's brownness removes his body from the history of white predations on the black male body, in particular the black male body that emerged after Reconstruction: the "free" black man ruled by savage and insatiable sexual appetites. This unremitting cultural fixation on the black penis needs to be understood as a legacy of lynching. The transformation of the black penis into a magic object requires that the racial-sexual violence become naturalized; in other words, the castrated penis must itself become fantastic in order to sanction genocidal violence. The culture of lynching continues to generate fresh enactments of its ritual violence: the separation of the man from the penis, the substitution of penis for the man, the impossibility of a "private" black sexuality, contempt for black humanity. His sexual voraciousness is located in his mythically proportioned manhood, the product of a white imagination that seeks to exterminate the black man for more reasons than it can ever allow itself to name. This white desire for a black male body, alternately manifested as love, disgust, fear, and murderousness, resides at the heart of U.S. sexual cultures, straight and queer.

The culture of lynching continues to generate fresh enactments of its ritual violence: the separation of the man from the penis, the substitution of penis for the man, the impossibility of a "private" black sexuality, contempt for black humanity.

The brownness conferred on Kiko when he is designated as "Latin" (itself an already ambiguous sign) circumvents troubling histories of racial oppression that are more immediate to the white imagination in the form of enslavement, lynching, and police brutality. Already forgetful about its history of state-sanctioned white-on-black violence, the United States remains blissfully amnesiac about its violent imperial history. The ambiguities of brownness function to unburden fantasies of black sexuality from their troubling histories; those same fantasies, and new ones, may be revisited on the brown body. In other words, one manifestation of the brown body occurs in the form of a black body un-*moor*ed, if you will, from material history and fixed instead to the landscape of a gay cosmopolitan imagination.

Kiko's dick was the biggest anyone had ever seen because it was that same mythic black dick dreamed by white desire, except for being transported to a location where desires are not so burdened by troubling histories. Gay shame's desire for Kiko seeks to humiliate Kiko, to symbolically annihilate him, but in order to mistranslate its own murderous desire as love, it must locate Kiko at the limits of civilization, where he is beautifully abject, where he is brown and shameless. Cosmopolitan gay male subjectivity is founded on the humiliation of "brown" primitives and thugs, a humiliation often subsequently misnamed as "love."

Kiko became brown within the contact zones of desire. His brownness functions in itself as a kind of traveling contact zone; it entertains all sorts of fantasies of the primitive. The brown body is a fetish for what the cosmopolitan has lost or forgotten at the other side (the brown underside) of civilization. Kiko is browned by the symbols that converge at his (and Gay Shame's) horizon: the moniker "Latin Inches"; the colonial schoolboy uniform; the nickname; his banjee-ness; his accessibility as spectacle. Once available to cosmopolitan consumption, the brown body generates desire, but only insofar as it is the location where different stories of desire become possible. The brown body's ambiguity is endlessly generative. It provides cosmopolitan gay male subjects with objects of desire and with the superabundant raw material from which to compose the story of that desire. The ambiguity of brownness contra the prevailing black/white opposition of U.S. race discourse secures for the contemporary cosmopolitan gay male a location in which he can materially and psychically flex his desire with impunity. He gets to have his brown body and eat it, too.

Dismissed as identity politics and a crude appeal to personal experience, my attempt to communicate the indignity and assault I experienced at the conference could not be heard. I propose that the resistance I confronted, articulated via post-structuralist critiques of identity, designates the need for white dominant culture to sustain the impossibility of a private black sexuality. The mythology of the black penis remains too deep-rooted in the popular imagination for me to convince the cock-struck attendees at Gay Shame that Kiko's privates were not the biggest they had ever seen. Euphemisms aside, Kiko's "privates" were not in any sense private, either. I did not advance an antipornography position at the conference, but I suspect that the defensiveness on the part of many queer theorists present, especially among the gay white men, resulted from an overdetermined misreading of my comments as just that. For example, one respondent insisted that I had contended in my remarks that he (a white man) "could not look at" nude images of Kiko. He perceived my criticism as a competing property claim on Kiko's body.

I was not there to make any such property claim, but it was made emphatically clear to me, by Hanson's presentation as well as by the reaction to my comments, that I am most certainly not entitled to do so. For the cosmopolitan gay male subject, the brown body constitutes communal property. As a site of communion for whiteness, the brown body realizes white indivisibility. My inquiry into the semantics of Kiko's body constituted a trespass. It represented for white desire an exercise of acquisitiveness on my part that is proper only to whiteness. To pose the question of the semantics of the brown body is to *take* meaning from the fetish-object of white desire, to infringe on the native acquisitiveness of whiteness.

The category "Latino," used as a racial descriptor rather than a political affiliation, is nearly as vague as "brown." Consider, for example, how easily "Latin" (or for that matter, "Spanish" and "Hispanic") may substitute for "Latino." However, most uses of "Latina/o" disregard the politics of that ambiguity, together with the differences that the category itself already collapses. Remarkably, queer theory understands the politics of difference as fundamental to its practice, yet it can participate in the circulation of categories like "Latin" without appreciating in the least its function within a complex web of identifications and desires. While the variations on the category "Latina/o" collapse innumerable differences, queer theorizing seems for the most part quite content to let that sameness alone. "Queer" needs to interrogate its own investments in sameness. Ironically, these investments deploy the rhetoric of difference precisely so that the presumed anti-identity of queer might dissimulate profiting by sameness. By this means, establishmentarian queer theory has colluded in rendering material and psychic violences of racialization unintelligible.

I agree that communities are bound by fictions, but that does not diminish the violences enacted in constituting those communities. Queer theory has exchanged too hastily the politics of identity for the politics of difference. To combat oppression it is necessary to theorize how communities are bound by shared fantasies and desires, in other words, how they are bound at some level by sameness. This is especially crucial where sameness makes itself transparent, as it does with whiteness. Sometimes, people are not so different from one another. Queer theory, when it privileges difference over sameness absolutely, colludes with institutionalized racism in vanishing, hence retrenching, white privilege. It serves as the magician's assistant to whiteness's disappearing act.

To combat oppression it is necessary to theorize how communities are bound by shared fantasies and desires, in other words, how they are bound at some level by sameness.

Hanson acknowledged that he had anticipated my response and had heard exactly the same protest before. Oddly, these repeated protests only invalidate one another. I should in fact feel shamed at this revelation of the commonplace nature of my thinking. Hanson's accusation constitutes a defensive posture, a way to dismiss criticism. However, I think the solace I received (much of it from white lesbian theorists) may similarly indicate a form of defensiveness. I absolutely experienced solidarity with white lesbian theorists at the conference, but there was also from some an expression of solace that I think masqueraded (and only just barely) as solidarity.[23] I am sure that reactions to the dispute between Hanson and me had to have been more complicated than the (apparent) polarization, the taking of sides that occurred after the final roundtable. But I also wonder if that (apparent) polarization did not in fact need to happen to preserve the status quo, to further bind queer theory's white indivisibility. As I alternately inhabited the body of an intransigent and vulgar savage as well as that of a noble one (depending on where you sat), as I performed my brownness—and what choice did I have really, fated to my performance of the unsophisticated and banal—I understood the rupture I witnessed as one that needed to happen in order to fortify that white body of queer theory, to strengthen its immunity against foreign agents. I did experience genuine intellectual engagement with colleagues. Otherwise, I would not waste my energy formulating this critique. However, that engagement was subsumed by a reductive polarization; like the brown body (poor Mario's, Kiko's, my own, and, most important, the brown body missing in action), it was an obligatory sacrifice to the status quo of Gay Shame's queer theorizing.

Although the ironies of Ellis Hanson's presentation were lost on me, I was keenly aware of another much crueler irony. The brown body in his schoolboy uniform, invited into the university classroom of a cosmopolitan gay male fantasy for a game of show and tell, remains simultaneously shut out of the university classroom. Increasingly, the brown body finds itself expelled from civil society—if not expelled outright from the nation. Seeing Kiko up on the screen, his dick hanging out of his khaki shorts, made the absence of gay men and lesbians of color at the conference all that much more pronounced. The brown body is variously sacrificed at the exigencies of white privilege and white desire. As peculiar as this may sound, I am not convinced that institutionalized forms of queer theory really care to investigate desire. An established group of queer theorists remain quite riled, understandably, about the normalization of queer. However, queer theory resists the critique of its own even more alarming normalizations. The dominant queer culture, like any dominant culture, demands assimilation. Queer theory does not want to be normalized, but neither does it want to be queered. Unruly subjects are expelled to its margins. This expulsion is telling. Establishmentarian queer theory, despite its oft-professed revulsion at mass culture assimilation, has also quite comfortably settled at the center or, rather, that comfortably furnished space just left of center. We would be deluded to think that queer theory is not invested in protecting the institutional structures that have accommodated it, including, most significantly, white patriarchal structures of knowledge. This does not call for abandoning the field but rather for greater vigilance, imagination, and accountability, as well as a reinvigorated inquiry into the complex trajectories of desire and identity.

Notes

I would like to thank David Eng and Judith Halberstam for their insights and patient editing. I am grateful to Mary Jane Smith for her invitation to share a very early draft of this essay, "What Color Is Brown? Troubling Desires, Troubling Identities," on 8 April 2004 as a guest of St. Lawrence University's U.S. Cultural and Ethnic Studies program. This essay has benefited significantly from conversations with Chris Cynn, Chris Danguilan, Kim Hall, and Sarita See.

1. For a cogent examination of how whiteness functions in the United States as property, see Cheryl I. Harris's essay, "Whiteness as Property," in *Critical Race Theory: The Key Writings That Formed the Movement*, ed. Kimberlé Crenshaw, Neil Gotanda, Gary Peller, and Kendall Thomas (New York: New Press, 1995), 276–91.

2. I identify Montez as Puerto Rican and Davis as black to illustrate the conference's race politics. However, I do so with some hesitation, as each figure's

race/ethnic identity needs further complicating in order to investigate the place of racialized desire in forming racial, ethnic, and sexual identities (and vice versa). Vaginal Creme Davis, for example, has produced work exploring her Chicana heritage. José Muñoz records Davis's history (or "legend"): "According to Davis's own self-generated legend, her existence is the result of an illicit encounter between her then forty-five-year-old African American mother and her father, who was, at the time, a twenty-one-year-old Mexican American. Davis has often reported that her parents only met once, when she was conceived under a table during a Ray Charles concert at the Hollywood Palladium in the early 1960s" (José Esteban Muñoz, *Disidentifications: Queers of Color and the Performance of Politics* [Minneapolis: University of Minnesota Press, 1999], 95). In the case of Montez, the category "Puerto Rican" can designate not only a national origin but also a racial identification; in either case, what "Puerto Rican" means is contingent also on historical context, place, and usage. I do not know for certain that Montez self-identified as "Puerto Rican," nor do I take for granted that the meaning of such an identification necessarily remains constant over one's lifetime.

3. Judith Butler and Biddy Martin, "Cross-Identifications," *Diacritics* 24 (1994): 3.

4. See Biddy Martin, "Sexualities without Genders and Other Queer Utopias," *Diacritics* 24 (1994): 104–21.

5. Butler and Martin, "Cross-Identifications," 3.

6. Harris, "Whiteness as Property," 277.

7. Hereafter cited as "the Patriot Act," the bill—passed 24 October 2001 by the 107th Congress—is officially titled the "Uniting and Strengthening America by Providing Appropriate Tools Required to Intercept and Obstruct Terrorism Act of 2001."

8. For a discussion of the U.S. military's "warrior caste," see David M. Halbfinger and Steven A. Holmes, "A Nation at War: The Troops; Military Mirrors a Working-Class America," *New York Times*, 30 March 2003.

9. The treatment of Iraqi prisoners of war and the histories of sexual humiliation of racially oppressed people in the United States are profoundly linked. The Abu Ghraib photos, like so many from the culture of lynching, function as postcards from a racial front. U.S. race ideology persists onto a world stage. Official responses to Abu Ghraib protect the race secrets of U.S. dominant and military cultures, which dictate the specifically sexual nature of the torture—at once sadistically homophobic and homoerotic. I elaborate on this "race secret" in a manuscript in progress. For this essay, I do, however, want to underscore cosmopolitanism's need for military occupation as a means of colonizing spaces for its material and imagined travels.

10. I am paraphrasing Kendall Thomas's invaluable formulation: "Race is a verb."

11. All race categories are, of course, regardless of their juridico-medical fixity, constitutively ambiguous. That ambiguity is relentlessly recuperated or even revoked by dominant culture (i.e., the one-drop rule, border patrol, determinations of dangerousness), but this same ambiguity perhaps also presents us with fertile ruptures in U.S. histories of systemic race oppression.

12. John Ashcroft's policy requiring male immigrants originating from any of twenty selected countries to register and periodically "check in" demonstrates how forms of governmentality adapt to endlessly and opportunistically mine the racial ambiguity of "brown," all the while professing to demystify it.

13. Howard Hughes, "Holidays and Homosexual Identity," *Tourism Management* 18 (1997): 6.

14. Quoted in Jasbir Kaur Puar, "Circuits of Queer Mobility: Tourism, Travel, and Globalization," *GLQ* 8 (2002): 102.

15. Ibid., 104.

16. This essay focuses on a troublesome gay cosmopolitanism that I argue characterizes establishmentarian queer theorizing. The 2003 Gay Shame conference provides the primary text for this investigation; however, Gay Shame occasioned various ruptures among the community of theorists, artists, and activists present. I attend to the significance of these divisions in the aforementioned manuscript in progress. For the purposes of this essay, I am more interested in how a queer community (despite numerous assertions about the fictitiousness of such community) was violently consolidated at Gay Shame, perhaps even by the very ruptures I mention. However, I do want to emphasize that Gay Shame witnessed not only predictable alignments of power but also numerous realignments, especially realigned masculinities. By focusing so exclusively on the construction of a gay male cosmopolitanism, this essay risks participating in the routine "subordination of alternative masculinities" that Judith Halberstam explores in her writing. What Halberstam describes as "lesbian counterproductions of female masculinity" needs to be appraised vis-à-vis Gay Shame just as any potential complicity with dominant white masculinity requires appraisal. I hope to expand my analysis in this direction, and I hope to read further elaborations of the various alignments of race, gender, and nation at Gay Shame and within queer theory. See Judith Halberstam, *Female Masculinity* (Durham, NC: Duke University Press, 1998).

17. The reference (made at the conference by Ellis Hanson) is to Eve Sedgwick's distinction between paranoid and reparative criticism in her essay "Paranoid Reading and Reparative Reading, or You're So Paranoid, You Probably Think This Essay Is about You." See Eve Kosofsky Sedgwick, *Touching Feeling: Affect, Pedagogy, Performativity* (Durham, NC: Duke University Press, 2003). I worry that Sedgwick's essay endorses the kind of unimaginative listening that protects a closed core of queer theory from unwelcome troubling. More significant, Sedgwick adopts the category "paranoid" without a consideration of the gendered and raced history of such pathologizing categories as they have been variously enlisted within the humanities and social sciences and within the everyday life of the academy in ways contingent on—yet exceeding—their clinical etiologies. If I may risk a generalization, an "essentialism" even: All colored academics know that expression of sincere yet dubious concern, that unmistakable *are you sure you're not just being too sensitive?* look on the faces of their trusted, good white liberal friends. Even when the question is articulated in that familiar, practiced tone of aggressive apprehension, it is never really a question at all, but rather an impervious accusation of paranoia. My other concern with Sedgwick's recycling of paranoia is its presumption that any criticism deemed "paranoid" was necessarily and naively directed at author intention, that is, Sedgwick means me, or my kind, harm. This ultimately provides a way to deflect criticism that confronts how words and images actually *do* injure people. It also minimizes the author's accountability with respect to the effects of her words. Witnessing too often the devastation exacted by the Left's "good intentions," I do not care much about the question of good or bad intentions. As a critic, I am concerned with the effects of words and images on lives. I do, however, also direct my analysis on motivation, which I understand as a

very different problem from intention. Motivation introduces different questions from the more atomistic problem of intention. Rather than positing individual consciousness as its end, the question of motivation looks to the dynamics of group identity formation and the fantasies and desires they generate.

18. Douglas Crimp, "Mario Montez, For Shame," in *Regarding Sedgwick: Essays on Queer Culture and Critical Theory*, ed. Stephen M. Barber and David L. Clark (New York: Routledge, 2002), 57.

19. In a manuscript in progress, I further pursue Martin's argument about the "fixity" of gender in queer theorizing, specifically in reference to Crimp's discussion of the "extraordinary cruelty" of Warhol's films. More specifically, I examine the treatment of Edie Sedgwick in *Beauty #2* in order to establish an indivisibility that binds white heterosexual and gay male identities. Although differently motivated, there are instances in which gay male and normative heterosexual desires may share in a patriarchal investment to annihilate the female body. Desire and identification are at once reverent and murderous. The humiliation of Edie Sedgwick in *Beauty #2* secures an ontological integrity for a white masculinity that is not particularly heterosexual.

20. Hanson contested this point. However, he conceded that he might have been *too ironic* (hence, my misunderstanding).

21. Hanson disagreed, characterizing the "move" to trauma as "easy."

22. See Kai Erikson, "Notes on Trauma and Community," in *Trauma: Explorations in Memory*, ed. Cathy Caruth (Baltimore, MD: Johns Hopkins University Press, 1995), 183–99. For a discussion of race shame and the value of trauma theory to theorizing black identity, see J. Brooks Bouson, *Quiet as It's Kept: Shame, Trauma, and Race in the Novels of Toni Morrison* (Albany: State University of New York Press, 2000).

23. I reiterate that the conference also suggested numerous alternative identity alignments. I also want to emphasize that my thinking on gay shame, race, and institutional queer theory benefited immeasurably from the papers, performances, and interventions by conference speakers and audience members, including George Chauncey, Deborah Gould, Judith Halberstam, Lisa Henderson, Holly Hughes, Liza Johnson, Joan Lipkin, Esther Newton, Nolan O'Dell, Elaine Roth, Bill St. Amant, Sarita See, Carroll Smith-Rosenberg, and many others.

JJ Chinois's Oriental Express, or, How a Suburban Heartthrob Seduced Red America

Karen Tongson

This essay was composed before eleven states—mostly red, but also blue—inscribed the cultural zeitgeist of homopanic into their state constitutions; before Ohio turned red and John Kerry conceded on 3 November 2004. Its tone is hopeful, forward-looking, one could even say devastatingly naive. Nevertheless, I hope that the project it initiates—reconceptualizing spatial imaginaries through the lens of a queer of color aesthetics and politics—can remain an important starting point for reconfiguring the representational strategies of our queer interventions in American electoral politics.

Hot Red and Blue: Queers and the Electoral Imaginary

> The pundits, the pundits like to slice and dice our country into red states and blue States: red states for Republicans, blue States for Democrats. But I've got news for them, too. . . . We coach little league in the blue states and, yes, we've got some gay friends in the red states.
> —Barack Obama, Illinois state senator, keynote address, 2004 Democratic National Convention in Boston

With references to gays and lesbians let alone to anything "queer" so few and far between at a 2004 Democratic National Convention carefully scripted to appeal to a minuscule margin of so-called moderate, undecided voters in the American electorate, Barack Obama's nod to "gay friends in the red states" scored a rousing ovation from the delegates on the convention floor. In a rhetorically skillful keynote address, Obama, a candidate for the U.S. Senate, revised a recurring topographical trope to diagnose the deeply fractured cultural, as well as political, American landscape.[1] In the wake of the hotly contested and catastrophically resolved 2000 presidential election that saw George W. Bush assume his first presidential term by the narrowest of margins (literally by one vote in a 5-4 decision issued by what could be called "activist judges" on the U.S. Supreme Court), the political punditry turned to the "sliced and diced" electoral map as it declared a "new culture war" defined geographically

Social Text 84–85, Vol. 23, Nos. 3–4, Fall–Winter 2005.

In our queer spatial imaginary about sexuality and race in the United States, we too have become attached to this paradigm that separates the rural and suburban from the urban.

by the distribution of votes. This new "uncivil war" purportedly rages between populations residing in Democratic "blue states" conspicuously intimate with large bodies of water (the Pacific, the Atlantic, and the Great Lakes), and Republican "red states"—the landlocked "flyover states" that appear formidable in their vast and contiguous territorial expanse.[2] The red state/blue state paradigm, recently renamed in a book by the eccentric liberal billionaire John Sperling as the "retro vs. metro" schism, is a geopolitical model both the Left and the Right have used to situate electoral politics within a broad cultural framework of conflicting "values." Pundits on both sides have agreed that the red, or retro, states are characterized by racially homogenous (primarily white) rural and suburban populations who preach economic and social conservatism, and fervently promote religion through local and statewide legislation. As Sperling describes retro Americans: "These are 'God, Family, and Flag' folks politically dominated by rural, conservative, white, Fundamentalist Christian populations. Retro America is not the land of co-habiting, unmarried, hetero, or same-sex couples, or of the young seeking cultural excitement in the large Metro cities."[3] Meanwhile, blue state, or metro, populations are depicted as racially and economically diverse, culturally "urban" and "tolerant" (even though not all metros necessarily live in metropolitan areas), and intellectually progressive. The neoliberal promoters of *The Great Divide* attempt to cast blue states in a thoroughly "modern" light as places "loosely held together by common interests in promoting economic modernity and by shared cultural values marked by religious moderation; vibrant popular cultures; a tolerance of differences of class, ethnicity, tastes, and sexual orientation; and a tendency to vote Democratic."[4]

While there is a problematic lack of nuance in these geopolitical and cultural designations, I would like for a moment to suspend judgment of these stark spatial contrasts to explain how Obama's remark about "gay friends in the red states" might help queer scholars rethink the spatial imaginaries that we ourselves take for granted in our efforts to redefine intellectual, cultural, and political discourse. In an American political landscape increasingly dominated by a jingoistic rhetoric of contrasts—of good versus evil, and the rallying cry that "you're with us or against us"—in a cultural climate in which thoughtful deliberation is deemed as weakness and in which complex answers unfit for sound bites are effectively mocked as flip-flopping, it behooves us to insist ever more powerfully, ever more distinctly on the importance of intricate intersections and encounters.

In our queer spatial imaginary about sexuality and race in the United States, we too have become attached to this paradigm that separates the rural and suburban from the urban.[5] We have become just as reliant on a self-congratulatory narrative about *our* territory—our urban havens—and just as self-righteous in our conviction that where we live affirms our beliefs as those self-professed "red-blooded," red state Americans who organize in school boards and state legislatures against our purported influence. Those of us lucky enough to live and work in urban hubs have become—dare I say it?—too proud of our own "safe" environs, too comfortable in our gentrified queer enclaves situated at a reassuring remove from the ignorant Wal-Mart shopping masses to consider the coalitional possibilities, intellectual and activist, with queers inhabiting rural and suburban spaces.

Obama's comment about "gay friends in the red states" brought this all home to me (to indulge in the folksy cadence of mainstream political rhetoric) while I was watching the DNC with a group of queer friends, mostly academics and artists, in my own comfortable if unaffordable "creative class" gay ghetto in a big city.[6] My informal, decidedly unscientific focus group responded to Obama's shout-out to "gay friends in the red states" with a barrage of pity and sarcasm:

> "Those poor things!"
> "Gay 'friends'—soon to be beaten by to a pulp by all of their neighbors."
> "All Log Cabin Republicans with bad haircuts, test-tube babies, and matching Subarus."

While I admittedly issued some of my own cynical barbs after hearing Obama's idealistic rhetoric about unity and common ground in a "*United* States of America," I have, in retrospect, begun to imagine how we might, at the very least, intellectually move beyond the geopolitical presumptions that concede vast territories of rural and suburban space—represented after the 2004 national election as swinging "purple counties"—to a homogenizing political and aesthetic imaginary. Writing off these large swaths of "red America," while not the only cause of the Democrats' demise in this year's national election, proved decisive in the failed if massive and impassioned efforts to depose George W. Bush before he could do more damage.

While the demographic data on unmarried gay and lesbian partners reported by the 2000 U.S. Census Bureau, the newly published *Gay and Lesbian Atlas*, and books like *The Great Divide* persuasively support the conclusion that our "gay friends in the red states" must be white, homonormative gays and lesbians fixated on causes like gay marriage, gay adoption, and other mainstreaming projects political and socioeconomic, there are significant interventions being staged by queer of color communities throughout the retro regions of the United States.[7] Groups like Southerners on New Ground (SONG), for example, have organized to foment a politically active queer regionalism in the United States by bringing together racially and socioeconomically diverse queers who live and work in states like Alabama, Arkansas, Florida, Georgia, Kentucky, Louisiana, Mississippi, North Carolina, South Carolina, Tennessee, Virginia, and West Virginia.[8] Founded by African American and white lesbians in the South, SONG's mission is to build a "movement across the South for progressive social change by developing models for organizing that connect race, class, culture, gender and sexual identity."[9] Rather than succumbing to social and cultural inevitabilities dictated by location, or investing all of its resources in pushing gay marriage, SONG strives to build queer constituencies that advocate simultaneously for civil rights, women's reproductive rights, and labor and antiwar causes.[10] What SONG enacts as political and organizational practice is what Roderick Ferguson has named "queer of color critique," a critical methodology that demands intersecting analyses of race, economy, gender, and sexuality in projects of intellectual and political reform.[11] Queer of color critique, as part of its larger intervention, also exposes the disturbing intimacies among "conservative" and "progressive" ideologies, and among both "normative" and "queer" formations.[12] Groups like SONG, with their insistence on practicing queer grassroots activism in locations that, to put it mildly, seem unfriendly at best, bring to the fore precisely this problematic symbiosis between normative spatial imaginaries like the red state/blue state paradigm, and a queer urbanity that focuses exclusively on blue state bastions of queer life like New York and San Francisco—our designated sites of progressive enlightenment and queer "safety." This "metronormativity," as Judith Halberstam described in a watershed essay on Brandon Teena, needs as its foil a "horror of the heartlands" mythology that perpetuates socioeconomic stereotypes about the "ignorant prejudices" bred by poverty and spatial alienation.[13]

While many others have begun to examine and celebrate rural queer lives as the distinct cultural formation emblematically Other to metronormative discourses,[14] I would like in this essay to turn to a murkier spatial designation that also performs a peripheral role in metronormative accounts of queer culture. I discuss a manifestation of queer subcultural life that is assumed to be literally subcultural, below, beneath, or even without "culture" in every sense of the word: an emergent queer and racialized suburban imaginary that traffics conceptually between rural and urban imaginaries while disrupting the symbolic continuities of each. My aim is to encourage the reconfiguration and reorientation of queer aesthetics and politics as it engages with the urban/rural binary conceived on a larger scale as the red state/blue state paradigm, yet enacted as a representational and political struggle on a microlevel among counties, and specific styles of lived environment. Rather than offering a demographic analysis of queer suburbanity, I instead focus on the cultural component of the topographical schism said to define the geopolitics of the United States by revisiting the concept of "style," the most recognizably urbane and popularized coordinate of queer culture. What comes as a passing remark in *The Great Divide* depicting metro inhabitants as purveyors of "vibrant popular cultures . . . tolerant [of differences in] ethnicity, class, *taste* and sexual orientation"[15] (my emphasis) carries with it the conceptual tools for reexamining, and ultimately dismantling, oversimplified topographies of sexuality in the United States. An underlying argument of *The Great Divide* is that taste remains an indicator of enlightenment both cultural and political. This is also an argument made explicitly and implicitly in a range of queer texts, primarily in literary and cultural theory composed mostly by gay white men. Yet a queer recourse to style and creativity, I argue, need not serve the exclusive function of mainstreaming urban gay white men with a keen eye for decorating skills into the popular imaginary as facilitators of the good life for all. Far from remaining innocuously provocative or entertaining, style can still provide an apparatus for examining uneven and uneasy, yet productive interclass and interracial encounters in spaces where we have limited ourselves to imagining only desperate outcomes for queer subjects. To achieve a new politicized function, however, style itself must be "re-Oriented" beyond the city in more ways than one.[16] This essay thus focuses on what functions as a queer developmental narrative of migration *within* the United States from amorphous suburban landscapes to welcoming and iconic urban centers.

This essay thus focuses on what functions as a queer developmental narrative of migration *within* the United States from amorphous suburban landscapes to welcoming and iconic urban centers.

My primary examples are taken from the Web and performance work of Lynne Chan, an artist who analogizes her own migration as a queer subject from the suburbs to New York City with her parents' immigration to the United States from Hong Kong. In the process, Chan humorously engages with how the narratives of local queer migration are interwoven with the tropes of U.S. immigration. Assuming the celebrity persona of JJ Chinois, a transgendered pop idol discovered in the cattle-ranching outpost of Coalinga, California, Chan endows JJ with a sanguine naïveté about rural risk and suburban ennui. She tests the urban boundaries of a queer topographical imaginary by routing JJ's storied discovery through strip malls and small towns in red counties and even some red states, culminating with a filmed, live appearance as JJ Chinois at a demolition derby in 2003. Chan's JJ Chinois projects, without eschewing the metropolitan histories and desires of queers, represent suburban spaces as potentially joyful and seductive spaces of a racialized and gendered self-stylization not fated to be marred by psychic despair at best, gruesome violence at worst. The climactic gut-busting lyrics of "New York, New York" tell us, "If I can make it there, I'll make it anywhere." Chan's work responds by insisting that making it there requires making anywhere—your characterless suburban nowhere—into a somewhere.

Suburban Imaginaries

> It turns out we overestimated the power of architectural determinism. The suburbs have proved flexible enough to accommodate working mothers . . . as well as a great many different kinds of families and lifestyles. Since I left the Gates, its white nuclear families have been joined by singles and gays, Asians and African-Americans, people operating home businesses and empty nesters. . . . The world that built the postwar suburbs has passed away, and yet those suburbs still stand, remodeled by the press of history. What they haven't been is reimagined or renamed, at least not yet.
> —Michael Pollan, "The Triumph of Burbopolis," *New York Times Magazine*, April 9, 2000

Despite the evolving architectural functions and demographics of the postmillennial suburbs, their twentieth-century mythos of homogeneity manages to endure. In *White Diaspora: The Suburb and the Twentieth-Century American Novel* (2001), a study of white, male suburban novels from the 1930s to the late twentieth century, Catherine Jurca explains how a "suburban aesthetics" was not only produced by the political and economic imperatives of a post–World War II America that inspired a "white flight" from cities to suburbs, but produced in turn a powerful cultural myth about suburban life that achieved salience as a master narrative for the white middle classes.[17] Encapsulating a sanitary ideal of white, middle-class homogeneity and "safety," as well as its dark underbelly of psychic dysfunction and suffocated privilege, the suburban aesthetic has only recently begun to account for a new wave of immigrants, queers, people of color, and working-class families (many of whom were displaced from urban centers by encroaching gentrification and skyrocketing property values[18]) who now form "minority majorities" in places like the California suburbs.[19]

Next Friday (2000), the second film in the hit *Friday* franchise created by and starring gangsta rapper turned Hollywood player Ice Cube, thematizes this shift in the suburban imaginary by boasting the tagline "the suburbs make the 'hood look good." Hijinks ensue when Ice Cube's character, Craig, moves to the Southern California suburb of Rancho Cucamonga with his lottery-winning Uncle Elroy and cousin Day-Day, in an effort to hide out from his former rival, Deebo, who escaped from prison and is looking for payback. The film unfolds amid the backdrop of the smoggy exurban enclaves east of Los Angeles dubbed the "Inland

Empire" and its stucco landscape of Spanish-style subdivisions where the "good life" is transformed into an extension of the "hood life." Unlike a slew of other recent novels and films that have transposed the white, upper-middle-class intrigue and ennui of the suburban aesthetic into dramas of immigrant assimilation (like Jhumpa Lahiri's celebrated 2004 novel *The Namesake*), or kinetic parables of overachievement gone bad (like Justin Lin's cinematic take on Asian American hooligan nerds, *Better Luck Tomorrow*, 2002), *Next Friday*'s romp takes on the interclass as well as interracial tensions that dismantle certain fixtures of the suburban mythos, namely, its claims to stability, seamlessness, and communal insularity.

Next Friday depicts a suburban "culture clash" as a series of slapstick encounters among blacks, Latinos, and Asians vying for their interpretation of the suburban landscape. This clash is also, fundamentally, a conflict among styles of living that rupture the architectural interchangeability and similitude that defines (often by failing to define) suburban space. *Next Friday* derives much of its humor from portraying ostensibly generic and unmarked tract houses and strip malls as "blinged-out" ethnicized lairs for the film's motley characters. Chinatown tchotchkes, lowriding minitrucks, and ghetto baroque furniture vacuum sealed in vinyl point to the endless varieties of class and "ethnically" inflected customization that have gradually transformed the suburban environment while putting a distinctly different spin on the competitive aspiration to "keep up with the Joneses."

By confounding white, bourgeois tastes with classed and racialized interpretations of "prosperity," *Next Friday* offers a critique of suburban aesthetics while reconfiguring the suburban imaginary with its parodic take on the stylistic markers of upward mobility. Whereas *Next Friday* explores how suburban spaces and communities have been altered by the mostly lateral migrations made by urban black and Latino families seeking more affordable housing, Chan begins with this reconfigured, racialized suburban landscape as a point of departure for her JJ Chinois projects. The mobility Chan tracks in her projects inverts the classic "good life" trajectory from the city to the suburbs by engaging and critiquing a queer developmental narrative in which the queer subject does not come out but comes *into* a queer scene by moving from a nowhere to a somewhere—from a placeless place like a suburb to "The City." Taking its cues from 1970s pop-cult films all the way up to *Next Friday*, the starting premise of Chan's revisionist narrative is to "re-Orient" her audiences to an otherwise disorienting suburban landscape: to show us that the "placeless place" is actually, already a "somewhere" with its own vexed if unarticulated relationship to race, sexual orientation, and orientalism.

The mobility Chan tracks in her projects inverts the classic "good life" trajectory from the city to the suburbs by engaging and critiquing a queer developmental narrative.

Chan's chosen proper name for her persona, JJ Chinois, is in and of itself a testimony to intersecting racialized and classed pop-cultural signifiers that invoke orientalism and imperialism. The initials are an homage to the mainstreaming of 1970s black popular culture, an echo of Jimmie Walker's signature character JJ, the ghetto-fabulous dandiacal lothario with a heart of gold from the sitcom *Good Times*.[20] The surname is an effete flourish accentuating a link between cosmopolitan and imperial projects of naming. Chan cribbed Chinois from her first wide-eyed encounter with the Asian restaurants of Paris, as well as the "fusion" Vietnamese restaurants of Southern California that attempt to convey "a touch of class" by evoking French colonial Vietnam and a Continental joie de vivre that makes "the ethnic" palatable to discerning consumers.[21]

In the various live and Web-based incarnations of her JJ Chinois projects, Chan works to transform her suburban imaginary from sprawl to specificity by trading on an idiosyncratic repertoire of place-names and strip mall sites to construct her suburban archive of worldly knowledge. The "worldliness" of this suburban archive is contingent on the classed, racialized, and nationalized tropes of popular culture, particularly television and Web culture, which function as the surrogate sites and circuits of sociability in an architecturally decentralized suburban context.

Where in the World Is JJ Chinois?

JJ Chinois's domain is a domain name. He can be found striking his signature soft-butch contrapostal pose at www.jjchinois.com. The borderless space of the World Wide Web plays on the fantasy of JJ's global appeal—even Chairman Mao is a fan—while spatially allegorizing the drama of JJ's narrative of origin in another borderless zone: the California expanse somewhere between and around Los Angeles and San Francisco. Because the contact enabled by street life and close quarters interactions in big cities is not available to the geographically isolated queer subject—the type of interclass, interracial, and intersexual contact valued by Samuel Delany in his homage to a precorporate Times Square[22]—the World Wide Web becomes the emblematic nonspace JJ Chinois uses to foment an intimacy among widely dispersed "teens," "dilettantes," "squares," "lesbians, "starlets," "celebrities," and "those who make them celebrities" who comprise JJ's fan base.[23] After the Macromedia Flash intro, the first page at which JJ's visitors arrive tells his biography. We learn about JJ's smashing debut in New York City engineered by the legendary impresario and original drag-king of comedy, Murray Hill, himself named after a little nowhere spot in Manhattan. It becomes apparent that JJ has already made it there and that we, luckily enough, are about to retrace his road to stardom.

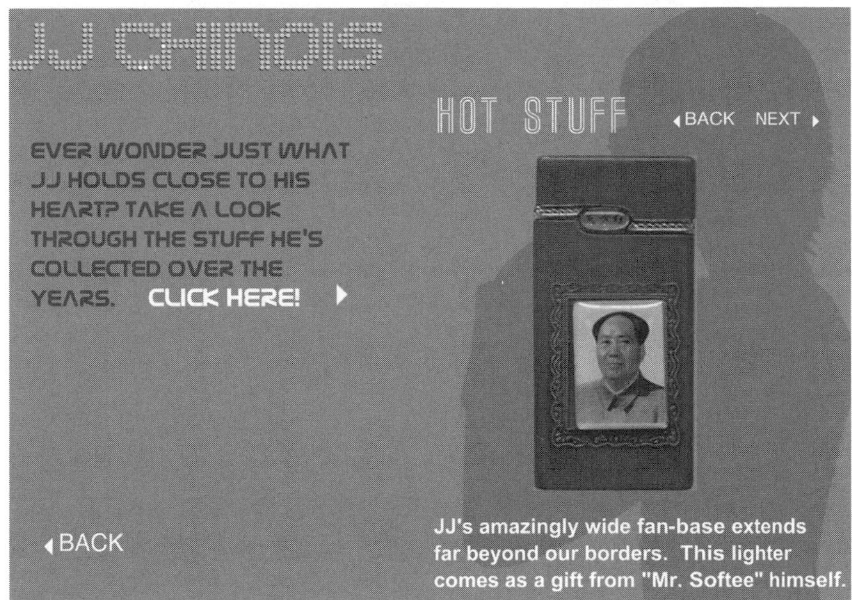

"Chairman Mao's Lighter." Lynne Chan (www.jjchinois.com)

The second page informs us that JJ's "story began a few years ago in Coalinga, California." Anyone who has ever taken a drive on Interstate 5 between San Francisco and Los Angeles, or who has read the *New York Times* article "The Dazed and the Bored on I-5,"[24] will recognize this place-name about midway through the route near a corporate cattle ranch, Harris Ranch. Coalinga is described on its city Web site as a place "nestled in Pleasant Valley . . . ten miles west of Interstate 5."[25] The Coalinga "local facts" community Web site situates the town at "the urban fringe of a large city"—Fresno, about sixty miles away, which the site boasts is "California's sixth largest city!"[26] Coalinga curiously situates itself as a "fast-growing suburb" to overcome outsider perceptions that it is a backwater wasteland somewhere in the Central Valley. What comes as a surprise in JJ's bio is not just that JJ uses the aspiring suburb, Coalinga, as his geographic springboard but, rather, the specific settings in Coalinga where JJ's "raw-throated vulnerability" is purportedly discovered. According to his bio, JJ squanders his "prodigious talents" as a "dim-sum cart pusher at the local Chinese restaurant." The setting for JJ's night shifts, the "Steer and Stein," is more likely to exist in Coalinga, yet the name itself is cribbed from an establishment now renamed the Spunky Steer in Riverside, a good 198 miles south.[27]

JJ CHINOIS
BIOGRAPHY
A lot has been said about JJ Chinois, and there's a lot more to be said about him. His popularity has grown enormously in the years since his first admirers started shouting, "Nice ass."
It began with the teenagers, of course. But at JJ's debut in New York City, it soon became obvious that it's easier to skin an amoeba than to catalog the "Typical JJ Chinois Fan". The teens were there, but so were the "dilettantes" and the "squares", the "lesbians" and the screen starlets, the celebrities and those who make them celebrities.
JJ Chinois is something special. His good looks, and raw-throated vulnerability bring an immediate response from fans and critics. But his story actually began a few years ago, in Coalinga, California.
JJ's talent was prodigious, but squandered in the morning shift as a dimsum cart pusher at the local Chinese restaurant and at the evening shift as the busboy at the local steak house, the Steer & Stein. But it was there that JJ was discovered by a then young Murray Hill, the legendary producer.

"JJ's Biography." Lynne Chan (www.jjchinois.com)

By conflating, confusing, and substituting one suburban site for the next, Chan uses a familiar humorous trope that plays on the suburbs' infinite interchangeability. Places, people, and things are so similar from one suburb to the next that it matters very little whether places like the Steer and Stein are actually in Riverside or Coalinga; some manifestation of the kitschy cowboy steak house will undoubtedly be found in either place. Chan's locational license, however, rewrites the punch line. JJ's biography actually substitutes one suburban site for the next for two differently situated audiences. As Chan explains, JJ Chinois's urbane audiences are expected to find a kind of sight-gag humor in the place-name *Coalinga* without even knowing exactly what it signifies and without realizing that another layer of humor can be derived from the decidedly outlandish notion that Coalinga harbors a dim sum restaurant.[28] The site of locational knowledge for a queer New Yorker in JJ's bio would be Murray Hill, recognizable as both an homage to a place-name in Manhattan and the *nom de stage* of a queer entertainer who has long been based in New York City.

Unlike the cosmopolitan reader of JJ's bio, the suburban reader might not necessarily find the name *Coalinga* in and of itself visually humorous. The suburban reader of JJ's bio, however, might revel in a deeper level of signification and recognition. To understand the joke fully requires living or having lived the demographic specificity and, indeed, the implicit misery of these suburban locales somewhere in the vast California expanse. A suburban audience in California would know that the suburban dim sum cart pusher would most likely be found in Monterey Park, the self-dubbed "Beverly Hills for Chinese," or maybe other densely populated Asian suburbs like Rowland Heights, Walnut, or Torrance, but not Coalinga.[29] Or, rather, the Asian suburban audience who lives in Monterey Park, or who drives there for dim sum from any one of a number of other Southern California outposts, would realize that this suburb is where you might find a JJ Chinois.

The inside joke is also for the queer suburbanite. JJ Chinois's ludic open secret is not that he is a queer transgendered Asian performer passing as a boy in a place that fails to recognize him but rather that Lynne Chan, the New York City artist who has created this persona and re-created these places, shares in an intimate knowledge of these mundane, shame-inducing suburban specificities. She at once pays tribute to, and is recognized by, the quirky queer suburbanite of color past or present who has shared the tragicomic reality of knowing the kinds of racial alienation that occur in the California suburbs, not just among whites and people of color broadly defined but among the varied ethnic groups that have settled in these enclaves and know in which generic sites to locate themselves and seek each other out. The cosmopolitan queer ethos, as Wayne Brekhus and Dereka Rushbrook have each suggested, relies on the repudiation of the suburbs and the glorification of urban hot spots for its veneer of stylistic and identitarian superiority.[30] Chan engages in a game of recognition with postsuburban queers while inviting a return of the repressed, encouraging another kind of "outing" altogether of a spatial familiarity with nowhere spaces. JJ Chinois's narrative insists that fabulous queers literally do come out of "nowhere"—from a myriad of specifically situated, and potentially embarrassing, nowheres thought to be at odds with the formation of the queer, racialized subject. The topographical knowingness that distinguishes the queer cosmopolitan[31]—where the best dim sum in the city is, or where the haute cuisine beef cheeks are perfectly done—is subverted by Chan's narrative of JJ Chinois's discovery. In an echo of her own personal narrative in which she longs to frequent sites like the corner 7-11, Denny's all-night restaurant, and other suburban outposts,[32] JJ Chinois is himself discovered in generic, suburban locales like the Payless Shoe Source. As Chan's revision of these sites suggest, you have to have cultivated the skills of seeking out places literally in the middle of nowhere, in the generic expanse of the suburbs, to ultimately find the right places now that you are somewhere—now that you have arrived *there* (in JJ's case, New York

Chan engages in a game of recognition with postsuburban queers while inviting a return of the repressed, encouraging another kind of "outing" altogether of a spatial familiarity with nowhere spaces.

City). JJ does not merely survive, but he thrives in strip mall settings and by virtue of his presence creates a "scene" in the suburban environment. As I show, the "buzz" surrounding JJ is generated in a series of settings beyond the orbit of the racialized, queer cosmopole.

Touring the Backroads: From Diaspora to "Dykeaspora"

Most of the JJ Chinois Web site is not devoted to the glamour of the big city that acts as glamour's geographic measure, New York. Neither does it narrativize JJ's ultimate arrival in New York City as a liberation or as an attempt to flee from his nowhere places of origin. JJ Chinois ultimately leaves sweet home California for New York City, although the route he takes after Murray Hill helps him cultivate his "ideal combination of talent and virility without bias in either direction" is not a straight shot from oblivion to bright lights, big cities. As JJ's tour dates show us, he weaves his way from the West Coast to the East by stopping at red states and red towns in between. His tour dates include the Payless Shoe Source in Hygiene, Colorado; the veteran's building in Protection, Kansas; OK Eggroll in Bowlegs, Oklahoma; the Sandollar RV Park in Sopchoppy, Florida; and the Doubletree Inn Recreation Center in Shanghai, West Virginia, among other locations.

All are places that seem as if they should not exist, yet all of them actually do. While not all of his tour stops are curiously orientalist in place-name or setting, there is a running motif in which the Asian is infused into unlikely locales. Here Chan riffs not only on the infinite substitution of the links in corporate chains but alludes to a racial imaginary informed by midcentury design's appropriation of "exotic" motifs for prefabricated environments in the suburbs. One publicity stunt employed by the developers of suburban residential outposts was to create theme environments to enliven otherwise cookie-cutter bedroom communities.[33] The proliferation of 1950s tiki-themed bars and oriental kitsch lounges in suburban outposts throughout the United States is but one example of how a Disney-inspired consumer imperialism manufactured a Pacific Rim exoticism that second-generation artists like Chan now exploit and celebrate as a significant component of their own racial imaginary. Chan's vision of her own Asianness through JJ Chinois, meanwhile, has been shaped by and in turn reshapes the suburban stereotypes of race she encountered in *her* homeland, Cupertino, California.[34] Chan's "drag" is racialized as well as gendered, and she exaggerates Asian and white iconographies of masculinity that circulated with suburban cache during her formative years. JJ's look is equal parts Bruce Lee, Steve Perry from Journey (the rocker who

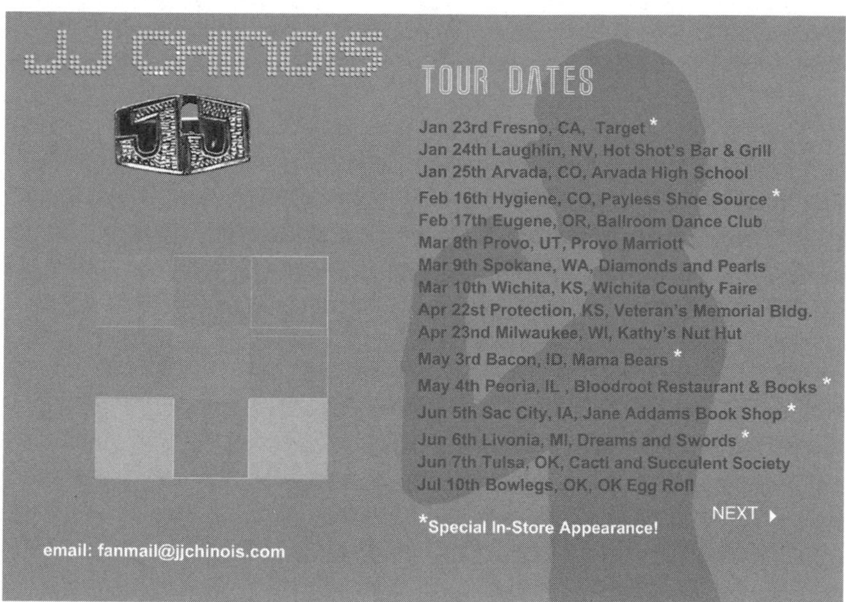

JJ CHINOIS
TOUR DATES
Jan 23rd Fresno, CA, Target *
Jan 24th Laughlin, NV, Hot Shot's Bar & Grill
Jan 25th Arvada, CO, Arvada High School
Feb 16th Hygiene, CO, Payless Shoe Source *
Feb 17th Eugene, OR, Ballroom Dance Club
Mar 8th Provo, UT, Provo Marriott
Mar 9th Spokane, WA, Diamonds and Pearls
Mar 10th Wichita, KS, Wichita County Faire
Apr 22st Protection, KS, Veteran's Memorial Bldg.
Apr 23nd Milwaukee, WI, Kathy's Nut Hut
May 3rd Bacon, ID, Mama Bears *
May 4th Peoria, IL , Bloodroot Restaurant & Books *
Jun 5th Sac City, IA, Jane Addams Book Shop *
Jun 6th Livonia, MI, Dreams and Swords *
Jun 7th Tulsa, OK, Cacti and Succulent Society
Jul 10th Bowlegs, OK, OK Egg Roll
NEXT
*Special In-Store Appearance!
email: fanmail@jjchinois.com

"Tour Dates." Lynne Chan (www.jjchinois.com)

implores "small town girls" to take the "midnight train going anywhere"), and Chan's own ideal of a hairless Asian masculinity.[35]

Chan experiments with representations of race from the suburban simulacral void; she does not turn to her parents' ancestral Hong Kong "homeland" to locate a model of Asian authenticity. In this sense Chan's work belongs simultaneously to a fin de siècle and postmillennial Asian American aesthetic (exemplified in literature by R. Zamora Linmark's *Rolling the R's*), which employs pop-cultural stereotypes of queer, ethnic sexuality to explode sentimental narratives of diasporic longing. Chan herself complicates the facile correlations made between the "suburbs" and stylelessness by exploring the relationship between the designated site of queer culture (named in Chan's project as New York City) and its most insidious other: the California suburbs, a vast sprawl of interlocking freeways and eight-lane "Main Streets" where no one walks and everyone drinks Slurpees and spends after hours at the all-night Denny's. By contrasting New York and California, Chan dramatizes the tension between traditionally urban topographical spaces—massive, vertical, centralized cities—and their sprawling counterparts on the California coastline.[36] With the exception of San Francisco, California's major cities such as Los Angeles and San Diego are incorporated into suburban topographical imaginaries, as Edward Soja's work, *Postmetropolis: Critical Studies of Cit-*

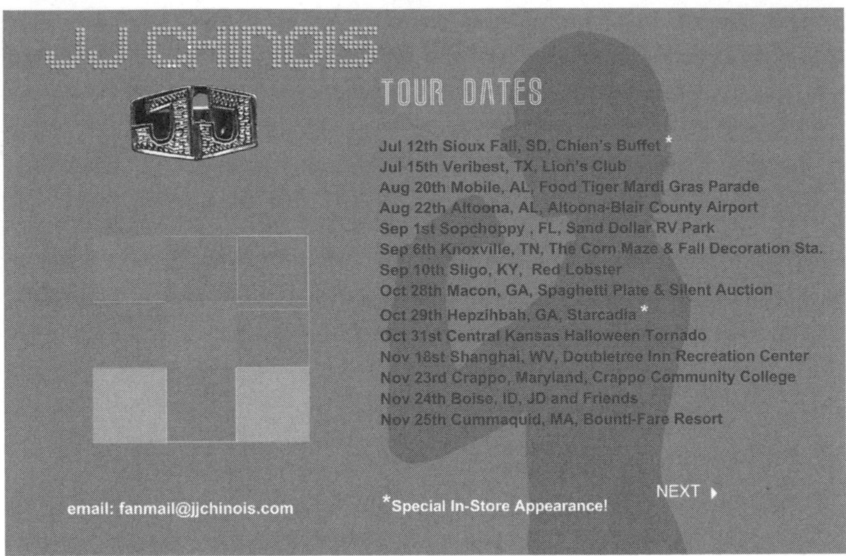

JJ CHINOIS
TOUR DATES
Jul 12th Sioux Fall, SD, Chien's Buffet *
Jul 15th Veribest, TX, Lion's Club
Aug 20th Mobile, AL, Food Tiger Mardi Gras Parade
Aug 22th Altoona, AL, Altoona-Blair County Airport
Sep 1st Sopchoppy , FL, Sand Dollar RV Park
Sep 6th Knoxville, TN, The Corn Maze & Fall Decoration Sta.
Sep 10th Sligo, KY, Red Lobster
Oct 28th Macon, GA, Spaghetti Plate & Silent Auction
Oct 29th Hepzihbah, GA, Starcadia *
Oct 31st Central Kansas Halloween Tornado
Nov 18st Shanghai, WV, Doubletree Inn Recreation Center
Nov 23rd Crappo, Maryland, Crappo Community College
Nov 24th Boise, ID, JD and Friends
Nov 25th Cummaquid, MA, Bounti-Fare Resort
email: fanmail@jjchinois.com
*Special In-Store Appearance!
NEXT

"Tour Dates." Lynne Chan (www.jjchinois.com)

ies and Regions, explains.[37] California shares with New York City a dense and complex history of immigrations and migrations, especially in the twentieth-century popular imaginary. Both New York City and California serve in Chan's work as national endpoints, not only at the coastal edges of the mainland American expanse but also within phantasmic trajectories of a still-extant American dream of "citizenship" in which queer subjects have also indulged. For different reasons, the urban and suburban serve both as last stops in a trajectory of triumph and fortune for the queer of color aspirant and as beacons for strangers from a different shore. Chan traces a pattern of queer migration from the suburbs to the cities in part to eschew her own immigrant parents' investment in an "American dream" of upward mobility that imagines a "good life" for children in the suburban context.

Yet what also distinguishes Chan's JJ Chinois project is that it refuses to pass over the points of transit to and from emblematic sites of migration and immigration like California and New York. By situating JJ's tour stops in chain stores and recreational centers within the "flyover zones" of the United States, Chan offers an imaginative mapping of queer local migrations to complement and complicate more global renditions of diaspora. The spatial and sexual orientations of dykes of color who cultivate their sexuality in the "middle of nowhere" are often misplaced and subsumed in perpetual reimaginings of global immigration rather than properly situated in their own histories of local migration. As Gayatri Gopinath predicted early on in discussions about queer diaspora, *diaspora* itself might be a limiting term and concept insofar as it relies on "conventional ideologies of gender and sexuality" while taking for granted the spatial and aesthetic hierarchies between first and third world spaces.[38]

In the interest of remapping the spatial terrain and the stylistic embodiments that come with queer topographies, I have chosen to concoct the neologism *dykeaspora* to describe the translocal homosexuality made legible by the movements within the United States depicted in Chan's JJ Chinois projects. *Dykeaspora* admittedly lacks the theoretical dignity of the word on which it plays, *diaspora*: a longing for a sense of home after the dispersion from "original" sites rich with "authentic" histories and cultures. A diasporic subject is burdened with an impossible desire for ancestral authenticity that looks elsewhere, to a place of origin, for a sense of stylistic and existential originality. The nostalgia that sometimes accompanies diasporic yearnings for a placeness imbued with originality both real and imagined is notably muted in my vision of the suburban dykeaspora, insofar as the suburban sites that serve as points of origin for the dykeasporic subject demand an ironized mimicry of longing, or a vigorous distancing from the point of first contact where the cultures imported by one's parents become assimilated into a suburban narrative of success. The etymological failing of *dykeaspora*, its excision of the "dia" that signifies movement and dispersion is, I would argue, precisely what opens the term to a queer of color critique that could challenge normative notions of space in queer as well as heteronormative contexts.

Literally, *dykeaspora* would translate into *dyke seed*, a phrase unfortunately evocative of the lesbian baby boom that belies a homonormative investment in bourgeois familial structures and lived environments. Yet I would like to suggest that the dyke seed contained within the term *dykeaspora* need not be subsumed by a reproductive imaginary. Instead, it makes legible the queer developmental narratives that underlie the queer subject's movements from suburbs and small towns to cities. Indeed, *dykeaspora* is an appropriately artificial term that can refer very precisely to the process of self-stylization and self-generation that initiates the movement with which Chan experiments in making the "star" persona, JJ Chinois. Chan's modulation of suburban ennui into a ludic key while repudiating the psychoanalytic familial sagas so often central to the "white diaspora" from cities to suburbs also disavows a homonormative, urban queer rhetoric of "danger" and despair about peripheral spaces.[39]

JJ's constant movements through suburban and rural landscapes equivocate the ideals of choice and liberation that normativize queer narratives of migration to big cities. As much as the JJ Chinois fan site

JJ Chinois becomes Chan's vehicle for expressing a willingness to return to and reclaim locations that we often quickly concede are "not for us."

documents how he ultimately "arrives" (in more ways than one) in Manhattan, JJ refuses to settle into the queer comfort that city life provides. JJ Chinois becomes Chan's vehicle for expressing a willingness to return to and reclaim locations that we often quickly concede are "not for us." What began as an experiment in self-stylization and topographical tracking using the phantasmic space of the World Wide Web became Chan's point of departure for a live demonstration of JJ's ability to make a scene in spaces beyond queer cosmopoles. In 2003 Chan introduced JJ Chinois to the townspeople of Skowhegan, Maine, where he entered the demolition derby at the Skowhegan State Fair, one of the nation's oldest country fairs established in 1818 to "improve the breeding of livestock, with particular emphasis being placed upon the betterment of breeds of horses and cattle."[40] Rather than focusing on the presumed "fear" or violence she might encounter as a queer subject entering the familial, heteronormative arena of the state fair setting, Chan instead viewed the demolition derby as an opportunity to examine the entertainment value placed on risk and violence:

> I liked the idea of this sort of niche arena of masculine competition that combines ridiculous comedy but real violence or real risk. I wanted to tap into that collective fascination with violence and entertainment. I think the Derby proved itself to be an important counterpoint to JJ's fansite. A fansite is ultimately a bit of a safe space: it's for the already seduced, and once it's set up that fiction is set in place. I think it's one thing to talk about the web as some utopian ideal of accessing a limitless audience. But closer to the truth, a fan community is also a fiction. Actually being in public space and introducing a persona taught me about people's assumptions, and my own assumptions.[41]

As I show, JJ's debut in the down-home environment of the Skowhegan State Fair—an annual event that boasts on its Web site live appearances by such figures as "Joey Chiltwoods [of] the auto thrill show, and the nation's popular country group, Asleep at the Wheel"[42]—provides a fascinating model of cultural "encounter" that presents a template for reimagining the geopolitical paradigms of space that have inhibited queer movements.

The taut and tan "Young Republican" in the besmirched muscle shirt hunched over his customized ride in this photograph is none other than JJ Chinois. While it echoes the alluring, animated silhouette of JJ featured on the first page of his fan site, this image from the Skowhegan State Fair indulges in a more earnest and effortless rendition of JJ's working-class masculinity as he moves from the representational space of the Web to a live arena. Many of the background images on JJ's fan site feature him in various shadowy, profiled poses, including one in which he strikes a classic muscle-mag bicep curl. In this photograph of JJ assessing his entry into

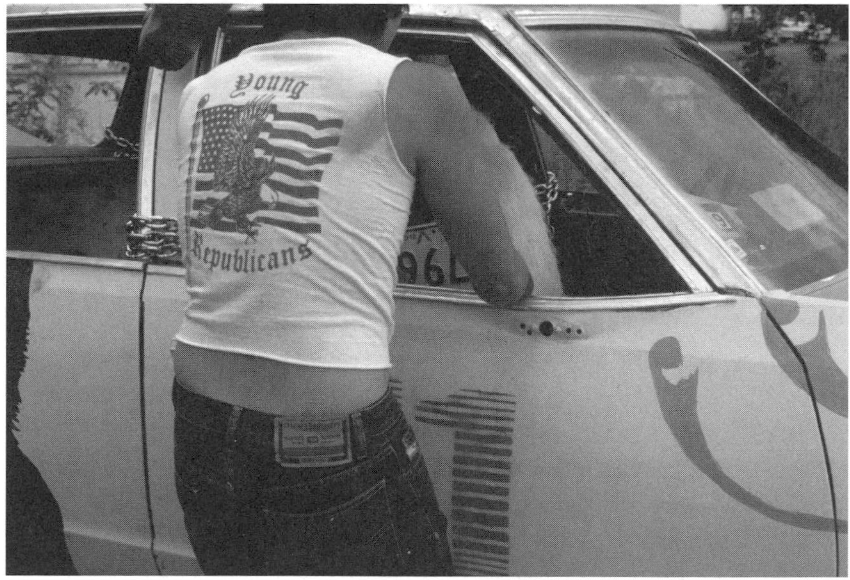

"Young Republicans." Still from JJ Chinois Demolition Derby film, Lynne Chan

the Skowhegan demolition derby, the campy bicep curl has been replaced with just enough cocky, virile lean to reveal naturally the toned contour of his upper arm. The photograph provides a study in unstudied masculinity, or at the very least, in a masculinity striving to achieve an unstudied presentation. As Chan explains, she chose JJ's demeanor and attire for the demolition derby in part as a response to whom she anticipated JJ's audiences might be at the fair: "The Young Republican t-shirt was an in-joke on my part. It kind of summed up the look I was going for . . . white trash, patriotic, macho. All the things I went in assuming my audience would be."[43]

Indeed, various other participants in the demolition derby at the Skowhegan State Fair entered the contest for patriotic causes like "raising money for the troops" in Iraq, so Chan's assumptions were not entirely off the mark.[44] Yet her experiences in Skowhegan in preparation for the derby and after the derby itself confounded Chan's own expectations about JJ's transition from the Web to a tour stop in live space:

> JJ's tour stops on the web were an imaginary journey across mid-America or all the supposed non-places across the country. I'd never experienced a state fair with a demolition derby. . . . My interactions with the friends I made in town, and the people in the crowd made me realize that I had my own assumptions about who my audience was. One of the most rewarding parts

of entering the competition was developing friendships with people in town who ended up helping me out immensely. I developed a genuine rapport with the old couple that sold me the car (Al and Betty). Ross, a mechanic in town, was the main person who helped me modify and tune-up my car. He also gave me important advice on derby strategy. He happened to be one of the finalists in the previous year and convinced me that the most important part of competing was "winning the crowd."[45]

Having talked the talk on the Internet, Chan wanted to walk the walk at the state fair and ultimately discovered that expectations on both sides of *The Great Divide* were open to reinterpretation. Chan acknowledges having entered the competition with a "cosmopolitan bias," a predisposition to assume her audiences might not have the critical capacity to "get the joke," even though the original Web incarnation of the JJ Chinois project deliberately indulged in a utopian fantasy about commonality and transformative encounters through fandom. She came to realize, however, that her cyberspace account of JJ seducing the masses in heartland settings was not entirely off the mark. She speaks warmly of "Al and Betty" and "Ross the mechanic," the local folksy figures who offered JJ support and encouragement in his quest to become the Skowhegan demolition derby champion. The quaint townsfolk who nurtured JJ's demo derby dreams are a far cry from the fan base described on the JJ Chinois fan site—the "teens, dilettantes, starlets, celebrities and those who make them celebrities." While JJ certainly seduced them, their earnest assistance with JJ's derby aspirations in turn seduced Chan and encouraged her to reenvision the range of JJ's fan community.

Yet even as some of these remarkable individual responses subverted Chan's assumptions about her audience, part of the thrill manufactured by JJ Chinois's participation in the Skowhegan demolition derby was not simply that certain expectations about locally marked subjects were frustrated. In fact, many of them were thrillingly affirmed even as JJ's encounters with some locals and retro crowds yielded unanticipated outcomes. As Chan reports, many of the state fair attendees were indeed white people gathered together from decidedly "red counties," some within the blue state of Maine, some from "red states" much further south along the Atlantic Coast. Many of the them came from suburbs, exurbs, and rural towns espousing the very ideals JJ ironically embodied in his Young Republican tee—a macho, chip-on-the-shoulder working-class patriotism more invested in the symbols of national belonging than interested in critiquing the national policies installed to keep class and regional stratification intact. In many respects, they fulfilled Chan's own queer fantasy of "the other," of the other as an archetype of contemporary Americana with all of the

NASCAR trappings. JJ, on the other hand, fulfilled his audience's fantasies about a stylish, and outlandish, celebrity glamour that had to have been imported from somewhere else and that had to represent different values: "People running the derby told me that they had 'figured I must be some kind of porn star' and Googled my website, which on some level seemed to confirm some belief about who they thought JJ Chinois was."[46]

Like her JJ Chinois site, which played with the signifiers of gender, race, and class in ways that moved beyond the drama of "passing," JJ's appearance at the Skowhegan State Fair left behind the paradigm of passing as a measure of success. Instead, Chan became more interested in staging a scene of seduction on a mass level by inviting, and potentially provoking, conflict as she inspired doubt, confusion, and even a kind of mimetic recognition with her appearance:

> I wasn't too concerned with "passing" in this setting. I kind of naturally pass to some extent a lot of the time, and I think that I did to varying degrees to different people through the event. Yet I think JJ really won over lots of new fans, by confusing expectations. I think many people probably realize on some level there was some kind of stunt going on with my appearance. Others seemed to simply accept my novelty whether it was because I was brown and dressed and acted like them, or ambiguously gendered. And then to small children I represented some kind of other-worldly or [maybe] just some kind of Other that they could project some kind of star-status onto . . . probably the most ideal reaction I would want.[47]

JJ Chinois's live demolition derby debut presents a novel notion of "demonstration" both stylistically and politically. While it has at its core a principle of confrontation—of exposing children and adults to "some kind of Other" in a normative, if spectacular setting—its larger political aim is not merely confrontation itself or an aggressively motivated staging of incongruous differences. Neither does it work exclusively on the principles of infiltration, assimilation, or passing. In other words, working with or wooing those who hold dear normative retro values does not require muting the markers of queerness and race to attain an acceptance that is itself a phantasmic ideal. Yet neither does an encounter with retro folks demand lapsing into a suffocating "Log Cabin" ethos to prove we can be just as normal, successful, and tax averse as "everyone else." This bourgeois approach probably would not fly in a setting like a state fair demolition derby. Even though JJ dons an eagle decal Young Republican muscle shirt and earnestly mimics the gestures and poses of white working-class masculinity, he retains an element of novelty and idiosyncrasy marked by race and his ambiguously gendered flourishes of style: "What I quickly learned is that most people are genuinely delighted to see JJ's pink

As JJ Chinois demonstrates, it might be possible for us to "win the crowd" even if we refuse to compromise the legibility of what is unapologetically, outlandishly queer.

car with gold wheels with a giant waving hand. I wasn't that concerned about 'fooling' the audience about who I was. On a mass level like that, people just start to assume that you are a man, or that 'Chinese boy,' or know that you are female and don't really care."[48] More than anything, JJ Chinois's appearance at the Skowhegan State Fair reminds us that the stylishly garish spectacle of queerness has a distinctly seductive potential, even as it stakes its own claim on spaces and settings that are not necessarily intended for us and even when it is not employed in the service of conferring the secret of style to heterosexuals who might envy it.

Yet JJ also reminds us that queers indulge too willingly in our own preconceived notions about space, that we rest too comfortably in our urban inhibitions to reimagine the geopolitical terrain and to have significant encounters with the rural and suburban others we fear most in the places we fear to tread. While JJ Chinois is not likely to single-handedly lure conservatives and elusive swing voters to rally around queer causes, Chan's JJ Chinois projects at the very least enable us to redraw the urban boundaries of a queer spatial imaginary in ways that invite a mutual respect or at the very least a potentially productive mutual curiosity.

Chan's projects offer a model of queer encounter distinctly optimistic about the queer's ability to move to, from, and through suburban and rural spaces without succumbing to the inevitable and self-fulfilling narratives of desperation and violence that haunt the spatial "peripheries." The crowds at the Skowhegan State Fair did not rip JJ to shreds or assail him with homophobic epithets and racial slurs as his pink, gold-wheeled car with a giant waving hand attached to the roof careened through the demo pit. They instead rallied around him as "the underdog" when his car began to take a beating in the derby.[49] Despite having lost the derby competition, JJ accomplished the kind of victory Ross the mechanic established as the ultimate goal for his demo derby apprentice: "It's about winning the crowd."

As JJ Chinois demonstrates, it might be possible for us to "win the crowd" even if we refuse to compromise the legibility of what is unapologetically, outlandishly queer. We are not obliged to transform ourselves into our tasteful, cuddlier made-for-TV versions in order to traffic through the American heartland unscathed. How we subsequently work to transform the political landscape after staging these close encounters, however, remains to be determined. At the very least, JJ poses the possibility that we can, at once, empathize with the other as well as invite the other's empathy—not just in our suffering but in our pleasures. Reflecting on JJ's "demo" in Skowhegan, Chan writes, "I wasn't so much making an ironic gesture, but finding a way of experiencing a genuine pleasure in shattering expectations about identity, race and gender in places we think of as scary, nowhere places. It was about having an audience react in confusion, but also delight."[50] This delightful confusion might only be ephemeral, might only last for the span of an evening in which irony and ridicule are suspended as the crowd sounds a roaring surge of respect for the underdog whoever he may be, wherever she may be from. But maybe we can find a morsel of possibility in the modest vision of victory that made buddies of Ross the mechanic and JJ Chinois. Maybe it is "about winning the crowd, even if it's just for an evening."[51]

Notes

1. The journalist David Brooks is credited with popularizing the red state/blue state paradigm in a December 2001 article titled "One Nation, Slightly Divisible" published in the *Atlantic Monthly.* A flurry of responses to Brooks's calculated oversimplification of the "new culture wars" was issued, among them a book-length study by Stanford political scientist Morris P. Fiorina (with Samuel J. Abrams and Jeremy C. Pope) titled *Culture War? The Myth of a Polarized America* (Harlow, UK: Longman, 2004), debunking the paradigm's cultural component. Nevertheless, the concept continues to have a considerable amount of play and has since been reconfigured as the retro versus metro paradigm in what amounts to a cultural template for electoral victory pitched to centrist Democrats. See John Sperling, *The Great Divide: Retro vs. Metro America* (Sausalito, CA: PoliPoint, 2004). Portions of the book are also available online for a free PDF download through a Web site run by PoliPoint Press, devoted to creating a buzz around the retro versus metro concept. See www.retrovsmetro.org. The political scientist Kimberly Nalder of California State University, Sacramento, is conducting a critical study and survey of these paradigms, and I thank her for her input on these geopolitical models.

2. See www.retrovsmetro.org/retrovsmetro/. These quotations are taken from a split-screen diagram explaining, in broad strokes, the crucial differences between retro and metro America.

3. Ibid.

4. Ibid.

5. The last twenty years have seen an abundance of cultural and social histories of queer urban life in the United States and abroad. While such texts are too numerous to list here, it warrants notice that a majority of urban queer histories, particularly those that have achieved canonicity in queer studies, have focused primarily on gay male communities in New York City. Perhaps most exemplary in this regard is George Chauncey's *Gay New York: Gender, Urban Culture, and the Making of the Gay Male World, 1890–1940* (New York: Basic Books, 1995). See also Charles Kaiser's *Gay Metropolis* (New York: Harvest Books, 1998). Recently, queer scholars have begun to critique the historical mythos of urban gay life by taking to task its complicity with projects of urban gentrification, and race and class segregation. Christina B. Hanhardt, a PhD candidate in American studies at New York University, is completing a dissertation titled "Safe Space: Sexual Minorities, Uneven Urban Development, and the Politics of Violence," which promises to be an important contribution to this field of inquiry.

6. In a series of books, Richard Florida has characterized an emergent "creative class" who populate specific cities (and neighborhoods within cities) that mirror the new economic lifestyle disentangled from the forty-hour work clock and industrial production. See Richard Florida, *The Rise of the Creative Class: And How It's Transforming Work, Leisure, Community, and Everyday Life* (New York: Perseus Books, 2002), and his recent follow-up, *Cities and the Creative Class* (New York: Routledge, 2004).

7. Much of the demographic information on gay and lesbian populations in *The Great Divide* and the newly published *Gay and Lesbian Atlas* is culled from the 2000 U.S. Census, which, for the first time, surveyed partnered gays and lesbians. Because the census only collected data on gay and lesbians using categories of normative social arrangements like couples and families, the *Gay and Lesbian Atlas* offers a limited portrait of gay and lesbian "communities" throughout the United States, despite its admirable geographic coverage. See Gary J. Gates, Jason Ost, and Elizabeth Birch, *The Gay and Lesbian Atlas* (Washington, DC: Urban Institute Press, 2004).

8. Information about SONG, its outreach networks throughout the southern United States, and its political objectives can be found on its Web site, www.southnewground.org.

9. See www.southnewground.org/page2.html.

10. Ibid.

11. Roderick Ferguson, *Aberrations in Black: Toward a Queer of Color Critique* (Minneapolis: University of Minnesota Press, 2004).

12. Ibid., 26. As Ferguson explains, "queer of color critique addresses minority cultural forms as both within and outside canonical genealogies" while nevertheless "pointing to the ruptural possibilities of those forms."

13. Judith Halberstam, "Telling Tales: Brandon Teena, Billy Tipton, and Transgender Biography," in "Queer Auto/Biographies," ed. Thomas Spear, special issue, *a/b*, 62–81. The article has since been republished in *Passing: Identity and Interpretation in Sexuality, Race, and Religion*, ed. Maria Carla Sanchez and Linda Schlossberg (New York: New York University Press, 2001), 13–37.

14. See James T. Sears, *Rebels, Rubyfruit, and Rhinestones: Queering Space in the Stonewall South* (New Brunswick, NJ: Rutgers University Press, 2001). See also works on the gay and lesbian Midwest, such as Beth Bailey's *Sex in the Heartland* (Cambridge, MA: Harvard University Press, 2002); and Karen Lee Osborne and William J. Spurlin, eds., *Reclaiming the Heartland: Lesbian and Gay Voices from the Midwest* (Minneapolis: University of Minnesota Press, 1996).

15. See www.retrovsmetro.org/retrovsmetro/.

16. One of the most compelling recent examples that remaps and reimagines queer, urban terrain is Martin Manalansan's new book, *Global Divas: Filipino Gay Men in the Diaspora* (Durham, NC: Duke University Press, 2004).

17. Catherine Jurca, introduction to *White Diaspora: The Suburb and the Twentieth-Century American Novel* (Princeton, NJ: Princeton University Press, 2001), 3–19.

18. For an account of working-class migrations into the suburban areas of Southern California, see Becky M. Nicolaides, *My Blue Heaven: Life and Politics in the Working-Class Suburbs of Los Angeles, 1920–1965* (Chicago: University of Chicago Press, 2002).

19. Recent social histories like Timothy Fong's *First Suburban Chinatown: The*

Remaking of Monterey Park, California (Philadelphia: Temple University Press, 1994) and Wayne Brekhus's *Peacocks, Chameleons, Centaurs: Gay Suburbia and the Grammar of Social Identity* (Chicago: University of Chicago Press, 2003) have powerfully argued that late-twentieth-century and postmillennial American suburbs are increasingly populated by "minority majorities" of queer and racialized subjects. Census data show that from 1980 to 1990 the Chinese American population more than doubled in the suburb of Monterey Park; by 1994, 56 percent of its inhabitants identified themselves as Chinese American.

20. Mimi Nguyen, a Mellon Postdoctoral Research Fellow in women's studies at the University of Michigan, has written extensively on Chan's celebrity persona and experimentations with 1970s "ethnic" masculinities, including Bruce Lee's internationally popularized brand of Asian masculinity. A specific portion of this work, "Star Personas and Fan Fictions: Bruce Lee, JJ Chinois, and the Queer Technologies of Celebrity," was presented at the Center for New Media at the University of California, Berkeley, in October 2004.

21. Chan began incorporating *Chinois* into her daily vocabulary after a visit to Paris and shortly thereafter invented the character of JJ Chinois (Lynne Chan, interview by author, New York City, October 2001).

22. Samuel Delany, *Times Square Red, Times Square Blue* (New York: New York University Press, 2001).

23. For an insightful analysis of the impact Internet technologies have on Asian American media arts, and on Chan's JJ Chinois projects in particular, see Eve Oishi, "Bad Asians, The Sequel: Continuing Trends in Queer API Film and Video," in "Gay and Lesbian Experimental Cinema," ed. Jim Hubbard, special issue, *Millennium Film Journal* 39 (2003): 34–41.

24. See Janelle Brown, "The Dazed and the Bored on the I-5," *New York Times*, 15 November 2002.

25. See www.coalinga.com.

26. Coalinga community Web site, www.digital-neighbor.com/city/ca/coalinga803b.htm (accessed November 2002; this site is no longer available). What are termed "cities" in the central valleys of California (like Fresno, and JJ's purported birthplace, Bakersfield) have recently been referred to as "edge cities," or hybrid suburban environments characterized by large civic governments and growing residential populations. Architecturally, these "edge cities," or exurbs, are more suburban in character than the classic, early-twentieth-century American notion of the vertical metropolis. See Joel Garreau, *Edge City: Life on the New Frontier* (New York: Doubleday, 1991).

27. Coalinga community Web site, www.digital-neighbor.com/city/ca/coalinga803b.htm.

28. Chan and I discussed her use of place-names in an interview conducted October 2001. Subsequent citations from that interview have been reviewed and approved by Chan.

29. See Fong, *First Suburban Chinatown*, 35–54.

30. Brekhus critiques these queer cosmopolitans in "Gay Suburbanites," in *Peacocks, Chameleons, Centaurs*, 5–7. See also Dereka Rushbrook's "Cities, Queer Space, and the Cosmopolitan Tourist," *GLQ* 8 (2002): 183–206.

31. Rushbrook, "Cities, Queer Space, and the Cosmopolitan Tourist," 188–90.

32. Chan, interview by author.

33. See Mike Davis, *City of Quartz: Excavating the Future in Los Angeles* (New York: Vintage, 1990), 84–88.

34. Chan, interview by author. Chan's parents found work in the software industry and relocated to Cupertino (in Silicon Valley) in the 1970s.

35. Ibid. Chan explains how the persona of JJ developed after a series of photographic experiments depicting Latino, "cholo" versions of racialized masculinity as part of her undergraduate work at the University of California, Davis, and UCLA. Chan subsequently began to think of ways to combine the iconically virile Asian masculinity of Bruce Lee with the stylistically androgynous but hypermasculine glam rock ethos of the same era.

36. A helpful resource on the sprawling topography of gay and lesbian life in Los Angeles is Moira Rachel Kenney, *Mapping Gay L.A.: The Intersection of Place and Politics* (Philadelphia: Temple University Press, 2001).

37. See especially Soja's chapters, "An Introduction to the Conurbation of Greater Los Angeles" and "Fractal City: Metropolarities and the Restructured Social Mosaic," in *Postmetropolis: Critical Studies of Cities and Regions* (Oxford: Blackwell, 2000).

38. Gayatri Gopinath, "Funny Boys and Girls: Notes on a South Asian Queer Planet," in *Asian American Sexualities*, ed. Russell Leong (New York: Routledge, 1996), 119–25. Gopinath's extensive body of work on "queer diaspora" has enriched this initially narrow and normative concept of *diaspora* while alerting us to the term's underlying nationalist limitations. At the same time, Gopinath points the way for a methodology that can interpret and make legible female queer desires subsumed by orthodox, diasporic imaginaries. My own account of JJ Chinois, however, does not easily fit within the rubric of queer diaspora that Gopinath describes in *Impossible Subjects: Queer Diasporas and South Asian Public Cultures* (Durham, NC: Duke University Press, 2005). I decided to use the neologism *dykeaspora* to offer a narrower, more locally situated notion of queer movements and migrations.

39. See Halberstam's critique of metronormativity in her essay "Telling Tales: Brandon Teena, Billy Tipton, and Transgender Biography." Teena's self-stylization as a chivalrous middle-class American male not only accounts for his trouble—his danger and risk—but also his pleasure. Yet Teena's failure to flee the Nebraska plains can only be read by his metronormative biographers as a failure rather than as a choice—as a failure to flee dangerous circumstances rather than as a strategy *for* survival and styles of living that Halberstam speculates might be "shared by many Midwestern queers [as] a way of staying rather than leaving."

40. For a local history of the Skowhegan State Fair, see www.skowheganstatefair.com/history.html.

41. Lynne Chan, e-mail interview by author, 15 October 2004.

42. Ibid.

43. Chan, e-mail interview by author. JJ has nevertheless consistently cited his political preference as "Republican," both on his Web site and in the *JJ Chinois* film. For another reference to JJ's Republicanism, see Oishi, "Bad Asians, The Sequel," 35.

44. The Skowhegan State Fair Web site offers links to local news articles about demolition derby participants raising money or offering tribute to American troops in Iraq (www.skowheganstatefair.com).

45. Chan, e-mail interview by author.

46. Ibid.
47. Ibid.
48. Ibid.
49. Ibid.
50. Ibid.
51. Ibid.

Shame and White Gay Masculinity

Judith Halberstam

When I first received an invitation to speak at the University of Michigan's "Gay Shame" conference, I felt immediately that this conference was not for me. The idea of gay shame felt anachronistic, even though I knew about the activist groups who organized under this rubric to critique the consumerism of gay pride festivals.[1] The more I thought about the conference and its theme, the more I became convinced that gay shame, if used in an uncritical way, was for, by, and about the white gay men who had rejected feminism and a queer of color critique and for whom, therefore, shame was still an active rubric of identification. A quick glance at the list of participants a few months before the conference confirmed this notion, as at least seventeen white gay men were scheduled to speak out of a list of about forty-five participants and only a handful of people of color were listed for the entire event. I considered sending an e-mail to the conference organizers to ask about their understanding of the place of race in queer studies today, but I thought better of it and presumed that the list of participants was still under construction and would look very different when the conference began. As it turned out, the list of participants did change slightly; one of the queer people of color invited, Samuel Delany, could not attend, and so Hiram Perez was one of two people of color at the event who was speaking on a panel (as opposed to moderating a panel). At a conference where disability studies was given a panel all its own (and an excellent panel at that) and the scope of the discussion was supposed to extend beyond the university and into activist and performance communities, the omission of people of color, or at the very least of queers explicitly working on race, was ominous.

How do we explain the absence of both a panel on race and sexuality and queer people of color at a major queer studies conference in the year 2003? Is it the case that gay shame is not a rubric that relates to racialization? Has there been no relevant work recently on gay shame and race? Is queer studies white? Is queer activism white? Is race somehow not an important rubric for queer studies? Obviously, the answer to each of these questions is "no": there has been a huge amount of work recently that foregrounds racial processes and indeed implicates shame in producing queer

Social Text 84–85, Vol. 23, Nos. 3–4, Fall–Winter 2005.

We cannot completely do without shame . . . shame can be a powerful tactic in the struggle to make privilege (whiteness, masculinity, wealth) visible.

identities. New books by Rod Ferguson, Robert Reid-Pharr, Juana Rodriguez, Licia Fiol-Matta, and David Eng immediately come to mind, and older work by José Esteban Muñoz, David Roman, and Jacqui Alexander provide the critical backdrop against which and from which this new work emerges.[2] Queer work on race has become central to the queer project in academia, and queer studies has moved far beyond readings of canonical white gay male authors and artists by tenured white gay male professors. So why, again, would a major national conference on queer studies include little to no work on queer race by published scholars in the field? I want to answer this question by providing here an expanded version of the paper I gave at the conference and then conclude with a brief summary of a series of skirmishes that developed at the conference around the topic of white gay male hegemony. In the course of this essay, some of my remarks, particularly those directed at white gay men, actually take on the form of shaming itself. While I realize that this performance of shaming is not the best way to dislodge its effects and influence, my argument throughout is that we cannot completely do without shame and that shame can be a powerful tactic in the struggle to make privilege (whiteness, masculinity, wealth) visible.

Let me say at the outset that some (not all) of the white gay men behaved as if they represented a block interest; at times the discussion was wholly dominated by white gay men discussing issues of interest to other white gay men, and the point was made, during one such discussion, that while women and people of color are willing to write and think about whiteness and masculinity, white gay men show very little interest in writing and thinking in reciprocal ways about race and gender.[3] This kind of narrow interest in the self can only be termed *identity politics*. My hope here is to use the conference to unravel and make visible the deeply invested identity politics of white gay men that have obscured more radical agendas; this is an identity politics moreover that, like the identity politics of other white male scholarship, hides behind the banner of "general interest" or simply "knowledge." The future of queer studies, I claim, depends absolutely on moving away from white gay male identity politics and learning from the radical critiques offered by a younger generation of queer scholars who draw their intellectual inspiration from feminism and ethnic studies rather than white queer studies.

Gay Shame: A White Gay Male Thing?

In my presentation at the Gay Shame conference, I offered some thoughts on "gay shame" intended to provoke and encourage discussion. I presented my remarks in three sections, each with its own polemical thrust, each with a set of questions, and each intended to add to a general concern about the romanticization of gay shame, a romanticization that, I believe, glosses over both the particularity of this formation and the damage of its myopic range.

Shame Is to Childhood as Queer Is to Adulthood . . .

> If queer is a politically potent term, which it is, that's because, far from being capable of being detached from the childhood scene of shame, it cleaves to that scene as a near-inexhaustible source of transformational energy.
> —Eve Kosofsky Sedgwick, *Shame and Performativity: Henry James's New York Edition Prefaces*

Eve Kosofsky Sedgwick,[4] and others who have written so eloquently about gay shame, posit an early childhood experience of sexual shame that has to be reclaimed, reinterpreted, and resituated by a queer adult who, armed with a theoretical language about his or her sexuality, can transform past experiences with abjection, isolation, and rejection into legibility, community, and love. Gay shame, in this scenario, becomes the deep emotional reservoir on which an adult queer sexuality draws, for better or for worse. The sexual and emotional scripts that queer life draws on, and that oppose the scripts of normativity, are indebted oddly to this early experience with shame, denial, and misrecognition. When we seek to reclaim gay shame and we oppose the normativity of a "gay pride" agenda, we embrace these awkward, undignified, and graceless childhoods, and we choose to make them part of our political future.

The annexing of shame to queer within the temporal space of "anteriority" has been a huge part of several influential projects in queer studies: Michael Warner's critiques of "normal," Sedgwick's theory of "shame," and Leo Bersani's work on "homos" all find rich archives of sexual variance in what Elizabeth Freeman has called "the temporal lag between homo and gay."[5] And in Douglas Crimp's new work, "Queer before Gay," queer is very explicitly the prehistory of gay, a history that must not be left behind in the rush to gay pride but which must be excavated in all its contradiction, disorder, and eros. While these projects make some useful disconnections between queer life and the seeming inevitability of homonormativity, there are also some problems that attend to characterizing shame as normal's "other" and then positioning it as a past that must be reclaimed. The three most obvious problems have to do with glorifying the pre-Stonewall past; idealizing youth itself, the territory of gay shame after all; and, as Lauren Berlant suggests in *Regarding Sedgwick: Essays on Queer Culture and Critical Theory*, focusing perhaps too much on interiority. Berlant asks: "Must the project of queerness start 'inside' of the subject and spread out from there?"[6]

Why are these things problematic? Well, focusing excessively on a mythic queer past or overinvesting hope in a queer future or building a queer project from the "inside of the subject" actually produces a romanticized notion of a gay past (this is what Raymond Williams calls "tradition")[7] and then neutralizes the potency of critiques of that past that emerge in the queer present; in a present-day context, for example, we may find that a contemporary antihomonormative queer politics emerges from racialized groups and immigrant communities specifically as a critique of the mythologizing of the queer past that goes on in white gay communities. For example, Martin Manalansan has already made a very different critique of North American gay pride celebrations (different from those critiques made by "gay shamers") and the traditions that they both mobilize and consolidate. In an essay about the twenty-fifth anniversary celebrations in 1994 of the Stonewall Rebellion titled "In the Shadows of Stonewall: Examining Gay Transnational Politics and the Diaspora Dilemma," Manalansan specifically took aim at the internationalizing of a U.S. gay movement: "Who bestows legitimacy on the narration of Stonewall as the origin of gay and lesbian development? What does this narrative of origins engender? What practices and locations are subordinated by a privileging of Stonewall as origin?"[8] His questioning of the "globalizing of gay identity" (502) reminds us of the global framework within which celebrations like gay pride take place, but it also reveals the problem of universalizing debates within which gay white men occupy all available positions: after all, the critics of homonormativity and pride are, like the homonorms themselves, white gay men.

Recently in gay and lesbian communities, we have witnessed a startling new focus on gay youth. Youth groups have sprung up everywhere along with gay schools and gay-straight encounter groups in high schools. Youth groups, to be very general, rescue young queers from the potential bullying and isolation that awaits the adolescent with same-sex desires or alternative gendering, and they offer a safe space among peers and counselors within which to develop contrary sexualities. Unfortunately, some youth groups also install, perhaps prematurely, both a sense of a fixed identity and a context of hurt and damage within which to understand that fixed sexual identity. Much of the organizing around gay shame in activist circles has come from queer youth who turn their rebellious instincts away from straight culture and direct many of their most searing indictments at older gays and lesbians. The generational conflict that gay youth groups inadvertently inspire works in turn to normalize the temporal rhythms of queer life.[9] While in the past, queer intergenerational dating allowed older men and women to pass on information, sexual practices, and historical information from one generation to the other, now gay youth are "protected" from the "predations" of older queers. In the past, oedipal dynamics could be avoided in queer communities because the divide between youth and older people was underemphasized; now, gay youth very much want to supplant an older generation's models of identity, community, and activism. Gay shame, again, with its emphasis on claiming the abject materiality that "pride" disregarded, increases these generational divides and enables young gays to direct their political anger at the very gay and lesbian activists who made gay youth groups possible in the first place.

In other words, gay shame has a tendency both in its academic and in its activist incarnations to become a totalizing narrative that balances out the consumer focus of "gay pride" with the faux-radical chic of white gay shame; because of its binary structure, shame/pride then seems to have covered the entirety of gay experience. When we make gay pride into the sum total of contemporary queer politics, we simply are not looking closely enough at the alternatives. Gay pride may well be a massive consumer opportunity as its critics have astutely pointed out, but not everyone is "buying." For some folks, gay pride is the only "gay" thing they do all year; for others, the opportunity to march within ethnic groups that tend to be marginalized by white gay communities makes gay pride an important site for the disruption of a monolithic association of gay identity with white gay masculinity. Gay groups like SALGA, TRIKONE, and the Audre Lorde Project are not merely offering themselves as new targets for niche marketing at gay pride, nor are they rounding out the diversity proclaimed by the ubiquitous rainbow flags; these groups come to queer politics with specific radical agendas, specific forms of queer culture, specific forms of queer world making, and in this respect they are far removed from the floats that advertise a new gay bar or a new gay church or a new gay hardware store.

So while gay shame stabilizes the pride/shame binary and makes white gay politics the sum total of queer critique, gay shame also has a tendency to universalize the self who emerges out of a "shame formation": at the microlevel, the subject who emerges as the subject of gay shame is often a white and male self whose shame in part emerges from the experience of being denied access to privilege. As I discuss later, shame for women and shame for people of color plays out in different ways and creates different modes of abjection, marginalization, and self-abnegation; it also leads to very different political strategies. While female shame can be countered by

The subject who emerges as the subject of gay shame is often a white and male self whose shame in part emerges from the experience of being denied access to privilege.

feminism and racialized shame can be countered by what Rod Ferguson calls "queer of color critique," it is white gay male shame that has proposed "pride" as the appropriate remedy and that focuses its libidinal and other energies on simply rebuilding the self that shame dismantled rather than taking apart the social processes that project shame onto queer subjects in the first place. This is why, as Berlant states, we might want to question the notion of a queer politics that begins "inside the subject." The notion that social change can come about through adjustments to the self, through a focus on interiority without a concomitant attention to social, political, and economic relations, can be a disastrous tactic for queer studies and queer activism.

Finally, discussions about gay shame, even those that want to counter a politics of pride, betray a kind of casualness about the effects of shame on others—Michael Warner warns about this when he writes, "What will we do with our shame? . . . the usual response is to pin it on someone else."[10] Warner is exactly right in describing how shame is projected away from the self and onto others; what he is less precise about is how the projection of gay shame elsewhere is neither random nor unpredictable. For example, in the infamous Warhol *Screen Test #2* that Douglas Crimp writes about in "Mario Montez: For Shame," which was screened at this conference, the body made to bear the visible marks of gay shame (Warhol's, the drag queen's, the viewer's), forced to squirm under the camera's gaze and be painfully vulnerable, belongs not to a white gay man like Warhol but to a Puerto Rican drag queen. In this excruciating screen test, the drag queen consents to be a kind of marionette for a "casting director" (not Warhol but Ronald Tavel) who manipulates Montez from behind the camera and only ever registers in the film as a disembodied voice. Crimp gives us an example of Montez's humiliation:

> Poor Mario. Now begins his humiliation. Tavel tells Mario to repeat after him, "For many years I have heard your name, but never did it sound so beautiful until I learned that you were a movie producer, Diarrhea." Mario is obliged to say "diarrhea" again and again, with various changes of inflection and emphasis. Then to lip synch, as Tavel says it. "Mouth 'diarrhea' exactly as if it tasted of nectar," Tavel instructs. Mario obeys, blissfully unaware of where this game of pleasing a producer named Diarrhea will lead.[11]

Crimp only mentions the fact that Montez was Puerto Rican in passing to point out that some of the religious abjection to which Tavel subjected Montez would have been very humiliating, but nowhere does Crimp address the racialized dynamic of the brown body dancing to the tune whistled by an invisible white director; and nowhere does he credit Montez with some agency in her own performance.

Crimp's interest in the Montez screen test, he says, has to do with the encounter it affords between the viewer and "the other's shame," a shame, nonetheless, that he claims: "We accept as also ours, but curiously also ours alone" (67). Curious indeed that this shame, the other's shame, so seamlessly becomes "ours"; how does this happen? Is it that the white viewer feels the racial shame of whiteness by watching the brown body squirm? Is it that the white gay viewer recognizes that his pride depends on another's abjection? Not exactly. Crimp implies instead that he (we?) accesses his own sense of vulnerability by watching it course through another body, and he affirms: "I am thus not 'like' Mario, but the distinctiveness that is revealed in Mario invades me—'floods me,' to use Sedgwick's word—and my own distinctiveness is revealed simultaneously. I, too, feel exposed" (67). How perfect! The white gay man, just like the white gay man in the Asian porn films described in Richard Fung's classic essay "Looking for My Penis: The Eroticized Asian in Gay Male Porn," does not have to be exposed because there is a racialized body well positioned to be exposed in his place. In the films that Fung described, the white gay male fantasizes his own vulnerability by imagining himself as an Asian man when he is being fucked.[12] David Eng has expanded on Fung's reading and provided us with a name for this process: racial castration.[13] In the scene that Crimp describes, Montez, the Puerto Rican drag queen, performs her castration so that Warhol/Tavel/Crimp can access the pleasure of humiliation without actually having to embody the shame himself. As Larry La Fountain-Stokes recently wrote to Douglas Crimp in an open letter: "For me the shame of Mario Montez becomes that of Frantz Fanon, faced by a child who stares at him in horror, the shame of Gloria Anzaldúa and Cherríe Moraga and Audre Lorde, of those Puerto Ricans and other diasporic people of color shamed every day for being a subjugated and racialized people, and particularly, the shame of the Puerto Rican queer."[14] At the conference, when asked about the racial dynamics of this scene, Crimp referred the audience to excellent work on Warhol and race by a graduate student, Taro Nettleton; while it was important for Crimp to refer to this work, it also had the effect of assigning the task of really poring over white gay shame elsewhere . . . yet again.

Shame Is to Femininity as Rage Is to Masculinity . . .

Obviously shame is multifaceted and can be brought on by psychic traumas as brutal as physical bullying and as seemingly benign as mute indifference. But the physical experience of shame records in dramatic fashion (a blush, vertigo, overwhelming panic) a failure to be powerful, legitimate, proper—it records the exposure, in psychoanalytic terms, of the subject's castration, be it racial, gendered, class-based, or sexual. Since

The physical experience of shame records in dramatic fashion a failure to be powerful, legitimate, proper—it records the exposure, in psychoanalytic terms, of the subject's castration, be it racial, gendered, class-based, or sexual.

gender is the dominant framework in psychoanalysis, one would be tempted to say that castration as theorized in psychoanalysis is central to shame and that shame is central to femininity. If the current social arrangements of power reserve and protect certain forms of legitimacy for white, phallic subjects, then, inevitably, those bodies neither white nor phallic will find that their maturation processes and even their adult lives must pass through the territory of shame. And, at the same time, white and phallic subjects will find that their only shame may lie in not claiming their historically mandated privilege. And so, the shame experienced by white gay men in childhood has to do with exposing their femininity and dramatizing their failure to access the privilege that has been symbolically reserved for them. The sissy boy is the incarnation of shame, and so we should not be surprised to find that the centerpiece of today's gay pride movements has to do with reclaiming gay masculinity.

It needs to be pointed out in any discussion of gay shame that for the butch lesbian, her masculinity is not in and of itself shameful when she is a child (hence tomboy tolerance). It is the butch's failure to become properly feminine at adolescence that prompts the shame, and so we should say that some lesbian subjectivities have much less to do with shame than most gay white male subjectivities, and indeed butch embodiment has been theorized by Butler in relation to "melancholy," and it is situated in the two most famous novels of lesbian masculinity, *The Well of Loneliness* and *Stone Butch Blues*, as defiant singularity in one and heroic isolation in the other.[15] Butchness gives rise to the blues, to rage, and finally to a political sensibility shared by other female subjects who experience themselves as disenfranchised—namely, feminism. Shame is, I am claiming, a gendered form of sexual abjection: it belongs to the feminine, and when men find themselves "flooded" with shame, chances are they are being feminized in some way and against their will. Feminists, over the years, have used consciousness-raising, support groups, political marches, and activist anger to counter the widespread effects of the shame associated with womanhood. Most often, feminists have produced complex analyses of the social structures that have inscribed certain forms of female and feminine embodiment with shame: we have analyzed the compulsions to feast and fast, to binge and purge, to fuck and be celibate, to harbor masochistic desires, to entertain thoughts of abuse. Feminism has thoroughly scrutinized shame because feminine subjects have so consistently lived in shame. And so now, at an event geared toward examining the particularities of gay shame, it becomes all too obvious that the only people really lacking a politically urgent language with which to describe and counter shame are gay white men.

Finally, while I see why people may want to hold on to shame, nourish and nurture a close relation to shame, build on the negative but deeply erotic nature of shame, I want to close by offering a caution against any deep investments in gay shame by quickly considering Pedro Almodóvar's film *Talk to Her* (2002). This film, which should have been given the subtitle "because she is in a coma and cannot talk back to you and she won't know or mind what you do to her even if you rape her while seeming to be basically a good guy if a little closeted," breaks its audiences down into those who hate it and those who love it. I would even offer a gross generalization and venture that lesbians hate it and gay men love it (straight women seem to like it and straight men could not care less, just for the record). Falling into the category of those who hate this film, who despise its pathetic dependence on aesthetic mastery to represent the most trite and insulting narratives about women and men, I nonetheless understand that *Talk to Her* has much to say about gay shame and its consequences.

Talk to Her opens with a gorgeous dance performance in which a woman stumbles blindly about a stage as a man scurries to move objects out of her path. In the audience sit two men, Marco (Darío Grandinetti) and Benigno (Javier Cámaro), who separately watch this performance unfold and then leave the theater to reenact it in some form or another. Each man idolizes a woman who remains unattainable, and each man harbors secret homoerotic desires that they repress out of some sense of shame. Benigno worships a ballerina, Alicia (Leonor Watling), and stalks her, and Marco is obsessed with a female bullfighter, Lydia (Rosario Flores). When Alicia is hit by a car and falls into a coma, Benigno takes care of her at the hospital, bathing her, moisturizing her prone body, and talking to her as she lies mute and unconscious. Marco inserts himself into Lydia's life after she has a fight with her boyfriend, another bullfighter. Marco clinches a romantic relation to Lydia when she sees a snake in her home, panics, and he comes to her rescue. When Lydia is gored in a bullfight and becomes comatose, Marco attends her bedside. He is befriended by Benigno, and the relationship between the two men, the central bond in the film, unfolds against the macabre backdrop of the two mute and comatose women. The silent women become the occasion for male bonding, and their presence provides an alibi for the enactment of desires that would otherwise be suppressed within the shame mechanism that we call "closeting."

Benigno's gayness is both hinted at in the plot and discussed overtly by nurses at the hospital. Marco regards Benigno with both wary skepticism and obsessive regard as Benigno cares for his dancer and chats away

What Almodóvar's film does do well, however, is to dramatize the precise mechanics of white gay male shame.

to her while encouraging Marco to do the same. Eventually, Benigno crosses a line, and he rapes the inert dancer. When Alicia is discovered to be pregnant, a short investigation by the police results in Benigno's arrest. He is abandoned by everyone except Marco, who visits him, and eventually Benigno kills himself. As even this brief plot summary reveals, the plot itself is a puerile, aggressive, and violent fantasy about the role of women in animating bonds between men. If there was any doubt at all that this was a regressive narrative, one sad scene confirms the viewer's worst fears. By way of hiding the sheer brutality of the rape scene, Almodóvar presents Benigno's assault on Alicia in the form of an animated sequence in which a tiny man clambers on the slopes of a huge naked woman. He travels down her body and enters her pubic area where, after some deliberation, he pushes his way into her gaping vagina. This is high-school-level misogyny in its miserably unimaginative understanding of the relations between men and women, its deep-seated fear of the female body, and its slick camouflage of ugly violence with seemingly benign cartoon representations.

A plot summary alone would not convince anyone that this was a film worth watching, contemplating, or celebrating; yet the critics (outside Spain) loved it, and *Talk to Her* was hailed as one of Almodóvar's best films. The richness of Almodóvar's aesthetic sensibility apparently makes up for the fact that the two lead women, women engaged in active and highly aestheticized professions, barely speak and in fact are inert through most of the film. The film's stunning colors, the clever use of camera angles, and the long pauses and moments of silence all gloss over the dramatic silencing and stilling of two very active women. What Almodóvar's film does do well, however, is to dramatize the precise mechanics of white gay male shame. Indeed, Almodóvar's film offers us three solutions to the discomfort of white gay male shame.

Work It Out or Normalize It The film, and contemporary gay pride politics, suggests that gay white men can work through gay shame by producing normative masculinities and presenting themselves as uncastrated, muscular, whole. This occurs by cleaving to the ordinary and the quiet; in the film, this role is fulfilled by Marco, the seemingly straight man who pursues the masculine woman, the bullfighter, and whose desire is triangulated through her onto her ex and Benigno. To distance himself from the shameful desires he may have for men, in other words, Marco first selects a masculine woman to stand in for the real object of his desire, and then later he uses her comatose form as a prop while he pursues his relationship with Benigno.

Project It Elsewhere or Aestheticize It The white gay male experience of shame is often managed through the act of projection, which Douglas Crimp describes so well in his essay on Mario Montez. There, Andy Warhol, the original "thin white duke," projects shame, castration, and vulnerability onto the feminized and racialized body of a Puerto Rican drag queen and in the process creates an illusion of mastery. In *Talk to Her*, it is Benigno who projects his shame elsewhere—onto the body of a mute woman, a dancer who lies in a coma after a car accident. And Marco preserves his facade of heterosexuality by lingering at the bedside of the "gored" phallic woman who fought bulls but feared . . . snakes (Symbolism 101 anyone?). The two women represent two different types of gay male projection directed specifically at women (as I have shown, white gay male shame may also be projected onto bodies of color). While the former female bullfighter is essentially the "fag hag," the castrated and unlucky woman whose castration stands in for the fag's own shame and who often becomes a source of humor, the former dancer occupies the role of the diva—Koestenbaum's Jackie Onassis or opera singer, Warhol's Marilyn Monroe—the idealized and phallic woman who often becomes an excuse for exquisite but dangerous investments in beauty and art.[16] While the fag hag is used and abused, the diva is cared for and talked to; the fag hag is an emblem, the diva a trophy, the fag hag is openly despised and secretly worshipped, the diva is openly worshipped and secretly despised. Both are summarily massaged, admired, and utterly destroyed.

Feminist Gay Shame An option that neither Almodóvar nor Warhol entertain is that gay shame can be used, in all its glorious negativity, in ways that are feminist and antiracist. The glory of the drag queen is that she takes pride in her shame: just the names alone—Vaginal Davis, for example—step in where others fear to tread.[17] The form of subject formation that José Esteban Muñoz, in reference to Davis's work, has called "disidentification" also leads us to a place where shame can be transformed into something that is not pride but not simply damage either. Muñoz uses the work of Davis to critique the gay/antigay binary that, like the pride/shame binary, critiques white homonormativity without really examining the racial and sexual politics that the homonorms and antihomonorms share. Muñoz writes: "The forms of 'anti-gay' thinking put forward by Vaginal Davis's work are vastly different in origin and effect than (Mark) Simpson's Anti-Gay. Davis's brand of anti-gay critique offers something more than a listless complaint. This additional something is a sustained critique of white gay male normativity and its concomitant corporate ethos."[18] Muñoz and Davis (whose name is taken as an homage to Angela Davis) find supple and vital models for identification in feminisms of color, and they cleave to an alliance with women rather than anxiously unyoking themselves from all things feminine, from the contaminating matter of feminine castration.

As if to remind us that the white gay male text, in all its aestheticism, does not necessarily have to detest and destroy women, Michael Cunningham's novel *The Hours* offers a counter to Almodóvar's *Talk to Her*. This novel helps us see how the sensibility of gay male shame can be routed through women without destroying them in the process. *The Hours* produces compelling schemas of queer temporalities as each woman—Virginia Woolf, Laura Brown, Clarissa Vaughn—lives through the cracks and broken moments in the lives of the others.[19] Each woman experiences a kiss with another woman, each takes care of a man she does not love, and each chooses whether to continue living at odds with time, art, life, and love. *The Hours* shows us vividly the meaning of queer before and after gay, and it depicts in unflinching detail the deaths of at least two of its main characters; but at its conclusion both shame and the woman have survived—a small triumph and a signpost to the next queer moment.

Conclusion

Even though the Gay Shame conference was quite enjoyable and had some great moments (the disability panel comes to mind), the plot summary of the conference resembled the script of *Talk to Her* more than the script of *The Hours*. In short, the conference fulfilled predictions that gay shame was a subject cultivated by white gay men but projected elsewhere, and this precise dynamic was acted out in several sessions. The implicit identity politics exercised by white gay men at the conference became explicit when Ellis Hansen chose to illustrate his talk about Plato's *Symposium* and desire between professors and students with images of his favorite Puerto Rican porn star. The images of the naked brown body immediately resonated with the excruciating visibility of Mario Montez that we had already witnessed and discussed, and it made clear the function of the brown gay male body in the narrative of white shame. Hansen was asked a few pointed questions about his presentation, but in general conference participants tried to forget what they had seen. It was left to Hiram Perez, one of the very few people of color presenting work at the conference, to address an angry and impassioned critique at Hansen when Perez finally had his turn to speak on the last panel of the conference. Hansen responded defensively to Perez, and shortly thereafter the conference disintegrated into the usual formulaic exchanges at the open mike about who was and who was not represented on the panels. The painful session only ended when Michael Warner grabbed the mike and mimicked Montez saying "diarrhea."

The spectacular dissolution of communication at Gay Shame was predictable and in a way inevitable. The punctuation of the conference by the apparently humorous but actually deeply offensive image of a white gay man (Warner) mimicking a drag queen of color (Montez) who is lip-synching to the voice of another white gay man (Tavel) captures perfectly the racial dynamics of the conference as a whole. Perez found himself very much in the position of Montez: he could speak, but he would always be read as a queer of color performing as a person of color and leaving the space of articulation open to the *real* gay subjects: white gay men. Hansen, Warner, and others left the conference unscathed, as the gay shame that they so "proudly" wanted to claim had been successfully projected elsewhere. Gayle Rubin's moving call earlier in the day for a little "humility" and Esther Newton's apology to Perez for leaving him with the task of upbraiding Hansen went unheard by the white gay men to whom these remarks were directed. And the story of the conference, soon after it was ended, began to circulate as the tale of another scholarly project hijacked by the identity politics of queers of color! The truth is, it is hard to find a more rigid identity politics than that articulated in Michigan by white gay men. If queer studies is to survive gay shame, and it will, we all need to move far beyond the limited scope of white gay male concerns and interests. As Sedgwick herself reminds us in *Between Men: English Literature and Male Homosocial Desire*, there is a thin line between homosociality and homosexuality, and white men (gay or straight) pursuing the interests of white men (gay or straight) always means a heap of trouble for everybody else.[20]

If queer studies is to survive gay shame, and it will, we all need to move far beyond the limited scope of white gay male concerns and interests.

Notes

1. I should add, however, that David Halperin was very gracious in his invitation to me and invited me to address my concerns about the rubric of "gay shame" at the conference itself. Halperin has been a dignified interlocutor for my less than cordial thoughts about this topic and the event it inspired, and I thank both him and Valerie Traub for the original invitation and for their editorial comments.

2. Jacqui Alexander and Chandra Talpade Mohanty, eds., *Feminist Genealogies, Colonial Legacies, Democratic Futures* (New York: Routledge, 1997); David Roman, *Acts of Intervention: Performance, Gay Culture, and AIDS* (Bloomington: Indiana University Press, 1998); José Esteban Muñoz, *Disidentifications: Queers of Color and the Performance of Politics* (Minneapolis: University of Minnesota Press, 1999); David Eng, *Racial Castration: Managing Masculinity in Asian America* (Durham, NC: Duke University Press, 2001); Robert Reid-Pharr, *Black Gay Man*

(New York: New York University Press, 2001); Licia Fiol-Matta, *A Queer Mother for the Nation: The State and Gabriela Mistral* (Minneapolis: University of Minnesota Press, 2002); Roderick Ferguson, *Aberrations in Black: Toward a Queer of Color Critique* (Minneapolis: University of Minnesota Press, 2003); Juana Maria Rodriguez, *Queer Latinidad: Identity Practices, Discursive Spaces* (New York: New York University Press, 2003).

3. Not all of the white gay men at this conference, obviously, felt loyal to white gay male identity politics. George Chauncey, for example, made some illuminating remarks about the interactions between men of color and white gay men in the history of gay New York.

4. Sedgwick was cast as the conference's intellectual progenitor, and her absence was cast as the most notable and palpable absence at the conference (as opposed to, say, the absence of people of color). Indeed, a decision was made to include an essay by Sedgwick in the conference volume, but similar essays were not requested from José Muñoz, David Eng, or Robert Reid-Pharr. I in no way want to suggest that Sedgwick's contribution will not be valuable and crucial, and I agree that her work, which I cite approvingly, has provided the most generative and insightful models for thinking about gay shame. However, the casting of Sedgwick as the absent center for this conference glossed over the more outrageous omissions of queer scholars working on race.

5. See Leo Bersani, *Homos* (Cambridge, MA: Harvard University Press, 1996); Michael Warner, *The Trouble with Normal: Sex, Politics, and the Ethics of Queer Life* (New York: Free Press, 1999); and Elizabeth Freeman, "Packing History, Count(er)ing Generations," *New Literary History* 31, no. 4 (2000): 1–18.

6. Lauren Berlant, "Two Girls, Fat and Thin," in *Regarding Sedgwick: Essays on Queer Culture and Critical Theory*, ed. Stephen M. Barber and David L. Clark (New York: Routledge, 2002), 74.

7. Williams insists that we regard "tradition" not in terms of inert fragments that survive from the past but as a narrative that shapes the past that a current ideology requires. He writes: "What we have to see is not just 'a tradition' but a *selective tradition*: an intentionally selective version of a shaping past and a pre-shaped present" (Raymond Williams, "Traditions, Institutions, Formations," in *Marxism and Literature* [Oxford: Oxford University Press, 1977], 115–20).

8. Martin Manalansan IV, "In the Shadows of Stonewall: Examining Gay Transnational Politics and the Diasporic Dilemma," in *The Politics of Culture in the Shadows of Capital*, ed. Lisa Lowe and David Lloyd (Durham, NC: Duke University Press, 1997), 486.

9. I have written about the problem, with an emphasis on youth in queer communities, in a book of essays on queer space and time: Judith Halberstam, *In a Queer Time and Place: Transgender Bodies, Subcultural Lives* (New York: New York University Press, 2005).

10. Warner, *Trouble with Normal*, 3.

11. Douglas Crimp, "Mario Montez: For Shame," in Barber and Clark, *Regarding Sedgwick*, 57–70.

12. Richard Fung, "Looking for My Penis: The Eroticized Asian in Gay Male Porn," *Q&A: Queer in Asian America*, ed. David L. Eng and Alice Y. Hom (Philadelphia: Temple University Press, 1998), 115–34.

13. Eng, *Racial Castration*.

14. Lawrence La Fountain-Stokes, "An Open Letter to Douglas Crimp," 22 March 2003.

15. Radclyffe Hall, *The Well of Loneliness* (New York: Anchor, 1990); Leslie Feinberg, *Stone Butch Blues: A Novel* (New York: Firebrand, 1993); Judith Butler, "Melancholy Gender/Refused Identification," in *The Psychic Life of Power: Theories in Subjection* (Palo Alto, CA: Stanford University Press, 1997), 132–66.

16. Wayne Koestenbaum, *The Queen's Throat: Opera, Homosexuality, and the Mystery of Desire* (New York: Vintage, 1994); Koestenbaum, *Jackie under My Skin: Interpreting an Icon* (New York: Farrar, Strauss and Giroux, 1995).

17. Vaginal Davis also sometimes goes by the name "Vaginal Crème Davis," the middle name having been given to him by a journalist. The fabulous embellishment of vaginal with crème suggests a total disregard for shame and its tortuous pathways.

18. Muñoz, *Disidentifications*, 111.

19. Michael Cunningham, *The Hours* (New York: Farrar, Strauss and Giroux, 1998).

20. Sedgwick, *Shame and Performativity*.

Gay Rights versus Queer Theory

WHAT IS LEFT OF SODOMY AFTER *LAWRENCE V. TEXAS*?

Teemu Ruskola

> In effect, we live in a legal, social, and institutional world where the only relations possible are extremely few, extremely simplified, and extremely poor.
> —Michel Foucault, "The Social Triumph of the Sexual Will"

> It is almost as if, starting from a certain point, every decisive political event were double-sided: the spaces, the liberties, and the rights won by individuals in their conflicts with central powers always simultaneously prepared a tacit but increasing inscription of individuals' lives within the state order, thus offering a new and more dreadful foundation for the very sovereign power from which they wanted to liberate themselves.
> —Giorgio Agamben, *Homo Sacer: Sovereign Power and Bare Life*

In 1986 the United States Supreme Court affirmed the constitutionality of a Georgia statute under which Michael Hardwick had been charged with committing "sodomy" in his home with another adult male. The Court began its analysis by disavowing any concern with "whether laws against sodomy between consenting adults in general, or between homosexuals in particular, are wise or desirable." Rather, the majority opinion in *Bowers v. Hardwick* formulated its judicial task in the following blunt terms: to determine "whether the Federal Constitution confers a fundamental right upon homosexuals to engage in sodomy."[1] The answer to *that* question could of course only be negative. An argument to the contrary was, in the Court's notorious phrase, "at best, facetious."[2]

Less than twenty years later, in June 2003, the Supreme Court reconsidered its earlier holding. In circumstances similar to those in which Michael Hardwick had been charged by the state of Georgia, John Lawrence had been arrested by the state of Texas for engaging in "deviate sexual intercourse with another individual of the same sex" in his own home.[3] In an impassioned endorsement of homosexual intimacies, the *Lawrence v. Texas* Court proclaimed breathlessly, "*Bowers* was not correct when it was decided, and it is not correct today. It ought not to remain binding precedent. *Bowers v. Hardwick* should be and now is overruled."[4] And by the instantaneous magic of a judicial pronouncement from the nation's highest

Social Text 84–85, Vol. 23, Nos. 3–4, Fall–Winter 2005.

With the fall of antisodomy legislation, have we finally been "liberated"? And if so, to what?

court, homosexuals could no longer be treated as presumptive criminals. Although *Bowers v. Hardwick* has not been literally erased—it still remains on the pages of *United States Reports*—its mean-spirited rhetoric has been deprived of constitutional force. It has become a mere historical artifact, a witness to its own powerlessness.

This is an astonishing reversal, and one that took many by surprise.[5] What made this judicial *volte face* possible? In this essay, I read the Court's opinion in *Lawrence v. Texas* rhetorically to look for answers to that question.[6] At the same time, I begin the critical evaluation of a post-*Hardwick* political landscape. With the fall of antisodomy legislation, have we finally been "liberated"? And if so, to what? From the perspective of queer theory, how should we view this victory of gay rights? Indeed, to what extent are commitments to queerness and liberal rights compatible? Or stated even more sharply, is "queer rights" an oxymoron?

The Question of Gay Rights: "Sodomy" or "Intimacy"?

It is a commonplace of legal advocacy that the framing of a legal question always already anticipates its answer. As Janet Halley observes, it has been "the virtually ubiquitous conclusion" in the literature criticizing *Bowers v. Hardwick* that "the *Hardwick* majority vitiated its credibility when it framed the question of the case"[7]—viz., "whether the Federal Constitution confers a fundamental right upon homosexuals to engage in sodomy."[8] In his dissent in *Hardwick*, Justice Blackmun was the first to make that claim[9] and Justice Kennedy, the author of the majority opinion in *Lawrence*, echoes Blackmun and likewise asserts that the *Hardwick* majority's reductive formulation of the constitutional question manifests their "failure to appreciate the extent of the liberty at stake."[10] Having established that the issue is emphatically not one of sodomy *simpliciter*, the *Lawrence* Court reframes the issue as follows: "The question before the Court is the validity of a Texas statute making it a crime for two persons of the same sex to engage in certain intimate sexual conduct."[11]

That is, the question is not one of "sodomy" but of "intimacy"—of "certain intimate sexual conduct," the precise nature of which the Court does not even specify for the purposes of stating the constitutional issue.[12] To paraphrase only slightly, by indicting the Texas sodomy law for interfering with same-sex lovers' "intimacy," the *Lawrence* Court effectively sets out to decide whether it is a crime to love someone of the same sex—and the answer to *this* question is as much a foregone conclusion as the *Hardwick* Court's futile search for the word *sodomy* in the Bill of Rights.

Given the unapologetically homophobic rhetoric of the *Hardwick* opinion, it may seem self-evident that the *Lawrence* Court's reframing of the constitutional question as a matter of interpersonal sexual intimacy rather than sodomy puts the nation's constitutional jurisprudence on the proper track. Like every right-thinking person of a progressive political orientation, I too am elated that *Hardwick*, so soon after its ugly appearance, has ended up in the graveyard of discredited constitutional precedents—in the company of cases such as *Dred Scott*, *Plessy v. Ferguson*, *Korematsu*, and others.[13] How could one *not* be stirred by *Lawrence*'s righteous proclamation, "*Bowers* was not correct when it was decided, and it is not correct today"?

In these circumstances, it may appear unseemly, not to mention politically unwise, to point to the critical limitations of *Lawrence*'s logic. Accepting that risk, I nevertheless want to suggest that *Hardwick*, after all, got the constitutional *question* right (with some important qualifications I consider below), even though the Court's answer to the question was obviously disastrously wrong. Admittedly, having been labeled as "sodomites" under the constitutional regime crowned by *Hardwick*, it is difficult to resist the *Lawrence* Court's interpellation of homosexuals as law-abiding subjects who are capable of intimacy and "are entitled to respect for their private lives."[14] We are now invited to a new world where homosexuals, too, can embark upon sexual relationships "in the confines of their homes and their own private lives, and still retain their dignity as free persons."[15]

But the "respect" and "dignity" offered by the Court will likely not come free. They will have to be earned, by leading respectable sex lives. Below, I first examine the rhetorical and political conditions attached to *Lawrence*'s offer of gay respectability and then turn to *Bowers v. Hardwick* and the possibility of redeeming its focus on "sodomy."

The Limitations of Intimacy

However, before examining critically the rhetoric by which *Lawrence* reaches its result, it is nevertheless appropriate to begin by commenting on some of its achievements. The opinion's revisionist account of *Hardwick*'s simplistic history of sodomy laws and its acknowledgment—however hesitant—of the historicity of sexual identity categories themselves are notable, not at all the kinds of analyses one typically finds in a judicial opinion.[16] Moreover, the *Lawrence* Court acknowledges not only some of the contributions of the academic study of sexuality but also the fact that virulent homophobia is not necessarily a global condition. The majority opinion cites, among other things, the decision by which the European Court of Human Rights struck down national laws similar to

Being in an intimate personal relationship should not be a *requirement* for having a constitutionally protected sex life.

those upheld in *Hardwick*. (To be sure, the Court gratuitously takes this as an opportunity to highlight the superior achievements of "*our* Western civilization.")[17]

To turn to *Lawrence*'s limitations, what, then, is the problem with how it frames the constitutional issue—namely, asking whether it should be permissible to make it "a crime for two persons of the same sex to engage in certain intimate sexual conduct"? Of course, it should not be a crime to love another person of the same sex and to express that love sexually. Rather, the problem with the Court's rhetorical formulation is not what it permits—intimate sexual association—but what it leaves out, beyond the sphere of sexual legitimacy. Being in an intimate personal relationship should not be a *requirement* for having a constitutionally protected sex life.[18] It should not be a crime *just* to have homosexual sex—anal or banal, oral or floral, intimate or not.[19]

In terms of its handling of constitutional doctrine, the *Lawrence* majority is careful not to say anything that might be seen as formalizing the legal status of same-sex relationships: "[This case] does not involve whether the government must give formal recognition to any relationship that homosexual persons seek to enter."[20] Justice Scalia is appropriately unmoved by this disclaimer, to which he responds laconically, "Do not believe it."[21] Indeed, in terms of its rhetoric and logic, the Court repeatedly and strenuously analogizes homosexual relationships to marriage. Scalia's outraged dissent is absolutely correct in evaluating the logical, if not strictly doctrinal, implications of the majority's reasoning. If homosexual "intimacy" is as deserving of protection as hetero sex, "what justification could there possibly be for denying the benefits of marriage to homosexual couples"?[22]

But what exactly is at stake in gay sex, according to the Court? Emphatically not "just" sex. The Court emphasizes that it was precisely in its reduction of same-sex intimacy to sodomy that the *Hardwick* Court "misapprehended" the object of its analysis.[23] Espousing an unabashedly positivist sexual ontology, the *Lawrence* Court is fully confident of its ability to apprehend correctly the nature of homosexual sex. Insofar as *Hardwick* thus failed to understand the true significance of sodomy laws, *Lawrence* proceeds to set the record straight.

Given that "heterosexual identity is the location from which the Justices decide the case without appearing to,"[24] it comes as no surprise that the Court's view of what homosexual sex is about (when properly apprehended) corresponds to normative heterosexual sex: "Intimate conduct with another person [which] can be but one element in a personal bond that is more enduring."[25] With (heterosexual) solicitude for misunderstood homosexuals, the Court announces, "To say that the issue in *Bowers* was simply the right to engage in certain sexual conduct *demeans* the claim the individual put forward, *just as it would demean a married couple* were it to be said that marriage is simply about the right to have sexual intercourse."[26] The wrong of *Hardwick* is ultimately its denial of dignity to homosexual relationships: sodomy laws "seek to control a *personal relationship* that, whether or not entitled to recognition in the law, is within the liberty of persons to choose without being punished as criminals."[27] Indeed, reading the opinion, one would think that homosexuals exist *only* in relationships, and that relationships are the *only* context in which homosexuals might conceivably engage in sex acts.[28]

It is certainly rhetorically satisfying when the Court grounds its holding not only in homosexuals' "spatial" liberty interest in being left alone in their homes but also in the "more transcendent dimensions" of liberty, which the Court associates with sexual expression. Yet this rhetoric leaves little or no justification for protecting less-than-transcendental sex that is not part of an ongoing relationship. In the end, the crucial rhetorical limitation of *Lawrence* is precisely its inability, or refusal, to imagine (legitimate) homosexual sex that does not take place in a relationship and does not connote intimacy. The implicit bargain the Court proposes is plain. The Court, and the Constitution, will respect our sex lives, but on condition that our sex lives be respectable.

This, one fears, is the new jurisprudential project inaugurated by *Lawrence v. Texas*: the normalization of gay sex, or as Katherine Franke puts it, the "domestication" of sexual liberty.[29]

The Possibilities of Sodomy

Liberal rhetoric aside, rights do not connote unqualified "freedom." Like everything else, they come at a price. That price is the disciplinary regime of political modernity. But so long as we recognize this, can we afford to turn down "dignity" and "respect" when they are being offered to us by the U.S. Supreme Court? After all, lacking those qualities can be positively hazardous to one's health.

Obviously I am in no way endorsing the *Hardwick* Court's answer to the question it posed. Sodomy laws *should* be unconstitutional, if for no other reason that—far beyond their symbolic effects—they have been used to deprive people with nonnormative sexual lives from their jobs and their children, for example, to mention only some of the more severe material consequences.[30] Rather, what I hope to recover from *Hardwick*, selectively, is a relative emphasis on sexual *acts*. I do so although I am not at all sanguine about the analytic distinction between acts and identities. Notoriously, the *Hardwick* opinion itself exploited the unstable relationship

An emphasis on acts can be a political tactic aimed at making certain acts available to the largest number of actors possible, rather than merely the respectable few.

between the two, as it opportunistically at various times both conflated and disaggregated "sodomy" and "sodomites."[31] Acts are always performed by actors who have identities, and identities are always consolidated in and through acts.[32] Yet it is a peculiar achievement of the liberal legal imagination to separate categorically things that are in fact indissolubly connected. (Notoriously, "if you can think about a thing, inextricably attached to something else, without thinking of the thing it is attached to, then you have a legal mind."[33]) Nevertheless, a return to a relative emphasis on acts rather than identities need not imply a metaphysical distinction between the two. Rather, an emphasis on acts can be a political tactic aimed at making certain acts available to the largest number of actors possible, rather than merely the respectable few.

Although it is useful to reevaluate the possibilities implicit in the way in which *Hardwick* framed the constitutionality of sodomy legislation, the Court's formulation has some crucial limitations as well. The most obvious, and most criticized, aspect of that formulation was its refusal to consider sodomy in its heterosexual aspect. The Georgia sodomy law under which Michael Hardwick was prosecuted defined sodomy capaciously as anal or oral sex between members of the same *or* opposite sex,[34] yet the Court gratuitously limited its analysis to "homosexual sodomy." The appropriate way to rephrase *Hardwick*'s question would be, then, to ask whether there is a constitutional right to engage in sodomy *tout court*—and a positive answer to that question would in turn afford the right to such sodomitical acts to men and women of any, all, or no sexual orientation.

Beyond questioning how *Hardwick* excluded heterosexuals from sodomy's embrace, one might also question the term *sodomy* itself. As Kendall Thomas observes, "The fact that the [*Hardwick*] Court did not choose an alternative characterization of the statutorily proscribed conduct is a textual register of how deeply the social voice of homophobia is inscribed in the institutional voice of the Constitution."[35] Insofar as "sodomy" is "an anachronistic, ideologically loaded appellation" burdened with overlapping sexual, political, and religious overtones,[36] one might reformulate the *Hardwick* Court's question more neutrally, as whether there is, or ought to be, a constitutional right to engage in, say, anal and oral sex.

Admittedly, an exclusive focus on sex acts can be rhetorically dehumanizing. Precisely for that reason, it is difficult to conceive the Supreme Court's asking the *Hardwick* question about heterosexual sex acts at all. Although the *Hardwick* Court was perfectly happy to analyze homosexuals' right to indulge in what it at one point called "acts of *consensual* sodomy" (as opposed to a constitutional right to male-on-male rape?),[37] it seems unlikely that the Court would ever frame questions of opposite-sex sexual acts in such a clinical manner—as, for example, "whether there is a fundamental constitutional right to insert a condom-covered (or even just a plain old) penis into a consenting vagina." Instead, constitutionally such questions are framed in terms of personal decisions about "procreation" and "family," not "vaginal intercourse."[38]

In the pre-*Lawrence* world, it made sense to respond to the dehumanizing language of *Hardwick* with a certain emphasis on the humanity of queers. Insofar as the *Hardwick* justices asserted patently counterfactually that there is "no connection between family, marriage, or procreation on the one hand and homosexual activity on the other,"[39] it was certainly important to remind the world that gay people, too, have families. (*Quelle surprise.*) Now, however, the Supreme Court has caught on to the fact that homosexuals too can, and do, exist in relationships with others. That, in itself, is a perfectly welcome observation. However, what should give us pause is the notion that the justices now purport to know the *truth* of homosexual intimacy: *it is just like heterosexual intimacy*, except between persons of the same sex. This is "compulsory heterosexuality" in its new, second-generation form, Adrienne Rich updated for the millennium.[40] Homosexuals are no longer faced with the impossible demand to literally *become* heterosexuals but merely to become *just like* heterosexuals. Imitation, after all, is the sincerest form of flattery.

Mere Rhetoric?

In Nan Hunter's apt observation, "The Supreme Court's decision in *Lawrence v. Texas* is easy to read, but difficult to pin down."[41] By no means does the opinion *require* that noncoupled homosexuals ultimately be treated legally as second-class citizens. As far as constitutional doctrine as such is concerned, *Lawrence* can indeed be read as removing "the last obstacle to the paradigm of consent, rather than the institution of matrimony, controlling the definition of when sex is presumptively legal."[42]

Yet, read more rhetorically, the ultimate jurisprudential project may turn out to be not that of destigmatizing *all* private consensual sex, but only certain kinds of intimacies, as I have suggested. Limiting legitimate sex to "intimate" relationships is admittedly not the same thing as state-sanctioned marriage, but it is its sociological analogue: although actual emotional intimacy is not a legal prerequisite for getting married, a "real" marriage is one where law reigns over a couple joined in sexually expressed love. Hence, even as the Court doctrinally delinks marriage and sex, rhetorically it recouples them, so that not all sexual subjects seem to be created equal, after all.

Nevertheless, and perhaps most strikingly, the couple whose dignity and respect the *Lawrence* Court works so hard to restore rhetorically is not a "couple" at all, but apparently just a one-night stand that got interrupted (as it were) by the state of Texas. How do we make sense of this dramatic disjunction between the Court's rhetoric and the legal effect of its holding? Why does the Court so willfully ignore the parties before it and insist on constructing an image of transcendental gay intimacy?

At the same time, if by virtue of the Court's fantastic rereading of the facts all sodomites—both the respectable and the not-so-respectable ones—are allowed to get on with their (sex) lives, why should we worry by what rhetoric the Court accomplishes that goal? As Franke emphasizes, in the end "the Texas sodomy statute was not found to violate a constitutional right to dignity, but rather a right to liberty,"[43] for the simple reason that in the United States "dignity" is not a constitutional right, only a social privilege, and terms such as "respect" and "dignity" have no precise legal meaning.[44] On the language of respect in *Lawrence*, James Whitman similarly insists that for better or worse "little of it can be said to count in any certain way as *law*."[45] Gay people's respectability or lack thereof is thus not a legally enforceable matter anyway.

Yet there are at least two reasons for concern. First, whether applicable to same- or opposite-sex conduct, *Lawrence*'s holding is nevertheless ultimately grounded in the principle of privacy. Insofar as we regard sex as an ultimately political and public issue, rather than a private one, *Lawrence* forecloses important avenues for political engagement. It permits the exclusion of nonnormative sexualities from the "world of public intimacy,"[46] which may remain reserved for manifestations of normative heterosexuality.[47]

Second, although the Court's singular insistence on making gay sex respectable does mean that one can in fact no longer be thrown in jail *just* for engaging in same-sex sexual conduct, that rhetoric may well come back to haunt us as homosexual sex, inevitably, becomes increasingly regulated by the state. So long as the Constitution permitted viewing *all* homosexual sex as presumptively criminal, there was little need to draw distinctions between kinds of homosexual sex—it was all bad (or at least not good and deserving of protection). But as Franke observes, after *Lawrence* gay sex takes place "in the underregulated space that lies between criminalization and legitimization through marriage."[48] New distinctions are likely to emerge to clarify the status of different sexual subjects in this ambiguous space. Those distinctions may not affect the interpretation of sodomy laws per se—under *Lawrence*, any unreconstructed sodomy statute *will* be unconstitutional—but *Lawrence*'s rhetoric may be a harbinger of the jurisprudence yet to come on the civil regulation of homosexual sex, with different treatment of "good" and "bad" homosexual sex.

At the very latest, if and when same-sex marriage arrives, we will know whose sex is good and whose is bad.

Tactical Acts

Given the prospect, embedded in *Lawrence v. Texas*, of the Supreme Court's defining the meaning of (normal) homosexual sex, it seems tactically wise to focus on liberating acts themselves, separating them away from their contexts and from the actors performing them. Sodomy, defined in the most expansive way, should be available to whoever desires to engage in it, for whatever reasons. Single people, especially single women, have as great a stake as queers in insisting on the legitimacy of engaging in sex outside of intimate relationships. As Halley insisted long before *Lawrence* overruled *Hardwick*, "We can form new alliances along the register of acts."[49]

It bears repeating, however, that whether we choose to focus on acts or identities, that choice is always only tactical, in the sense in which Michel de Certeau uses the term. Distinguishing tactics from strategies, de Certeau defines a strategy as a "calculus of force-relationships" that is performed by a "proper" subject that occupies a definite discursive location; it is in relation to his or her own relatively fixed location that a "proper" subject assesses others in the social field. A tactic, in contrast, is a calculus of those without such a location:

> It has at its disposal no base where it can capitalize on its advantages, prepare its extensions, and secure independence with respect to its circumstances. The "proper" is a victory of space over time—it always depends on the watch for opportunities that must be seized "on the wing." Whatever it wins, it does not keep. It must constantly manipulate events in order to turn them into opportunities. The weak must continually turn to their own ends forces alien to them.[50]

Queer sexual subjects are obviously not "proper" subjects speaking from a position of relative power and fixity. Indeed, it is the peculiar discursive privilege of heterosexuality that it can opportunistically define and redefine homosexuality from moment to moment as either merely a set of acts or an identity possessed by certain people. Therefore, as Halley's reading of *Hardwick* shows, those labeled "homosexuals" continually face a discursive double bind that offers no simple exit: "You cannot win because your victorious opponent is willing to be a hypocrite and to 'damn if you do and damn if you don't.'"[51] Applying the act/identity framework to *Law-*

It is time to focus not on the love but on the acts that dare not speak their names.

rence, it is evident that both decisions exploit this discursive ambivalence, strategically treating "homosexuality" as a practice and as an identity.

However, in *Hardwick* homosexuality as identity is a minor rhetorical key and homosexuality as acts a major one, as the opinion relentlessly seeks to reduce homosexuals to sodomy (never mind that, tautologically, the stigma of sodomy ultimately derives from the identity of the actors).[52] In *Lawrence*, in contrast, identity is the major rhetorical mode, as the Court seeks to justify sexual conduct by the actors' identities: capable of intimacy and hence deserving of respect, homosexuals should be permitted to engage in the acts that define them in the first place. Tactically, then, there were certain opportunities in resisting *Hardwick*'s reduction of homosexuals to their acts and insisting on queers' humanity, as I have suggested. However, with the discursive 180-degree turn of the *Lawrence* Court and its celebration of homosexual intimacy, we are clearly far beyond a "love that dare not speak its name," and a rhetoric describing simply the humanity of that love no longer has the traction it once did. The circumstances have shifted, and so has our discursive location. We ought therefore to reconsider our tactics as well, as we confront a new judicial landscape. It is time to focus not on the love but on the acts that dare not speak their names.

There is no doubt that, in the political order of the United States, being a respectable subject of rights is preferable to being a sexual abject. Even if rights do not signify pure, unadulterated "freedom,"[53] and even if they impose their own normalizing discipline on their subjects,[54] in the contemporary political world they are surely preferable to a regime of homophobic violence sanctioned by sodomy laws. As Gayatri Spivak observes with artful ambivalence, liberal rights are something that "we cannot not want":[55] without them one has no legal and political existence.

But as we emerge from the closet and our sex lives begin to turn into entitlements recoded as part of universal human intimacy, we need to consider the ways in which such new sexual rights institute their own regime of normalcy, their own code of sexual behavior. Given homosexual subjects'—and abjects'—still uncertain claims to humanity, we ought to be alert to the continuing exclusions of this humanist logic even as we (or at least those in qualifying "intimate relationships") are embraced by it. It is in this context that it seems politically useful to insist on liberating sexual *acts* for use by any individual—without regard to his or her relationship status.

As always, there are costs to this tactic as well. Insofar as we insist that the right to "sodomy," in any one of its multiple definitions, pertains to individuals *qua* individuals, rather than partners in an intimate relationship with another individual, we are implicitly supporting the legal fiction of a transparent, freestanding subjectivity—the legal subject of liberal individualism that the law so presumptuously calls the "natural person." Ironically, in *Lawrence* the Supreme Court promises to rehabilitate homosexuals as sovereign subjects of law precisely because it seems to have finally gained faith in our ability to *surrender* our individuality in intimate relationships with other homosexuals, to become one in love.

Indeed, a liberal legal order treats its subjects as atomistic individuals insofar as it regulates their political and economic lives: the abstract bearer of political rights and the abstract *homo economicus*, respectively. The intimate sphere of the family, in contrast, is the one place where a liberal society not only permits but expects its citizens to shed their individuality and connect with others. And the privileged intimate bond in this most private of spheres is the sexual one between a man and a woman—a feature of the liberal organization of society that Martha Fineman aptly criticizes as the "sexual family."[56] *Lawrence v. Texas* is thus an instance of the conceptually indissoluble and politically indispensable liberal contradiction between individuality and connectedness. It is only when the state is able to imagine legitimate homosexual intimacies entitled to "privacy" that homosexuals become deserving of "dignity" and "respect" in the public spheres of the liberal polity as well. Ultimately, it is this dichotomized public/private schema that *Lawrence* invites queers to join—with the noteworthy, though increasingly contested, restriction that two men or two women cannot be legally married.

Although this humanizing gesture is hard to resist, we nevertheless ought to insist on separating sexual acts from identities as much as we can, at least for the purposes of legal categorization.[57] *Lawrence v. Texas* is a rhetorical symptom of the risk that the invitation to join the "intimate public sphere," to use Lauren Berlant's term, is being ultimately offered "only for members of families,"[58] whether gay or straight.

Yet a family need not be built around a relationship that is defined by a sexual bond, and a sexual connection need not constitute an embryonic family. After all, sex need not be about connection at all; sex can signify intense alienation and separation as much as connection.

Notes

I would like to thank Ritu Birla, David Eng, Katherine Franke, Nan Hunter, Aamer Mumtaz, Nancy Polikoff, Elizabeth Schneider, Hinrich Schuetze, Marc Spindelman, Kendall Thomas, James Whitman, and two anonymous reviewers for their comments.

1. *Bowers v. Hardwick*, 478 U.S. 186, 190 (1986).

2. 478 U.S. 194.

3. *Lawrence v. Texas*, 123 S. Ct. 2472, 2475 (2003).

4. 123 S. Ct. at 2484.

5. That is, while many observers did expect the ultimate outcome—the Court's striking the Texas statute—few expected the sweeping rhetorical and doctrinal reversal by which the Court achieved the result. As Nan Hunter observes, in reversing itself the Court ordinarily prefers to rely on bland and technical rhetoric, so as to minimize the disruption of constitutional continuity. *Lawrence*, in contrast, is "a reversal of more than law," as the majority sets out passionately to reconfigure not only the relevant constitutional doctrine but also "the social meaning of homosexuality" (Nan D. Hunter, "Living with *Lawrence*," *Minnesota Law Review* 88 [2004]: 1125).

6. In what follows, I draw methodologically as well as substantively from the classic rhetorical readings of *Bowers v. Hardwick* by Janet Halley, "Reasoning about Sodomy: Act and Identity in and after *Bowers v. Hardwick*," *Virginia Law Review* 79 (1993): 1721–73; and Kendall Thomas, "Beyond the Privacy Principle," *Columbia Law Review* 92 (1992): 1431–516.

7. Halley, "Reasoning about Sodomy," 1747.

8. 478 U.S. at 190.

9. The very first sentence of Blackmun's dissent is "This case is no more about a 'fundamental right to engage in homosexual sodomy,' as the Court purports to declare, than *Stanley v. Georgia* . . . was about a fundamental right to watch obscene movies, or *Katz v. United States* . . . was about a fundamental right to place interstate bets from a telephone booth" (ibid., 199).

10. 123 S. Ct. at 2478.

11. Ibid., 2575.

12. The opinion does eventually specify the criminal act in question—"deviate sexual intercourse, namely anal sex, with a member of the same sex (man)"—but the very first substantive section of the majority opinion that sets out the constitutional question refers only to "certain intimate sexual conduct." In terms of its relative emphasis on sodomy, rather than intimacy, the majority opinion in *Hardwick* finds occasion to use the term *sodomy* a total of thirty-three times, whereas it resorts to the word *intimate* only once. In contrast, the *Lawrence* majority opinion uses the words *intimate* or *intimacy* a total of twelve times.

13. *Dred Scott v. Sandford*, 60 U.S. 393 (1856); *Plessy v. Ferguson*, 163 U.S. (1896); *Korematsu v. United States*, 323 U.S. 214 (1944).

14. 123 S. Ct. at 2484; emphasis added.

15. Ibid., emphasis added.

16. Ibid., 2478–80. From the amicus briefs of scholars from various disciplines, the Court culls references to Katz's *Invention of Heterosexuality* as well as d'Emilio and Freedman's *Intimate Matters: A History of Sexuality in America*—hardly conventional legal authorities (ibid., 2479). Yet even as we welcome this attention to scholarship, its blessings may be mixed. The law can undoubtedly benefit from academic insights, yet there is also something disturbing in seeing scholarly positions translated into judicial pronouncements. Once embedded in a chain of judicial citations, they may be used justify the exercise of state authority in unanticipated and wholly unqueer ways.

17. Ibid., 2481, citing *Dudgeon v. United Kingdom*, 45 Eur. Ct. H.R. (1981), paragraph 52; emphasis added. To be sure, as constitutional law scholars have

observed, the reference to the European Court of Human Rights is primarily a rhetorical embellishment, not an acknowledgment of the binding nature of human rights law on the constitutional question at issue. As Gerald Neuman puts it, "The Supreme Court's invocation of human rights law in *Lawrence v. Texas* represents a rather modest use of international law in aid of constitutional interpretation" (Gerald Neuman, "The Uses of International Law in Constitutional Interpretation," *American Journal of International Law* 98 [2004]: 89).

18. Needless to say, the words *relationship* and *intimacy* have multiple meanings. For example, there are surely kinds of intimacies that are possible even in a one-night stand, and even the briefest sexual encounter takes place in the context of some kind of relationship—it is, after all, exceedingly difficult to commit sodomy alone. However, rather then resignifying the key terms, for the purposes of this essay I take them in the mutually constitutive senses in which the Court uses them, with "relationship" connoting intimacy of long duration and "intimacy" connoting sexual activity occurring in the context of an ongoing relationship.

19. I borrow my formulation from Gore Vidal's irresistible reference to "anal and banal sex as well as oral and floral sex," in "Pink Triangle and the Yellow Star," in *United States: Essays 1952–1992* (New York: Random House, 1993), 595.

20. 123 S. Ct. at 2484.

21. Ibid., 2497 (Scalia, J., dissenting).

22. Ibid. As Scalia correctly points out, " 'Preserving the traditional institution of marriage' is just a kinder way of describing the State's *moral disapproval* of same-sex couples" (ibid., 2496; Scalia, J., dissenting).

23. Ibid., 2478.

24. This is Halley's description of the *Bowers* majority, but it is an apt description of the *Lawrence* justices as well—indeed, of all constitutional jurisprudence ("Reasoning about Sodomy," 1767).

25. 123 S. Ct. at 2478.

26. Ibid.; emphasis added.

27. Ibid.; emphasis added.

28. Tellingly, in describing the history of sodomy legislation, the Court observes that "American laws targeting same-sex *couples* did not develop until the last third of the 20th century" (ibid., 2479; emphasis added).

29. Katherine M. Franke, "The Domesticated Liberty of *Lawrence v. Texas*," *Columbia Law Review* 104 (2004): 1399–426. Franke's comment on *Lawrence* makes an argument parallel to that of this essay. We both analyze the ways in which the Court rhetorically narrows the constitutionally protected liberty that it doctrinally upholds; Franke emphasizes the Court's rhetoric of "privatizing" and "domesticating" that liberty, while I focus on the Court's demand for "respectability" as the price at which the liberty has to be earned.

30. See, for example, Ryan Goodman, "Beyond the Enforcement Principle: Sodomy Laws, Social Norms, and Social Panoptics," *California Law Review* 89 (2001): 643–740; and Christopher R. Leslie, "Creating Criminals: The Injuries Inflicted by 'Unenforced' Sodomy Laws," *Harvard Civil-Rights—Civil-Liberties Law Review* 35 (2000): 103–81. On the denial of custody to gay parents, see also Teemu Ruskola, "Minor Disregard: The Legal Construction of the Fantasy That Gay and Lesbian Youth Do Not Exist," *Yale Journal of Law and Feminism* 8 (1996): 291–96. On the wider implications of sodomy laws, such as the construction of sodomy as a tax crime, see, for example, Anthony C. Infanti, "The

Internal Revenue Code as Sodomy Statute," *Santa Clara Law Review* 44 (2004): 763–804.

31. See Halley, "Reasoning about Sodomy." As Halley demonstrates elsewhere, the military's "don't ask, don't tell" policy similarly exploits the instability and incoherence of the homosexual status/conduct distinction. See Janet Halley, *Don't: A Reader's Guide to the Military's Anti-Gay Policy* (Durham, NC: Duke University Press, 1999).

32. See, for example, Judith Butler, *Gender Trouble: Feminism and the Subversion of Identity* (New York: Routledge, 1990); and Butler, *Bodies That Matter: On the Discursive Limits of "Sex"* (New York: Routledge, 1993).

33. Thomas Reed Powell, quoted in Lon L. Fuller, *The Morality of Law*, rev. ed. (New Haven, CT: Yale University Press, 1969), 4.

34. 478 U.S. at 188.

35. Thomas, "Beyond the Privacy Principle," 1434 n. 4.

36. Ibid., 1433 n. 4. For a problematization of "sodomy," see also Katherine M. Franke, "Putting Sex to Work," in *Left Legalism/Left Critique*, ed. Wendy Brown and Janet Halley (Durham, NC: Duke University Press, 2002), 290–336.

37. 478 U.S. at 192; emphasis added.

38. See, for example, *Griswold v. Connecticut*, 381 U.S. 479 (1965); *Eisenstadt v. Baird*, 405 U.S. 438 (1972).

39. 478 U.S. 191.

40. See Adrienne Rich, "Compulsory Heterosexuality and Lesbian Existence," *Signs* 5 (1980): 631–60.

41. Hunter, "Living with *Lawrence*," 1103.

42. Ibid., 1112.

43. Franke, "Domesticated Liberty of *Lawrence v. Texas*," 1401.

44. On the role of "dignity" in the South African Constitution, see Franke, "Domesticated Liberty of *Lawrence v. Texas*," 1404–5; and Hunter, "Living with *Lawrence*," 1136.

45. James Q. Whitman, "The Two Western Cultures of Privacy: Dignity versus Liberty," *Yale Law Journal* 113 (2004): 1214. Robert Post also notes that while "themes of respect and stigma are at the moral center of the *Lawrence* opinion," they are "entirely new to substantive due process doctrine" in which the Court grounds its opinion doctrinally. Robert C. Post, "Foreword: Fashioning the Legal Constitution: Culture, Courts, and Law," *Harvard Law Review* 117 (2003): 97.

46. The phrase is from Lauren Berlant, *The Queen of America Goes to Washington City: Essays on Sex and Citizenship* (Durham, NC: Duke University Press, 1997), 5.

47. Kendall Thomas makes an expanded version of this argument in his remarks at the Association of American Law Schools Panel on *Lawrence v. Texas* (San Francisco, CA, 4 January 2004).

48. Franke, "Domesticated Liberty of *Lawrence v. Texas*," 1426.

49. Halley, "Reasoning about Sodomy," 1722.

50. Michel de Certeau, *The Practice of Everyday Life*, trans. Steven Rendall (Berkeley: University of California Press, 1984), xix.

51. See Halley, "Reasoning about Sodomy," 1748.

52. As Halley observes, in most of the opinion (the fundamental rights holding) the Court defines homosexuality primarily as a set of acts and secondarily as an identity. In its briefer discussion (the rational basis holding), the Court switches these primary and secondary rhetorics ("Reasoning about Sodomy," 1748). Yet

within the overall structure of the opinion, the rhetoric of acts predominates over the rhetoric of identity.

53. This does not reflect a failure of rights as a technology of freedom, but rather the nature of freedom itself. As Iris Murdoch observes, "Freedom is not an isolated ability, like the ability to swim, which we can 'exercise' in a pure form. . . . Freedom is a matter of degree and a mode of being" (Iris Murdoch, *Metaphysics as a Guide to Morals* [London: Penguin Books, 1992], 326).

54. I analyze law's role as a ritual of "subjection," in the Althusserian sense, in Teemu Ruskola, "Legal Orientalism," *Michigan Law Review* 101 (2002): 179–234. On discipline and governmentality as hallmarks of political modernity, see Michel Foucault, *Discipline and Punish*, trans. lan Sheridan (New York: Vintage Books, 1977); and Graham Burchell, Colin Gordon, and Peter Miller, eds., *The Foucault Effect: Studies in Governmentality* (Chicago: University of Chicago Press, 1991).

55. Gayatri Chakravorty Spivak, *Outside in the Teaching Machine* (New York: Routledge, 1993), 45. For an extended discussion of the dilemma of liberal rights, inspired in part by Spivak's aphorism, see Wendy Brown, "Suffering the Paradoxes of Rights," in Brown, *Left Legalism/Left Critique*, 420.

56. Martha Albertson Fineman, *The Neutered Mother, the Sexual Family, and Other Twentieth-Century Tragedies* (New York: Routledge, 1995).

57. Much of the commentary on *Lawrence* has responded enthusiastically to its promise to rehabilitate homosexuality as an identity. Laurence Tribe, for example, applauds the decision for emphasizing "not the *set of specific acts* that have been found to merit constitutional protection, but rather the *relationships* and *self-governing commitments* out of which those acts arise—the network of human connection over time that makes genuine freedom possible" (Laurence Tribe, "*Lawrence v. Texas*: The 'Fundamental Right' That Dare Not Speak Its Name," *Harvard Law Review* 117 [2004]: 1955 [emphasis in original]).

58. Berlant, *Queen of America Goes to Washington City*, 3.

Uncivil Wrongs

RACE, RELIGION, HATE, AND INCEST IN QUEER POLITICS

Queer Limits

Michael Cobb

Something curious has happened over the past fifteen years. For queers, in the words of John D'Emilio, "the world turned," and now they are a central focus of mainstream politics and culture.[1] Because of this increasing familiarity, queers are at once present and still despised. Gays—particularly white, affluent, stereotypical gays—experience visibility in shows such as *Will and Grace* and *Queer Eye for the Straight Guy*; homosexual sodomy has been legalized in the United States by the U.S. Supreme Court decision in *Lawrence v. Texas*; Massachusetts's highest court has ruled twice in favor of same-sex marriage, not civil union, rights; and renegade counties, towns, and cities in California, Oregon, New Mexico, and New York are defiantly marrying same-sex couples. But if the reelection of George W. Bush and the rise of values voters should signal anything, it is that we should hesitate to agree with the optimistic words of George Chauncey, who exclaimed, in the *New York Times*, that the battle for gay visibility has clearly "been won."[2] We are visible, perhaps, but definitely not victorious.

When queers push for civil rights such as marriage, they routinely confront that old symbolic and sentimental terrain called the "family." These confrontations are citizenship contests, in which so much of the American national sphere intimately, as the past November reminded us, reconsolidates its most conservative tendencies.[3] The queer, especially when she or he asks to be let into politically legitimate, state-approved family making, discovers that she or he is still a suspicious and criminalized citizen. Look at the words of the conservative Christian Family Research Council (FRC), which defends "family, faith, and freedom" as the Judeo-Christian principles of a strong and solid culture. It has a list of core principles that queers jeopardize:

> God exists and is sovereign over all creation. He created human beings in His image. Human life is, therefore, sacred and the right to life is the most fundamental of political rights.

Social Text 84–85, Vol. 23, Nos. 3–4, Fall–Winter 2005.

> Life and love are inextricably linked and find their natural expression in the institutions of marriage and the family.
>
> Government has a duty to promote and protect marriage and family in law and public policy.
>
> The American system of law and justice was founded on the Judeo-Christian ethic.
>
> American democracy depends upon a vibrant civil society composed of families, churches, schools, and voluntary associations.[4]

This list is not just another example of an extreme ideology of an evangelical religious fringe. The FRC has substantial clout in the GOP (it was started during the Reagan years, with many prominent members of the Republican Party). It is also quite typical of the guiding principles of many mainstream religious Right organizations, in that it concisely explains why the Right still opposes the legal enfranchisement of queers in those institutions cast as most at risk: families, churches, and schools. The religious ethic of the American system of law and justice, which relies on virtuous families drenched in correct faith, cannot be violated by substantial policy gains made by queers. In response, a massive fund-raising and activist initiative by the FRC, "Family, Faith, and Freedom: The Battle for Marriage," has been created to help in the pursuit of the Federal Marriage Amendment. The same-sex marriage issue, one of many issues dear to the FRC and the religious Right (such as abortion, contraception, stem-cell research, Internet pornography, decency laws), is now *the* boutique issue, successfully drawing on the revulsion many still feel against queers.

It is within the context of this confrontation that I want to reassert something that should be obvious: queers currently function as one of the major limits of the American nation-state and, as such, cannot ever fully be included.[5] The use-value of the sex panic that still occurs around homosexuality and rights cannot be underestimated. For the purposes of this essay, I want to focus on one genre of queers' creative engagements with the nation-state, which occurs when queers are confronted with an emotion they experience when they push the limits of liberal inclusion: religiously articulated hate. Remember, not long before *Will and Grace* debuted, when the Reverend Fred Phelps, pastor of the infamous Westboro Baptist Church, gained notoriety for protesting Matthew Shepard's funeral? Phelps still maintains his Web site, God Hates Fags, which features the "Perpetual Gospel Memorial to Matthew Shepard," in which an image of Matthew screams electronically and counts the number of days Matthew has been in hell—a biblically just punishment for the "Satanic lifestyle"

Matthew lived as a "homosexual."[6] Phelps's church radically asserts on this site what lesser explicit, but fundamentally and evangelically influenced, Protestants have long thought of queer sexuality: "'GOD HATES FAGS'—though elliptical—is a profound theological statement. . . . The three words, fully expounded, show" that severe punishments await those who go against the scriptural and foundational laws of a holy society: "The only lawful sexual connection is the marriage bed. All other sexual activity is whoremongery and adultery, which will damn the soul forever in Hell."

Rather than dismiss Phelps as an extremist, I would like to relate this outrageous hyperbole to the kinds of public, doctrinal, financial, and political gains the rhetorical opposition to "homosexuality" has provided (and will continue to provide) for powerful Christian organizations such as the FRC and less-explicitly Christian organizations (such as the U.S. government) in the late twentieth and early twenty-first centuries.[7] The moral panic over traditional values also saturates the agenda of the mainstream Christian media giant, Focus on the Family. Its Web site's "Hot Topics" section raises a familiar and malicious question about homosexuality and human rights: "Homosexual activists claim their lifestyle, which in some cases includes thousands of sexual partners, should be sanctioned, protected, and granted special rights by society. Would you critique this stance?"[8] The answer, of course, is "yes," and one should make that "yes" heard by protecting traditional, heterosexual morality, reinforcing the explicit mission of Christian family values that makes Focus on the Family such a large and cherished media outlet for all sorts of conservative Christians throughout the world.[9]

But queers have also made similar gains from the same rhetoric of hate. Virulent language often has a peculiar use-value in oppositional politics. Judith Butler's *Excitable Speech: A Politics of the Performative* is a subtle exploration of hate speech and the ways that we must "question for a moment the presumption that hate speech always works, not to minimize the pain that is suffered as a consequence of hate speech, but to leave open the possibility that its failure is the condition of critical response."[10] Provoked by Butler's insights, I want to suggest that antiqueer religious language, what often amounts to queer hate speech, does not necessarily hurt queers. Queers have long used such hateful expressions as the condition for a circumspect publicity in a U.S. religious public sphere, a sphere that necessarily always shapes the positions from where anyone, especially queers, can speak in culture and politics. But rather than produce, as Butler proposes, a "resignification of speech . . . [that] opens new contexts, speaking in ways that have never been legitimated, and hence producing legitimation in new forms,"[11] queers mine the hostility and politics of hate that does not resignify as much as repeat

I want to suggest that antiqueer religious language, what often amounts to queer hate speech, does not necessarily hurt queers.

the traditional forms of political sphere access, but to perverse advantage, using the limits of liberalism to achieve something more. Queers mine the hate, through a religious language of hate, to provoke important feelings that can understand and manipulate the limits of liberal inclusion in a severely restricted U.S. public sphere.

In the following pages, I argue that much of queer politics and rights, which seem so mainstreamed,[12] also circulate at the limits of liberalism and specifically do so in a recognizably scandalous sphere of religious hatred. Hate speech erupts at one liberal impasse that always serves as a major factor "limiting" queers from entering fully into citizenship—our forced association, through a religious language of hate, with pedophilia and incest. For it is through the connections to antifamily incestuous and pedophilic leanings that many who want to prohibit queer inclusion are able to cast queers as those who are "incompatible with personal and public senses of the moral and the criminal."[13] I study the creative manipulations of the religious language of queer incest, which, quite surprisingly, linguistically affiliates the scandals of queer kinship crisis with the national crises of race and racial civil rights in an entirely "problematic" fashion, and necessarily so.[14] Such a link between race and sexuality (and there are many kinds of links between race and sexuality) is notoriously troubling. Janet Halley, among numerous others, has been helpful in the critique of much minority modeling ("like race" arguments) in queer activism and politics. I understand such critique as hope for the emergence of less lethal and exclusive models of citizenship and politics, and I share such criticism and desire. But for the purpose of this essay, and for the urgency of our ultraconservative times, I am interested in how queers create rhetorical forms of democratic coping, of survival, amid so much hate by using the "like race" analogy—forms made possible by a religious verbal attack on queers that makes the hatred experienced by them not unlike the hatred experienced by racial minorities. This politics, moreover, is very much a rhetorical politics that is not as reliant on conventional and literal conceptions of civil rights predicated on the accurate testimony of exclusion from an unsatisfying and coercive nation-state. Instead, the queer push for civil rights uses the hateful religious language to indicate the uncivil wrongs of being marked as queer, recalling the dramas of political, social, and cultural exclusion. What I hope to show is that some civil rights discourses, as they now operate within contemporary minority politics, often function as rhetorics of suffering, pain, and minority emotion that can be used by the politically and culturally disenfranchised to announce and bother people, from inside and outside the queer community, into some kind of transformative action, even if that action is simply feeling that something is wrong and that something else should be done.

Children, Church, and the Outraged Nation

A knee-jerk response to the outrage over pedophilia overshadowed the fact that a man had been killed, and by someone who has long hated homosexuals.

In 2003 Joseph Druce murdered John Geoghan, a notorious "pedophile priest." Druce, a man whom the Worcester, Massachusetts, district attorney described as being "so consumed with hatred toward homosexuals," considered Geoghan a "prize" worth killing.[15] Druce was already serving time for the strangulation of a man he had believed was gay. Geoghan's killing, which occurred within the confines of the Souza-Baranowski Correctional Center, was gruesome and has been reported in vivid detail, but, curiously, little moral outrage occurred. After all, this was a pedophile who was killed, a man convicted in January 2002 for groping a ten-year-old boy in 1991, just one incident among many. In September 2001 the Archdiocese of Boston paid a reported $10 million to settle a suit by eighty-six plaintiffs, all charging Geoghan with sexual assault. A Notre Dame historian, Scott Appelby, told CNN that Geoghan was "clearly a troubled soul," a "sick man and a predator priest. An icon for the scandal that has rocked the church."[16] The defrocked priest was certainly no martyr, and so his violent end, at the hands of an unrepentant homophobe, is not easily mourned. He is a "sick" and "perverse" icon of the increasingly infamous Catholic Church.

Certainly it is hard to defend the actions and life of a pedophile, especially with all the harmful and tragic stories of real abuse that comprise Geoghan's history as well as the many histories within dioceses worldwide. Among numerous quarters and casual conversations, however, a knee-jerk response to the outrage over pedophilia overshadowed the fact that a man had been killed, and by someone who has long hated homosexuals. Real justice, I have been repetitively told, was served behind bars. Appelby explained, "While some may say, sadly, he got what's coming to him. I think the prevailing feeling is one of sadness for what he did, for the state of his own soul."[17] Instead of being let to feel shock and anger over the actions of Druce, we are directed to the "real" story—one with priests who pray and prey on little boys, priests whose sicknesses must be lamented, if not "cured" by death. What escapes our attention is the fact that Druce made the mistake that many often make: that pedophilia is just another example of homosexuality and that some kind of hatred toward gays can find an acceptable expression in the violent punishment of the predator, pedophile priests. The lack of the child's consent is an upsetting part of Geoghan's sex abuse and should not be diminished; nor should we be unconcerned with the aftereffects of any act of sexual violence. But that kind of abuse cannot be so easily conflated with homosexuality, and the hatred of homosexuality should not be permitted, or even celebrated, when the homosexual victim is a pedophile. Instead, we should be worried about the public uses and abuses of pedophilia, and wonder why so much hatred can be deemed justifiable or acceptable when questions of children, of religion, and of family seem threatened. And usually threatened by someone considered "homosexual."

This murder and the reactions to it are by no means isolated. The proliferation of church sex scandals, along with the regimented outrage that even permits homophobic violence to occur within state institutions such as the prison, are not just accidental occurrences, aberrations in a public that seems to be more tolerant and accepting of gays. One should look at the not-infamous-enough comments of U.S. Senator Rick Santorum, who makes many of the links between homosexuality and pedophilia that contemporary queer politics needs to worry about. In a 7 April 2003 interview with the Associated Press, Santorum connected the decline of the traditional, heterosexual family with the "moral relativism" brought on by "liberalism," which is, according to the senator, one of the root reasons why there are so many church sex scandals. With the acceptance of a variety of "different lifestyles," Santorum explained, the dangerous case is made that "you can do whatever you want to do, as long as it's in the privacy of your own home." When he made these remarks, he was concerned about the impending *Lawrence v. Texas* ruling, with its specific issues about who has the right to privacy. For Santorum, there is the dangerous possibility that privacy granted to all, twinned with consent, would allow for any type of behavior: "You're sending signals that as long as you do it privately and consensually, we don't really care what you do." Bizarrely, this fear of private permissiveness inspired Santorum to characterize the Catholic Church sex scandals as "basic homosexual relationships" between consenting, private adults because in these cases, "we're not talking about priests with 3-year-olds, or 5-year-olds." If we think about this assertion, suddenly, the pedophiles are no longer pedophiles, they are homosexuals, and Santorum quickly makes the association Druce makes: pedophilic priests engage in "basic homosexual relationships," which are revolting and worthy of our disdain.[18]

When questioned by the AP reporter about his bias against homosexuality, Santorum parroted a typical Christian response that, as a Christian, he "has no problem with homosexuality" per se. His problem is actually with "homosexual acts." And homosexual acts done privately and with consent signal the descent of decent, American society:

> We have laws in states, like the one at the Supreme Court right now, that has sodomy laws and they were there for a purpose. Because, again, I would argue, they undermine the basic tenets of our society and the family. And if the Supreme Court says that you have the right to consensual sex in your

home, then you have the right [to] bigamy, you have the right to polygamy, you have the right to incest, you have the right to adultery. You have the right to anything. Does that undermine the fabric of our society? I would argue yes, it does. It all comes from, I would argue, this right to privacy that doesn't exist in my opinion in the United States Constitution, this right that was created, it was created in Griswold [v. Connecticut]—Griswold was the contraceptive case—and abortion [*sic*]. And we're just extending it out. And the further you extend it out, the more you—this freedom actually intervenes and affects the family. You say, well, it's my individual freedom. Yes, but it destroys the basic unit of our society because it condones behavior that's antithetical to strong, healthy families. Whether it's polygamy, whether it's adultery, whether it's sodomy, all of those things, are antithetical to a healthy, stable, traditional family.

Every society in the history of man has upheld the institution of marriage as a bond between a man and a woman. Why? Because society is based on one thing: that society is based on the future of the society. And that's what? Children. Monogamous relationships. In every society, the definition of marriage has not ever to my knowledge included homosexuality. That's not to pick on homosexuality. It's not, you know, man on child, man on dog, or whatever the case may be. It's one thing.[19]

The persistent and all-too-familiar connections between homosexuality and the decline of the family seem inescapable. For Santorum, as well as many others, homosexuality is the family's apocalypse; the basic foundations of "family" as monogamous, heterosexual union will shake as we become more private and tolerant. Most worrisome is that children might be most at risk. Of course, children are not just children, they are the future, and these children should not be hurt by the progressive move to change the nation's most cherished institution—marriage.

Perhaps this is one reason, beyond the scandal of sexual abuse, that pedophilia so quickly becomes the story of homosexuality. Homosexuality, in its illogical conflation, is always an affront to children—it is pedophilic preying on the nation's future voting citizens, who might otherwise become so tolerant as to accept any social behavior, who might allow for Gayle Rubin's long-held wish for "benign variation" of sexual identities and behaviors.[20] Or, these children might simply not be "there" at all, if we ignore the realities of queer parenting and reproductive technologies and, instead, believe the conservative Christian lie that homosexual families are nonprocreative families. In any case, we are led to worry, in a sentimental way, about the future loss of children; we are told to worry about the violent world they will be forced and coerced into accepting if homosexuals are permitted to thrive in privacy, in consensual relations, in marriage, and, especially, in the church, which is increasingly synonymous, through the pervasive presence of conservative, evangelicals in the United States, with "the family."[21]

Among his worries, Santorum confuses not only homosexuality with pedophilia but also pedophile homosexuals with a demand for incestuous rights. He does so to further circumscribe the precarious "nature" of families in a too tolerant world. Incest has certainly long been a vexing issue, a constitutive taboo, which has touched most arenas engaged in understanding the makeup and maintenance of family, if not all, social structures. Many fascinating works in psychoanalysis, anthropology, and feminist anthropology, as well as literary criticism in the American context, have already investigated the "right" of incest and its precious placement in the constitution of families, societies, nations, and individual psyches.[22] In a study of Greek tragedy and *Antigone*, Judith Butler, for an example that understands Santorum's hysteria, explains that "alternative kinship arrangements [such as same-sex kinship relations] attempt to revise psychic structures in ways that lead to tragedy again, figured incessantly as the tragedy of and for the child. No matter what one ultimately thinks of the political value of gay marriage . . . the public debate on its legitimacy becomes the occasion for a set of homophobic discourses that must be resisted on independent grounds."[23] I agree with Butler. Such resistance, however, is increasingly difficult to resist on "independent grounds." The tragedy of queer rights is the tragedy for the child, and this figuration of tragedy engenders the kinds of hateful rhetoric so laboriously used by religious politicians such as Santorum. Church sex controversies quickly transform into homosexual controversies, then into gay marriage controversies, threatening traditional, very national, and patriotic kinship systems, which are "incessantly," or "incest-antly," the child's potential loss.

We most certainly can describe this tragedy as sentimental, providing conservative politicians with an emotive occasion to become quite hateful toward the pedophilic, if not incestuous, "Father" of the child: the homosexual. Butler rightly states, "Consider that the horror of incest, the moral revulsion it compels in some, is not far afield from the same horror and revulsion felt toward lesbian and gay sex, and is not unrelated to the intense moral condemnation of voluntary single parenting, or gay parenting, of parenting arrangements with more than two adults involved. . . . These various modes in which the oedipal mandate fails to produce normative family all risk entering into the metonymy of that moralized sexual horror that is perhaps most fundamentally associated with incest."[24] Santorum's comments certainly experience and manipulate that sexual horror. I would push Butler's argument even further: that incest—which is also so closely aligned with pedophilia—and homosexuality are so frequently thought

Among his worries, Santorum confuses not only homosexuality with pedophilia but also pedophile homosexuals with a demand for incestuous rights.

together that the horror of incest is now also the horror of homosexuality, the horror of what a permissive, private, and queer friendly society might permit. In other words, the horror of incest is the current way to mark, to figure, the limits of what kinds of sexual tolerance toward gays, lesbians, and bisexuals the current, extremely conservative political climate can accommodate. It is thus perfectly acceptable for a leading politician to voice, in a national way, his hatred of homosexuality, in part because the specter of homosexuality is not "far afield" from the destruction of the family, the fabric of a great nation, and the onslaught of a too permissive liberalism that believes "anything goes."

It is also perfectly acceptable for U.S. Supreme Court Justice Antonin Scalia in his dissent in *Lawrence* to fret similarly over the foundations of the American nation. Anxious that the Court's antisodomy ruling might deform U.S. marriage laws, Scalia believes that the "homosexual agenda" now hurts many Americans who "do not want persons who openly engage in homosexual conduct . . . as scoutmasters for their children, as teachers in their schools"; indeed, these Americans are at peril and will not be able to protect "themselves and their families from a lifestyle that they believe immoral and destructive."[25] The new social tolerance of the homosexual agenda, again and again, puts our moral/religious country, our moral/religious families, and especially our moral/religious children at destructive risk. The specter of the pedophile, the specter of incest, is lurking perniciously within this apocalyptic vision of the nation's future. And this position does not cause enormous outrage because the hateful connections between the homosexual as sexual predator of children are always so present, always so potently upsetting, that no amount of flair and comedy from the "Fab Five" Queer Eyes can yet alleviate the country's rhetorical convulsions over the possibility that homosexuals might come into destructive contact with children. So here are the questions I have, given the incestuous and pedophilic affiliation we have not chosen and cannot avoid: how do we address the nation, from this pedophilic, incestuous position that preys on the nation's innocent children? How do we respond to this argument, this version of religious hate?

A Fictional Case for Civil Wrongs

The most common response I know, as I suggested above, is also full of religious hate. But this genre of hate is twisted into a kind of sentimentality that conjures up another history of national intolerance. Chauncey, in the *New York Times*, is quoted as saying: "What strikes me . . . is how closely the resistance to same-sex marriage resembles white people's fears about interracial marriage, which were the emotional core of their fears about integration in general. Now, as in the 1950s and 60s, much of the objection to legally extending marital rights takes the form of religious warnings about a declining 'moral order.'"[26] Chauncey brings the current concerns over queer rights into alignment with the emotional core of race relations, which is by no means a novel tactic. Certainly we should be cautious: the "like race" argument has already been extensively critiqued by the important critical legal work of Janet Halley.[27] Without diminishing her crucial insights, I want to suggest a different analytic route, one that investigates the tenacity of why so many thinkers and activists make queers "like" race. I must caution that by fixating on the analogy, I do not mean to imply, as one reader of this piece worried, that race and queer sexuality are not fully entangled concepts, and the explosion of sophisticated work by and about queers of color certainly reminds us as much.[28] Instead, I want to think of the identity categories as rhetorical positions in a limited grammar of body styles we must use rightly or wrongly, with varying degrees of success and failure.[29] Race has an especially complicated and powerful status: for race, indeed, is an identity *category* or rhetorical *name* that the public sphere grudgingly acknowledges has had a traumatic, painful, and hostile treatment in the United States, a history that is serious and in need of at least limited reparations, civil rights, and recognitions. We can take those racial and religious words of hate, those public condemnations saturated with religious morality and family panic, and use them for our advantage.

Think of, for instance, queer moral outrage—even my own personal outrage—over Santorum's hating and Geoghan's killing. My rhetoric must also be interrogated as a strategy pushing my own Left and prohomosexual agenda. Curiously, the God Hates Fags Web site is correct when it asserts, "Fags shamelessly use the deaths of fags to promote their sodomite agenda,"[30] for I am using the moral panic, the manifest expressions of queer hatred (for example, Matthew Shepard's murder), to a perverse, queer advantage: it is the display of intolerance, of such conservative sentimental worry over restricted national notions of families and especially children, that permits me to reassert what is still minor about queerness, especially at a moment when "gay visibility" has been heralded as winning the battle. I am using the horror of incest, but for a different purpose. By drawing attention to the sentimental hysteria of figures such as Santorum, by drawing attention to the perversity of religious commentary on national futurity and the nation's important children, I start to manipulate the hateful feelings of the religious Right as a "structure of feeling" that can describe the position of queer in contemporary U.S. politics and culture.[31] I can take on that form of hate speech as a form of self-expression of the queer as a minority. I am asserting something as strange as: I am still a minority because I am so quickly affiliated with incest, pedophilia, and the destruction of functional, productive families. I am still a minority because I have to figure the apocalyptic vision of liberal ruin, and, as an incestuous, pedophilic figure, I can so readily and calmly be defiled at the lowest and highest levels of U.S. government and culture—on the floor of the Senate or the floor of a jail cell, as it were, all while the conservative and religious public sphere gives such derision its religious blessing. What is more, positioned at the nation's limits, I have no choice in the matter—the associations and anxieties are there, no matter how much I wish they were not. So, in negative, in obverse, I am still using, and not really changing, the terms set by the Right, if not the religious righteous: my claims of recognition also worry over the family, child loss, and the future of the nation—a nation so predicated on the conservative, Christian values.

Moreover, these emotional, irreverent concerns—family, child loss, and the future of the nation—belong to a kind of racialized sentimental politics we have often seen in the history of LGBTQ politics. As many others have argued, the manipulation of emotion for social movements and political change in the United States since at least the nineteenth century has been concerned with the problem of race as it was articulated by the tragedy of slavery and the struggles for citizenship's enfranchising possibilities for those who were once excluded—especially African Americans and women.[32] I might be overstating the case, but this version of sentimental minority politics is primarily and persistently racial in tone, which might account for why so many struggles to define the frustrated emotional claims of those who have not achieved full citizenship or equality in the United States, frequently evoke, as Lauren Berlant does, a quick mention of the Fourteenth Amendment to make articulate that the "history of civil rights in the United States shows that gaining the franchise is both an event and a process, a zone of individualization that always crackles with contingency."[33] I would modify this claim a bit and describe that the achievement of adequate recognition of full citizenship in the United States is also a feeling, a sentiment, that "crackles with contingency," one that usually uses the African American race, more than gender, as the default "font" or form of difference to make the urgency of difference felt. Despite its obvious and upsetting pitfalls (there are vastly different experiences of racism and homophobia, even if they often overlap), queers often take on the feelings of race to describe social injustice, to assert that they are still queer and in need of the limited, restricted, and normative protections offered by a public sphere. And they take on those structures of racial feelings not because they forget the analogy and forget that there is deliberate, if not very fictitious play of rhetoric, of language, but quite

Instead of a truthful and careful queer story, we often have the manipulation of a hateful emotion that belongs to another minority category—"the emotional core" of race.

the opposite: there is a useful strategy that is not about a faithful utterance, the precise naming of the minority situation in which they persistently find themselves; there is use in being fictitious, imaginative, if not downright dishonest when it comes to one's publicity in a coercive and hostile nation. Instead of a truthful and careful queer story, we often have the manipulation of a hateful emotion that belongs to another minority category—"the emotional core" of race.

It is no wonder that Butler, soon after she argues that the horror over incest is so often associated with the horror of gay sex, rushes into a discussion of Orlando Patterson's influential book, *Slavery and Social Death: A Comparative Study*, and his useful concept of "social death," a "status of being a living being radically deprived of all rights that are supposed to be accorded to any and all living beings."[34] The social death of slavery is a social death that can be applied to the kinds of deaths queers are given in the United States, especially when they are so closely aligned with the horrors of incest, also known as the horror of the eroding tradition of the American family. In the current queer political and cultural climate, the complicated rhetoric of emotion provokes us into politics; we are struggling, as we long have, with social injustice in terms of loss, of slavery, of incest, and strong feelings that aggregate the queer with race. So let us now chart that struggle with an instructive, queer instance.

Ann Cvetkovich describes Dorothy Allison's *Bastard out of Carolina* as a "powerful" examination of "the intimate connections between sexual trauma and sexual pleasure, and by implication the connections between incest and, if not lesbianism explicitly, then, perverse sexuality."[35] For this "lesbian" narrative, and I will call it as much, does articulate some difficult connections that belong to this constellation of homosexuality, incest, hate, and, quite poignantly, race and religion that I have been describing in this essay. The central character, Bone, a victim of incest and a failing and poor white family, struggles and embodies "hardscrabble" existence. At key moments in her story, moreover, Bone is overcome by the power of gospel music, by the power of preachers' words, wondering how she could possibly belong to these moments of public, collective expression about what is supposed to be private: one's soul, one's personal story, or one's faith. The words she hears during one church gathering are characteristically religious in that they are both obscure and yet potent: "Revivals are funny. People get pretty enthusiastic, but they sometimes forget just which hymn it is they're singing. I grinned at the sound of mumbled, unintelligible song."[36] Despite the lack of specific words and message, and despite the way that this mumbling occasions men close to the Revival tent to "punch each other lightly and curse in a friendly fashion," Bone finds the religious utterances deeply moving:

> *You bastard.*
> *You son of a bitch.*
> The preacher said something I didn't understand. There was a moment of silence, and then a pure tenor voice rose up in the night sky. The spit soured in my mouth. They had a real singer in there, a real gospel choir.
>
> *Swing low, sweet chariot . . . coming for to carry me home . . . swing low, sweet chariot . . . coming to carry me home.*
>
> The night seemed to wrap around me like a blanket. My insides felt as if they had melted, and I could taste the wind in my mouth. The sweet gospel music poured through me in a piercing young boy's voice, and made all my nastiness, all my jealousy and hatred, swell in my heart. . . . The world was too big for me, the music too strong. I knew, I knew I was the most disgusting person on earth. I didn't deserve to live another day. I started hiccupping and crying. (135–36)

Initially, it might be hard for a reader to see how on earth the language provoking the feelings of being "the most disgusting person on earth" might actually foster a radical politics. But surely the redeployment of the word *queer* demonstrates that negatives still might generate some unforeseen and positive developments. Emotionally charged language can be twisted and wrestled in some very curious ways, especially religious language.[37] Thus Allison here emphasizes through italics the song-quality of gospel music, just as she also starts the quotation of meaningful rhetoric with curses that call attention to Bone's status as a "bastard," as someone outside legitimate kinship systems. With italics, Allison grants a significant status to the religious words, which are drawn into equivalence of the "friendly curses" to give importance to the form and rhetoric of gospel rather than to the message of the words. Direct religious words from the preacher, theological messages, are not understood; precise meaning is not as important as the visceral, affective state the gospel words provoke in Bone. She is wrapped up by the night, her insides melt, her spit sours, her nastiness and jealousy and hatred swell in her heart. She has an extreme emotional response that is indexed by her intense, corporeal reaction, which calls forth all the feelings of shame, abuse, anger that make her feel at once full of grandiose self-disgust and empty of significance. Moreover, the gospel music leads her through a series of images of her family into a realization of the way the world is "too big": "I remembered Aunt Ruth's fingers fluttering birdlike in front of her face, Uncle Earle's flushed cheeks and lank black hair as they'd cried together on the porch, Mama's pinched, worried face and Daddy Glen's cold, angry, eyes" (135). It is significant that the eyes that give Bone her particularly confusing insight into her own complicated disgust are the eyes of her incestuous abuser. His eyes enable her perspective, give her eyes. This victim of incest has a family that has quite simply made her feel terribly wrong, out of place, out of scale, not belonging to this large, strong world.

But Bone's response to gospel is not simply witnessed by either the reader of the novel or Bone herself. She outlines a linguistic structure of these provocative emotions. The religious words are not merely vehicles for the expression of a paralyzing hatred and self-disgust. For Bone astutely tells us something important at another point in the novel: "Salvation was complicated" (148). And part of that complication, Bone explains, are the religious words, exemplified by gospel, which are there to "make you hate and love yourself at the same time, make you ashamed and glorified" (136). It is a musical language of ambivalence, which provides a particularly important form in which to express extreme emotions. Listen to the way Bone describes her Uncle Earle's insistent need to blaspheme:

> What I really liked was how he talked about Jesus in a way I understood even when I couldn't put it together with all he said. He talked about Jesus like a man dying for need of him, but too stubborn to sit down to the meal spread within his reach. Earle talked the language of gospel music, with its rhythms and intensity. I heard in his drawled pronouncements the same swelling rough raw voices, the red-faced men and pale sweating women moaning in the back pews. "Lord, Lord!" Moaning and waiting, waiting and praying, "to be washed, *Lord Jesus*! washed in the blood of the Lamb!" The hunger, the lust and the yearning was palpable. (148)

Bone's sense of words that "could not be put together" into a coherent theological message is subordinate to the fact that she understands the "language of gospel music" to be a language of intensity, moaning, waiting, lust, hunger, and yearning—emotional states somehow made "palpable" by the music. Bone needs this language of love and hate because it helps her to understand. More important, this language of love and hate helps her to feel.

Tellingly, the moment when Bone most feels the power of gospel, what she immediately describes as "real gospel" (169), is when she encounters a clapboard church in the woods. This church provides the occasion for Bone to hear where gospel comes from—from the overwhelming sentiment of African Americans. "At that I froze, realizing that such a church off such a dirt road had to be . . . a colored church" (170). And this moment also provokes a difficult moment of Bone encountering racist hate speech. Her companion, Shannon, uses the slur "Nigger." In response, Bone acknowledges, "My voice was shaking. The way Shannon said 'nigger' tore at me, the tone pitched exactly like the echoing sound of Aunt Madeline sneering 'trash' when she thought I wasn't close enough to hear" (170).

Bone's white-trash status—a status most tragically marked by her status as a victim of incest—has made her vulnerable to the kinds of hate speech attacks she so readily identifies as sharing the same pitch as "nigger"; both are slurs that are also experienced as the language of injury. But it is the African American slur in particular that helps her understand that language can tear. The language of slur is so closely associated with the language of "real gospel," and Bone, here, can feel and understand the kind of hate she must also endure as a subject systematically blocked from full or legitimate status in the hostile world that hates its "niggers" and its "trash." Hortense Spillers regards "African American sermons [and the religious language they contain] as a paradigm of the structure of ambivalence that constitutes the black person's relationship to American culture and apprenticeship in it."[38] Bone similarly regards sermons and gospels, particularly African American gospels, as paradigmatic of the ambivalence she must confusingly negotiate as she circulates within a culture and society in which she is not legitimate (she is a bastard, an incest victim, a minor girl, and white "trash"). The agony of African American experience so deeply feels like Bone's agony. There are powerful analogies, occasioned by the penetrating feeling and power of religion, between "race" and other forms of social exclusion that are hard to articulate, especially if one is a young girl without any status at all.

Bone's white-trash status—a status most tragically marked by her status as a victim of incest—has made her vulnerable to the kinds of hate speech attacks she so readily identifies as sharing the same pitch as "nigger."

It is no wonder that theorists and activists, and not just characters in a book, excavate this emotive connection, this high pitch of hatred, feeling, agony, hunger, and lust to communicate the "tragedies of a child." Butler, as I mentioned above, suggestively manipulates childhood tragedies, such as incest, to propose the productive qualities of an unexpected resistance we can and should call a racialized politics. She concludes her arguments with a lyrical appeal to the "social death" and the "shadowy realm" of those who fall outside the boundaries of normative, public sphere. "Giorgio Agamben has remarked that we live increasingly in a time in which populations without full citizenship exist within states; their ontological status as legal subjects is suspended," writes Butler. "These are not lives being genocidally destroyed, but neither are they being entered into the life of the legitimate community in which standards of recognition permit for an attainment of humanness." But rather than see these populations as helplessly moribund, something about this status is productive, or useful. Butler wonders:

> How are we to understand this realm, what Hannah Arendt calls the "shadowy realm," which haunts the public sphere, which is precluded from the public constitution of the human, but which is human in an apparently catachrestic sense of that term? Indeed, how are we to grasp this dilemma of language

> that emerges when "human" takes on that doubled sense, the normative one based on radical exclusion and the one that emerges in the public sphere of the excluded, not negated, not dead, perhaps slowly, yes, surely dying from a lack of recognition, dying, indeed, from the premature circumspection of the norms by which recognition can be conferred?[39]

The shadowy realm, the realm of the haunting death of those who do not belong to the public sphere, poses a "dilemma of language," a dilemma summarily described as the "melancholy of the public sphere." Bone feels this melancholy of her own lack of positive recognitions that are more valuable of derivative, palpable appellations of trash, which are akin to nigger. But through love-hate gospel, her existence in the shadowy realm of noncitizenship produces a melancholy language, full of the ambivalence that cannot let go of the pain, that must love and hate, and that must produce a rawness that is not as intelligible as much as it is felt.

Somehow this religious language—which functions more as a dilemma of language rather than clear, theological messages—produces defiance in Bone. She describes, in terms that could be the very definition of melancholy,[40] what she likes about the way religion expresses the incoherency of her shadow existence. Bone responds to her inability to be "saved" in various Baptist congregations; she knows there was no magic or guilt that would be purged from herself. Nevertheless, religion provides some kind of comfort, and it is a hostile comfort:

> I sneezed and coughed for a solid week, lying limp in my bed and crying to every gospel song that came over the radio. It was as if I were mourning the loss of something I had never really had. I sang along with the music and prayed for all I was worth. Jesus' blood and country music, there had to be something else, something more I could hope for. I bit my lip and went back to reading the Book of Revelation, taking comfort in the hope of the apocalypse, God's retribution on the wicked. I liked Revelations, loved the Whore of Babylon and the promised rivers of blood and fire. It struck me like gospel music, it promised vindication. (152)

What Bone enjoys, here, is that religious words provide a reversal of the dire circumstances in which she finds herself, in which she experiences the wicked as those around her who tear into her, much like Shannon's disdain for "nigger," which is so much like the disdain thrown at Bone by other words. Rather than be "saved," Bone enjoys the power and force of the words that promise some kind of intense opposition to those who oppress her. In this way, she affiliates herself with something the shadowy realm of noncitizen often deeply evokes: a language of blackness. In an inquiry into Ralph Ellison's *Invisible Man*, Spillers argues: "By revising and correcting 'blackness' into a *critical* posture, into a preeminent site of the 'multicultural,' long before the latter defined a new politics and polemic . . . Ellison harnessed 'blackness' to a symbolic program of philosophical 'disobedience.' . . . [his works] make 'blackness' a *process*, a *strategy*, of cultural critique rather than a condition of physiognomy and/or the embodiment of the *auto-bios-graphe*."[41] In this provocative formulation, blackness is the symbolic, critical posture that anyone, as Spillers believes, can inhabit as an intense and necessary form or figure of opposition—a posture that looks perhaps in utopian ways to another future, one full of blood and vindication, when certain wrongs might be made right. Blackness, for Spillers (and Ellison), should not be captured and overly infused with narratives of authenticity and essentialism—blackness should not merely be testimony or autobiography. Blackness, instead, functions most effectively as a powerful language of critique. And Bone speaks as if she is black in order to make a forceful opposition to the public sphere, the liberal nation-state, that despises and excludes her.

Bone speaks as if she is black in order to make a forceful opposition to the public sphere, the liberal nation-state, that despises and excludes her.

Butler's own writing reveals similar rhetorical emphases, optimistic about what the shadowy realm of confusing language might permit in terms of its oppositional potential. In describing Antigone's incestuous, promiscuous claim on the human, when she is supposed to be excluded, we know that Antigone "is not of the human but speaks its language. . . . She speaks within the language of entitlement from which she is excluded, participating in the language of the claim with which no final identification is possible."[42] Antigone, much like Bone, has no right to speak in the ways she does, but nevertheless, she does, and as she does, produces the possibility of her own dark, blackening opposition to that language the two women are forced to inhabit. Antigone speaks the language of the state, and Bone, we can argue, does the same: the language of the American State, despite claims to the contrary, is still very much a religious language. As Janet R. Jakobsen and Ann Pellegrini provocatively and correctly assert, "To be traditionally American is to be traditionally Christian in a certain way,"[43] so we can argue that the public sphere is certainly also a religious public sphere with an official religious language. Both female figures of incest speak authoritative languages, but undermine those languages, forcing them "into perpetual catachresis, showing . . . how a term can continue to signify outside its conventional constraints."[44] An outlaw figure such as Bone or Antigone "acts, she speaks, she becomes one for whom the speech act is a fatal crime, but this fatality exceeds her life and enters the discourse of intelligibility as its own promising fatality, the social form of its aberrant, unprecedented future."[45]

Certainly this is dangerous, *figurative* territory. But the figuration, the style of queer expression, is often where much of contemporary politics about sexuality is and needs to engage as we move toward the "aberrant, unprecedented future" when homosexuals pedophilically and incestuously defile the American family with demands for things like marriage rights. After all, a U.S. senator and other fundamental Christians are making much of the homosexual, incestuous, pedophilic panic up in their heads; they are being inventive and fictitious, rhetorical, and effectively so, with very real consequences. What I want to stress is that queers are similarly making themselves up, with similarly real consequences. All of which makes sense, since the U.S. government is a *representative* government, relying on the manner in which people describe (or are described) and spin themselves (or are spun) into publicity as they push for civil rights and legal enfranchisements from the nation-state.

Whether we like it or not, the U.S. public sphere and its citizens still work, on a daily basis, with a rights-based model, which presupposes the American revolutionary ideal that informed the complicated and incomplete transformation of the United States by its Declaration of Independence, Constitution, and its now, precarious, Bill of Rights: the "revolutionary claim that the subject of post-monarchism is the subject of birth . . . the subject of universal, inalienable rights."[46] From the vantage point of the "like race" rhetorical strategy, the simile for public sphere access is not one of similitude, not a born-that-way assertion, or even a claim of fixed minority status, but rather a point of dangerously, perhaps harmfully productive affiliation with the emotions of racial distinction, with an agreed-on minority status and its sentimental effects, with legibly *not*-belonging to the public sphere, of being violently and painfully excluded—of being made oppositional or "raced" by the malicious associations between homosexuality and pedophilia, figuring the ruin of traditional American civil, political, and cultural society. Queers are hated. Queers, in a suggestive word, are "raced." For the race claim made in the United States is that shadowy realm often inflected with legible language pain and suffering—a form of sentimental language of an excluded and factionalized group within the United States, conjuring up memories of slavery and segregation that should no longer be tolerated in a country and a public trying to make amends and adjust to "true" equality.

Berlant's work on citizenship helps us understand the "sentimental politics" that persists as we make the public sphere respond to difference, an emotional politics "by which mass subaltern [minority] pain is advanced in the dominant public sphere, as the true core of national collectivity."[47] The pain and suffering described by the hateful plight of those who feel oppressed or stripped of basic citizenship rights increasingly takes absolute importance in a conflict over whether one belongs equally to the United States. "National sentimentality is more than a current of feeling that circulates in a political field: the phrase describes a longstanding contest between two models of U.S. citizenship," instructs Berlant. "In one, the classic model, each citizen's value is secured by an equation between abstractness and emancipation: a cell of national identity provides juridically protected personhood for citizens regardless of anything specific about them" (128–29). And "in the second model, which was initially organized around labor, feminist, and antiracist struggles in the United States in the nineteenth century, another version is imagined as the index of collective life. This nation is peopled by suffering citizens and noncitizens whose structural exclusion from the utopian-American dreamscape exposes the state's claim of legitimacy and virtue to an acid wash of truth-telling that makes hegemonic disavowal virtually impossible at certain moments of political intensity" (129).

These two versions of citizenship—the abstract/utopian versus the suffering/loud—leads to a form of politics that relies on the functional citation of pain: "Identification with pain, a universal true feeling, then leads to structural and social change." This citation thus reasserts the value of the classic model of abstract equality: "In return, subalterns scarred by the pain of failed democracy will reauthorize universalist notions of citizenship in the national utopia, which involves believing in a redemptive notion of law as the guardian of public good. The object of the nation and the law in this light is to eradicate systematic social pain, the absence of which becomes the definition of freedom" (129). Queer activism and minority complaint most certainly belong to the traumatic model of the pain of citizenship; as victims of hate, as target members of society, queers use their injuries to mark, sentimentally, the failures of the classic citizenship's promise, with an eye on, but perhaps not yet a handle on, eventually becoming "classic" rather than merely a "subject of true [and painful] feeling."

Berlant has a whole host of reservations about these competing models of citizenship, all of which make enormous amounts of sense, especially if one wanted to move beyond the hierarchy and histories of violent exclusion implied in these versions of constitutional personhood, a hierarchy in which "the counterhegemonic deployments of pain as the measure of structural injustice actually sustain the utopian image of a homogenous national metaculture, which can look like a healed or healthy body in contrast to the scarred and exhausted ones" (129). The current system of appeal and complaint is seriously wrong, and Berlant and others are

Perhaps an even queerer understanding of the figurations of representational politics will evacuate, at least for a little while, the need for holding out for sweeping, utopian transformation of the public sphere and its neoliberal ruses.

holding out for other "democratic possibilities,"[48] ones that acknowledge the complexity and diversity of minority emotion and minority status. Berlant hopes that the subaltern will recognize "that the signs of subordination they [minorities] feel also tell a story that they do not feel yet, or know, about how to construct the narrative to come."[49] The future and the utopian promise of a better, less coercive articulation of marginalization in the national culture fuels much queer, critical work, to be sure. There is an understandable mistrust, one I frequently feel, in the deployment of conventional and often abusive forms and relationships of citizenship in advancing any demand for social and structural change. But while we are in the useful and necessary mood to hope and imagine and offer excellent criticisms and theories about what could be otherwise, it is also crucial to think about the less-detectable, even the less-desirable, strategies of coping with the confines of dominant culture, of the already established nation-state that, as I have said, does not seem to be going anywhere else anytime soon. Perhaps an even queerer understanding of the figurations of representational politics will evacuate, at least for a little while, the need for holding out for sweeping, utopian transformation of the public sphere and its neoliberal ruses.

When queers reference, as I have throughout this essay, the avarice of the religious righteous who make queers assume the burden of being incestuous and pedophilic, we demonstrate that the religious hate of queers is a position in rhetoric as much as it is an immediate and upsetting emotion—a position that affiliates us with oppression that is perhaps more legible within a neoliberal public sphere that is religious, not ready to transform and lend full, civil rights to queer people: a raced position that has at least captured the emotive attention of a nation that did make some—but not nearly enough—strides to make racial minorities more fully members of society. It makes sense, then, that members of a four-hundred-something coalition of progressive clergy called the Religious Coalition for the Freedom to Marry has signed a declaration that states, "From the shameful history of slavery in America, the injustice of forbidding people to marry is evident as a denial of basic human rights."[50] The Supreme Court of Massachusetts, in its second ruling on same-sex marriage on 4 February 2004, rhetorically and explicitly references the history of segregation, racial civil rights, and *Brown v. Board of Education*: "This history of our nation has demonstrated that separate is seldom, if ever, equal."[51] Where would we be without this kind of language, this kind of sentimental jabbing? It is an allusion, a reference, and not an explicit or specifically articulated queer testimony.

I am hopeful that this kind of emotional, racially inflected language is the twist we need for a political sphere that is hyperemotional, full of suspicion and hate, and not willing to be rational. In the current climate where religious opinions about homosexuality's dangerous connections to incest, pedophilia, liberal ruin, and moral decline flourish, it is especially important to understand the ways that these words can be merely and only words, a literary "dilemma of language,"[52] and how those words make queers hated in the most sentimental ways. It is certainly a civil wrong to claim that religious hate speech makes us like a racial minority. But perhaps, by engaging civil rights in such an uncivil manner, we can then begin to give our outrage back to ourselves and push up against liberalism's impasses into understanding the creative and radical copings of queers who have to do something about the persistent subordination they are forced to feel everyday. We might also get something as peculiar as twisted enfranchisement, short-circuiting the liberal quandaries that require we remain forever outside the liberal nation-state, in a public sphere that is always ready to despise and "Fab Five" us.

Notes

1. See John D'Emilio's optimistic, but still very nuanced, arguments about LGBTQ issues moving from margin to center in the American national consciousness in his collection of essays, *The World Turned: Essays on Gay History, Politics, and Culture* (Durham, NC: Duke University Press, 2002).

2. George Chauncey, quoted in Frank Rich, "And Now, the Queer Eye for Straight Marriage," *New York Times*, 10 August 2003. For a necessary critique and deep investigation of the concept of visibility, especially lesbian visibility, see Amy Villarejo's *Lesbian Rule: Cultural Criticism and the Value of Desire* (Durham, NC: Duke University Press, 2003). See also D'Emilio, *World Turned*, and Urvashi Vaid, *The Mainstreaming of Gay and Lesbian Liberation* (New York: Anchor/Doubleday, 1996).

3. For a recent study of the complicated and commodified transformation of evangelical message and media, see Heather Hendershot, *Shaking the World for Jesus: Media and Conservative Evangelical Desire* (Chicago: University of Chicago Press, 2004). For greater insight into the conservative forces of the "intimate public sphere," see Lauren Berlant, *The Queen of America Goes to Washington City: Essays on Sex and Citizenship* (Durham, NC: Duke University Press, 1997).

4. Family Research Council, www.frc.org/get.cfm?c=ABOUT_FRC (accessed 6 July 2004).

5. For a compelling and perhaps contradictory reading of queer politics and certain forms of neoliberalism, see Lisa Duggan, *The Twilight of Equality? Neoliberalism, Cultural Politics, and the Attack on Democracy* (Boston: Beacon, 2003).

6. See www.godhatesfags.com/memorial.html (accessed 15 May 2002).

7. In her *Between Jesus and the Market: The Emotions That Matter in Right-Wing America*, Linda Kintz persuasively demonstrates the persistent connections between religious and right-wing conservative movements in the contemporary United States. Kintz argues that "the tenets familiar from religious conservatism

help shape market fundamentalism by sacrificing certain groups to the purity of the market while displacing attacks on workers, people of color, gays, and lesbians into the abstractions of economic theory" (Linda Kintz, *Between Jesus and the Market: The Emotions That Matter in Right-Wing America* [Durham, NC: Duke University Press, 1997], 4). This market focus is important to keep in mind. My study is more involved in detailing the ferocity of the rhetoric of Jesus and should be read as a companion piece to Kintz's work.

8. See www.family.org/married/topics/a0025114.cfm (accessed 9 February 2004).

9. For a fascinating study of vision and Christian thinking, see Didi Herman, *The Antigay Agenda: Orthodox Vision and the Christian Right* (Chicago: University of Chicago Press, 1997).

10. Judith Butler, *Excitable Speech: A Politics of the Performative* (New York: Routledge, 1997), 19.

11. Ibid., 41.

12. For well-discussed debates of queer mainstreaming, see Vaid, *Mainstreaming of Gay and Lesbian Liberation*; Andrew Sullivan, *An Argument about Homosexuality* (New York: Vintage, 1996); and Michael Warner, *The Trouble with Normal: Sex, Politics, and the Ethics of Queer Life* (Cambridge, MA: Harvard University Press, 2000).

13. Elizabeth Povinelli, *The Cunning of Recognition: Indigenous Alterities and the Making of Australian Multiculturalism* (Durham, NC: Duke University Press, 2002), 4. Povinelli is interested in "national subjects [who] find that no matter the heroic rhetoric of enlightenment understanding, 'their ways,' cannot cease to make 'us' sick. And this sickness scatters the self (I, us) across contrasting obligations to public reason and moral sensibility. It is this cauldron of competing social impulses that interests me, because of the way it generates new ethics and metaethics of national and international life" (5).

14. Just a quick note. It is with great relief that stunning work about race and ethnicity has taken a hold of queer studies in the most productive ways. I am thinking of projects such as Samuel Delany, *Times Square Red, Times Square Blue* (New York: New York University Press, 1999); José Esteban Muñoz, *Disidentifications: Queers of Color and the Performance of Politics* (Minneapolis: University of Minnesota Press, 1999); Mary Pat Brady, *Extinct Lands, Temporal Geographies: Chicana Literature and the Urgency of Space* (Durham, NC: Duke University Press, 2002); Robert Reid-Pharr, *Black Gay Man: Essays* (New York: New York University Press, 2001); David Eng, *Racial Castration: Managing Masculinity in Asian America* (Durham, NC: Duke University Press, 2001); and Philip Brian Harper, *Are We Not Men? Masculine Anxiety and the Problem of African American Identity* (Oxford: Oxford University Press, 1998), among other great studies.

15. Michael S. Rosenwald and Stephen Kurkjian, "Monthlong Plot to Kill Geoghan," www.boston.com/news/local/articles/2003/08/26/monthlong_plot_to_kill_geoghan/ (accessed 10 October 2003; this site is no longer available).

16. "Sex Abuse Priest Killed in Prison," 25 August 2003, edition.cnn.com/2003/US/08/24/geoghan/ (accessed 20 October 2003).

17. Ibid.

18. See www.sfgate.com/cgi-bin/article.cgi?file=/news/archive/2003/04/22/national1737EDT0668.DTL (accessed 24 October 2003).

19. Ibid.

20. See the iconic essay by Gayle Rubin, "Thinking Sex: Notes for a Radical Theory of the Politics of Sexuality," in *The Lesbian and Gay Studies Reader*, ed. Henry Abelove, Michèle Aina Barale, and David M. Halperin (New York: Routledge, 1993), 3–44.

21. Ellis Hanson is working on many of these connections, and he claims that discourses around pedophilia and incest and "child love" so quickly conjure up not-so-distant discourses around the homosexual. Some work that helps him make this point, as well as some work that helps us understand the hysteria around children, includes James Kincaid, *Child-Loving: The Erotic Child and Victorian Culture* (New York: Routledge, 1992); Eve Kosofsky Sedgwick, "How to Bring Your Kids Up Gay: The War on Effeminate Boys," in *Tendencies* (Durham, NC: Duke University Press, 1993); Pat Califia, "The Age of Consent: The Great Kiddy-Porn Panic of '77" and "The Aftermath of the Great Kiddy-Porn Panic of '77," in *Public Sex* (Pittsburgh: Cleis, 1994), 39–70; Lela B. Costin, Howard Jacob Karger, and David Stoesz, *The Politics of Child Abuse in America* (New York: Oxford University Press, 1996); and Elaine Showalter, *Hystories* (New York: Columbia University Press, 1997).

22. I am particularly indebted to debates of kinship theorists, especially dynamic feminist anthropologists. See, of course, Gayle Rubin, "The Traffic in Women: Notes on the 'Political Economy' of Sex," in *Toward an Anthropology of Women*, ed. Rayna R. Reiter (New York: Monthly Review, 1975). But see also *Reproducing the Future: Essays on Anthropology, Kinship, and the New Reproductive Technologies* (New York: Routledge, 1992); and Jane Fishburne Collier and Sylvia Junko Yanagisako, eds., *Gender and Kinship: Essays toward a Unified Analysis* (Stanford, CA: Stanford University Press, 1987).

23. Judith Butler, *Antigone's Claim: Kinship between Life and Death* (New York: Columbia University Press, 2000), 70–71.

24. Ibid., 71.

25. *Lawrence v. Texas* 539 U.S. 558,606 (sec. 3).

26. Chauncey, quoted in Rich, "And Now, the Queer Eye for Straight Marriage," 16.

27. See Janet Halley, "'Like Race' Arguments," in *What's Left of Theory: New Work on the Politics of Literary Theory* (New York: Routledge, 2000).

28. See note 21.

29. See throughout Spiller's volume for this point, which is stubbornly ignored by so many critics. See especially "The Crisis of the Negro Intellectual: A Post-Date" and "Interstices: A Small Drama of Words," in Spiller, *Black, White, and in Color: Essays on American Literature and Culture* (Chicago: University of Chicago Press, 2003).

30. See www.godhatesfags.com/main/index.html (accessed 10 January 2004).

31. Of course, I am referring to Raymond Williams's oft-quoted concept.

32. See Shirley Samuels's useful edited collection, *The Culture of Sentiment: Race, Gender, and Sentimentality in Nineteenth-Century America* (New York: Oxford University Press, 1992). Lauren Berlant has been critical in her work on the afterlife of sentimentality as it has traversed the centuries and made its indelible mark on many contemporary, pain-inflected minority political gestures. Among many essays of hers, see "Uncle Sam Needs a Wife: Citizenship and Denegation," in *Materializing Democracy: Toward a Revitalized Cultural Politics*, ed. Russ Castronovo and Dana D. Nelson (Durham, NC: Duke University Press, 2002).

33. Berlant, "Uncle Sam Needs a Wife," 149.

34. Butler, *Antigone's Claim*, 73.

35. Ann Cvetkovich, *An Archive of Feeling: Trauma, Sexuality, and Lesbian Public Cultures* (Durham, NC: Duke University Press, 2003), 101.

36. Dorothy Allison, *Bastard out of Carolina* (New York: Plume, 1992), 135, hereafter cited in text.

37. See my "Pulpitic Publicity: James Baldwin and the Queer Uses of Religious Words," *GLQ* 7 (2001): 285–312. See also Judith Butler's "Critically Queer," in *Bodies That Matter: On the Discursive Limits of Sex* (New York: Routledge, 1993).

38. Spillers, *Black, White, and in Color*, 254.

39. Butler, *Antigone's Claim*, 81.

40. Slavoj Žižek writes, "In short, what melancholy obfuscates is the fact that the object is lacking from the beginning, that its emergence coincides with its lack, that this object is *nothing but* the positivization of a void/lack, a purely anamorphic entity which does not exist 'in itself'" (Slavoj Žižek, *Did Somebody Say Totalitarianism?* [New York: Verso, 2001], 143).

41. Spillers, *Black, White, and in Color*, 5.

42. Butler, *Antigone's Claim*, 82.

43. Janet R. Jakobsen and Ann Pellegrini, *Love the Sin: Sexual Regulation and the Limits of Religious Tolerance* (New York: New York University Press, 2003), 13.

44. Butler, *Antigone's Claim*, 78.

45. Ibid., 82. I am also reminded here of Sharon Holland's work on representations of race and death, *Raising the Dead: Death and "Black" Subjectivity in Twentieth-Century Literature and Culture* (Durham, NC: Duke University Press, 2000).

46. Paul Downes, *Democracy, Revolution, and Monarchism in Early American Literature* (Cambridge: Cambridge University Press, 2002), 8–9.

47. Lauren Berlant, "The Subject of True Feeling: Pain, Privacy, and Politics," in *Feminist Consequences: Theory for the New Century*, ed. Elisabeth Bronfen and Misha Kavka (New York: Columbia University Press, 2001), 129, hereafter cited in the text.

48. Jakobsen and Pellegrini, *Love the Sin*, 17.

49. Berlant, "Subject of True Feeling," 154.

50. Quoted in Jane Lapman, "Gay Marriage: Clergy Gear for Amendment Battle," *Christian Science Monitor*, online edition, www.csmonitor.com/2004/0109/p13s01–lire.html (accessed 9 February 2004).

51. Text of majority opinion of question presented by the Massachusetts Senate, www.boston.com/news/specials/gay_marriage/sjc_020404/ (accessed 5 February 2004).

52. Butler, *Antigone's Claim*, 81.

Policing Privacy, Migrants, and the Limits of Freedom

Nayan Shah

In June 2003 the U.S. Supreme Court delivered a landmark ruling that decriminalized consensual sodomy. *Lawrence and Garner v. Texas* protected the liberty to engage in "certain intimate conduct" as a dimension of a person's privacy and autonomy. Justice Kennedy, writing for the 6–3 majority, expounds on the constitutional meaning of liberty. He begins with the tenets of classical liberalism, that the state recognizes and makes visible the "dwelling," the "home," and "other private places" to protect "persons" from the state's own intrusive policing. And then Kennedy argues that this liberty and freedom "extends beyond spatial bounds. Liberty presumes an autonomy of self that includes freedom of thought, belief, expression, and certain intimate conduct. The instant case involves liberty of the person both in its spatial and more transcendent dimensions."[1]

The *Lawrence* decision repudiated the 1986 *Bowers v. Hardwick* ruling and explicitly extended the rights of privacy and sexual freedom to adult consenting homosexuals. Justice Kennedy's decision drew on over thirty years of Supreme Court decisions that limited government intervention in the reproductive choices of women (in terms of both contraception and abortion).[2] In *Lawrence and Garner v. Texas*, the terrain of privacy and sexual freedom shifted from heterosexual reproduction to adult sexual intimacy more broadly:

> Adults may choose to enter upon this relationship in the confines of their homes and their own private lives and still retain their dignity as free persons. When sexuality finds overt expression in intimate conduct with another person, the conduct can be but one element in a personal bond that is more enduring. The liberty protected by the Constitution allows homosexual persons the right to make this choice.[3]

Significantly, Kennedy's decision broadened the constitutional protections of privacy beyond the married heterosexual couple and their bedroom, which had dominated the reproductive freedom cases of the 1960s to early 1990s, to encompass the homosexual couple in their home, and perhaps beyond. The parameters for exercising liberty and privacy from govern-

Social Text 84–85, Vol. 23, Nos. 3–4, Fall–Winter 2005.

ment interference required that the relationship be between consenting adults.

The Supreme Court ruling in *Lawrence* produced a privacy shield for homosexual couples. Kennedy's opinion focused on redressing the inequality between heterosexuals and homosexuals. Yet the historical dynamics of inequitable policing and prosecution feasted on distinctions of race, nationality, and class. As both the historian's amici brief and Kennedy's decision explain that sodomy prosecution in the twentieth century has intensified to target homosexuals, our own historical and legal analysis must recognize the social inequities and prejudices, and the dynamics of social space, that shaped the policing of sodomy.[4] *Lawrence and Garner v. Texas* offers an important opportunity to consider where and for whom does privateness apply historically and legally. Under what circumstances does a person have privacy, mobility, and freedom of intimate contact unfettered by government policing?

The specific circumstances of the arrest of John Geddes Lawrence and Tyron Garner explicates the Supreme Court's focus on individual autonomy and privacy of homosexual conduct in the home. On the night of 17 September 1998, John Lawrence, a fifty-five-year-old white medical technician; Tyron Garner, a thirty-one-year-old black unemployed man; and Robert Royce Eubanks, a forty-one-year-old white neighbor, were socializing in Lawrence's apartment in the suburbs of Houston, Texas. Later that evening Eubanks called the police and reported that a man was behaving erratically with a gun. The police met Eubanks in the parking lot, and Eubanks directed them to Lawrence's eighth-floor apartment. The police barged into the unlocked apartment and discovered Lawrence having anal intercourse with Garner. The police arrested Lawrence and Garner for "homosexual conduct," handcuffed them, and hauled them off to jail. Eubanks later served fifteen days in jail for making a false police report. Lawrence and Garner were convicted of "deviate sexual intercourse" in Harris County Justice Court, and five years later they successfully appealed their conviction in the U.S. Supreme Court.[5]

The location of the arrest—John Lawrence's apartment—and the Texas statute that explicitly criminalized homosexual sodomy have much to do with the legal and political tension of how the presumed privacy of the home is at odds with homosexual sodomy. Texas had in 1973 repealed sex laws that criminalized all anal sodomy and oral sex and adopted a homosexual conduct statute that prohibited oral and anal sex when performed by persons of the same sex. At the time of the 1998 conviction, nineteen states had sodomy statutes that barred consensual anal or oral sex, but Texas was only one of five states that had laws targeting same-sex partners.[6]

In the actual case of *Lawrence and Garner v. Texas*, interracial relations may be important, yet unremarked, circumstances in the details of the police action that led to the legal case. Historically, concerns about interracial sodomy aggravated fears of sexual and social danger and catalyzed anxieties about the undermining of the social order.

In the actual case of *Lawrence and Garner v. Texas*, interracial relations may be important, yet unremarked, circumstances in the details of the police action that led to the legal case.

The power of a U.S. Supreme Court ruling is the ability to abstract the specific circumstances into far-ranging rules of law, doctrine, and juridical governance, and yet much of the texture and tensions of social life are lost when we lose sight of the historical context. My own research of early-twentieth-century sodomy court cases in the western United States and Canada shows that sexual identity is not the determining factor in prosecuting sodomy, but, rather, differentials of class, age, and race shape the policing that leads to sodomy and public morals arrests. Pursuing these social and spatial dynamics illuminates the social and spatial dimensions of difference that regulate sexual relations and privilege individual autonomy and sexual liberty in public, semipublic, and private spaces.

During the first decades of the twentieth century, thousands of men and boys from all over the world converged on small towns and new cities in western North America. These male migrant laborers took on seasonal work in sawmills, farms, and canneries from British Columbia to California. Migrants from India, Poland, China, Armenia, Mexico, and the midwestern United States lived together in boardinghouses, bunkhouses, and work camps. Male migrant sociability was entangled into the culture and mobility of the streets. The geography of the rapidly urbanizing town and city provided the settings and spaces for casual, fortuitous, and dangerous encounters between men and boys of different ethnicities, classes, and ages. Migrant males encountered each other on the streets, alleys, and parks, at the train and stage depots and other public spaces where men congregated. They socialized and drank in saloons and brothels as well as the bunkhouses and hotels rooms they rented for a day or weeks.

Police walking their neighborhood beats observed public activity and the social relations of the street. The policing of potential criminal activity included the regulation of improper social and sexual activity such as vagrancy, soliciting prostitution, loitering, public drunkenness, and lewd and lascivious conduct. Many of the court cases that I have researched were brought forward through the policing of migrant sociability. For example, in Marysville, California, in the early morning of 4 February 1928, two police officers drove by a Ford coupé parked in a secluded spot, about a block from residences farther down the street. The officers' suspicions were aroused by someone inside the car, leaning against the passenger window, asleep, who "looked like a Mexican." They pulled Rola Singh out and discovered Harvey Carstenbrook, a "young man [who] was lying in the seat with his head under the wheel, his pants . . . down to his knees, his union suit underwear split . . . open, his coat . . . turned up and his rectum . . . exposed."[7] The officers grabbed Carstenbrook and roused him from a deep sleep; Carstenbrook started throwing punches as they jerked him out of the car.

What had begun as police curiosity on a routine patrol became amplified by racial suspicion. Apparently, the presence of a dark man in a parked car at night was enough cause for suspicion. Although one officer had initially mistaken Singh for a "Mexican" and later testified that he was a "Hindu," the officer treated his initial confusion about Singh's racial identity as irrelevant.[8] The police presumed that neither a Mexican nor a Hindu, both of whom were typically migrant laborers, would own an automobile. Racial suspicion quickly turned into police investigation when they discovered a white male partially undressed and unconscious in Singh's company. The police officers arrested both men and hauled them to the police station for observation and medical examination. Eventually, Singh was charged with a "crime against nature."

In court, Singh testified that he had met Carstenbrook near the stage depot on Second Street. Carstenbrook was sitting in his car and asked if Singh wanted a ride. Singh responded that he "wanted to go to Yuba City." They drove to the secluded spot where the officers had found them. Carstenbrook claimed that he was too drunk to drive home.[9] When he was called to the stand, Carstenbrook could not remember anything of the evening until he had been brought to the police station. He did not remember picking up Singh and denied that anything happened between them. All he could recall was that he was drunk.[10]

Carstenbrook's denial of sexual assault did not hinder the prosecution's case, nor did it impede the jury's conviction. In the appeal, the defense attorney reasoned that "had Carstenbrook's person been subjected to such an assault, it is reasonable to say he would have experienced therefore some uncomfortable or unusual injury, and would have been eager to testify to such injury. There is no reason why he should be inclined to protect a strange Hindu, with whom he had no previous acquaintance. On the contrary, had he even suspected such an assault, he would have felt himself humiliated and outraged."[11] (One could well argue that Carstenbrook would have suffered more humiliation by public acknowledgment of sexual relations with Singh.) During the trial, he was repeatedly referred to as the "Carstenbrook boy," treated as the underage victim of sexual assault, and thereby protected from any public interrogation of his solicitation of Singh.

There are several puzzling elements that emerged in the trial testimony but occasioned little comment by the attorneys or judges. First, there was no reference made to the ownership of the car; second, during the lunch break of the trial, the prosecutor urged Carstenbrook not to turn up as a defense witness; and third, his parents or guardians were conspicuously absent. As it turns out, Carstenbrook was a member of a prominent small-business family in Marysville that had lived in the region since the late nineteenth century. Harvey's father and uncle were landowners and had a history of contracting service work from the city. Probate records reveal that in May 1927, nine months prior to the sodomy arrest, Carstenbrook's father died. Carstenbrook, twenty-seven at the time, was named executor of the will.[12] Voting records, probate records, and the biographical detail in the testimony all point to Carstenbrook as a twenty-eight-year-old former lineman for PG&E who lived in Marysville in 1928 during the trial proceedings.[13]

In many ways, the very possibility of having a private sphere was precarious for migrant male laborers. Bodily autonomy was questionable, and privacy did not obtain in the government's understanding of the interracial and interclass male migrant world. How can we rethink the spaces, practices, and cultures of public sex and the pursuit for contact uninhibited by state surveillance and intervention? Queer studies scholars of the public have raised an array of theoretical questions and problems that resonate with this early-twentieth-century history of sodomy cases. Prior to the *Lawrence* decision, the late-twentieth-century Supreme Court rulings about privacy narrowly promoted heterosexual domesticity and sexual expression. The "zone of privacy" argument applied from the *Griswold v. Connecticut* decision to *Bowers v. Hardwick* limited what spaces could be considered constitutionally protected. According to the queer studies scholar Michael Warner, "The 'zone of privacy' was recognized not for intimate associations, or control over one's body or for sexuality in general but only for the domestic space of heterosexuals. The legal tradition tends to protect sexual freedom by privatizing it, and now it reserves privacy protections for those whose sexuality is already normative."[14] Warner further argued that "your zone of privacy requires the support of an elaborate network of state regulations, judicial rulings, and police powers, and if it is based on the prejudicial exclusion of others from the rights of association or bodily autonomy you take for granted, then your privacy is another name for armed national sex public to which you so luckily belong."[15]

Richard Mohr in *Gays/Justice: A Study of Society, Ethics, Law* challenges the reasoning in Bowers by arguing that sex is "inherently private" and should be protected no matter where it occurs. Instead, scholars like Warner and William Leap argue that the practices of public sexual culture involve "not only a world-excluding privacy but a world-making publicness."[16] This public sexual culture has its "own knowledges, places,

Public sexual culture is a counterpublic to the norms of public morality, which offer public status exclusively to privatized heterosexuality.

practices, languages, and learned modes of feeling." One learns the codes of subculture, its rituals, typologies, and "improvisational nature of unpredicted situations." Public sexual culture is a counterpublic to the norms of public morality, which offer public status exclusively to privatized heterosexuality. Its publicness is constituted in transmitting and circulating sexual knowledges that are made cumulative. The erotics and bodily sensations are both public and extremely intimate.[17]

The migrant sociability of the early twentieth century that I have described—with its public meeting, offering, drinking, conversing, and sexual trysts—may have its corollary in the late-twentieth-century practices of cruising. The kind of belonging that cruising creates (according to Warner) is "directly eroticizing participation in the public world of the intimate." He explains that, "contrary to myth, what one relishes in loving strangers is not mere anonymity, nor meaningless release. It is the pleasure of belonging to a sexual world, in which one's sexuality finds an answering resonance not just in one another, but in the world of others. Strangers have the ability to represent a world of others in a way that one sustained intimacy cannot."[18]

The gay male subject Warner assumes has both free access to participate in the public world of the intimate and may also retreat to a private realm of intimacy. The class and race privileges of this undifferentiated subject do not anticipate any inequality or difference in the rapport, subjectivity, and opportunities for this male subject's "world making publicness" among other males. In his analysis, Warner ignores the diversity of social relations, the relative differences and privileges, status, opportunities, and constraints. The axis of disenfranchisement is prominently and significantly sexual in Warner's analysis. Class and race differences, the differences of access and opportunity, the differential relation to public spaces and how that might impact the dynamics of sociability, erotics, and subjectivity are not discussed.

Samuel Delany's queer ethnography and memoir of the radical transformation of Times Square, however, situates inequality and interclass and interethnic contact at the center of his analysis of public sex and sexual publics. Delany valorizes cross-class contacts in public space that encompass a range of random, interclass, and interethnic social encounters in urban public spaces, which he heuristically distinguishes from the professional, motive-driven, intraclass practices of networking. He contrasts bar going and other institutional social practices of networking from the broadly social, random practices of contact, which, he argues, include the endless variety of casual sex and public sexual relations. As an "outdoor sport," contact is "contoured, if not organized by earlier decisions, desires, commercial interests, zoning laws, and immigration patterns."[19] However,

Delany observes that the 1990s campaign to "clean up" and "gentrify" Times Square is drastically narrowing the "varieties of erotic life," "dampening interclass contact, and foreclosing the promise and necessities of a democratic city." He proclaims that in a "democratic city it is imperative that we speak to strangers, live next to them and learn how to relate to them on many levels, including the sexual." Delany further emphasizes that the vitality of queer public life and sexuality has thrived on the abundance of "interclass contact" despite decades of marginalization and policing by dominant heterosexually normative society.[20]

The intimate contact of migrant men interfered with the boundaries of a race- and class-segregated society. The vision of free movement and association, the mingling of the races, that some may have presumed was the promise of democratic citizenship and civic belonging, however, was under the conspicuous suspicion and surveillance of the middle-class district attorneys and police magistrates and working-class police officers. They interpreted the activity as enhancing and leading to immorality that required surveillance, particularly at any moment when the migrant males attempted to remove their social activities from public visibility into the murky arena of the semiprivate.

In the early twentieth century it was impossible for migrant men to pursue "privacy" or to enjoy freedom from state surveillance of those spaces removed from public view, such as automobiles, boardinghouses, bars, and gambling houses. These countersites and landscapes of queer contact and communities were shaped by both the activities of migrant men and policing. These queer sexual publics exposed the contradictions of normative expectations and fluidity at the borders of public spaces. The queer and homoerotic presence can unsettle the very demarcations of public and private.[21] In this context what does public space mean? Is the middle-class framing of public space, as the site of safe public spectacle of middle-class citizens' domestic status, being challenged and resisted by the many ways that squares, streets, alleys are creating a spectacle of migrant social life? A promenade of fortuitous encounters and juxtapositions allows masculinity, class status, and physicality to be displayed and to test sensibilities and expectations of the migrant males and the working-class and middle-class women, children, and men who also travel and use the same locations. Queer studies scholars have vigorously questioned how modern nationalist citizenship, entitlement, and valued public experience is contingent on the public performance of respectable domesticity and coupled, heterosexual intimacy.[22]

In the twenty-first century, the Supreme Court's *Lawrence* ruling has potentially accorded freedom for privacy within the parameters of a homosexual domestic identity. The decision has been widely hailed as a

The decision keeps intact the public sphere idealization that protects the liberties of those who possess a recognizable home and their public communicative expression.

victory for gay rights. And yet some sexual relations and social contact remain unprivileged and unprotected. Scholars of ethnic studies, colonial studies, gender studies, and queer studies have questioned how the usage of minority "identity" and "community" tends to ignore social variety and flatten differences. Incommensurate lives, acts, politics, and ways of knowing are frequently subsumed into a unitary category, such as "lesbian," "gay," "homosexual," and "transgender." Legible identities and social taxonomies—those of race, class, religion, sexual orientation, and gender—have shaped much of what we think of as minority history within the nation-state. As historians, much of our preoccupation has had to be the documentation of "deviance," "difference," "queerness," and "alerity" that is both prohibited and incited in law, policing, markets, local embodiments, and cultural expression.[23] "Gay" identity and community as an urban U.S. and Western European formation has underwritten the epistemology and knowledge production of the queer past. Throughout the twentieth century, social movements of protest and subcultural communities have demanded, reshaped, and expanded the scale and scope of this civic culture of sexual liberty, association, and expression. The heterogeneity and contradictory terrain of sexual dissidence has been impossible to contain in a unitary gay identity and community. Yet government and civil society—the police, the courts, interest groups, and the media—have framed the debate as a contest between heterosexual norms and homosexual resistance, one that the Supreme Court in the *Lawrence* decision seeks to resolve.[24]

In sharp contrast to *Bowers*, which denied any rights of privacy and any respected public status to gay men, the *Lawrence* decision provides recognition to "homosexuals" in coupled relationships as visible subjects that can be managed, governed, and afforded the liberty of "certain intimate conduct." However, this only embraces a segment of the persons, groups, and communities that have been vigorously policed. The immense heterogeneity of how persons live—in social relations, locales, practices, and cultures—counters, confounds, and queers the norms of coupled households. The decision keeps intact the public sphere idealization that protects the liberties of those who possess a recognizable home and their public communicative expression. Homelessness or temporary habitations such as bunkhouses, SROs, and vehicles may or may not be privacy protected. Queer knowledge projects and politics must continue to destabilize the assumptions that personhood and citizenship emanate from the "domestic private" and coupled intimacy, either heterosexual or homosexual. For those who do not possess such attributes, the "transcendent" possibilities of liberty in intimate conduct, expression, and civic life are all curtailed. In the early twentieth century "foreign" and racialized migrants, tramps, and hoboes were subject to heightened police surveillance and arrests of vagrancy and sodomy. In the early twenty-first century "illegal" migrants, homeless, "enemy combatants," and refugees awaiting asylum proceedings may be the most visible and vulnerable subjects of state power. For those identified outside norms and normativity, the liberties to pursue "certain intimate conduct" remains unfathomable in a liberal ethos that links private intimacy with respected and protected public status.

Notes

1. *Lawrence and Garner v. Texas*, 539 U.S. 1 (2003).

2. Ibid., 3–4, 13–14. The Supreme Court decisions on reproductive freedom include *Griswold v. Connecticut* 381 U.S. 479 (1965); *Eisenstadt v. Barid* 405 U.S. 438 (1972); *Roe v. Wade* 410 U.S. 113 (1973); *Planned Parenthood of Southeastern Pa. v. Casey*, 505 U.S. 833 (1992).

3. *Lawrence v. Texas*, 6.

4. George Chauncey, Nancy F. Cott, John D'Emilio, Estelle B. Freedman, Thomas C. Holt, John Howard, Lynn Hunt, Mark D. Jordan, Elizabeth Lapovsky Kennedy, and Linda P. Kerber, "Historians' Case against Gay Discrimination," amicus brief, 1–3.

5. "Two Men Charged under State's Sodomy Law," *Houston Chronicle*, 5 November 1998; "Houston Case May Test Sodomy Law: Lawyer Says His Clients' Privacy Invaded," *Dallas Morning News*, 7 November 1998; Steve Brewer, "Texas Men Post Bonds, Challenge State's Sodomy Law," *New York Times*, 20 November 1998; "Arrests Will Put Sodomy Law on Trial," *San Francisco Chronicle*, 2 December 1998. The context of the case has been imaginatively reconstructed in Dale Carpenter, "Colloquium: The Boundaries of Liberty after *Lawrence v. Texas*: The Unknown Past of *Lawrence v. Texas*," *Michigan Law Review* 102 (2004: 1464–1527.

6. *Lawrence v. Texas*, 7–8, 12; Chauncey, "Historians' Case against Gay Discrimination," 1–3.

7. *People v. Rollo* [*sic*] *Singh*, Third Court of Appeals, Transcript of Testimony, District Court, Yuba County, 5, 6, 7, 10, 12, 13, California State Archives, Sacramento, APWA #359 (June 1928).

8. "Hindu" was both the formal and informal racial category used to describe migrants from colonial India. Most early-twentieth-century migrants were Punjabi Sikhs; however, "Hindu" less explicitly designated religious identity and more frequently was short for "Hindustani," a geographic or national identity.

9. *People v. Rollo* [*sic*] *Singh*, 43–44.

10. Ibid., 48–50.

11. *People v. Rollo* [*sic*] *Singh*, Appelent's Opening Brief, 7, California State Archives, Sacramento.

12. Harry J. Carstenbrook Probate Case #3226, Yuba County Superior Court, Marysville, California, filed 18 May 1927.

13. Great Register of Yuba County, General Election, 1928 Marysville Library; *People v. Rollo* [*sic*] *Singh*, Clerk's Transcript of Testimony, 48, California State Archives, Sacramento.

14. Michael Warner, *The Trouble with Normal: Sex, Politics, and the Ethics of Queer Life* (Cambridge, MA: Harvard University Press, 1999), 174.

15. Ibid., 175.

16. Richard Mohr, *Gays/Justice: A Study of Ethics, Society, Law* (New York: Columbia University Press, 1988), 110–116; Warner, *Trouble with Normal*, 177; William Leap, ed., *Public Sex/Gay Space* (New York: Columbia University Press, 1999).

17. Warner, *Trouble with Normal*, 177–79.

18. Ibid., 179.

19. Samuel R. Delany, *Times Square Red, Times Square Blue* (New York: New York University Press, 1999), esp. 126–42.

20. Ibid., 186–92.

21. David Bell, "Sexual Citizenship," in *Mapping Desire: Geographies of Sexualities*, ed. David Bell and Gill Valentine (London: Routledge, 1995), 306; Lawrence Knopp, "Sexuality and Urban Space: A Framework for Analysis," in Bell and Valentine, *Mapping Desire*, 149–61.

22. Lauren Berlant, "Intimacy: A Special Issue," *Critical Inquiry* 24 (1998): 281–86; Lauren Berlant and Michael Warner, "Sex in Public," *Critical Inquiry* 24 (1998): 547–58; Elizabeth A. Povinelli, "Notes on Gridlock: Genealogy, Intimacy, Sexuality," *Public Culture* 14 (2002): 215–31; Lisa Duggan, *The Twilight of Equality? Neoliberalism, Cultural Politics, and the Attack on Democracy* (Boston: Beacon, 2003).

23. Jennifer Terry, "Theorizing Deviant Historiography," *Differences* 3, no. 2 (1991): 55–74; David Halperin, "Forgetting Foucault: Acts, Identities, and the History of Sexuality," *Representations* 63 (1998): 93–120.

24. Janet R. Jakobsen, "Queer Is? Queer Does: Normativity and the Problem of Resistance," *GLQ* 4 (1998): 511–36.

Sex + Freedom = Regulation

WHY?

Janet R. Jakobsen

Sexual regulation has played a crucial role in American politics over the last several decades. Here are a few snapshots of sexual politics in action: (1) in the summer of 1996, to establish his credentials for reelection, President Bill Clinton signed the Defense of Marriage Act, a draconian "welfare reform" bill, along with a stringent "immigration reform" bill, legislation that placed sexual regulation at the center of a connected neoliberal agenda;[1] (2) the impeachment of President Clinton based on charges of lying under oath about a sexual affair with Monica Lewinsky;[2] (3) the remaking of the Republican Party over the last twenty years as an alliance between fiscal conservatives and social conservatives who do not share the same economic interests, yet are nonetheless willing to vote for the same candidate based on a mutual conservatism around gender, sexuality, and race;[3] (4) the recent controversies over the role of moral values—values that the *New York Times* described only in terms of gender and sexuality—in the 2004 election.[4]

In short, sex is not just a private matter; it matters—a great deal, in fact—in American public life. Sex is neither the truth of ourselves nor a frivolous concern of the privileged. It is rather a social relation constituted by and constitutive of the various social relations that have made this historical moment possible.

But why? Why is sexuality—and sexual regulation in particular—such a crucial part of the fabric of American politics? Why isn't the vaunted American value of freedom one of the "moral values" that applies in the realm of sexuality? And why is the story of religiously based sexual regulation so naturalized that both the Democrats and the mainstream press accepted the "moral values" explanation of George Bush's victory in the 2004 election despite the fact that this explanation was based on dubious evidence?[5]

Religion, Secularism, and Queer Possibility

The commonsensical notion as to why sexual regulation is so central in U.S. public life is that it has something to do with religion and with

Social Text 84–85, Vol. 23, Nos. 3–4, Fall–Winter 2005. © 2005 by Duke University Press.

In fact, sexual regulation is such a passion in U.S. politics because sexual regulation is constitutive of (secular) American freedom.

the specific religious heritage of the United States. "Puritanical" is the name not just for the religious tradition that has historically dominated U.S. politics; it is, at least in the popular imagination, also a synonym for sexual repression.[6] While I agree in part with the idea that religion is at the base of sexual regulation in the United States, I think the traditional story misleads us as to how this regulation works.[7]

In the traditional view, religious repression is the root of sexual regulation and hence freedom from religion is the answer to the problem. This traditional view plays into the larger Enlightenment narrative in which freedom from religion brings about human liberation. In contrast to this view, however, I argue that our problem is as much secular freedom as it is religious regulation.

In fact, sexual regulation is such a passion in U.S. politics because sexual regulation is constitutive of (secular) American freedom. It is not that religious regulation and secular freedom are the same, but they are mutually constitutive. I make this argument because modern freedom, even the Enlightenment freedom that is first and foremost supposed to be liberated from religion, has its own religious roots. Those roots can be found in the Protestant Reformation, and they inform the specifically Christian secularism that marks U.S. culture and politics.[8]

We know from Max Weber's 1930 book *The Protestant Ethic and the Spirit of Capitalism* that the freedom that dominates life in the United States is dependent on the regulated activity that makes the market possible, activity that Weber names "worldly asceticism." As Weber notes, this form of freedom requires both immense self-discipline—the disciplines that Foucault chronicles as indicative of modernity—and regulation—what Weber documents as "earnest enforcement."[9] Freedom in this sense—and this market-based sense of freedom becomes dominant in modernity—is not the repression of activity, but it is the regulated enactment of activity along particular lines.

While the disciplinary nature and even religious roots of market-based freedom may be familiar, less commented on is the fact that the Reformation also marked a major change in sexual relations, one that instituted a particular form of sexual freedom. As I show in detail below, this sexual freedom is intertwined with the market and is constituted through its own forms of regulated activity. Specifically, the Reformation ties the idea of individual freedom to the institution of marriage. The free individual is the individual whose sexual activity is regulated in marriage—a relation earnestly enforced by the reformers.[10] This connection between freedom and sexual regulation is maintained in the shift to a modernity that remains marked by the Protestant ethic. Regulation, then, is internal to the meaning of modern freedom, including the meaning of sexual freedom. Most important, in a United States dominated by Christian secularism, religion is not just responsible for our ideas of sexual repression; it has also crucially formed our understanding of sexual liberation.

What, then, of our politics? Do we give up on freedom, or the more movement-oriented term of liberation, as a possible site for organizing and political action? Do we move, for example, from gay liberation to queer resistance? While queer politics initially promised an alternative to the problematics of gay liberation, as a number of scholars and activists have now concluded, and as the editors of this special issue make clear, queer politics has often failed to live up to that early promise.[11] Queer resistance has all too rarely embodied the possibility of connections across multiple identities that the shift from gay to queer hoped to produce. And resistance has proven to be a term too thin to organize diverse and wide-ranging politics.[12] Even the progenitor of the concept of resistance, Michel Foucault, turned at the end of his career toward questions of ethics to explore alternative possibilities that could not be subsumed under the imperative to resist.[13]

This "turn to ethics," which has been taken up in a number of fields of critical theory, suggests a need to reengage with a set of questions that the queer critique had at one time hoped to bypass.[14] In particular, if freedom is at least part of the answer to the question, "why sex?" then we need to rethink our relationship to freedom. Moreover, this rethinking of the value of freedom may also allow us to rejoin the alternative affinities that constituted part of what was supposed to distinguish queer politics. In the hope of exploring this possibility of what is queer about queer theory now, I first turn back to the genealogy of freedom's role in the sexual obsessions of American politics.

The Politics of Sex

These are not just theoretical questions. Accepting religious repression as the answer to the question "why sex?" and failing to engage our implication in freedom sets up a number of pragmatic problems. The traditional view of religious repression underwrites a form of gay politics that appears to be necessarily secularizing, an appearance that has been extensively exploited by the political Right, whether by Jerry Falwell when lumping gays and secularists together in the blame for the September 11 attacks or by Bill O'Reilly claiming that the Massachusetts Supreme Judicial Court decision on gay marriage is another victory for the secularists. This association between gay rights and secularism was used by the Republicans in the effort to bring out conservative votes in the 2004 election, even though John Kerry also opposed legalizing gay marriage and tried to espouse faith.[15] It seems one cannot be both gay and religious, a disjunction that is belied by the lives of many gay persons and that splits gay rights movements from progressive religious movements that might provide crucial alliances.

Yet gay politics has all too often bought into the idea that because the problem of sexual regulation seems based in religion, the answer is to defend secular freedom. Following the path laid out by modern ideas of freedom can clarify why whatever gains made through this approach have been accompanied by an increasingly powerful and religiously identified right wing. John D'Emilio first identified the import of these issues in his now-classic essay "Capitalism and Gay Identity," arguing that gay liberation participates in a dialectic between repression and liberation such that liberation, as exhilarating as it is, also leads to further repression. D'Emilio's essay, first published in 1983 in *Powers of Desire: The Politics of Sexuality*, edited by Ann Snitow, Christine Stansell, and Sharon Thompson, was prescient in its prediction of an increasingly conservative politics organized around the ideology of "family," which did indeed develop throughout the 1980s and 1990s alongside a vibrant movement for gay liberation.

D'Emilio is specifically concerned with a dialectic between gay visibility and political repression. D'Emilio's stated reason for writing the essay was a political one. He argues that understanding the dialectic of visibility and repression will allow us to see that the politics of visibility—specifically of coming out—is not in and of itself adequate, nor is a gay identity politics. Such a political focus, he warns, will only perpetuate the dialectic, creating a right-wing backlash organized around the ideology of "family." He argues instead for a broad coalitional politics to connect all those with "shared interests" in expanding the social space for lives outside the bounds of the heterosexual nuclear family. These interests include a set of issues he names as "the availability of abortion and ratification of the Equal Rights Amendment, affirmative action for people of color and for women, publicly funded daycare and other essential social services, decent welfare payments, full employment, [and] the rights of young people" (110). Yet those political lessons were not heeded, and I, for one, am sorry for it.

D'Emilio could not, it seems, have been more perceptive. The 1980s and 1990s saw massive leaps forward in terms of gay visibility, along with the extension and eventual solidification of right-wing politics, most of it under the sign of "family values." With the Bush administration we have found Republicans in control of both houses of Congress and the executive branch for the first time in decades. Familial conservatism also appeared in various gay rights movements during the 1980s and 1990s, as asserting that "we have families, too" became more and more a part of mainstream politics.[16]

Why would American politics develop in this way—why would a movement in the 1980s that was greatly fueled by pro-sex responses to the AIDS crisis, a crisis that radicalized many pro-sex advocates to make connections across issues like access to health care, poverty, and housing, produce a vision that has culminated twenty years later in the most narrow version of "gay rights"? Why have we, despite D'Emilio's warnings in a widely read, indeed foundational, essay and countless other interventions, including those of queer politics, moved so far over the last twenty years down the path of gay visibility and single-issue politics?

To reinvigorate the type of politics that D'Emilio recommends, I think we must also reconsider our analysis. We need a sharper analysis of what connects the issues that D'Emilio names, and we also need a clear sense of how to form movements that address these interconnected issues. I suggest that the idea of "shared interests" is an insufficient basis for these connections. While interests may be shared across identities, they may also conflict, and overcoming these conflicts has proven to be particularly difficult. Finally, we need a more extended analysis of why the dialectic between the politics of gay visibility and the politics of family values seems to be so powerful, supporting not only the conservative politics of the last twenty years but also inducing so much gay political activity along its path. Given the evident appeal and supposed effectiveness of single-issue politics, we need a better vision of what we are fighting for. If not freedom from repression, then what? Here, a better understanding of the role that religion plays on both sides of the dialectic—in sexual regulation *and* in our understanding of freedom—would help us reformulate contemporary politics outside the grasp of the dynamics that have driven both the successes and failures of recent decades.

A better understanding of the role that religion plays on both sides of the dialectic—in sexual regulation *and* in our understanding of freedom—would help us reformulate contemporary politics.

Rethinking the Dialectic of Freedom

Because it is both so clear and so prescient, D'Emilio's essay provides a crucial starting point. D'Emilio argues that the problem lies in the dialectic between material life and ideology. In a story that is now familiar to us because of the wide influence of this essay, he argues that materially, capitalism creates the conditions that allow "individuals to survive beyond the confines of the family" (105) and, thus, to organize their lives around erotic interests not accommodated by the nuclear family structure. More than that, in a point that will become crucial for his later argument, capitalism actually creates conditions that undermine the family. When it comes to gay identity, because the "freedom" of wage labor allows people to make a living outside the structure of the family, people who might have engaged in homosexual practices or merely had same-sex inclinations or interests can now pursue these interests as a central part of their lives. Hence capitalism creates the material conditions not for homosexual practice, but for gay identity. The identity and community formation that flourished immediately after World War II also created the conditions for a gay liberation movement: "A massive, grass-roots liberation movement could form almost overnight [after the Stonewall riots] because communities of lesbians and gay men existed" (107).

The part of the argument that is less familiar has to do with the dialectical repression that accompanies this flowering of gay identity and eventual liberation movement. D'Emilio begins with a dialectic between visibility and repression that was particularly evident in the politically repressive 1950s:

> Although gay community was a precondition for a mass movement, the oppression of lesbians and gay men was the force that propelled movement into existence. As the subculture expanded and grew more visible in the post-World War II era, oppression by the state intensified. The Right scapegoated "sexual perverts" during the McCarthy era. . . . The danger involved in being gay rose even as the possibilities of being gay were enhanced. Gay liberation was a response to this contradiction. (107–8)

But this back-and-forth between social action that creates gay visibility and repression that leads to further social action in the form of a social movement is not a sufficient explanation for repression. After all, if capitalism creates the conditions for the "freedom" of gay identity, why does it not establish a laissez-faire attitude toward sexuality? Why isn't freedom simply "free"? D'Emilio locates the answer in "the contradictory relationship of capitalism to the family." On the one hand, capitalism undercuts the "economic functions that created ties between family members." On the other hand, "the ideology of capitalist society has enshrined the family as the source of love, affection, emotional security, the place where our need for stable, intimate relationships is satisfied" (108).

This still does not tell us why capitalist ideology should enshrine the family in this manner. Why should the capitalist ideology of personal satisfaction be a familial one? This is a profound question, given the sharp and increasing disjunction between the way that Americans live their lives and this ideology. If the nuclear family fails so many Americans, why is it so enshrined and ideologically enduring? After all, as a number of histories recognize, particularly feminist histories like Stephanie Coontz's 1992 *The Way We Never Were: American Families and the Nostalgia Trap* and

Elaine Tyler May's 1988 *Homeward Bound: American Families in the Cold War Era*, even the 1950s, the supposed time of familial bliss, were not as dominant ideologies have imagined them. Today, more than half of marriages (including those of many right-wing pundits and policymakers who promote family values) end in divorce. If many, in fact most, people do not get from families the type of emotional sustenance that allows them to get up and go to work each day, why does capitalist ideology not support, and even enshrine, the various types of relationships that allow for personal satisfaction despite the exploitation and alienation of wage labor?[17]

I argue that while "family," and the dominations of race, gender, and sexuality that it entails, may not be directly necessary to the exploitation of labor, they are necessary to the complex whole that is capitalist social relations. When we think of material life, we should think not just of relations of production but also of the material embodiments of social relations. After the Foucauldian revolution in sexuality studies, we know that sexuality and family values are not the ideology of capitalist materiality; they are the discourses through which capitalist social relations are embodied. Thus production and reproduction are not two separate spheres that mirror each other; rather, both are the materiality of capitalist social relations. What we need to explain, then, is not the relation between materiality and ideology, between what D'Emilio has named as the relatively free material relations of personal life and the ideological constraints of the family. We need to explain the relation between the exploitation of wage labor and the domination of social relations. The question is not, why is the family ideologically enshrined when many people live their personal lives outside its bounds? but rather, why do some forms of sexual relation dominate over others? And why must those forms, as D'Emilio points out, also entail gender and racial domination?

In thinking through the problem that D'Emilio puts for us—why is the sexual freedom induced by capitalism accompanied by sexual regulation—we need to consider the possibility that we are not facing a dialectic between capitalist freedom and dominative regulation, but rather regulation is internal to the capitalist notion of freedom itself. From this perspective, sexual regulation is not the antithesis of modern freedom; it is constitutive of freedom as we know it.

Most important for our purposes, insofar as our ideas of gay liberation are predicated on capitalism and gay identity, this liberation may contain dominative relations within it. The very idea of gay liberation—that which we are fighting for—contains within it the domination that we are fighting against, because the freedom enabled through the exploitation of wage labor is itself enabled by the dominative disciplines of sexual regulation. Exploitation and domination are not in this sense two separable problems,

The role of Protestantism in modernity is an important piece in the puzzle of sexual freedom.

nor is one the ideological constraint of the other. They are both materially and ideologically intertwined.[18]

Freedom and the Protestant World Order

To understand how modern freedom comes to entail a concomitant regulation, specifically sexual regulation, I have turned to the initial moment in developing the economic market as a site of freedom: the Protestant Reformation. My argument is not that sexual attitudes have not changed since the Protestant Reformation. Rather, if the United States as a nation is an "imagined community" in Benedict Anderson's terms,[19] then the dominant imagination of that community is Protestant and, in fact, specifically Calvinist. The consolidation of that national imagination has also entailed the consolidation of a particular sexual imagination, so that practices, like marriage, that may have been diffuse and scattered, observed unevenly and less frequently than is currently imagined, were brought into the center of national life.[20] This imagination is found not just in the explicitly Christian discourse of America but also in dominant secular discourse, including those institutions, like the U.S. Supreme Court, that are charged with maintaining the putative "separation of church and state."[21]

The role of Protestantism in modernity is an important piece in the puzzle of sexual freedom because it shows that the religious heritage of the United States does not just provide for sexual regulation; it also provides a particular imagination of freedom from that regulation. In particular, the freedom from the family offered by the market that D'Emilio makes so much of remains fundamentally Protestant. It is this, religiously derived, but now secularized, notion of freedom that drives liberation, including sexual liberation, to produce further regulation. It is this notion of freedom that drives capitalist ambivalence about the family.

One of the major changes instituted through the Reformation was a shift in the ethical ideal for sexual life. From the twelfth century onward, the sexual ideal for religious life in Christendom was the celibate life of the clergy and those with religious vocations—monks and nuns. The Reformers, most notably Luther and Calvin, denounced celibacy as part of what they depicted as the Church's perversion of the Gospel and encouraged marriage as the ideal of even the most religious life. While today's discourse of Christian family values makes it hard to recognize, this was a major shift in Christian understandings of the ideal of sexual relations.[22] Both Luther and Calvin took the position that everyone should enter a married state, and Luther, who had himself been part of a religious order, was especially adamant that clergy should marry. Marriage, then, like the market, is part of the freedom from the church that marks the beginning of modernity.

Like the discipline of the market, the elevation of marriage as the ideal—and free—organization of sexual life also invokes disciplines. In particular, this change highlights what Foucault tells us is a new form of moral discourse in which the moral ideal and what we now call the statistical norm converge. When it comes to sex, marriage was long the norm in terms that we would now define statistically, but it was not the ideal of sexual morality within the Christian societies. Foucault is so interested in this convergence because it sets up a particular type of moral problem. Normative discipline—rather than, for example, the cultivation of virtue—becomes the centerpiece of moral life. The normative regulation of sex is not a remnant of premodern periods that is progressively removed by modernity but is, if not new, significantly reformed in the modern period.

The move toward ideal as norm/norm as ideal is also a move toward the particular understanding of individual freedom that reaches full flower in the Enlightenment, particularly in the Kantian understanding of the individual who gives the law to himself. For Foucault, this freedom as autonomy requires self-discipline in which—to put it crudely—the ideal of freedom induces us to produce ourselves through the norms of the human sciences. Those are the norms of autonomous individualism, including the discourse of sexuality. We become autonomous individuals by freeing ourselves from the imposition of the law, but we also give the law to ourselves. Thus self-discipline becomes the hallmark of the modern individual and, importantly, of modern freedom.

In Luther and Calvin we can see versions of freedom that stand in between juridical law and self-discipline. Luther, in the preface to his translation (into German) of Paul's Letter to the Romans states that the freedom from the law offered to Christians does not mean that Christians do not follow the law: "Our freedom is not a crude, physical freedom by virtue of which we can do anything at all. Rather this freedom is a spiritual freedom; it supplies and furnishes what law lacks, namely willingness and love."[23] Christians follow the law, but they do so because they want to.[24] For Luther, spiritual freedom is wanting to do the right thing. It is a discourse of desire.

The disciplines of this form of freedom become apparent in Luther's next paragraph, which is a reading of an analogy in Romans between the position—and freedom—of a wife after the death of her husband and the position of Christians who have "died to the law." This is a strange analogy in many ways. First, if Christians are in the position of the wife, the law would have died to them, not they to the law. But Luther's gloss adds

In other words, Protestant freedom is an incitement to sexuality over against the celibacy of priestly and monastic life, and it is an incitement specifically to matrimonial and reproductive sexuality.

another twist: "The point is that [the wife] is quite at liberty for the first time to please herself about taking another husband."[25] It is an interesting moment because the Pauline author is not at all concerned about the wife pleasing herself.[26] The only concern that the biblical text expresses is that the wife would be called an adulteress if she lived with another man while her husband was alive, and now she is free to marry again and live with a second man without fear of adultery. Luther, however, nowhere states whether the woman will or will not take another husband. In fact, he explicitly states, "The woman is not obliged, nor even merely permitted to take a husband," but rather she is at liberty to please herself. Yet, in Luther's conclusion to the analogy, Christians are free to "really cling to Christ as a second husband and bring forth the fruit of life."[27] The analogy only makes sense if it is obvious to Luther that in her freedom to please herself, the woman will not only choose the conjugal relation of matrimony for a second time, but she will also procreate with this new husband, bringing forth the fruit of life.

In other words, Protestant freedom is an incitement to sexuality over against the celibacy of priestly and monastic life, and it is an incitement specifically to matrimonial and reproductive sexuality. Clergy and those with religious vocations are now free to marry, but there are losses in this freedom. There is a loss of alternatives to marriage, a loss that has particular implications for how women might please themselves. As a number of feminist historians have noted, the Protestant destruction of monastic life meant an end to a major alternative to marriage for women.[28] It is not that marriage is bad—that people, including women, in their freedom would never choose marriage—but that marriage becomes the only expression of sexual freedom. The choice between marriage and monastic celibacy is not necessarily a wide range of options, but monastic celibacy was an alternative way of life, one that allowed some women access to education and empowerment within the Church. And there might have been other options. Modern freedom might have offered more.

The shift to marriage is also a shift from communalism to individualism. Monastic celibacy was itself a communal way of life and was also part of broader networks of communities. In the reformed world, however, the Christian who clings to Christ and the widow who chooses a new husband are first and foremost individuals. But, as with modern freedom, individualism need not have been the only possible answer to the strictures of the Church's communalism. Various forms of affinity—neither communal in the Church's sense, nor individualistic in the modern sense—are possible, but these possibilities are lost in the narrative of progress and freedom.

The switch to marriage as both norm and ideal, then, is part of the production of the modern individual, and of that individual as free. A "free" country like the United States might tout its own sexual liberation, but ambivalence and regulation will remain because a specific sexual relation—marriage—is crucial to right social relation in the form of individualism. This is one reason that the path of gay identity, which starts with freedom from the family, has led us so inexorably back toward gay marriage. It is through marriage—by being able to say who we freely choose to marry—that gay people fully become individuals.

Calvin takes the further step of connecting this freedom to economic relations. Protestant marital life indicates that the individual will not be excessive in either his relation to God or to worldly goods. In enumerating his "considerations against ancient monasticism," Calvin makes clear that monasticism is a problem not because of its self-denial, but because it is spiritually and materially excessive.[29] Calvin finds "ancient monastics" to be somewhat better than his contemporaries, whom he accuses of "superstition" in their way of life, meaning that they follow the ritual and edicts of the Church without appropriate reference to what the Gospel actually says. They follow the community, rather than reading the Gospel for themselves. The early monastics, those early Christians who practiced celibacy before the edifice of the Church was constructed, cannot be accused of superstition: "Yet, I say that [ancient monastics] were not without immoderate affectation and perverse zeal. It was a beautiful thing to forsake all their possessions and be without earthly care. But God prefers devoted care in ruling a household, where the devout householder, clear and free of all greed, ambition, and other lusts of the flesh, keeps before him the purpose of serving God in a definite calling" (1258, 4.12.4). The ideal of the moderate householder is, of course, the connecting point between sexual life and economic life, showing the interdependence of the two. Marriage, devotion to a family and to a calling, allows this individual to be free—free from greed, ambition, and other lusts of the flesh.

This ideal, of the married householder, condenses in the single individual the world of Reformed social relations, allowing Calvin to use his critique of the vow of chastity to stand in for a critique of all monastic vows. He chooses not to discuss his objections to the other two vows—of poverty and obedience—but, rather, finds such critique unnecessary after the error of celibacy has been demonstrated. Having completed his long critique of celibacy, he concludes: "I shall not stop to assail the two remaining vows. I say only this: besides being, as conditions are today, entangled with many superstitions, these vows seem to have been composed in order that those who have taken them may mock God and men. But lest we seem to criticize every little point too spitefully, we shall be content with the general refutation that has been given above" (1274, 4.13.19). The claim—"lest we seem to criticize every little point too spitefully"—is made in a text that in its English translation is over fifteen hundred pages long. It is no accident that Calvin chooses this point on which to restrain himself. In the end he does not need to criticize the other two vows—of poverty and obedience—because sex comes to stand in for right relation to the material world and right relation between God and community. The Protestant can find prosperity in ruling a household rather than poverty in communal living, and the Protestant relation to God is defined by the individual freedom to marry rather than by obedience to the community.

In the newly formed Protestant social relations, the right relation to the (immaterial) spiritual world is no longer guaranteed by the (material) institution of the Church. Rather, the individual stands alone before God, and his (a word I use advisedly) right relation to the spiritual world is guaranteed by the immaterial substance of faith alone. This shift is particularly acute in Calvinism's system of predestination in which the rule of God is so complete that one's salvation is already determined by God's will. One can never know for certain whether one will be among the saved or the damned. A good life that is materially rewarded is an indicator of salvation, but it is no way a guarantee. We have two major shifts here: the materialization of God in the world is now accomplished primarily through the individual rather than the community, and this materialization is itself spiritualized. Transubstantiation no longer occurs, and faith alone embodies God in the world. At the same time, this new relation also carries the spiritual more into the material world. As Weber points out, because good works in the world no longer directly produce salvation, work and the discipline of work produce goods that are primarily material rather than spiritual.

This reworking of the relation between the immaterial and the material—a reformation symbolized and embodied through sex and marriage—allows for the formation of capitalism. Capitalism is itself a reworking of the relationship between the material and the immaterial. Capitalism, we must remember, is more than a set of material relations, it is fundamentally dependent on abstraction, the abstraction of labor into labor power. It is not that people did not labor before capitalism, it is that their labor, when not abstracted into labor power, did not produce surplus value and, hence, did not produce capital. The shift to Protestantism allowed for the shift to capitalism not because of a moral superiority inherent in Protestant self-discipline as contemporary moralists on the political Right would have it, but because the Reformation was a moment that allowed for the reworking of both symbolic and material relations. The Reformation produced a symbolism that allowed capitalism to make sense. It is not that material and immaterial relations are not present before the Reformation, it is that this interrelation worked differently after the Reformation—the way that the immaterial is made manifest in the world is different.

Thus sexual relations, and marriage in particular, come to epitomize the Protestant ordering of the world. Sex embodies the remaking of the relation between material and immaterial worlds, and sexual relations are key to producing the individual, rather than a community, as the primary site of relation to God. Sex, like the commodity, is fetishized in modernity; it replaces food as the sin extraordinaire, the sign of gluttony and dissolution, and it also replaces the vows of poverty and obedience as the sign of right relation to both God and community. Sex becomes the premier site of morality.[30] Sex is not a realm analogous to the realm of production, but rather a necessary part of productive relations. And what sex produces is the individual, specifically the autonomous and free individual.

Thus sexual relations, and marriage in particular, come to epitomize the Protestant ordering of the world. Sex becomes the premier site of morality.

For D'Emilio individualism is the source of the freedom that makes gay identity possible. Capitalism creates the conditions for gay identity because it allows "individuals to survive beyond the confines of the family."[31] This same individualism is the basis for the freedom promised by Protestantism. The individual stands alone before God. And the individual's religious vocation is freed from the confines of the community—of poverty, chastity, and obedience. Given Weber's connection between the Protestant ethic and the spirit of capitalism, this coincidence should not surprise us, but the connection between freedom and sex is a profound one. This Protestant freedom is accomplished in part through the elevation of marriage to the normative ideal. Luther and Calvin do not encourage those with a religious vocation to leave the monastery and convent and live alone in their faith, as pure autonomous individuals. Luther and Calvin encourage them to get married, and this is because, as feminists have long pointed out, autonomous individuals do not actually exist autonomously.[32] Rather they depend on the labor of others, and in what is now called the traditional family, they depend on the labor of wives and servants. Capitalist exploitation depends on domination, not just to provide a reserve pool of labor, but because the free and autonomous individual depends on domination. The progress that modernity is supposed to provide by which more and more people can become autonomous individuals, until eventually all are equal, will always be a contradictory movement, because there is no such thing as an autonomous individual, a person who is free from all dependence on others. The same freedom that encourages the formation of gay identity also encourages sexual regulation. It specifically encourages the disciplines of marriage.

This analysis helps explain why sex has dominated U.S. public discourse. The particular conceptualization of freedom in the Protestant imagination combines the idea of individual liberation with a particular emphasis on sexual regulation. This analysis also suggests that the way out of this conundrum, out of the cycle that D'Emilio so presciently described, is to focus not on gay liberation but on remaking social relations in ways that undercut the individualism that enables capitalist exploitation and requires sexual regulation. The point at which gay liberation and sexual regulation meet is in individualism. It is individualism that sustains both liberatory and regulatory discourses, and it is individualism that sustains the relation between them. Thus it is this modern individualism that we must resist if we hope to slip the constraints of freedom.[33]

Alternative Possibilities

The freedom of individualism need not be the only freedom that we seek. It is not the case that individualism does not allow for change. In the modern period it is better to be an individual than not, just as it is better to have rights than not. The types of changes allowed by gay liberation and chronicled by D'Emilio are very real, and they are importantly better than repression. But the type of change that leads to gay rights also traps us in the discourse that also calls out increased regulation. This is because change, including liberatory change, when within the discourse of autonomous individualism works for capitalism. Capitalist exploitation allows for individual freedom, but the value of that freedom is defined by regulation, including sexual regulation, that makes the individual open to both exploitation and domination. The danger to capitalism is that exploitation will not be experienced as freedom or, perhaps more accurately, that when people seek relief from the alienation of capitalism they will search for something other than an increase in individual autonomy.

Freedom need not be defined only by an increase in individualism; freedom could also be constituted through alternative social formations. We can, for example, imagine different forms of freedom, forms based not in individualism or communalism but in various affinities, and forms that challenge the Christian secularism, of the United States. While the root of American sexual regulation may be religious, salvation is not to be found in simply seeking freedom from that religion. Such a search is based on the imagination of freedom from the Church sought by the Reformers, the very imagination that fuels the unspoken assumptions of Christian secularism. The problem is not a failure to be secular enough, but the fact that our public imagination of a central value like freedom is dominated by one particular tradition. While freedom is a contested term, progressive social movements still frequently play into the dominant imagination, oftentimes apparently without realizing that they are doing so.[34] We can, however, develop alternative values that can enable a subjectivity based in and through affinities that are neither those of individualism or community.

From Shared Interests to Alternative Affinities

But how are we to build these new social formations? How do we build the type of politics that D'Emilio recommends? D'Emilio's answer is to bring together all those who share an interest in living outside the bounds of the heterosexual nuclear family. For him, shared interests, rather than shared identity, are the basis of radical politics. Interest is supposed to provide a means of transcending identity; yet this argument did not bring into being the alliances that it called for, nor have the many similar arguments that were articulated throughout the 1980s and 1990s actually produced widespread alliance politics. This suggests that shared interests may not be an adequate means of conceptualizing how to build alliances.

We have not considered fully, nor adequately addressed, the ways in which interests among those various persons and communities who might not live within the bounds of the nuclear family are not necessarily shared. If interests are socially constituted, the wide-ranging repression of the 1950s on which D'Emilio focuses gives us a prime example of how interests that might have become broadly shared are instead constituted as opposing.

The 1950s were a time of massive social change that involved the reworking of relations among groups. As the United States emerged from World War II a superpower, the question of how this new power would be used was a fundamental one. The answer, as we all know, was to spread capitalism.

This was accomplished through the formulation of the Cold War, a war with both international and intranational implications that allowed the reworking of relations within the United States as well as across the globe. U.S. national identity was reconstituted and reconsolidated in relation to a new world order, and the repression of sexuality was central to this process. It was used as the "sin extraordinaire" that could taint other struggles, as civil rights or labor leaders were tarnished through sexual accusation. It was also a part of a network of "evils." Invocation of this network—whether in the troika of "godlessness, communism, and homosexuality," or in suspicious pairs like "communists and integrationists"—mutually constituted gender, race, class, and sexual relations in the context of U.S. nationalism.

The mutual constitution of identities is often drawn on in feminist and queer theory as a reason for connecting identities and issues, but, as the history of the 1950s shows, mutual constitution can also be used quite effectively in repressive discourse to create conflicting interests. These conflicts have frequently taken precedence over the shared interests named by D'Emilio, and they have blocked the realization of alternative affinities.

The network as a whole helps ensure that alienation will be experienced as a problem of gender, race, and/or sexuality, rather than as a problem in the relations of production. The American political fetishization of sex within such a network helps manage the relations between materiality and immateriality that both constitute and burden the autonomous individual. For capitalism to work, the alienation caused by the abstraction of labor into labor power must be experienced as freedom. In fact, alienation does produce the form of freedom that enables the modern self. It is the market that offers opportunities for the development of the self, including the development of gay identity. But the market also demands discipline and regulation, and this burdensome aspect of freedom is obscured by the very structure of autonomy. If the self is understood only as autonomous, then "others" threaten the self. The understanding induced by this discourse is that I would reap the benefits of capitalism without suffering the alienation I experience were it not for those others.

Importantly, the sense that others are a threat is not merely a displacement of the feeling of alienation of capitalism, it is a reflection of the individual's status as produced through capitalism. The independence of the autonomous individual is produced through a hierarchal—a dominative—dependence on others. Thus these others can threaten the self, not just by actively attacking the self but simply by asserting their own autonomy. If this sense of threat from others were only displacement, it would be easier to expose. Like commodity fetishism, these attributions are so powerful, because they are not merely illusions: they hook into real relations.

Rereading the narrative of the 1950s provides a perfect example of how such relations produce separated rather than shared interests. In this light, to understand fully the period's repression of sexuality, we cannot focus only on the dialectic between gay identity and its repression. We have to place gay identity in relation to the network of repressions that were instigated during the decade, and we have to place the production of gay identity and subsequent liberation in relation to the nascent social movements of the immediate postwar period.

We can see these dynamics at work by looking at examples from the articles appearing in the *New York Times* in the 1950s that mention homosexuality. The network of threats to the "American public" is reiterated so as to show these threats as mutually constituting when the *Times* reports on a conference of the Association for Group Psychology. The *Times* focuses on a paper by Dr. Cornelius Beukenkamp Jr., which claims that women's liberation produces "a primitive situation" that results in both homosexuality and violence:

> [In the case of women's liberation] the son is presented with a mother who is the absolute authority in the home, who dominates where the father once did. . . . In this position, the youngster is placed on a see-saw, swinging between physical violence against one or both parents, and overt homosexuality, which Dr. Beukenkamp thinks this ambivalent situation produces. . . . Dr. Beukenkamp saw this situation in the family as resembling primitive society. The youngsters, too, who increasingly participate in tribal warfare (gang activities) and acts of violence, are primitive.[35]

In this scenario problematic gender relations are negatively associated with both pathological sexuality and ethnically tinged violence, as the primitivist trope of tribal warfare provides an ethnic specter to modern-day gang activities.

This potential for guilt by association is one reason that contemporary theorists have focused on the need for and possibility of alliance across identities, issues, and interests. But the associations built by such conservative discourses are often more effective in separating than in connecting issues.

For instance, in another article from 1959 the potential for guilt by association is used to promote the idea that segregation is in the interests of everyone, especially those segregated. In the example above, homosexuality is deployed as a cause of ethnic violence, but in a description of "tension" in Greenwich Village also from 1959 the *Times* portrays homosexuals as potentially innocent (and also potentially guilty) bystanders to violence over "racial mixing."[36]

In this fairly long article, the history of immigration into the Village area is described in great detail from the first half of the nineteenth century, when the area "thrived as the home of the well-to-do and respectable," through waves of Irish and African Americans moving into the neighborhood until finally we reach the period of Italian American prominence. This history establishes the current problems as the result of "newcomers" entering the neighborhood. Specifically, the article is concerned with the arrival of the "beat generation"; "at the same time the freedom that the Village offered began to attract a new type of Negro from Harlem. In contrast to the Negro artists and writers already in the Village, the newcomers had no literary or artistic aspirations." These newcomers participated in sexualized racial mixing, which the article portrays as the triggering mechanism for much of the violence, including beatings of African American men and violence against businesses that are open to both African American and white patrons.

The description of racial mixing pits African Americans against Italian Americans, who in this situation are representative of "whiteness" and yet are also differentiated from the earlier period of "respectable" whiteness.[37] Finally, the specter of homosexuality is brought into this mix, which I quote in its entirety:

> Another cause of friction in the neighborhood is the homosexual. As a rule the homosexuals practice their own kind of segregation. They had their own section of Washington Square Park until the police evicted them recently. They patronize particular bars and particular street corners, and usually keep to themselves. Sometimes, however, they put on a more flamboyant show of their homosexuality. At times street brawls result, but homosexuality at present is much less an immediate cause of rowdiness than is the matter of racial mixing.

The incentive to counteridentify is more than apparent in this particular description. Peace is best maintained when both racial and sexual relations are organized through segregation. This arrangement means that there are "good" African Americans, those with literary aspirations who mingle only with other outsiders (the "beats"), and "bad" African Americans, those who mingle sexually with white women. There are also good homosexuals and bad homosexuals: those who keep to themselves (even apparently after they have been evicted from their separate space by the police) and those who flagrantly display their sexuality to others. The clear message of the article is to create a set of "interests" for homosexuals to keep to themselves; specifically, they should not mingle with other sexual outsiders—those whose sexuality crosses racial boundaries.

The system is arrayed around a center, and yet no one who resides in the central space is named as an actor, nor are their interests ever named.[38] The issues as presented are only the relations among others, and the violence that may ensue is portrayed as depending only on the behavior of these others. Moreover, homosexuals are here constructed as a group entirely separate from African Americans, Italians, and even the racially mixed beats. The racial mixing of homosexual life in the Village during this period is erased as homosexuals are constituted as putatively white. Sexuality and race are, thus, simultaneously interconnected and utterly distinct issues. Most important, the way that the interconnection is formulated—as sexualized racial mixing that leads to violence—tends to disaggregate rather than connect sexualized and racialized others in the system.

Moreover, homosexuals are here constructed as a group entirely separate from African Americans, Italians, and even the racially mixed beats.

Alternative Affinities and Reconfigured Values

Shared interests, while real, are not enough to overcome the simultaneous division of those interests. There were major effects from the repression of the 1950s, effects that are rarely counted in the relief brought on by the social movements of the decades that followed. Building on responses to the Great Depression and World War II, the 1940s represented a time of social openings on a number of issues—gender, race, class, sexuality—and these openings were sometimes addressed by movements that crossed the boundaries of identities. The repressions of the 1950s undercut these nascent alliances. The historians Catharine Fosl, Patricia Sullivan, and John Egerton have all argued, for example, that as Fosl put it, "the Red Scare of the post-WWII years throttled the black-white alliances that had budded during the depression."[39]

What was destroyed in the 1950s is not the emergence of gay identity per se, but the possibility of allied social movement of which gay identity is a part. The flowering of possibility in the last half century is a profound testament to the possibilities that were sustained even through this repressive period. As D'Emilio points out, the reason that gay liberation could burst on the scene after the Stonewall riots was because gay communities had been forming and growing through the 1950s. These gay communities were not necessarily organized around familial forms or even around couples. Some of these communities included cross-racial or cross-class alliances. Queer communities at moments overcame the race and class segregation of the dominant culture, and 1940s and 1950s social movements for racial justice also included cross-racial or cross-class alliances that were later destroyed. These nascent alliances and the glimmerings of openness might have been strengthened over time. What the repression of the 1950s accomplished was the channeling of the possibilities embodied in these formations toward single-issue identity-based movements that were separate from each other and that could coexist with familial forms, so that even in the resurgence of social movements in the 1960s, these alliances could not be fully realized.

Although late 1960s and early 1970s groups like the Gay Liberation Front understood themselves as connected to worldwide liberation struggles—hence the name "liberation front," all too soon these connections broke down in favor of the single-issue politics that D'Emilio criticizes in 1983. Gay rights groups have been led to pursue this path because the freedom that they most often seek is ultimately organized around individualism and individuals' rights. It is not that we are trapped in a dialectic between liberation and oppression, but that we have been induced to seek a liberation that contains the discourse of constraint within itself. Because

If, in modernity, sex plus freedom equals regulation, then one of the jobs of queer theory now is to change the arithmetic of our politics.

of this fact, the shared interests of multiple groups in liberation have been coconstructed with a set of divided interests that have blocked alliances. To recognize these divisions is not simply a misperception; the divisions are real and need to be addressed. But we do not necessarily have to remain trapped in them.

A shift is needed, but not just from identity politics to shared interests. Rather, our movements need to shift from identities and interests to alternative affinities, different values, and reconstructed interests. This does not mean doing away with either materialist politics or identity politics. Alternative affinities do not do away with identity politics, because goods and interests, punishments and disciplines are divided along identity-based lines. Materialist politics continue to be crucial because capitalism continues to form the context of political possibility. But, if capital depends on values like freedom to produce value—if the material is intertwined with and embodied through (im)material values—materialist politics needs to rework values as well as interests.

Just as it is not enough to shift from identities to interests, a shift from gay identity to queer resistance is also insufficient to produce the type of new politics that the turn to queer initially promised. The great hope of queer politics was to produce alternative affinities and complex political commitments that were not trapped in singular identities. But, as with the failure to produce alliances, this hope was not realized. Deployed against us were not just the norms of normative identity formation but also the values of a supposedly value-free market. The value of freedom is precisely that it is productive of both economic value and a particular set of moral values—values that include both the idea of human liberation and of the need for discipline, regulation, and domination.

We cannot develop a successful queer politics if we just resist the discipline and regulation. We need to change values as well as resist norms. Changing values also provides possible sites for building alternative affinities. Rather than simply resisting freedom, queer politics might connect to those alternative genealogies of freedom, like the ones described by Robin Kelley in *Freedom Dreams: The Black Radical Imagination*, that are not trapped in discourses of modern individualism, the market, and Christian secularism.[40] If, in modernity, sex plus freedom equals regulation, then one of the jobs of queer theory now is to change the arithmetic of our politics.

Notes

1. Lisa Duggan, *The Twilight of Equality? Neoliberalism, Cultural Politics, and the Attack on Democracy* (Boston: Beacon, 2003), has documented the role of sexuality in neoliberalism. Clinton saw sexual regulation as vital to his own reelection and hence signed both the Defense of Marriage Act and the welfare reform act in the summer before the 1996 elections. Importantly, welfare reform was a fundamental change in U.S. economic policy, but it was accomplished not through a discussion of economics but through a discourse that focused on young women and their sexuality, who were always presumed to be women of color (even though statistically more white women than women of color have drawn welfare benefits). For an analysis of how welfare reform worked in a network of social relations that included economics, sexuality, and racial politics, see Janet R. Jakobsen, "Family Values and Working Alliances: The Question of Hatred and Public Policy," in *Welfare Policy: Feminist Critiques* (Cleveland: Pilgrim, 1999).

2. For an in-depth analysis of Clinton's impeachment and its ramifications, see Lisa Duggan and Lauren Berlant, eds., *Our Monica, Ourselves: The Clinton Affair and the National Interest* (New York: New York University Press, 2001).

3. For a full analysis of the alliance between fiscal and social conservatives, see Jakobsen, "Family Values and Working Alliances."

4. In describing these "moral values" the *New York Times* mentions only two issues: opposition to abortion and to "recognition of gay and lesbian couples" (Kate Zernike and John M. Broder, "War? Jobs? No, Character Counted Most to Voters," *New York Times*, 4 November 2004).

5. The percentage of voters claiming "moral values" as their primary concern was actually "down from 2000 (35 percent) and 1996 (40 percent)," so the "moral values" voters were not the factor that ensured that George Bush won this time (Frank Rich, "The Great Indecency Hoax," *New York Times*, 28 November 2004).

6. Historians have long resisted this popular stereotype when documenting the sexual practices of the Puritans. For example, John D'Emilio and Estelle B. Freedman in their history of sexuality in America state, "Even among the Puritans and their Yankee descendants, sexuality exhibited more complexity than modern assumptions about their repressiveness suggest" (D'Emilio and Freedman, *Intimate Matters: A History of Sexuality in America* [New York: Harper and Row, 1988], 15). And, in a point which is important for my later argument, they continue, "Early Americans did indeed pay close attention to the sexual behavior of individuals. . . . They did so, however, not in order to squelch sexual expression, but rather to channel it into what they considered to be its proper setting and purpose: as a duty and a joy within marriage, and for the purpose of procreation" (16).

7. Ann Pellegrini and I demonstrate the religious, and specifically Protestant, basis of sexual regulation in U.S. law in Jakobsen and Pellegrini, *Love the Sin: Sexual Regulation and the Limits of Religious Tolerance* (New York: New York University Press, 2003).

8. For a full explanation of the Christian nature of U.S. secularism, see Janet R. Jakobsen and Ann Pellegrini, "Introduction to World Secularisms at the Millennium," *Social Text*, no. 64 (2000): 1–28.

9. Max Weber, *The Protestant Ethic and the Spirit of Capitalism*, trans. Talcott Parson (New York: Charles Scribner's Sons, 1930), 36.

10. On these enforcements, see Merry E. Wiesner, "Nuns, Wives, and Mothers: Women and the Reformation in Germany," in *Women in Reformation and Counter-Reformation Europe*, ed. Sherrin Marshall (Bloomington: Indiana University Press, 1989), 8–28.

11. See the introduction to this special issue by David Eng, Judith Halberstam, and José Esteban Muñoz. For a different set of problems with the development of queer politics, see David Halperin, *Saint Foucault: Towards a Gay Hagiography* (New York: Oxford University Press, 1995), 64–65.

12. For a description of some of the inadequacies of critical theories that rely solely on "the critique and exposure of dominant ideologies," see Eve Kosofsky Sedgwick, "A Response to C. Jacob Hale," *Social Text*, nos. 52–53 (1997): 237.

13. See, for example, Foucault's third volume of *The History of Sexuality*, *The Care of the Self* (trans. Robert Hurley [New York: Vintage Books, 1986]), and the writings and interviews collected in the volume *Ethics: Subjectivity and Truth* (ed. Paul Rabinow, trans. Robert Hurley et al. [New York: New Press, 1997]), which was interestingly the first volume of the Essential Works of Foucault series.

14. On the turn to ethics in critical theory, see Marjorie Garber, Bernice Hanssen, and Rebecca Walkowitz, *The Turn to Ethics* (New York: Routledge, 2000).

15. Kerry was the first to raise the issue of faith in the third presidential debate and then later in the debate pointed out that he had done so. For the debate transcript, see www.npr.org/templates/story/story.php?storyId=4108590 (accessed 30 November 2004).

16. The ultimate culmination of this "family values" idea of gay rights was summarized when Elizabeth Birch, then head of the Human Rights Campaign, claimed, shortly after adopting children, that the real dividing line in American life was not between hetero- and homosexuals but between "people who are parents, and people who aren't" (Tim Weiner, "Public Lives; Gay-Rights Leader Sees Shift Toward Public Acceptance," *New York Times*, 24 April 2000).

17. D'Emilio rejects functionalism, and his answer depends on an analogy between production and reproduction: "The elevation of the nuclear family to preeminence in the sphere of personal life is not accidental. . . . The privatized family fits well with capitalist relations of production. Capitalism has socialized production while maintaining that the products of socialized labor belong to the owners of private property. In many ways, childbearing has been progressively socialized over the last two centuries with schools, the media, peer groups, and employers taking over functions that once belonged to parents. Nevertheless, capitalist society maintains that reproduction and childrearing are private tasks, that children "belong" to parents, who exercise rights of ownership." D'Emilio can hardly be blamed for appealing to such an analogy in 1983, but it never quite worked. Attempts to bring together Marxism and feminism in this analogical manner always seem to make reproduction a mirror image of the production process. Once again the concerns of women were reflections of the real concerns of the world (and of men), in this case production. This type of analogy also could not explain the ways in which gender oppression operates with "relative autonomy" from capitalist functionalism, as Cornel West has said of race ("Marxist Theory and the Specificity of Afro-American Oppression," in *Marxism and the Interpretation of Culture*, ed. Cary Nelson and Lawrence Grossberg [Urbana: University of Illinois Press, 1988], 17–30). Gender oppression, like racial oppression, seems to flourish even when it is not in the best interests of capitalism. While racism and sexism

often work for capitalism, they also have lives of their own. Neither functionalism nor analogy will ultimately serve as explanation. For a critique of analogy that includes a trenchant critique of D'Emilio, see Miranda Joseph, "Family Affairs: The Discourse of Global/Localization," in *Queer Globalizations: Citizenship and the Afterlife of Colonialism*, ed. Arnaldo Cruz-Malavé and Martin F. Manalansan IV (New York: New York University Press, 2002).

18. This analysis of the intertwining of exploitation and domination is based on a reading of Gayatri Chakravorty Spivak's "Scattered Speculations on the Question of Value," in *In Other Worlds: Essays in Cultural Politics* (New York: Routledge, 1988), 154–75, which I provide in Janet R. Jakobsen, "Can Homosexuals End Western Civilization as We Know It?" in Cruz-Malavé and Manalansan, *Queer Globalizations*.

19. Benedict Anderson, *Imagined Communities: Reflections on the Origin and Spread of Nationalism* (London: Verso, 1983).

20. Nancy F. Cott, *Public Vows: A History of Marriage and the Nation* (Cambridge, MA: Harvard University Press, 2002). Cott, however, assumes marriage is central to national life, rather than seeing the consolidation of marriage at the center of Americanness as part of the *process* of consolidating the nation.

21. Jakobsen and Pellegrini, *Love the Sin*.

22. Some would argue (although you would not know it from today's Christian Right) that marriage is not a biblically based ideal. By example, Jesus was not a family man and the Pauline epistles prefer celibacy to marriage. The Pauline author suggests that marriage is merely necessary: most people cannot resist sex, and so marriage is the best alternative to fornication. The Reformation's intensified focus on the sinful nature of humans allows for a slippage in interpretation where everyone is now seen as best off in marriage.

23. Martin Luther, *Martin Luther: Selections from His Writings*, ed. John Dillenberger (New York: Doubleday), 30.

24. This is the precursor to Kant's good will (and we cannot forget that Kant is deeply influenced by German pietism. He should not simply be read as a "secular" philosopher).

25. Luther, *Martin Luther: Selections*, 30.

26. Biblical scholarship has shown that the canonical letters written under the name "Paul" were not all written by a single individual. See Elizabeth Castelli, *Imitating Paul: A Discours of Power* (Louisville, KY: John Knox/Westminster, 1991).

27. Luther, *Martin Luther: Selections*, 30.

28. See, for example, Merry Wiesner's account in "Nuns, Wives, and Mothers" of how strictly the Reformers enforced the idea that marriage represents women's calling. While some women voluntarily left their convents to become Protestants and marry, others in areas controlled by Reformers fought to keep their religious communities together even when cut off from the Catholic Church. Wiesner also reports that the Counter-Reformation Church moved to restrict some of the freedoms that women in religious orders had experienced, thus further narrowing women's possibilities.

29. Calvin elaborates a morality that runs counter to both the specific vows of the Catholic religious life and the process of taking vows itself. For him, the interior intention of the individual, rather than vows taken before the community, is the crucial indicator of morality. Calvin, for example, precedes Kant in arguing

that the moral value of an action depends not on one's relation to the community but on intention: "For, because the Lord looks up on the heart, not the outward appearance, the same thing (as the purpose in mind changes) may sometimes please and be acceptable to him, sometimes strongly displease him" (John Calvin, *The Institutes of the Christian Religion*, ed. John T. McNeill, trans. Ford Lewis Battles, 2 vols. [Philadelphia: Westminster, 1960], 1258, 4.12.4, hereafter cited in the text).

30. I am not arguing that sex is simply analogous to the commodity, but rather that sex, too, goes through the process of fetishization. It is important to note that in Marx fetishism is a process of which the commodity is the elementary form, but fetishism is not necessarily restricted to the commodity.

31. John D'Emilio, "Capitalism and Gay Identity," in *Powers of Desire: The Politics of Sexuality*, ed. Ann Snitow, Christine Stansell, and Sharon Thompson (New York: Monthly Review, 1983), 105.

32. Carole Pateman, *The Sexual Contract* (Stanford, CA: Stanford University Press, 1988), makes this point in her critique of liberal political theory.

33. This does not require giving up the freedoms that have been so hard won in modernity. It does not require denying the value and the power of modern accomplishments, but it does require remaking these freedoms, because the fact that freedom is accompanied not just by exploitation but also domination is not an accident or a mistake that will simply be remedied by progress. Domination is internal to both exploitation and modernity.

34. For a history of contests over the term *freedom*, see Eric Foner, *The Story of American Freedom* (New York: Norton, 1998); for an in-depth exploration of alternative visions of freedom that have fueled radical politics, see Robin D. G. Kelley, *Freedom Dreams: The Black Radical Imagination* (Boston: Beacon, 2002).

35. In fact, one of the subject headings within the article is "A Primitive Situation" (*New York Times*, 22 February 1959).

36. *New York Times*, 29 September 1959.

37. The *Times* describes the period of Italian American prominence before the arrival of "the beats" as a time when "the neighborhood was a closed community with a village elder presiding. He administered neighborhood justice, and little outside interference, even by the police, was tolerated." This description effectively locates Italian Americans as immigrants who control the neighborhood beyond the bounds of the police and outside the limits of the law.

38. The *Times* names the dominant group—"the well-to-do and respectable" (and presumably white and straight)—only in reference to the past.

39. Catherine Fosl, *Subversive Southerner: Anne Braden and the Struggle for Racial Justice in the Cold War South* (New York: Palgrave Macmillan, 2002), 200. See also Patricia Sullivan, *Days of Hope: Race and Democracy in the New Deal Era* (Chapel Hill: University of North Carolina Press, 1996); and John Egerton, *Speak Now against the Day: The Generation before the Civil Rights Movement* (New York: Knopf, 1994).

40. On possibilities for connecting alternative genealogies, see Janet R. Jakobsen and Elizabeth Lapovsky Kennedy, "Sex and Freedom," in *Regulating Sex: The Politics of Intimacy and Identity*, ed. Elizabeth Bernstein and Laurie Schaffner (New York: Routledge, 2004).

Call for Papers

War is back and seemingly forever. In recent years the pacific neoliberal rhetoric of globalization has been replaced by the Hobbesian war of all against all. This pervasive metaphorization of war blurs the boundaries between military and civilian, combatant and noncombatant, state and war machine, wartime and peace. But war discourse also operates as a strategy that partitions, separates and compartmentalizes knowledge, offering a highly seductive, militarized grid through which to interpret the world. Though the contemporary scene shows striking parallels with the neocolonialism, counterinsurgency, and "dirty wars" of the Cold War era, the current proliferation of war discourse often masks older continuities and material interests. Like a virus, it seems, war tropes have spread throughout the body politic and global economy.

What are the ends of war? This special issue of *Social Text* invites contributions that engage this critical question by challenging teleological narratives of endless conflict, by confronting the seductions of metaphorization and militarization, and by analyzing the historic and material interests that they serve. "The Ends of War" will insist on the contingent and instrumental nature of war discourse and on the need to think beyond its global reach. Contributors are invited to challenge the hegemonic force of war and contest its tendency to compartmentalize knowledge.

Contributions that link the work of gender or postcolonial studies, area studies, or political economy to analyses of war culture and technology will be particularly welcome. Possible areas of interest might include the gendered imaginary of war; the Left's ambivalent relationship to the seductive metaphorization of war; the colonial genealogy of contemporary war discourse; race and the military; buried histories of *postmodern* war culture in other conflicts; the arms trade and the permanent war economy; the militarization of intellectual life; media consolidation, censorship, and the reporting of war; and the economic and environmental impact on the Global South.

Deadline for submissions is **1 May 2006.** Essays of 7,000–10,000 words, including endnotes, and following *The Chicago Manual of Style*, 15th ed., should be sent by e-mail as Microsoft Word documents to Livia Tenzer, Managing Editor, ltenzer@rci.rutgers.edu. Send hard copies to:

Social Text
8 Bishop Place
New Brunswick, NJ 08903

Extent and Nature of Circulation

Average number of copies of each issue published during the preceding twelve months; (A) total number of copies printed, 889; (B.1) sales through dealers and carriers, street vendors and counter sales, 69; (B.2) paid mail subscriptions, 382; (C) total paid circulation, 451; (D) samples, complimentary, and other free copies, 66; (E) free distribution outside the mail (carriers or other means), 0; (F) total free distribution (sum of D & E), 66; (G) total distribution (sum of C & F), 517; (H.1) office use, leftover, unaccounted, spoiled after printing, 372; (H.2) returns from news agents, 0; (I) total, 889.

Actual number of copies of a single issue published nearest to filing date: (A) total number of copies printed, 1023; (B.1) sales through dealers and carriers, street vendors and counter sales, 100; (B.2) paid mail subscriptions, 352; (C) total paid circulation, 452; (D) samples, complimentary, and other free copies, 66; (E) free distribution outside the mail (carriers or other means), 0; (F) total free distribution (sum of D & E), 66; (G) total distribution (sum of C & F), 518; (H.1) office use, leftover, unaccounted, spoiled after printing, 505; (H.2) returns from news agents, 0; (I) total, 1023.